8/13

WHAT CHANGED WHEN EVERYTHING CHANGED

JOSEPH MARGULIES

What Changed When Everything Changed

9/11 AND THE MAKING
OF NATIONAL IDENTITY

Yale

UNIVERSITY PRESS

NEW HAVEN & LONDON

Yale University Press books may be purchased in quantity for
educational, business, or promotional use. For information, please e-mail
sales.press@yale.edu (U.S. office) or sales@yaleup.co.uk (U.K. office).

Set in Scala and Scala Sans types by Integrated Publishing Solutions.
Printed in the United States of America.

Library of Congress Cataloging-in-Publication Data

Margulies, Joseph.
What changed when everything changed : 9/11 and the making
of national identity / Joseph Margulies.
pages   cm
Includes bibliographical references and index.
ISBN 978-0-300-17655-1 (cloth : alk. paper)   1. National characteristics,
American.   2. Nationalism—United States.   3. September 11 Terrorist
Attacks, 2001—Influence.   4. Terrorism—United States—Prevention—
Social aspects.   5. United States—History—21st century.   I. Title.
E169.1.M264 2013
973.93—dc23
2012049865

A catalogue record for this book is available from the British Library.

This paper meets the requirements of ANSI/NISO Z39.48-1992
(Permanence of Paper).

10 9 8 7 6 5 4 3 2 1

To Sid Tarrow
and CVW

CONTENTS

PART THREE: PRESERVATION AND TRANSFORMATION

PREFACE

MY HEAD IS FILLED WITH VERY SIMPLE questions. Some people describe questions like these as unwelcome distractions. "It was nagging at me," we might hear someone say, as though she were dealing with a toddler tugging at her sleeve in the grocery store. But my questions don't nag at all. They are my constant companions. They sit with me at coffee shops, join me for lunch, wait patiently while I tend to other matters, and always seem awake when I am. By and large, they provide delightful company, and all they ask in return is that I try to answer them.

This book is my attempt to do right by two such questions, both of which have been with me for more than a decade. First, I wanted to know what is meant by the insistence that the attacks of September 11 "changed everything." It was impossible to sort this out in the first years after 9/11. When a tsunami hits, we wait until the water recedes before trying to assess the damage. Now, with the benefit of some time and perspective, we can begin the more sober task of figuring out what September 11 has meant to national identity.

One often hears that to be an American means to believe in a small cluster of shared ideals. "There is no American race," George W. Bush often said. "There's only an American creed." This creed has been described in different ways, but at its core it has always been understood to mean an attachment to liberty, equality, limited government, the rule of law, and the dignity of the individual, all of which are embedded within a commitment to civic virtue. These are the timeless ingredients of national identity. They fill the pages of our most revered texts and give us the symbols and stories that define national life.

Because the words themselves have been so stable, it is also customary to hear that national identity is unchanging, as though what it means to be an American is the same today as it was at the Founding. But this is not remotely true. Though we have long invoked the same values and traditions to describe our national identity, we have fought endlessly over what these words mean and the role they should play in national life. The ideals that make up national identity are not fixed stars in an unchanging sky but immensely powerful symbols that are manipulated and redefined to justify competing social arrangements. They are verbal weapons in a continual struggle to make one or another vision of national life dominant in the public square. National identity is what we make of it.

And what have we made of it since 9/11? What I found was not at all what I expected. I had imagined at the start of my research that September 11 would have thrown us from our true path and that the long decade since then would have been spent in a struggle to find our way back. The book, as I originally imagined it, would be an attempt to map our present location and point the way home. All of this reflects the conventional wisdom about the American response to crisis—we are supposedly tossed off course, do foolish things because we've lost our bearings, and eventually return to normal, chastened if not much wiser. I call this the myth of deviation and redemption.

Perhaps this myth is an accurate description of the response to other traumatic events in American history, but it certainly does not describe the course of history since September 11. The most striking feature of the immediate reaction to that day is not the extent to which the nation lost its way but the great extent to which it resolved not to do so. The attacks were instantly cast as a challenge to our shared values, which was taken to mean the values *as they were understood at the time.* This led to a widely shared insistence that those values should remain unchanged. It was not until years later that the impulse to change our national identity took hold.

What's more, the preference for draconian policies was not some spontaneous and uncontrollable reaction to September 11. At the moment of greatest perceived threat, when fear of another attack was at its peak, favorable attitudes toward Muslims and Islam were at record highs throughout all segments of the population, the suggestion that America might torture suspects in custody was mocked and ridiculed in the public square, and many of the counterterror policies pursued by the Bush administration were met with widespread opposition.

Today, by contrast, tens of millions of Americans denounce Islam in the most incendiary terms, more than half the population accepts the idea of torture, and counterterror policies that President Bush apparently never dreamed of have been codified into law. Again and again, an initial determination within society to *preserve* national identity has been replaced by a determination to *transform* it. Still more surprisingly, these repressive attitudes have taken hold even though the threat from transnational jihad in general and al Qaeda in particular has diminished significantly.

My goal in the book is to explain how all this came to pass. Some insight into the process comes from the answer to my second simple question: How does the United States justify the betrayal of its professed values? I was less interested in how the country explains its transgressions years after the fact than in how it accounts for them at the time. The answer is that it doesn't. When Americans come upon a social arrangement they want to preserve, they do not alter their behavior to fit their values; they alter their values to fit their behavior. They change what it means to be an American, reshaping the meaning and content of shared ideals like religious liberty, community membership, personal dignity, the rule of law, and the other elements of national identity. In that way, the behavior itself is always imagined as completely congenial to the creed. Turns out it was a trick question.

ACKNOWLEDGMENTS

TO ANSWER MY QUESTIONS, I FOUND IT necessary to consult the accumulated lessons of a number of disciplines: law, which is my own background, but also history, political science, sociology, and social psychology. And this is one of the reasons why my questions are such pleasant companions— they bring me into close contact with a great many exceptional scholars who have devoted themselves to answering their own simple questions. Four in particular inspired me with their ability to see beyond the ordinary: the political scientist Murray Edelman, the sociologist Robert Wuthnow, and the historians C. Vann Woodward and Daniel Rodgers. Edelman and Woodward have since left us, and I have never met or communicated with Wuthnow or Rodgers, but their insights fill the pages of this book, and I hope I have done them justice.

My greatest intellectual acknowledgment, however, is to my friends and collaborators at Cornell. I do not know quite how it came to pass, but a number of Cornell scholars figure directly or indirectly in these pages. They listened patiently as I tried to introduce and describe my questions, and did their best to help me answer them. I am particularly pleased to thank Tamara Loos in the history department, Aziz Rana in the law school, and Eric Cheyfitz in American Studies. I am especially indebted to Mary Fainsod Katzenstein and Sid Tarrow in the government department, whose help to me has gone well beyond what a writer can fairly ask of another. Both have been exceptionally gracious and supportive, and Sid has been so patient and helpful that I recognized some time ago I would never have completed this book were it not for him, and for that reason, to him it is also dedicated.

When it comes to acknowledging influences, now is as good a time as any to point out that I have been professionally involved in some of the events I discuss in this book. I was counsel of record in *Rasul v. Bush*, involving the rights of foreign nationals held at Guantánamo, and *Munaf v. Geren*, which involved the rights of American citizens held in Iraq. Both were decided by the Supreme Court during the Bush administration. As I write this, I am counsel of record for Abu Zubaydah, for whom the infamous torture memo was written. It would be folly to pretend this work has not influenced me. I certainly imagine no such thing, and in these matters take my lead from H. G. Wells, who in the course of his mammoth *Outline of History* warned that "the teller of modern history is obliged to be at once cautious and bold. He has to pick his way between cowardly evasion on the one hand, and partisanship on the other. As far as possible he must confine himself to facts and restrain his opinions. Yet it is well to remember that no opinions can be altogether restrained. The writer has his own very strong and definite persuasions, and the reader must bear that in mind."

A number of students devoted a great many hours to this project. I cannot thank them all here, but I am most grateful to Mary Novak and Luke Herrine, whose contributions sometimes transcended those of a student or research assistant and became much more those of a collaborator or coauthor. Northwestern University has provided a congenial setting for my intellectual wanderings, and I was very fortunate to have Mike Sherry and Bonnie Honig in the history and political science departments to help keep me on track. I also owe a great debt to Heidi Kuehl in the law library for helping me get my hands on a great deal of esoteric material from libraries and archives all over the country. Ray Bonner has labored long and hard to get me to write less like a lawyer.

As with my last book, I am grateful to Rick and Solange MacArthur, whose support for the Roderick MacArthur Justice Center at Northwestern has given me the platform from which I have been able to meander so enjoyably. Thanks also to my colleagues Locke Bowman, David Bradford, and Alexa Van Brunt for bearing extra burdens while I completed this book. Bill Frucht and Dan Heaton at Yale University Press are exceptionally gifted editors, who improved the manuscript a great deal by their careful attention to the sound of words on a page. My agent Peter Matson at Sterling, Lord Literistic once again deserves a great deal of credit for having the uncanny ability to grasp my very simple questions more clearly and more quickly than I did. Several of my Chicago friends put up with too many hours listening to me ruminate about the mysteries of the American Creed, but I am particularly happy to thank Alex Kotlowitz, next to whose writing all of us are just monkeys pounding on the keys, and Scott Hibbard, whose great wisdom bridges the gap not only between religion and politics but also between friend and scholar.

My last and most profound debt is to my wife, Sandra Babcock, without whom even the most simple questions have no answers.

"What the United States of America Is All About at Our Core"

I

A CAMPAIGN THAT SEEMED ENDLESS WAS at last coming to a close. On October 11, 2000, Texas Governor George W. Bush and Vice President Al Gore took their seats at a table on the stage of Wait Chapel at Wake Forest University in Winston-Salem, North Carolina, for their second presidential debate. The event was billed as a conversation, with Jim Lehrer, the polished public television anchor, as the moderator. He took the candidates through an eclectic assortment of national issues, from gay marriage to education reform. On foreign policy, Lehrer asked how the rest of the world should view the United States. "It really depends," Bush said, "upon how our nation conducts itself in foreign policy. If we're an arrogant nation, they'll resent us. If we're a humble nation, but strong, they'll welcome us." Gore agreed. The "idea of humility is an important one," he said, but humility was not enough. America had to have "a sense of mission in the world." Its status as the world's only superpower created an obligation to "project the power for good that America can represent."[1]

Midway through the event, Lehrer asked the candidates whether they would support a federal law banning racial profiling at all levels of government. "Yes, I would," Gore answered. "I think that racial profiling is a serious problem. . . . Imagine what it—what it is like for someone to be singled out unfairly, unjustly, and feel the unfair force of law simply because of race or ethnicity. Now, that runs counter to what the United States of America is all about at our core." Gore promised that as president, he would make a law banning racial profiling "the first Civil Rights Act of the 21st century."[2] Bush agreed. "I can't imagine what it would be like to be singled out because of race and stopped and harassed. That's just flat wrong, and that's not what America is all about. And so we ought to do everything we can to end racial profiling."[3] But he went farther. The problem, he said, was not just in law enforcement. "It's an issue throughout our society. And as we become a diverse society, we're going to have to deal with it more and more. Arab-Americans," he said, "are racially profiled in what is called secret evidence"—a reference to the use of secret evidence in immigration proceedings. "My friend Senator Spencer Abraham of Michigan is pushing a law to make sure that Arab-Americans are treated with respect." Bush placed his confidence in the decency of the American people. "I believe, as sure as I'm sitting here, that most Americans really care. They're tolerant people. They're good, tolerant people. It's the very few that create most of the crises, and we just have to find them and deal with them."[4]

Bush's remarks were part of a calculated strategy. Longtime Republican activist Grover Norquist, who was advising the campaign, understood that many American Arabs and Muslims were social and fiscal conservatives who were uncomfortable with the Democratic platform on issues like abortion, gay rights, and tax policy. He also knew that the Democratic ticket was staunchly pro-Israel. When Lehrer asked a question about the Middle East, Gore's first words were, "Well, we stand with Israel."[5] Bush, by contrast, said that any lasting peace between Israel and the Palestinians must "be good for both sides." He pledged to work with moderate Arab states like Egypt, Jordan, Saudi Arabia, and Kuwait; Gore never mentioned an Arab nation except to demand that Syria release three recently captured Israeli soldiers.[6] Norquist also knew that Muslims were the fastest-growing religious group in America. Though reliable numbers are hard to come by, some estimates put their number at six million, concentrated in such key battleground states as Michigan, Illinois, and Florida.[7]

The Bush campaign's strategy to woo Muslim and Arab-American voters fixed on two issues: racial profiling and the use of secret evidence in immigration proceedings. The latter was the subject of a bill introduced by Senator Spencer Abraham, a cofounder of the conservative legal group the Federalist Society. In 2000, as the only Arab-American in the Senate, Abraham had introduced the Repeal Secret Evidence Act, which would have barred the Immigration and Naturalization Service from deporting a person based on undisclosed evidence. Many in the Arab-American and Muslim communities believed the INS used such evidence to discriminate against Muslim and Arab immigrants. Parallel legislation had been introduced in the House by David Bonior (D-MI). By the time of the presidential debate, Bonior's bill had one hundred cosponsors from both sides of the aisle. The ACLU had warmly supported both the Abraham and Bonior bills. Three days after the debate, Gore added his support.[8]

The bipartisan political sentiment mirrored the consensus within society. Americans were overwhelmingly opposed to racial profiling. A 1999 Gallup poll, for instance, showed that eight in ten whites and nearly nine in ten African-Americans were opposed to the practice.[9] Mindful of this consensus, the Republican camp correctly judged that Bush could appeal to conservative Muslims and Arab-Americans on an issue that mattered deeply to them while also appealing to moderates and independents who were worried that he might be too conservative. He worked hard to implement this strategy during the campaign. He issued a statement entitled "Governor George W. Bush's Record of Inclusion." Regarding secret evidence, he said he was "troubled" that "new immigrants, often Arab or Muslim immigrants, face deportation or even imprisonment based on evidence they've never seen and never been able to dispute. That's not the American way." While Bush agreed that national security was "of course the foremost consideration," he insisted that a legitimate concern about national security "doesn't justify a disregard for fairness, dignity, or civil rights."[10]

Days before the debate, Bush had met with more than two dozen Arab-American and Muslim leaders in Dearborn, Michigan. Located on the banks of the River Rouge southwest of Detroit, Dearborn is the center of Arab-American life in the United States. Nearly 30 percent of the city's 100,000 residents are of Arab descent, by far the highest concentration in any American city.[11] In this meeting as well, Bush had pledged to end ethnic profiling and the use of secret evidence. He named Khaled Saffuri, the deputy director of the American Muslim Council, to be the campaign's

national adviser on Arab and Muslim affairs. He sent his top national security adviser, Condoleezza Rice, to meet with another delegation of Muslim and Arab-American leaders.[12] At the Republican National Convention
in Philadelphia, Talat Othman, a third-generation Muslim-American and
businessman from Chicago, closed one session by offering the *duaa,* a
Muslim prayer of benediction. It was the first Muslim benediction ever offered at a major party's national convention.[13]

These efforts paid off. Barely two weeks before the election, the political
action committee of the American Muslim Political Coordination Council—
an umbrella organization made up of the four largest Muslim organizations in the country—formally endorsed Bush for president. Dr. Agha
Saeed, head of the council, praised Bush for taking "the initiative to meet
with local and national representatives of the Muslim community. He also
promised to address Muslim concerns on domestic and foreign policy issues."[14] Dr. Yayha Basha, president of the American Muslim Council, said
Bush had shown an "elevated level of concern in regards to secret evidence
and airport profiling and bringing it to the national political debate."[15] On
election day, Muslims sided with the GOP in record numbers, by some accounts favoring Bush over Gore by a ratio of 8:1. In Florida, a state Bush
carried by only 537 votes, some polling data showed that 80 to 90 percent of
the roughly 55,000 Muslim voters cast their lot with Bush. In an article in
the *American Spectator,* Norquist boasted that "George W. Bush was elected
President of the United States of America because of the Muslim vote."[16]

Muslim and Arab-American groups celebrated Bush's victory and looked
forward to movement on racial profiling and secret evidence as well as
greater presidential access. Their hopes were buoyed as Bush filled out
his cabinet. Senator Abraham, who had lost his reelection campaign, was
named secretary of energy. Khaled Saffuri landed a position in the White
House. The day after Bush was sworn into office, a group of prominent Republicans, including Newt Gingrich, John Sununu, and Grover Norquist,
met with representatives of the Muslim community to discuss secret evidence legislation, the role of the Muslim community in the election, and
bringing Muslims into the Bush White House.[17] Signs remained positive as
the administration settled in. In an address to a joint session of Congress
on February 27, President Bush said that "too many of our citizens have

cause to doubt our Nation's justice when the law points a finger of suspicion at groups instead of individuals. All our citizens are created equal and must be treated equally."[18] Bush said he had charged Attorney General John Ashcroft with developing "specific recommendations to end racial profiling. It's wrong, and we will end it in America." Days later, Ashcroft said he was "very eager" to answer the president's call.[19]

In June, Democrats in both houses of Congress introduced the End Racial Profiling Act. In July, in videotaped remarks to the NAACP, President Bush repeated that "racial profiling is wrong, and it must be ended in America." In August the Senate held hearings on the pending legislation. Even opponents of the bill spoke in favor of ending racial profiling. Senator Orrin Hatch (R-UT) said, "Racial profiling is an issue that has generated widespread public concern. Fortunately, unlike many of the issues we confront here in Washington, there has emerged a consensus concerning the fundamental point of the debate. Racial profiling, also known as bias-based policing, is wrong, it is unconstitutional, and it must not be practiced or tolerated."[20] In addition, Muslim leaders were eager to meet with the new president. They wanted to remind him of their support and hold him to his campaign promises. Twice the meeting was scheduled, and twice put off. Finally, it was set for a Tuesday afternoon in the second week of September. The president would be flying up from Florida and would meet with the group at 3:30. But the September 11 meeting never took place, and when it was finally rescheduled, the president's priorities, like those of the nation, had changed.[21]

II

We are often told that September 11 "changed everything." But this is a sentiment more repeated than explained. The so-called war on terror has now entered its second decade. It has lasted more than twice as long as either the Civil War or the Second World War, and more than five times as long as our involvement in the First World War. Yet aside from the occasional dramatic event—the killing of Osama bin Laden, for instance—terror no longer dominates the news. By the time Barack Obama was elected, only 2 percent of the population ranked terrorism as the most important problem facing the country, and by late 2011, the fraction had fallen to fewer than one in a hundred. Americans do not much fear another attack (though that would no doubt change if one were to occur), and it is no longer necessary for people to form judgments about a post-9/11 world in an emotional state (though some still do). Enough time has passed for people to have taken the long second look.

Having taken that look, we may ask how September 11 has changed "what the United States is all about at our core," as Vice President Gore put it in the 2000 debate at Wake Forest. How have these attacks altered the meaning and content of our shared national values? How have they changed the stories we tell that give these values their shape and substance—stories about immigrants and diversity; about membership and belonging; about tolerance and dignity? In the hundreds of books written about September 11, these questions have largely escaped attention.

Answering them requires that we take a very different look at post-9/11 debates. Many writers have studied what politicians and other cultural leaders have said. Vice President Cheney's infamous line that September 11 would carry us to "the dark side" has been endlessly reprised and provided the title of a best-selling book.[22] But few writers have examined how these debates have been linked to different visions of "what America is all about," as Governor Bush said in the 2000 debate. To do this, we must have a very clear understanding of how national identity comes into being.

Many people seem to believe that American national identity is a fixed condition, timeless and unchanging since the Founding. That is certainly how it is described by our political leaders. "We believe in and fight for our principles," Jimmy Carter said in 1980, "and they'll never change."[23] Carter was certainly right that Americans "fight for" their principles, but they also fight over what those principles mean and entail. National identity takes shape as these contests resolve themselves in the public square and we settle, if only for a time, on how our shared values and traditions will be expressed. National identity, in other words, is dynamic. It depends vitally on which arguments and constructions about American life acquire the exalted status of *common sense*.

Consider, for example, the idea of America as a Judeo-Christian nation, with its unmistakable implication that national identity is more closely connected to certain religious traditions than others. Today this idea is so deeply embedded in the national consciousness that if we think about it at all, we might imagine that leaders in the United States have *always* described the country in these terms. Yet until the middle of the twentieth century, the expression would have struck most Americans as bizarre and many as blasphemous. As a term used to describe the values and beliefs shared by Jews and Christians, it originated in the 1930s and did not appear in presidential remarks until late 1952, when President-Elect Eisenhower famously pronounced that "our form of government has no sense unless it is founded in a deeply felt religious faith, and I don't care what it is. With us of course it is the Judeo-Christian concept but it must be a religion that all men are created equal."[24] Thus the many people who bristled at the insistence by President Bush and other cultural leaders right after September 11 that Islam is a third partner in our national religious heritage were clinging not to a timeless reality of American life but to a recent creation.[25]

This example helps illuminate something important. Because it is impossible to understand *after* without a keen understanding of *before*, our task requires that we give considerable thought to national identity as it had taken shape by the end of the twentieth century. Yet with notable exceptions, this too has been overlooked in the vast literature on September 11. Instead, the attacks have led to a great many studies of American behavior during periods of armed conflict. We became much more familiar with the sentiment that led to the internment of Japanese-Americans during the Second World War and the suppression of dissent during and immediately after the First World War. The thought was that we are most apt to overreact immediately after a crisis begins, and that this impulse could perhaps be restrained by careful attention to past crises. Writers turned their worried gaze to these moments in the hope that inquiry into the past could prevent misery in the present.

But scholars also studied these periods out of a sincere belief that moments of real or perceived threat (even those separated by decades or centuries) have more in common with one another than with periods of relative calm (even when calm and chaos are separated only by the time it takes for a plane to crash into a building). And it is certainly true that, at least on occasion, post-9/11 rhetoric seemed to echo the language of earlier times, skipping across the years like a rock skipping across a pond. Only the proper nouns were new. Yet there is something intuitively unsatisfying about this approach to history. It imagines that the American response to threat is somehow free-floating, cast loose from time and place and uninfluenced by existing beliefs and social arrangements. It supposes, for example, that we can learn more about Congress's decision to suspend the writ of habeas corpus in 2006 by examining the suspensions during the Civil War—made under the leadership of a very different president during a very different war at a very different moment in our history—than we can by studying "peacetime" events during the second half of the twentieth century, which collectively shaped the worldview of the actors who suspended the writ in 2006.

This approach to history is dangerously incomplete. The response to real or imagined crisis in the United States has always been shaped by a number of factors that vary substantially over the years. For one thing, American policy makers always believe they are acting in conformity with the nation's values; but as I will stress throughout, the meaning and content of those values has never been etched in stone. National identity is forever a work in progress. The response to crisis will be governed in very large part by what those ideals mean at the time of the response. The internment of the Japanese during the Second World War, for instance, was made substantially easier by the fact that "equality" meant something very different in 1941 than it does today. A nation at home with Jim Crow while at peace, with its rigorously enforced insistence on second-class status for African-Americans, was not likely to be particularly troubled by legally enforced discrimination against Japanese-Americans while at war.

On a smaller scale, the direction of any response will be shaped by the formative life experiences of those in a position to influence events. As Henry Kissinger reminded us, "the convictions that leaders have formed before reaching high office are the intellectual capital they will consume as long as they continue in office."[26] The great majority of cultural leaders and opinion makers active in the United States today came of age after the civil rights movement. Many others reached adulthood after the triumph of modern conservatism in the 1980s. Tom Brokaw's "greatest generation"—the cohort that fought the Second World War and launched the baby boom—has passed from the national stage. Their successors, the Korean War generation, are close behind: A person who finished college in 1957, the year President Eisenhower sent federal troops to Little Rock, Arkansas, to desegregate the public schools, was nearing retirement on September 11, 2001. George W. Bush was seventeen in June 1964, when his fellow Texan Lyndon Johnson signed the Civil Rights Act that finally ended Jim Crow. Barack Obama was a toddler. Today's leaders, products of their time, have developed distinctive habits of mind and intellectual convictions that shape the way they understand and respond to the world and its problems. These habits and convictions are very different from those that prevailed during the New Deal or at the height of the anticommunist hysteria of the 1950s, let alone in the middle of the nineteenth century.

Thus we cannot understand how September 11 has changed national identity without a clear sense of what national identity was on September 10. The understanding of our shared values most Americans held on that day is the one they brought to bear on the post-9/11 debates. Unless we grapple with this history, we cannot understand what September 11 has meant to national identity.

To accomplish all this, we need a firm foundation, which I lay in the first half of the book. In the two chapters of Part One I describe how national identity is made. In Chapter 2 I introduce the elastic and manipulable language of national identity, the language of the American Creed, while in Chapter 3 I demonstrate how this language is deployed by cultural leaders to give content and shape to shared national values. Using the arguments for and against Jim Crow, I show in Chapter 3 that the lofty rhetoric of national identity, of "what the United States is all about at our core," can just as easily be deployed to construct and defend something wretched as put in service of something exalted. Though we may now wish it otherwise, both are equally "true" to national identity.

In Part Two I look at the construction of national identity in the recent pre-9/11 past. In Chapters 4 and 5 I take a close look at race, religion, and risk in the latter half of the twentieth century. When nineteen Arab followers of a particular interpretation of Islam commandeered four planes and caused so much destruction, these elements of American life were instantly thrown into play. And as some of the most fractious and divisive features of modern society, the debates surrounding race, religion, and risk have contributed much to the content and meaning of equality, liberty and religious tolerance, individualism and civic virtue, the rule of law, and limited government. In the first half of the book, then, I describe how national identity is made, and what it had been made into before the attacks.

Part Three describes the course of national identity since September 11. Contrary to what is often imagined, the most noteworthy aspect of our immediate reaction to that day is not the extent to which the nation set out to change its identity as a result of the attacks but the great extent to which it resolved to preserve its identity intact. September 11 was immediately constructed as an attack on national values, which was naturally taken to mean the values as they were understood at the time. This gave birth to a profound determination on both sides of the aisle and throughout society that those values should remain unchanged—an insistence that September 11 would not cause a radical reconstruction of "what the United States is all about." Only later did the impulse to change our national identity take hold.

In Part Three I examine three critical aspects of the post-9/11 world. In every case, an initial determination within society to *preserve* national identity was followed by a determination, sometimes coming years later, to *transform* it. In Chapters 7 and 8 I look at the treatment of Islam in post-9/11 thought. Immediately after September 11, cultural leaders, including most importantly President Bush, valiantly resisted any attempt to demonize Islam and struggled to preserve the dominant understanding of equality and religious liberty that prevailed in the United States before the attacks. Attempts by the radical right to equate Islam with terrorism were instantly denounced as un-American. But then, with gathering intensity, a very different vision of national identity began to take shape—a vision that is far more exclusive, more frightened, and more brittle. Millions of Americans have now embraced this darker vision, and mock the sentiment that prevailed immediately after September 11 as dangerously naïve.

In Chapters 9 and 10 I examine the most direct challenge posed by the post-9/11 era to "what America is all about." Very soon after September 11, civil society began to consider whether torture could be reconciled with American values. Overwhelmingly, the answer was no. Even at the height of the anthrax scare, when national hysteria was at its peak, a bipartisan consensus insisted that torture was utterly irreconcilable with national ideals and that not even September 11 could force the country to embrace it. In the initial phase of this debate, the Bush administration was largely silent. Later, after the Abu Ghraib prison scandal and the release of the torture memos, the administration took ambiguous positions, eventually coming down in favor of "enhanced interrogations"—torture by another name. By the end of the Bush administration, torture had become an enduring symbol of the extent to which the administration had lost its way. Still, the Bush administration's vigorous public defense of the enhanced techniques had the important effect of creating the first government-led attempt to reconcile torture with national values, which in turn allowed torture to compete in the public square. Though this narrative was largely drowned out by the criticism that overwhelmed the Bush administration in its final years, it came roaring back with the election of President Obama. Support for torture became part and parcel of the opposition to the new president. By the second half of 2012, a significant fraction of the population—and a great majority of Republicans—endorsed the idea of torture as official American policy.

In Chapters 11 and 12 I consider counterterror policy, which is the label I have given to the cluster of policies adopted by the federal government to meet the challenge of al Qaeda in particular and transnational jihad in general. The Bush administration's response to this challenge generated a heated national debate about the limits of the rule of law and limited government in American life. Attempting to preserve the prevailing understanding of these values, civil society rebelled against the Bush administration's prosecution of the war on terror, especially its claim to unilateral and unfettered power, a rebellion captured in the rise of the epitaph "the imperial presidency." In contrast to its treatment of Islam, here the Bush administration planted its flag on a hill it ultimately could not defend, a misjudgment that contributed to the Republican drubbing in 2008. But the Obama administration's initial determination to make good on its campaign promise to reform these practices invigorated the right and summoned it to action. Once again, the right integrated its opposition to Obama's counterterror policies into its broader narrative about the new president, and opposition to one became synonymous with opposition to the other. Before long, the Obama administration capitulated to this opposition, relinquishing the claim to unilateral power but preserving most of the counterterror policies instituted by its predecessor.

Thus, while the Bush years were in general characterized by a determination within civil society to *preserve* national identity, the Obama presidency has seen the dramatic rise of powerful impulses to *transform* it. By the end of Obama's first term, anti-Islamic sentiment was more openly and viciously expressed than at any time during the Bush administration; a substantial fraction of the American population had come to support torture; and counterterror policies that the Bush administration never even proposed have achieved the force of law. In each case, the new narrative is more repressive and alarmist, and more determined to change national identity, than anything that achieved prominence during the prior administration.

This state of affairs is both surprising and significant. Perhaps most important, it completely contradicts the standard wisdom about the American response to crisis, which is that repressive behavior is greatest immediately after the event that summoned it forth and declines as the threat recedes. This is simply not how events have unfolded since September 11. When the perceived threat was greatest, so too was the attachment to preexisting values. Only after the threat had diminished did attachment to those values loosen. By 2012 the accepted wisdom had been turned almost completely on its head: Tens of millions of Americans seem determined to embrace ever more draconian policies, even as national security experts describe al Qaeda as nothing more than "a shadow of its former self." What's more, much of this shift took place after President Obama swept into office in a landslide that gave Democrats control of both chambers of Congress—that is, precisely when political support for the shift seemed at its weakest.

Accounting for the paradox of the Obama era is a major goal of this book. Partisanship is part of the answer, naturally, but it does not tell the whole story. Saying that the right took a different view from the left does not explain why one view prevails over another, why preferences change over time, or why the change would be inversely related to the level of threat. Nor does it account for why the change would tend toward the view of the party that had just been decisively beaten at the polls. Furthermore, if change were merely a matter of partisanship, one would expect support for the policies of the right to be no greater than the size of the Republican Party, or at most no greater than the sum of independents and Republicans. That, however, is not the case. Democrats support certain parts of the new order in great numbers. Partisanship is a clue to the puzzle, but not a solution.

In solving this riddle, I will return to the suggestion that September 11 "changed everything." The lesson of the past decade is that it doesn't have to, but will if we let it. In the debate at Wake Forest, Governor Bush said he thought Americans were "good, tolerant people," and so they are. But just as much and just as often they are cruel and nationalistic, shallow and manipulable, frightened and ethnocentric. These are the Janus-faces of national identity. Gazing on these faces, the left sees too much ugliness and the right too much beauty. But both are genuine, and both may be summoned by (and justified in) the lofty language of American ideals. National identity is what we make it. There is an endless contest in the public square to claim "what the United States is all about at our core." And woe unto them who abandon the struggle, for the soul of the nation is at stake.

PART I

MAKING NATIONAL IDENTITY

2

"The Ceaseless Striving to Live Out Our True Creed"

DET. JAMES "JIMMY" McNULTY: Let me understand. Every Friday night, you and your boys are shootin' crap, right? And every Friday night, your pal Snot Boogie . . . he'd wait till there's cash on the ground and he'd grab it and run away? You let him do that?

KID: We'd catch him and beat his ass but ain't nobody ever go past that.

McNULTY: I've gotta ask you: if every time Snot Boogie would grab the money and run away . . . why'd you even let him in the game?

KID: What?

McNULTY: Well, if every time, Snot Boogie stole the money, why'd you let him play?

KID: Got to. This is America, man.

—The Wire, *opening dialogue to season 1, episode 1*

I

SCHOLARS AND SOCIAL CRITICS HAVE LONG pondered the seemingly unbridgeable divide between lofty ideal and lived reality. The many dark chapters in American history—slavery, Jim Crow, and the periodic bursts of xenophobia, nationalism, discrimination, and nativism—have continually prompted debates that challenge whether the United States is genuinely committed to its stated values. This is certainly a sensible object of study; the political scientist Theodore Lowi recently observed that political illegitimacy "can be measured simply as the distance between form and reality."[1] Because the distance endures, the debates continue. But we must recognize their limits. Whatever worried commentators may think, the great majority of Americans entertain no doubts whatsoever about the country's intrinsic greatness.

Polling data in late 2011 revealed that 48 percent of all Americans believe the United States is the greatest country in the world, and another 40 percent say it is certainly one of the greatest.[2] Earlier polls show much the same thing. In 1996, for instance, four in five Americans agreed that "generally speaking, America is a better country than other countries," and nine in ten reported they would rather be American citizens than citizens of any other country.[3] Pollsters have uncovered similar findings for decades. Even before opinion polling came of age in the second half of the twentieth century, the public and private sentiments expressed by Americans—from private diaries and letters to political speeches, editorials, and sermons—all point to the same conclusion. Americans are exceptionally proud of their country. When they gaze at themselves in the national mirror, they do not suffer the sort of angst that might come from living a lie.

When asked what makes their country so special, Americans of every station have long pointed to a set of ideals. They will refer vaguely, but with considerable pride, to "the American Way of Life," which some writers have considered so distinctive as to deserve capital letters.[4] Attempts to distill this sentiment often culminate in a list that has been remarkably stable for centuries: To be an American means to embrace certain principles and traditions, including a commitment to individual liberty as guaranteed by a written Constitution; a complementary attachment to universal equality; respect for the dignity and integrity of the individual; and an abiding distrust of centralized authority, which often expresses itself in the idea that government should be limited in reach and restrained by the rule of law.[5] Many will also point to an intangible commitment to the welfare of the community, however it is defined—a tradition that does not easily reduce itself to a phrase, though "civic virtue" comes close. Americans cling to these values and traditions with a pugnacious intensity that defies not only argument but fact. As the historian Richard Hofstadter famously put it, "It has been our fate as a nation not to have ideologies but to be one."[6]

The idea that national identity reflects a commitment to a set of shared values and traditions is what writers mean by the American Creed. The expression itself was popularized by the Swedish economist Gunnar Myrdal and his coauthors in their enormously influential 1944 study of southern racial inequality, *An American Dilemma: The Negro Problem and Modern Democracy.*[7] But the essential idea of the Creed long predates Myrdal. Visitors have commented upon it for centuries, scholars have studied it nearly as long, and those who live here have experienced it every day.[8]

To be sure, the writers who have tried to reduce the Creed to words have not been entirely consistent. But the differences in their accounts can generally be traced to their own idiosyncrasies and biases. For instance, Myrdal, whose purpose was to point out the many ways in which Jim Crow was a betrayal of what he believed was the irreducible core of American identity, tended to emphasize the Creed's egalitarian and humanistic aspects. He wrote that the Creed captured "the essential dignity of the individual human being, of the fundamental equality of all men, and of certain inalienable rights to freedom, justice, and a fair opportunity."[9]

In *American Politics: The Promise of Disharmony*, the political scientist Samuel Huntington described the "core" values of the American Creed as "liberty, equality, individualism, democracy, and the rule of law under a constitution."[10] But two decades later, in *Who Are We? The Challenges to America's National Identity*, Huntington lamented what he saw as the waning influence of our Anglo-Protestant heritage in American culture. Unlike his earlier treatment, in *Who Are We?* he stressed the distinctive contribution of this heritage to the shared values of the Creed.[11] By contrast, when the historian Arthur Schlesinger, Jr., wrote his broadside against a multiculturalism that he felt slighted the European contribution to national identity, he tended to minimize religious influences and spoke instead of "the great Western ideas of individual freedom, political democracy, and human rights."[12]

The sociologist Seymour Martin Lipset thought the Creed could be described "in five terms: liberty, egalitarianism, individualism, populism, and *laissez-faire*."[13] To Lipset's list, many others add the rule of law. The United States is an intensely legalistic society and its reverence for the Constitution is almost limitless. As the legal scholar Mary Ann Glendon has observed,

Americans "look to law as an expression and carrier of the few values that are widely shared in our society: liberty, equality, and the ideal of justice under law. . . . Legality, to a great extent, has become a touchstone for legitimacy."[14] Others have often made similar observations.[15]

In their emphasis on the American Creed's classical liberal values, these and other writers stand with Alexis de Tocqueville, the nineteenth-century French observer of American society whose *Democracy in America* remains required reading about American life. Others, however, like the sociologist Robert Bellah and the journalist E. J. Dionne, have identified another tradition that has coursed through American thought. This tradition stresses the well-being and integrity of the community and the virtuous citizen's obligations to the community's welfare.[16] "Many in our country do not know the pain of poverty," George W. Bush once said. "But we can listen to those who do. And I can pledge our Nation to a goal: When we see that wounded traveler on the road to Jericho, we will not pass to the other side."[17]

This commitment to civic virtue, with or without the religious symbolism, has a long history in American thought.[18] The more secular version is captured in the title of Hillary Clinton's book *It Takes a Village*.[19] It was a central theme of Barack Obama's 2012 State of the Union address, when he appealed to our "common purpose" and "our common resolve." "No one built this country on their own," he said in his closing remarks. "This nation is great because we built it together. This nation is great because we worked as a team. This nation is great because we get each other's backs. And if we hold fast to that truth, in this moment of trial, there is no challenge too great; no mission too hard. As long as we are joined in common purpose, as long as we maintain our common resolve, our journey moves forward, and our future is hopeful, and the state of our Union will always be strong."[20] On other occasions, Obama has tried to wed the individualistic and communitarian strains in American thought. Throughout our history, he told a Florida audience in 2011, "what has distinguished us from all other nations is not just our wealth, it's not just our power. It's been our deep commitment to individual freedom and personal responsibility, but also our unshakeable commitment to one another, a recognition that we share a future, that we rise or fall together, that we are part of a common enterprise that is greater, somehow, than the sum of its parts."[21]

These differences in the account of the American Creed should not be taken as proof of deep disagreement about shared values. No doubt Myrdal recognized limited government as a value of some significance to American identity, though it did not make his list, and it is impossible to imagine that Huntington considered freedom irrelevant to the American experience or that he was indifferent to civic virtue and the welfare of the community. In their account of the Creed, the political scientists Herbert McClosky and John Zaller used freedom and liberty interchangeably. "No value in the American ethos is more revered than freedom," they wrote, but added almost immediately, "Equality and popular sovereignty, of course, are given their due, but liberty is more deeply embedded in the nation's system of values than any of the others."[22]

Omissions and quirks like these merely underscore that the words are meant to stand in for an inherently imprecise idea—namely, that cluster of core values widely shared by the great majority of Americans and identified by them as integral to national identity. It is this imprecision that allowed the historian Daniel Boorstin to write an entire book about Americans' tendency to view our defining values as "a given," without pausing to articulate what those values were (and to give his book the immodest title *The Genius of American Politics*).[23] The list of values, in other words, is less important than what those values are meant to convey, which is the answer to the question asked more than two centuries ago by Hector St. Jean de Crèvecœur in his letters to Europe: "What then is the American, this new man?"[24]

Because lists of this sort are mere words, they can no more give us the full meaning of a lived experience than a skeleton can provide the full measure of a man. To compensate for this imprecision, Americans have always enlarged the list into a set of morality tales—richly symbolic stories we tell ourselves to get a better picture of who we are as a nation. Consider the story of Rosa Parks, whose brave decision in December 1955 to remain seated when the driver of a Montgomery, Alabama, bus ordered her to give up her seat for a white rider helped launch the boycott that played such an important role in the civil rights movement. Today her story is remembered as a lesson about personal courage in the face of gross injustice. But at a more fundamental level it is about equality, the rule of law, and civic membership. Parks is celebrated today as part of a larger movement in American society that used the rule of law (the federal civil rights legislation) as a sword to strike a blow at the barriers to equality imposed by the Jim Crow South in order to restore African-Americans to full participation in the civic life of the community.

American life is full of these tales. For example, millions of immigrants have become an object lesson, their countless experiences flash-frozen into a single story about an open society and a bountiful land. Emerson captured the essence of the tale when he described the glorious new world that supposedly awaited the immigrant. "Opportunity of civil rights, of education, of personal power, and not less of wealth; doors wide open . . . to every nation, to every race and skin, . . . hospitality of fair field and equal laws to all. Let them compete, and success to the strongest, the wisest, and the best. The land is wide enough, the soil has bread for all."[25] This is a story of equality and individual liberty, of course, but also of the rule of law and limited government, which combine to create the conditions that allow individualism to thrive. And this story has produced another, which the political scientist and sociologist Alan Wolfe has called the tale of "the good immigrant," who comes to this country, works hard, embraces its values, assimilates its traditions, contributes to its rich diversity, and ascends into its middle class. We recognize this story as a tribute to a particular conception of civic membership.[26]

Or consider the "self-made man." His success is considered a testament to the virtue of American life, where the accidents of caste and clan do not prevent a person from making the most of his talent and ambition. But the story is also a paean to the ideals of liberty, equality, and individualism: liberty because all are free to make and remake themselves as best they can, unconstrained by the past; equality because one person has as much claim to the prize as the next; and individualism because the sole predictor of success is, and should be, individual effort and ingenuity. Of course, the fact that the tale refers to a man is just one way in which it has never reflected reality for a majority of the population, but that does not prevent it from becoming a deeply embedded and dearly prized story about American life.

Most of us recognize that these tales of national identity are embellished and enriched as they are continually retold. Rosa Parks is transformed from flesh and blood to national symbol. In the process of becoming symbols, these stories come to occupy that uncertain ground between myth and truth, a place the historian William McNeill called mythistory.[27] They become the legitimating tales of national life. Still, to label something as part myth is not to denigrate it. A country cannot long survive without a set of tales that provide national cohesion and purpose, which is the role of myth. And myth should not be confused with legend or fairy tale. John Henry is a legend, Pinocchio a fairy tale, but the Founding Fathers were real people whom we have endowed with mythic qualities in order to enhance the moral lesson of their contribution to the American experience. Myth is truth burnished to a brightness, durability, and perfection not found in nature. Each new generation commits to protect our national myths, recognizing that they carry within them an important truth, until finally we cherish the myths rather than the truth, and the two become one in the national understanding. The myth becomes our representation of the truth—not entirely the truth, and sometimes dangerously removed from it, but certainly not a lie.[28]

These stories should also alert us to the fact that national identity is not static. Though Americans have long invoked the same values and traditions to describe their national identity, they have given these words very different meanings and prioritized them differently over time. The bus driver who told Ms. Parks to give up her seat, the police officer who arrested her when she refused, and the judge who convicted her of violating a Montgomery ordinance and fined her ten dollars almost certainly had a different conception of equality, and assigned it a different priority in American life, than we do today. Yet their view was widely shared throughout the South, at least among whites, and indeed throughout most of the country for most of the nation's history. Equality means something very different today from what it meant during the heyday of Jim Crow, and in fact, as two historians have shown, its meaning today bears only a distant "family resemblance" to its meaning at the time of the Founding.[29]

What is true for equality is no less true for the other values that make up American identity. Historians have long understood that the key ingredients of national identity are both socially constructed and hopelessly abstract. Words and phrases like "equality," "liberty," "freedom," "the state," and "the rule of law" have acquired radically different meanings over the years as partisans have battled to make one or another understanding dominant in the public square.[30] "The meanings of freedom," wrote the historian Eric Foner, "have been constructed not only in congressional debates and political treatises, but on plantations and picket lines, in parlors and bedrooms. . . . The history of freedom is really the history of contests over its constructions and exclusions."[31] What we mean by liberty, writes Cornell's Michael Kammen, has likewise "changed and broadened over time, . . . ranging from constraints upon authority to improvements in the conditions of social justice, of privacy, and a growing concern for the protection of personal liberty."[32] This process is not only natural but inevitable. As Supreme Court Justice Felix Frankfurter once observed, "Great concepts like . . . 'due process of law,' 'liberty,' [and] 'property' were purposely left to gather meaning from experience. For they relate to the whole domain of social and economic fact, and the statesmen who founded this Nation knew too well that only a stagnant society remains unchanged."[33]

In addition, these values will invariably clash, stimulating and encouraging the endless process of redefinition. One of the most prominent and enduring conflicts has been between liberty and equality, since the full expression of one inevitably runs up against the demands of the other. The ideals of laissez-faire capitalism, with its insistence on limited government, unregulated markets, and private control of property and contract, and the egalitarian ideals of democracy, with its reliance on law and the coercive power of the state to assure equality of treatment and opportunity, are inherently at odds.[34] Either one, taken to an extreme, tramples on the other, and the precise moment when arrangements have reached that trampling extreme is ever in the eyes of the beholder.

Other conflicts arise from the complex origins of our shared values. Some writers, like Samuel Huntington, place great emphasis on the religious foundations of American society, in particular on its Anglo-Protestant heritage.[35] Others tend to slight religious influences and stress the tie to Enlightenment thought, with its emphasis on the rule of law and natural rights.[36] Even the most casual observer of contemporary American society is familiar with the debates that result when these two perspectives collide, which they occasionally do with great passion. That was certainly the case in 2004, when the Supreme Court was asked to consider whether the last line of the Pledge of Allegiance ("one Nation under God, indivisible, with liberty and justice for all") improperly endorsed religion and therefore violated the Establishment Clause of the First Amendment.[37] The last six words ("with liberty and justice for all"), which have been part of the pledge since it was written by the socialist Baptist minister Francis Bellamy in 1892, obviously reveal the influence of Enlightenment thought and liberal ideals. The words "under God," by contrast, were added in 1954, when Cold War tensions induced Congress to emphasize the distinction between the United States and godless communism.[38] (Shortly thereafter, Congress also made "in God we trust" the national motto.) The bitter controversy that erupted when it appeared the Court would decide whether God had any place in the pledge testifies eloquently to the enormous and potentially divisive power of both traditions. In the end, the Court avoided the question.[39]

Still other conflicts center on the competing demands of the individual and the community. This particular clash has been especially prominent in the past several decades. We often hear that an extravagant concern for the rights of one class of claimants—for instance, criminal defendants—threatens the welfare of the entire community.[40] Yet we also hear that an overweening concern for the well-being of some imagined community threatens individual liberty, which is at the core of much of the Tea Party rhetoric.[41] These debates are among the ugliest in American society, since they lend themselves so easily to polemics about who is in, who is out, and why. Only when one group is perceived as "outside" the rest are its claims viewed as a demand *on* the community, rather than a demand *by* the community. At a fundamental level, therefore, these debates—the most fractious and contentious arguments of all—are about national membership.

Yet if words like "liberty," "equality," and "community" are imprecise, if their meanings change over time, they are nonetheless among the most symbolically potent words in American life. No cultural leader who holds out hope of influencing the course of public debate in this country can say that the rule of law is unimportant, that liberty is overrated, that centralized control is better than individual freedom, or that Thomas Jefferson had it all wrong—men are *not* created equal. To say such things in America is to court instant marginalization. The most this would-be leader can say is that perhaps in this particular situation one value has proven itself more useful than another, and should therefore be given pride of place. But that is a very different matter from suggesting that a time-honored ideal, cherished for generations and revered by the Founders, can ever be deliberately cast aside.

The obligation to speak in the shared language of symbol and myth generally poses no difficulty for our leaders. They do not expound on the wonder of American ideals merely because that is what one must say to get ahead. All evidence suggests that they, like the great majority of Americans, genuinely believe in the myths they repeat. Their faith in the symbols they invoke is deeply felt. Southern slaveowners in the antebellum era gave rousing speeches in defense of equality as they understood it, which moved the hearts and stirred the souls of whites throughout the region as they prepared to die in defense of the Peculiar Institution.[42] We do a great disservice to the historical record if we pretend that, simply because their vision of the nation no longer predominates, it was therefore false or insincere.[43]

This brings us to one of the core contentions of the book. The values and beliefs that make up national identity are best understood not as fixed stars in an unchanging sky but as a set of immensely powerful symbols that are manipulated, deployed, and redefined to justify competing social arrangements. The rule of law, to take just one example, is not some unchanging state of affairs whose meaning is universally agreed upon. It is a symbol that partisans invoke to rally support, justify a policy, or explain an attack, and its use has changed dramatically over time. And the idea of the rule of law embraces other symbols that are similarly powerful and equally malleable. The Constitution, for instance, is the master symbol of the rule of law and moral legitimacy in American life. For many people, it is the trump card that settles all arguments. But snippets associated with the Constitution can play a similar role. Phrases like "separation of powers," "the Bill of Rights," "the right to bear arms," "due process," and "habeas corpus," all of which come directly or indirectly from the Constitution, or even an expression like "We the People," which is part of the preamble, are infused with such great symbolic power that most Americans consider them worth defending even if they do not know exactly what they mean.[44] Like the other key elements of the American experiment, they are *rhetorical resources*, weapons in the verbal battle to achieve dominance in the public square for one or another vision of national life.

These symbols are not infinitely elastic. As the fate of American socialism attests, they cannot be combined in a way that would justify *any* social arrangement.[45] And some combinations, though perhaps theoretically available, have become so thoroughly discredited that they are no longer part of what the sociologist Ann Swidler calls the cultural tool kit.[46] It is hard to imagine, for instance, that anyone will once again argue that women have no place in the workforce and even more difficult to suppose that such an argument, if advanced, would gain credence. Demographic and economic forces have simply left it behind. But within the broad range of allowable forms, American national identity is not given to us by divine Providence or entrusted to us as a covenant from our ancestors. It is fought for and won in the public square. Though Americans have always defined their national identity in terms of a core set of shared values, the meaning of those values—their shape and content at any one time; what they demand of the citizen and her society; whom they protect and to what degree; whom they exclude and why; how they are prioritized when they inevitably conflict— these vital questions are endlessly contested. In short, when it comes to shared values, the words may be stable and timeless, *but their meaning is constructed and changing.*[47] As he so often did, Tocqueville well captured this odd habit of thought:

> Men living in democratic countries . . . are apt to entertain unsettled ideas, and they require loose expressions to convey them. As they never know whether the idea they express today will be appropriate to the new position they may occupy tomorrow, they naturally acquire a liking for abstract terms. An abstract term is like a box with a false bottom; you may put into it what ideas you please, and take them out again without being observed.[48]

In a Fourth of July address to the National Education Association in 1924, President Calvin Coolidge said, "American ideals do not require to be changed so much as they require to be understood and applied."[49] But what Coolidge failed to appreciate was that the process by which we understand and apply these ideals is precisely what changes them. Bill Clinton may have been more correct than he realized when he said, during his first inau-

gural address, "Every generation of Americans must define what it means
to be an American."[50]

II

The determination to define national identity in terms of a small set of
shared values, which are in turn communicated through widely shared legitimating myths and symbols, has enormous consequences. For one thing,
it imparts a characteristic manner of speech, a way of speaking American.
It is the universally recognizable language of the American Creed. When
Vice President Gore said in the 2000 Wake Forest debate that racial profiling was "counter to what the United States is all about at our core," and
Governor Bush said it was "not what America is all about," they appealed to
the now widely shared egalitarian principle that no person shall be judged
based on the color of his skin, which draws on the ideals of equality and
civic virtue. When Governor Bush denounced the use of secret evidence in
immigration proceedings as "not the American way," he joined his position
to the equally powerful belief that Americans are committed to "fairness,
dignity, [and] civil rights." When he expressed confidence that Americans
are "good, tolerant people," he attached himself to the ideal of an open and
welcoming culture that treats everyone with respect. And when Gore said
America has to have "a sense of mission in the world," he appealed to the
deep-seated belief that the nation has a special role in spreading its values
across the globe.

But there is a flip side. Some rhetoric will simply strike the American ear
wrong and therefore win no followers in the public square. The political
scientist Louis Hartz gave the example of George Fitzhugh, the antebellum southern social theorist who defended slavery but thought the condition should extend to both blacks and poor whites. Fitzhugh also accepted
the inevitability of an aristocracy in the United States.[51] Defenses of slavery
were certainly common enough in the antebellum South, but Fitzhugh's
justification set him at odds with the pillars of American identity as it
had been constructed in the antebellum South, particularly the distinctive
meaning of equality, which put all white men on an equal plane. His work
was well received only by a small planter and academic elite.[52] Examples

like this can be readily multiplied; if Fitzhugh is too obscure, we could easily substitute Marx. In a country where "socialist" is an epithet on a par with
"harlot," Groucho is the only Marx one can safely endorse.

Sometimes the language of the Creed takes the form of an ambitious
attempt to capture the whole of the national story in a few short sentences.
"The promise of America," Bill Clinton said in 1997, "was born in the 18th
century out of the bold conviction that we were all created equal."

> It was extended and preserved in the 19th century, when our Nation spread
> across the continent, saved the Union, and abolished the scourge of slavery.
> Then, in turmoil and triumph, that promise exploded onto the world stage
> to make this the American Century. . . . America became the world's mighti-
> est power, saved the world from tyranny in two World Wars and a long cold
> war, and . . . reached out across the globe to millions who, like us, longed for
> the blessings of liberty.[53]

Here, in one hundred words, is nearly the entire national experience as it
is commonly told—the great rise from humble birth to "mightiest power,"
the beacon to immigrants across the globe, the savior from tyranny, the
enduring commitment to liberty and equality, and the undefined link between American values and divine "blessings." The entire passage, spoken
in the language of the Creed, is instantly recognizable and congenial to
nearly every American as a tale of triumph, innocence, and virtue. Dark
chapters that cast an unwelcome shadow across a hallowed national myth
understandably get no space.

Other times, speakers stress the Creed itself, the idea of shared and uni-
fying principles. The second President Bush was particularly fond of this.
At a Fourth of July celebration in 2002 at Ripley, West Virginia, he told
the cheering crowd that "unlike any other country, America came into the
world with a message for mankind that all are created equal, and all are
meant to be free."

> There is no American race. There's only an American creed: We believe
> in the dignity and rights of every person; we believe in equal justice, lim-
> ited government, and in the rule of law; we believe in personal responsi-
> bility and tolerance toward others. This creed of freedom and equality has
> lifted the lives of millions of Americans, of citizens by birth and citizens by

choice. This creed draws our friends to us. It sets our enemies against us and always inspires the best that is within us.[54]

On other occasions, speakers tap into the part of the Creed that suits their purpose at the moment, using the words and symbols that Americans recognize and revere. Martin Luther King, Bill Clinton said at his second inaugural address, "told of his dream that one day America would rise up and treat all its citizens as equals before the law and in the heart. Martin Luther King's dream was the American dream. His quest is our quest: the ceaseless striving to live out our true creed."[55]

Because it is meant to describe a shared national identity, the language of the Creed is entirely bipartisan. All political speech is couched in its terms, sometimes in ringing tones:

> Let the word go forth from this time and place, to friend and foe alike, that the torch has passed to a new generation of Americans, born in this century, tempered by war, disciplined by a hard and bitter peace, proud of our ancient heritage, and unwilling to witness or permit the slow undoing of those human rights to which this nation has always been committed, and to which we are committed today at home and around the world. Let every nation know, whether it wishes us well or ill, that we shall pay any price, bear any burden, meet any hardship, support any friend, oppose any foe to assure the survival and success of liberty.[56]

It is this bipartisan quality that allowed Richard Nixon to channel Lyndon Johnson in his appeal to equality and civic virtue:

> No people has ever been so close to the achievement of a just and abundant society, or so possessed of the will to achieve it. . . . Those who have been left out, we will try to bring in. Those left behind, we will help to catch up. . . . No man can be fully free while his neighbor is not. To go forward at all is to go forward together. This means black and white together, as one nation, not two. The laws have caught up with our conscience. What remains is to give life to what is in the law; to insure at last that as all are born equal in dignity before God, all are born equal in dignity before man.[57]

And it led George W. Bush to sound like Jimmy Carter when he said, "In the quiet of American conscience, we know that deep, persistent poverty is unworthy of our Nation's promise. . . . Where there is suffering, there is duty. Americans in need are not strangers; they are citizens—not problems but priorities. And all of us are diminished when any are hopeless."[58]

In addition to providing a common "creedal" language, the belief in shared values has other vital consequences. Most important, Americans tend to describe their cherished social arrangements as entirely harmonious with the Creed. Daniel Boorstin made this point more than half a century ago. When describing what they hope to preserve, Americans will almost always say things *are* precisely as they *ought to be.*[59] For example, those who labored so hard to deny women the right to vote—whatever we think of them today—did not see themselves as bad Americans; neither did the members of the virulently anti-Catholic Know Nothing Party in the first half of the nineteenth century. On the contrary, they believed they stood for the very essence of American ideals. Their cause was not a lie or a sham. It was a struggle to protect and sustain national identity as they understood it. We risk the worst sort of historical misunderstanding if we think they looked themselves in the mirror and saw their cherished beliefs as morally bankrupt. They thought their beliefs represented America at its very best.[60]

The converse is also true. When a segment of the population comes to believe the country has fallen out of sync with the Creed, it causes palpable discomfort, like fingernails scraping across a national blackboard. Things are no longer as they ought to be. It is not that the values of national identity are themselves archaic, but that the nation has turned its back from what those values demand. As the political scientist Samuel Huntington observed, these are likely to be periods of intense political and social turmoil, producing what Huntington called episodes of "creedal passion."[61] In these moments, people see the country as cutting a path against the familiar grooves of its true nature, and even those with no prior history as activists may be roused to protest and resist. The Tea Party movement, with its odd cry that President Obama is a Muslim Socialist, is the latest example of this phenomenon. Yet many people view President Obama's economic policies with relief and his religion with indifference. What some see as a dire threat to economic individualism, others view as a welcome affirmation of America's historic commitment to the welfare of the entire community. What some view as a challenge to our Judeo-Christian identity, others view as a testament to religious diversity. Both sides invoke the Creed, and all participants believe they speak for the "true" America.

It is easy to underestimate how pervasive the Creed and its distinctive rhetoric have become in American society. Its language permeates our founding documents—the Declaration of Independence, the Constitution, the Bill of Rights—and is distilled in the clichés memorized by every child and recited by every adult: "with liberty and justice for all"; "all men are created equal"; "life, liberty, and the pursuit of happiness." For centuries, the Creed has been taught in the schools and preached from the pulpit. Editorial pages pronounce endlessly on whether government and private actions demonstrate an appropriate fidelity to the Creed and its principles: Do they advance the inexorable march of equality; do they contribute to the inalienable rights of man; do they honor the intent of the Founders; are they faithful to our sacred texts? The Creed defines the limits of popular culture and sets the bounds of socially acceptable behavior. It raises some to prominence and relegates others to shame. We celebrate Dr. King for the courage of his dream and deride Governor Wallace for the wickedness of his defiance. Entirely without conscious effort, Americans across every stratum of society absorb the national story, told in the language of the Creed, in everything they see, hear, and read. Most times, Americans are no more conscious of the American Creed than a man is of his own bones. But a lack of conscious awareness should not be mistaken for indifference. The Creed pervades American thought and dominates public debate. It is the shared language by which Americans express their national identity.

Almost no opportunity is too trivial to reinforce the Creed, as I learned when I had to get extra pages for my passport. The supplement featured brief quotes from historic figures at the top of each page. Much in the way directors will put a can of Pepsi into a movie scene, it was product placement for the Creed:

> The nation has a banner . . . it is the banner of Dawn. It means Liberty . . .
> Every color means Liberty; every thread means Liberty.
> —Henry Ward Beecher

Democracy is based upon the conviction that there are extraordinary possibilities in ordinary people.
—Harry Emerson Fosdick

The God who gave us life, gave us liberty at the same time.
—Thomas Jefferson

It is immigrants who brought to this land the skills of their hands and brains to make of it a beacon of opportunity and hope for all men.
—Herbert H. Lehman

That this nation, under God, shall have a new birth of freedom.
—Abraham Lincoln

Each quotation captures part of the familiar imagery of the national story; each is written in the language of the Creed: the idea of the nation embarked on an endless journey; the egalitarian faith in "ordinary people"; the tribute to the land as "a beacon of opportunity"; the unseverable but unexplained link between God and values; the paean to symbolically potent words ("democracy," "liberty," and "freedom"); and, of course, homage to the wisdom of past leaders. The sentiments expressed in these snippets are so familiar that they can be quoted by any speaker or dropped onto any page without explanation or context, as they are on the pages of my passport, and elicit nods of agreement from nearly any American audience.

III

This habit of speaking in the language most apt to secure agreement from the most people is perfectly understandable. The elastic language of the Creed is filled with symbols, sentiments, and images shared by the great majority of Americans. It therefore produces an illusion of national consensus and permits us to present a single face to an uncertain world. And tied as it is to the most potent symbols of national identity, it is a faith to which people cling with a fierce passion.

Yet it is nonetheless ill-rewarded. Americans may broadly agree on basic values, but they have often been deeply divided over what those values mean at any given moment, how they should be prioritized, and what they demand by way of concrete action. These differences can be readily translated into competing visions of how things ought to be—that is, of the "true" nature of American identity. For instance, both the fundamentalist Christian who condemns homosexuality and the gay rights activist who defends it will deploy the language of the Creed to make his case. By one light, homosexuality is a threat to the family and a departure from a long and unbroken tradition of Judeo-Christian values, passed down without interruption since the memory of man runneth naught. By another, discrimination against homosexuals offends our fundamental commitment to equality and involves the state in a person's most intimate private choices. (The 2012 election campaign produced a variant of this precise exchange. Shortly before the New Hampshire Republican primary, Mitt Romney was asked by an elderly local resident and veteran whether he supported gay marriage. Romney answered that he did not. "I believe marriage is between a man and a woman," he said, adding that he believed this was also the view of the Founders. "It's good to know how you feel," his questioner responded, "that you do not believe that everyone is entitled to their Constitutional rights." Both speakers claimed the Creed as their polestar. Both claimed to speak for the genuine American experience.)[62]

Or consider the example of a national health care policy. It is either assailed as socialized medicine and therefore contrary to our commitment to individualism, limited government, and personal choice; or it is embraced in the spirit of civic virtue, an overdue acknowledgment that a community thrives only along with its members. One view is individualistic, the other communitarian, but both speak the language of the American Creed and both are faithful to national ideals.[63] Likewise, supporters of affirmative action cast it as essential to the ideal of equality. "In order to get beyond racism," Supreme Court Justice Harry Blackmun wrote in *Regents of the University of California v. Bakke,* "we must first take into account race. There is no other way. And in order to treat some people equally, we must treat them differently."[64] But of course, many people believe that trying to achieve equality by treating people unequally amounts to moving backward in order to advance. Opponents of affirmative action frame it as "reverse discrimination," relying on the same egalitarian ideal to press for the opposite result. The language of the Creed thus becomes a kind of national Ror-

schach blot, justifying a kaleidoscope of conflicting, sometimes contradic-
tory positions. In fact, apart from moments of acute national crisis, when
a spirit of cooperation briefly settles on the land like fresh snow, we detect
this cacophony in all public debate over national issues. In any national
controversy where participants hope to influence the direction of American
thought, all sides will invoke the language and symbols of the Creed. No
argument can succeed without it.

〉 This points to another, even more serious consequence of our reliance
on the language of abstract national symbols: the risk of elite manipulation. National controversies are remote from most Americans' daily lives.
As the political scientist Murray Edelman put it nearly five decades ago, for
the vast majority of Americans the issues exist only as "a series of pictures
in the mind, placed there by television news, newspapers, magazines, and
discussions."[65] (Today we would add the Internet and social media.) National policy is distant and opaque to most of us, operating in a world set
apart from our daily existence and beyond our power to control. We have
no direct access to the relevant information and cannot assess which of the
many contested claims are true. Does raising the U.S. debt ceiling imperil
individual liberty by constantly feeding the insatiable maw of the federal
government, as members of the Tea Party warned in 2011? Or is it a routine
step, essential to running the government and maintaining the confidence
of the international markets? Should the federal government regulate Wall
Street? What should be done about global warming? Just what are Korean
and Iranian nuclear ambitions, and how should they be met?

The great majority of Americans cannot answer these questions for
themselves, so they look to cues and messages from trusted insiders who
they believe have access to the facts they lack. They form judgments about
what they "want" with respect to these issues, and whether those wants are
being met, not by independent study but from cues and messages provided
by perceived elites: national politicians, prominent journalists, television
and radio personalities, public intellectuals, religious leaders, and others
recognized as experts. These people are believed to have digested the information for and against a particular policy in order to arrive at a position that
is most congenial to the values they share with their audience. They can be
counted on, in other words, to reach the position that a like-minded person

would come to if she had the time to review the evidence herself.[66] As two
careful students of the process recently put the matter:

> Citizens aren't in a position to figure out through personal investigation
> whether the death penalty deters, gun control undermines public safety,
> commerce threatens the environment, *et cetera*. They have to take the word
> of those whom they trust on issues of what sorts of empirical claims and
> what sorts of data supporting such claims, are credible. The people they
> trust, naturally, are the ones who share their values—and who . . . are pre-
> disposed to a particular view.[67]

Illustrations of this abound in the post-9/11 era, but few are more candid
on the matter than Robert Spencer. Spencer is undoubtedly one of the most
outspoken critics of Islam participating in the post-9/11 debates. He is a
prolific author, producing a new book almost every year, the titles of which
tell us both his orientation and his target audience: *Religion of Peace? Why
Christianity Is and Islam Isn't; The Myth of Islamic Tolerance: How Islamic
Law Treats Non-Muslims; The Politically Incorrect Guide to Islam (and the
Crusades); The Truth About Muhammad, Founder of the World's Most Intolerant Religion; Stealth Jihad: How Radical Islam Is Subverting America Without
Guns or Bombs.* In his 2009 book, *The Complete Infidel's Guide to the Koran,*
he asked rhetorically, "Why not just read the Koran on your own? Why does
any self-respecting infidel need a guide?" Because, he helpfully answered,
the Koran is confusing. It "isn't easy for non-Muslims." According to Spencer, it follows no discernible narrative structure or chronological order and
gets repetitive and boring. "But never fear," he says, "I read the Koran so
you don't have to."[68]

"Experts" like Spencer do not simply articulate a solution for whatever
problem is at hand. They inform people *what the problem is,* and communicate it in the symbolically potent language of national values. An excellent
illustration of this occurred at a town hall meeting in 2012, when conservative Tea Party Congressman Joe Walsh (R-IL) warned, in classic creedal
language, about the threat to individualism posed by government "handouts," which he views as a sort of opium, narcotizing people into a condition of dependency that saps them of their will to be free and independent

citizens. His comments were part of an extended monologue about the virtues of limited government and individual liberty and the complementary need to shrink the federal government and cut taxes. "I really am scared," he thundered at one point, "that we're past the point—we have so many people now dependent on government, so many people want handouts." The Democratic Party, he continued, "promises groups of people everything. They want the Hispanic vote, they want Hispanics to be dependent on government, just like they got African-Americans dependent on government. That's their game." In case anyone missed the implication, he later told a radio host, "Once you're dependent on government, you'll continue to vote for the party of government." Civil rights activist Jesse Jackson, he added, "would be out of work" if African-Americans "weren't dependent on government."[69]

With this diatribe, Walsh both named what he saw as the problem (government "handouts" that threaten individual liberty by making people "dependent" on a particular political party) and offered the solution (lower taxes, less regulation, and support for the Republican Party). His supporters, self-selected to share his values, were apparently not offended by his remark that all African-Americans were "dependent on government." Instead, like Walsh, they were focused on his other creedal message, about individual liberty and smaller government, which they found congenial to their own values. Yet when news of his remarks spread, his opponents named a very different problem (Walsh was a racist who openly traded in false stereotypes about African-Americans and thus betrayed the creedal commitment to universal equality), and offered a different solution (the need to support Democrats in order to defeat Walsh at the polls). They made no mention of Walsh's support of individual liberty and limited government.[70] Each side, in short, identifies the problem to suit its needs and proposes a solution designed to satisfy the values held by its audience. And all of this is communicated in the malleable language of the American Creed.

But remote attachments can be paradoxical. Because the issue exists only as "a series of pictures in the mind," the image in the mind's eye depends on the pictures. The remoteness is what makes the attachment malleable. Bombard a person with a new set of pictures, and her attachment can change. Scholars often do not pay sufficient heed to this malleability and its implications for the formation of national identity. The Princeton sociologist Robert Wuthnow, for instance, in his otherwise excellent account of religious diversity in the United States, quoted a California woman (herself an immigrant) who asked, "Is it the Islams or whoever who believe in Allah? And they will kill and murder for Allah because they go straight to heaven if they kill for Allah? That is an extreme bad religion, I think." Another man expressed a similar sentiment: "I didn't realize a religion could tell people to kill. And then we have all these bombings and terrorist attacks." Wuthnow's book appeared in 2005, and the interviews were conducted in 2002 and 2003.[71] Although it is remotely possible these people came to their mistaken judgments based on their own study of Islam and its tenets, it is far more likely they were simply repeating what they had heard and accepted as true in a post-9/11 world. As we will see, sentiments like theirs are now quite common. Yet the people who hold them think they are good Americans, steeped in the values and traditions of the American Creed.

Sometimes, remote attachments change with dizzying speed even when they seem to have been thoroughly entrenched. History presents a ready supply of such transformations. The classic example is the post–World War II reimagining of Germany and the Germans from demonic incarnation of evil to democracy-loving, anticommunist stalwarts and allies—a metamorphosis that provided one of George Orwell's inspirations for his novel 1984.[72] But an even more striking illustration, if perhaps less commented upon, was the juxtaposition in the perception of the Japanese and our former allies the Russians and Chinese. As the historian John Dower has artfully shown, within weeks of the war's end, the iconic wartime image of the Japanese—the rapacious, blood-soaked, and savage ape—was replaced with the inquisitive, imitative, and childlike chimp, resting on the broad shoulders of his American protectors, who would educate him in the ways of democracy.[73] General Douglas MacArthur later made this relationship explicit, explaining to the Senate that his philosophy during the occupation of Japan had been to treat the Japanese as twelve-year-olds: "Measured by the standards of modern civilization," he said, "they would be like a boy of 12. . . . Like any tuitionary period, they were susceptible to following new models. You can implant basic concepts there. They were still close enough to origin to be elastic and acceptable to new concepts."[74]

Meanwhile, as the Japanese were reimagined as eager and harmless students of the American Way, the Russians were cast in the old wartime stereotypes. "Traits which the Americans and English had associated with the Japanese, with great empirical sobriety, were suddenly perceived to be really more relevant to the Communists (deviousness and cunning, bestial and atrocious behavior, homogeneity and monolithic control, fanaticism divorced from any legitimate goals . . .)." When China joined the communist camp, the favorable traits attributed to the Chinese during the war—their individualism and love of democracy—suddenly disappeared, replaced by "the old, monolithic, inherently totalitarian raiments the Japanese were shedding. They became the unthinking horde; the fanatics; . . . the new Yellow Peril." Experts quickly emerged to explain their "true" character. Edmund Chubb, a diplomat and leading China specialist, assured Americans that the Chinese "do not think like other men" but act out of a "madness born of xenophobia."[75]

Such eye-popping transformations are not uncommon, nor are they confined to matters of national security. In 1972, in *Furman v. Georgia,* the Supreme Court struck down then-existing death penalty statutes. In the years prior to *Furman,* the death penalty had come under attack from leading intellectuals, prominent politicians, editorialists, and religious organizations.[76] Juries had been sentencing fewer and fewer people to die, and protracted appeals had prevented executions. There were 105 executions in 1951 but just 56 in 1960. Five years later there were only 7, and in June 1967, Colorado carried out what would be the last execution in the United States for a decade.[77] State legislatures responded to these developments with a flurry of activity. By 1969, fourteen states had abolished the death penalty and several others came close. In 1957 the California and Illinois Assemblies passed six-year moratoria on executions, and the Illinois Assembly renewed theirs in 1967. Meanwhile, public opinion polls showed decreasing support—and more important, no apparent enthusiasm—for the ultimate sanction.[78] By 1972 there seemed to be a growing national consensus against capital punishment.

Yet the day after the Supreme Court decision in *Furman,* legislators in five states announced their intention to introduce bills to restore the death penalty. President Nixon asked the FBI for the names of convicted killers who had committed a second murder after being released from prison. That November the California electorate, which had hardly reacted when its Assembly passed its moratorium, now overwhelmingly supported an amendment to the state constitution to allow for capital punishment. By 1976, thirty-five states plus the federal government had enacted new death penalty statutes.[79]

The shift in public opinion was equally dramatic. A few months before *Furman*, supporters of capital punishment outnumbered opponents by only 8 percentage points; a few months after, the number grew to 25 points. By the time the Court revisited the issue in 1976, supporters outnumbered opponents 65 percent to 28 percent, the widest gap since the early 1950s.[80] As the legal historian Stuart Banner observed, "*Furman* suddenly made capital punishment a more salient issue than it had been in decades, perhaps ever. People who previously had had little occasion to think about the death penalty now saw it on the front page of the newspaper. *Furman*, like other landmark cases, had the effect of calling its opponents to action."[81]

To be sure, public opinion is not Silly Putty, and some views are more firmly fixed than others. One reason why attitudes about the death penalty could be manipulated so easily is that widespread opposition to capital punishment had emerged only in the decade before *Furman*, which meant the attachment to the sentiment was fragile. Likewise, anti-German sentiments did not have nearly the historic pedigree of anticommunism, which facilitated the shift in thought from "Germany as totalitarian enemy" to "Germany as anticommunist ally." But as views and attachments spread through society and enter the received wisdom, beyond credible criticism— as they become part of how things *ought to be*—they grow steadily more difficult to dislodge. By the unassailable power of the American Creed, they become part of "what the United States is all about at our core." They become our national identity.

National identity is what we make it. And sometimes, let us be fair, we make a hash of it. We are just as capable of creating an identity that causes untold damage to unnamed millions as we are of creating its opposite. Yet at the time, that identity will be defended with the same tenacity as any other. Its supporters will claim it represents the one "true" America and insist that things *are* as they *ought to be*. Though Americans are loath to admit it, there is a darkness to national identity that must be examined more closely. Even the most horrific forms can be justified in the lofty language of American ideals—as the post-9/11 debates would prove.

3

The Dark Side of the Creed

I

EVERY NATION BELIEVES IN ITS OWN VIRTUE. There is nothing inherently wrong with this, though at the margins it risks an ugly turn to nationalism. In the main, however, it endows a country with a necessary sense of national unity and moral purpose. But such a belief is not without consequences, the most prominent of which may be a curious approach to history. Certain interpretations of the past may become sacrosanct. When historians uncovered evidence suggesting that the bombings at Nagasaki and Hiroshima were as much a warning to the Soviet Union as a blow to Japan, and were perhaps more the start of a cold war than the end of a hot one, they cast an unwelcome shadow across the sacred national memory of "the Good War," when a selfless nation saved democracy from the evil of totalitarianism. Their thesis was met with derision, and scholars who promoted it were publicly damned as unpatriotic revisionists.[1]

But no amount of historic scrubbing can erase the stain left by certain elements of the American experience. To protect the belief in national virtue from the destructive reality of these shameful periods, we relegate them to a dark and regrettable past. That was then and this is now. History takes on a teleological glow, becoming an endless journey toward the fulfillment of our unique national promise. Deviations from the path are walled off in the national memory as aberrations. We hold them up as cautionary lessons that mark how far we can fall should we ever again stray from the Creed. And we assimilate them into the myth of national virtue by using them to gauge our progress in our eternal march toward "a more perfect Union."[2]

But it takes time to reshape the past, to erase mistakes from the national memory and transform them from settled understandings into temporary misjudgments. In September 1992 Lynne V. Cheney, then chair of the National Endowment for the Humanities, was the principal author of an angry little pamphlet called *Telling the Truth*, which excoriated liberals in academia for their over-glum assessment of the American experience.[3] Cheney applauded the State of California for its decision to teach its students the "common truth" that Americans were united by a shared "belief in equality and freedom." She quoted approvingly from the California curriculum, which put the matter in the immediately recognizable language of the Creed:

> The American Creed is derived from the language of the Constitution, the Declaration of Independence and the Bill of Rights. . . . The Creed provides the unifying theme of Martin Luther King, Jr.'s oration, "I have a dream that one day this nation will rise up and live out the true meaning of its creed: *We hold these truths to be self-evident, that all men are created equal. . . .* This will be the day when all of God's children will be able to sing with new meaning, 'My Country, Tis of Thee, Sweet Land of Liberty.'"[4]

It is all perfectly good today to believe that Dr. King's vision of the Creed is shared by all Americans, but that was certainly not evident in April 1963, when Alabama Governor George Wallace told Attorney General Robert Kennedy that it was King who was "advocating . . . lawlessness" by demanding civil rights for African-Americans.[5] Nor was it evident later that year when Attorney General Kennedy authorized J. Edgar Hoover and the FBI to tap King's phones. Hoover firmly believed that King's private conversations would confirm Hoover's public insistence that King was connected to the Communist Party.[6] And it was not evident for many years after King's assassination in 1968, when Representative John Conyers (D-MI) annually introduced legislation to make King's birthday a national holiday, only to have it derailed in committee or defeated on the House floor. Even in 1983, when the bill passed both chambers by an overwhelming margin and was reluctantly signed into law by President Reagan, it was still not evident to Senator Jesse Helms (R-NC), who voted against the measure and attacked King for "action-oriented Marxism."[7] Cultural change calls upon us to create new champions and to mold flesh and blood into mythic symbols. Today we celebrate Dr. King for the courage of his dream. But we deceive ourselves if we pretend it was always so.

Countless books have been written about the darker episodes of the American past. But less attention has been paid to how a nation so deeply committed to the values of the American Creed justifies its misdeeds. Certainly the fact that we view things differently in the fullness of time provides a partial answer: Problems that seem trivial today once loomed large in the public imagination. But this merely states the obvious—priorities change and perspective is a virtue—without telling us how American thought justified illiberality at the time. How do Americans avoid the damning charge of hypocrisy? When confronted with the chasm between ideal and reality, what do they say?

Lincoln's famous observation on this score is instructive. In June 1857, in a speech at Springfield, Illinois, Lincoln said the drafters of the Declaration "meant to set up a standard maxim for a free society which should be familiar to all, and revered by all; constantly looked to, constantly labored for, and even though not perfectly attained, constantly approximated."[8] Like so many of Lincoln's insights, this one has much to commend it. A nation reared to believe in something can be roused to protest its absence, and the inevitable gap between lived reality and cherished ideal can be a powerful catalyst for change. In that way, our ideals have become the North Star by which we guide our national ambition.

Yet the notion of ideals as aspirations supposes that we recognize "un-American" behavior when it happens. It suggests, in other words, a conscious willingness to betray the Creed. Yet for the great majority of Americans the great majority of the time, illiberality is *not* viewed with regret or twangs of conscience. It is accepted as a routine feature of life, perfectly consistent with American ideals. A moment's reflection is enough to show why this is the case. Americans who grow fond of a particular social arrangement are unlikely to say to themselves and others that their attachments are a fraud and a sham or that they are contrary to our foundational principles and sacred beliefs. The very ubiquity of the Creed in national life means that American thought will nearly always cast itself as fundamentally harmonious with American values. So Lincoln's memorable expression still does not tell us how a people so deeply committed to certain ideals can face themselves in the national mirror.

Paradoxically, the answer lies in the very malleability of the American Creed, which provides all the space a nation could need to construct, justify, and come to accept whatever social arrangement it wants. One period that reveals the dark side of the Creed with tragic clarity is the struggle of the civil rights movement to end Jim Crow, for the same Creed that inspired Dr. King stoked the angry fires of George Wallace.

II

The popular image of the southern segregationist (at least, outside the South) looks vaguely like Bull Connor, the scowling, jowly, potbellied commissioner of public safety in Birmingham, Alabama, who gave the order to unleash attack dogs and fire hoses on peaceful civil rights marchers in 1963. Myth can work that way, waving a kernel of truth like a magic wand to make nuance and complexity disappear. But recent scholarship has been unkind to this image. Segregationists were not at all monolithic. From the virulent racism of the Ku Klux Klan to the more moderate and considerably more popular White Citizens' Councils (who nonetheless insisted on "massive resistance" to desegregation), to still more moderate leaders like the Atlanta and Charlotte business elite (who favored minor strategic compromise as a way to prevent racial violence and avoid federal intervention), to liberals who hated Jim Crow but considered it a necessary evil, defenders of the practice were a complex and diverse group.[9] Still, diversity should not be confused with disagreement. On the fundamental question of the day— whether the South should be desegregated—whites in the Jim Crow South thought with one mind and spoke with one voice. As the liberal southern journalist Hodding Carter, Jr., put it in 1948, "The white South is as united as 30,000,000 people can be in its insistence on segregation."[10]

This alone should dispel any idea that segregationist ideology thought itself at odds with American ideals. When nearly every white man, woman, and child in an entire quarter of the country holds to a single view for generations—through two world wars, years of public education, scores of July Fourth celebrations, and hundreds of other national holidays, as well as countless sermons, editorials, and speeches extolling the virtue of "the Southern Way of Life"—it is impossible to imagine that they considered themselves anything other than good Americans. And as the historian Paul Gaston has explained, Jim Crow was conceived and designed precisely in order to resolve the inherent tension between the lofty ideals of the American Creed and the lived reality of southern life—that is, between "the Southern faith in white supremacy" and "the American image of itself as a just and humane society."[11]

The solution to this dilemma was an ingenious but perfectly sincere exercise in rationalization. The first challenge was thrust upon the South by the Fifteenth Amendment, which prevented the States from denying any citizen the right to vote "on account of race, color, or previous condition of servitude."[12] This forced the South to square white supremacy with black voters. In resolving this conundrum, the champions of the New South accepted the liberal principle of universal adult male suffrage. At the same time, however, the view was commonplace (at least among whites) that African-Americans, owing both to their prior servitude and innate inferiority, were not yet ready to exercise the franchise responsibly. Political participation, they insisted, required virtuous citizens who could take the needs of the entire community into account, and must therefore rest "with men of wealth, character and intelligence."[13] The creedal values of civic virtue and community welfare figured prominently in their rhetoric and worldview. If African-Americans would simply place themselves under a benevolent "white tutelage," they could gradually be equipped for the demands of responsible citizenship. When that day came, the vote would be theirs. "This, they believed, did no violence to the American commitment to freedom and was the only way to make the Fifteenth Amendment a working reality."[14] Of course, most white southerners were confident such a day would never come yet were untroubled by this lacuna in their argument. And in this way, "freedom, universal manhood suffrage and white supremacy" not only were compatible "but were mutually bound together."[15]

The second challenge facing southerners was the Fourteenth Amendment's command that "all persons" receive the "equal protection of the laws."[16] Yet almost no white southerner and precious few whites anywhere in the country remotely imagined that African-Americans and whites were equals, regardless of what Congress might have declared.[17] It was widely believed at the time that God, in His infinite wisdom, had made the races different and had obviously made the Anglo-Saxon superior. And let no man "tinker with the work of the Almighty," warned Henry C. Grady, the powerful editor of the *Atlanta Constitution*.[18] If African-Americans and whites were forced unnaturally to compete in the same arena, the innate superiority of the Anglo-Saxon race would be the black man's ruin. This "reality" created an obligation to shelter African-Americans from a race they could never win; in African-Americans, it created a sense of gratitude (or so whites believed) that they had been spared the humiliation of a hopeless contest. In both, it created a shared preference for segregation. A desire for racial preservation was perfectly natural and led blacks and whites to prefer their parallel spheres, producing deep, "inbred instincts toward separation."[19] So was born the southern principle of "separate but equal," which allowed whites to "create their desired image of a rational and humane system that rested on consent, not force," even as it permitted them "to limit the areas of movement of Negroes and restrict contacts between the races."[20]

For decades, the rest of the country did not much trouble itself with the regional oddity of Jim Crow, especially after 1896, when the system received the Supreme Court's blessing in *Plessy v. Ferguson*.[21] As segregation endured, southern society seemed increasingly foreign to the rest of the country. That was perfectly fine with the South, which came to prefer its unique approach to race relations, believing the familiar was also the good. Things were precisely as they ought to be.[22] If the rest of the country didn't like it, that was too damn bad. And as the storm clouds of civil rights began to appear and intensify, southerners wondered why sovereign states could not be left to develop their society as they saw fit. So long as "the Southern Way of Life" did not violate the Constitution (and the Supreme Court had said it didn't), what business was it of Washington? So took shape a third argument in favor of Jim Crow, the twentieth-century version of the great antebellum contention: states' rights.

Throughout the civil rights era, segregationists would find support for their world in the Bible as much as in science, in ancient history as much as modern sociology.[23] But the core and most enduring arguments were these: The right to suffrage depended on evidence of civic responsibility, which was not yet present in African-Americans; segregation was a natural state of affairs that both races wanted and did no violence to equal protection; and the rest of the country should mind its own business. "We in the South are not trying to tell the West how to handle their Indian problem," Louisiana's Russell Long said in a 1960 Senate debate, "and we are not trying to tell people in New York or Chicago how to handle their affairs. But . . . we might have occasion to point out that they have a civil rights situation of such proportions that they ought to look after their own problems before trying to tell us what to do."[24] Each of these arguments drank deeply from the well of shared values and traditions that have always been at the core of national identity: civic virtue, equal rights, and limited government. Together, they created the myth of a genteel and peaceful South that did no violence to American ideals. Jim Crow, the South would argue, was entirely compatible with national values and traditions, and it was the assault on Jim Crow, not its defense, that threatened the American Creed.

III

One of the many ways in which Jim Crow systematically disenfranchised African-American voters was the poll tax. Alabama, Georgia, Mississippi, South Carolina, Tennessee, Texas, and Virginia required payment of a fee, which varied from one to two dollars, to vote in federal, state, and local elections. In some states, the tax was cumulative; a single year's failure to pay could dig a poor man into a hole from which he might never escape.[25] Though the precise impact of the tax is a matter of some dispute, studies undertaken during the Second World War indicated that roughly ten million otherwise eligible voters stayed home election day because of it.[26] Federal legislation to outlaw the poll tax had been introduced before, but the first serious challenge came in 1944, when legislation easily cleared the overwhelmingly liberal House and came to the Senate with broad bipartisan support. Debate in the Senate began that May.[27]

Patrick McCarran (D-NV), the legislation's chief Senate sponsor, opened deliberations with a simple statement of the American Creed. "This country," he said, "is a democracy. The right to vote is a part of the democratic privilege, guaranteed to every citizen of the United States. . . . To deny that privilege is to deny that this country is a democracy."[28] He insisted the poll tax was contrary to the nation's cherished ideal of equality. "To say to one man that because he has money he may vote, and to say to another man that because he does not have money he may not vote, is to preclude the idea of equality before the law. We would be putting our democracy on the basis of wealth and of wealth alone. . . . That was not the contemplation or in the contemplation of those who wrote the Constitution which is basic to this country."[29]

Other supporters spoke in similar terms, invoking the time-honored image of the nation's steady march toward "a more perfect Union," which was taken to include universal suffrage. James Mead (D-NY) argued that ending the poll tax was "in keeping with the trend of our times; namely, to expand, to become more liberal, to add to the number of those who may vote, and to add to the interest in voting."[30] This trend had been continuous: "From 1789 all the way down to 1943, while the democratic experiment was proving itself, the Congress, in response to the will of the people, has been eliminating one obstacle after another so that the masses of our citizens could participate in the basic privileges that go with citizenship."[31] And of course, Mead contrasted the present with a benighted past when the country had not been faithful to the Creed. "There was a time in the early history of our country, when democracy had not yet proved itself, when traffic in slaves was still tolerated, when education was costly and not the prerogative of the poor. There were in those days defenders of such impositions as the poll tax, as we know it. But those days are past, those times are gone."[32] The time had come to finish the course that destiny had set for this country.

When southern politicians fretted that repeal of the poll tax would bring chaos, their opponents mocked the fear of too much democracy. "As long as any group of people in a democracy or anywhere in this world are deprived of the right to vote, are segregated, Jim Crowed, discriminated against, and treated as second-class citizens, so long will there be unrest; so long will

those conditions cause unrest, and what is more, those conditions are in-
tolerable as long as we remain a democracy."[33]

These arguments against the poll tax are classic expressions of the American Creed. They describe a nation committed to the universal application
of fundamental rights in order to break down barriers of class and race and
thereby attain a more equitable and representative democracy. Because this
position ultimately prevailed, contemporary readers may find these sentiments so self-evidently true that they cannot imagine another argument.
But that was certainly not the case in the 1940s and any suggestion that
this view had a monopoly on American ideals and creedal rhetoric simply
cannot be maintained. The Senate's defenders of Jim Crow—the "Southern
Caucus"—launched a sustained and eloquent argument against the repeal
of the poll tax that relied on an entirely different vision of "what the United
States is all about at our core." Yet this argument is no less recognizable
as an expression of the American Creed, and no less faithful to American
ideals.

To begin with, Walter George, the senior senator from Georgia, pointed
out that the United States is obviously *not* a democracy. "It never was a
democracy," he said, "and I hope that it never will be one. Pure democracy
means dictatorship. It is impossible for 130,000,000 people to get together
and govern a country. It is impossible for 50,000 people to get together and
govern the city in which I live. Washington would be perfectly unbearable
if the attempt should be made to govern the city by a democracy composed
of everyone in the city."[34] The Founders had established "a representative
democracy in which representatives of the people administer the laws,
conduct the business of legislation, and give an account every 2, 4, or 6
years to those who elect them. That form of government is representative
democracy. It is American republicanism. That is what we mean by 'the
Republic.'"[35]

The genius of the Republic, George continued, was its careful balance
between local, state, and federal power. "Human liberty depends finally
and at last upon local self-government, upon government administered
by local officials, selected by the people of the community, responsive to
public opinion in the community. The farther we travel away from self-
government, even local self-government, the farther we travel away from

freedom itself."[36] This fragile balance of power, members of the Southern Caucus warned again and again, is the unambiguous command of the Constitution, the obvious intent of the Founders, the only guarantee of liberty and a virtuous citizenry, and the last bulwark against tyranny.

Much of the southern argument was devoted to the constitutional text and its interpretation. Members of the Southern Caucus parsed the Constitution to show that the drafters, "all the great and brilliant men who adorned the Convention at Philadelphia by their presence," meant to leave this question to the various states.[37] They recounted in great detail the Supreme Court's consistent interpretation of this language to demonstrate that the matter had always been understood as a question exclusively for the states. But a careful reading of the debates suggests that the Caucus rested its case less on particular provisions of the Constitution than on the whole document—on the idea of the Constitution as a symbol. Tom Connally of Texas, for instance, urged his colleagues to read the text and "listen to these words which were inspired, and which have come ringing down to us through the corridors of 150 years. They have come down to us with the veneration of a great people. They have come down to us with blood and tears all over them, blood and tears which have been shed in the defense and in the maintenance of the rights which were guaranteed."[38]

The Southern Caucus also emphasized the obligations of citizenship and civic virtue. This ideal envisions government by an enlightened and responsible citizen who places the community's well-being ahead of his narrow self-interest. The members of the Southern Caucus spoke at length about the poll tax as a means both to support the community and to mold good citizens. The able-bodied man who is not willing to make the very modest annual sacrifice of a few dollars to help support the community, they argued, is not the sort of person who deserves a say in its affairs—and this had nothing to do with discrimination, since the tax applied to white and black alike. It was a matter of demonstrating a commitment to the community, of doing one's part to help defray the cost of roads, police, schools, and hospitals.[39] If you relieve the good citizen of this obligation, you tempt him to favor "a free ride," and that "is a hurtful thing to the citizen." "I am saying something," Connally warned, "about the hurt done the self-respect of any able-bodied person by making him believe that if he is not permitted to have a free governmental ride a great injustice is done to him. That does not make for good citizenship in a democracy."[40]

The Caucus also invoked the right of the states to be different and decried the determination of meddlesome northerners to subjugate the South for its own good.

> Because some State in the Union [Connally said], such as my own State of Texas, does not conduct its affairs as the State of New York thinks it should conduct them, these crusaders, these Sir Galahads, mount their steeds and come down into Texas to "modify" us, and to Christianize us, and to liberalize us, and to modernize us, and to intelligence-ize us. [Laughter.] Mr. President, we do not think it is right. We do not think it is just. We do not think it is in accordance with the proper concept of the Constitution and the traditional political equality of the United States.[41]

Finally, the Southern Caucus spoke with great passion about the risk to the liberties of every American should Congress take this step. If it can order states to eliminate the poll tax, Connally predicted, "then Congress has the power to prescribe any other qualification it may see fit to prescribe. It not only has the right of prohibition or denial, requiring that voters shall possess certain qualifications, but it has the affirmative power to require the States to impose certain conditions or requirements with respect to suffrage within the States."[42] "In effect," granting Congress the power to repeal the poll tax "would amount to a delivery by the States to the Federal Government of the control of suffrage, the very root, the very foundation, the very subsoil of liberty and free government itself."[43] Richard Russell, the junior senator from Georgia, who would soon replace Connally as leader of the Southern Caucus, was no less apocalyptic. "Whereas today the victim on the rack might be Texas, tomorrow it might be any other State. We would have a Federal clerk presiding over the enforcement of a Federal law, to be enforced, if necessary, at the point of a Federal bayonet. Such a system could eventually eliminate the States as subdivisions of government. . . . When that day comes, democracy will, indeed, be dead in this country."[44]

The southern arguments did not betray American ideals, nor did they represent some foreign tradition unknown to American political culture. The constituent pieces—veneration of the Constitution, the rule of law, and the Founding generation; the tribute to the virtuous citizen and the welfare of the community; and the fear that an oppressive federal government will rob the states of their rights and the people of their liberties, "if necessary at the point of a Federal bayonet"—are as much a part of American identity as arguments in favor of fundamental rights and universal equality. The Southern Caucus would repeat these arguments for decades. And on this occasion, as they so often did, they succeeded. The anti–poll tax legislation was defeated.[45]

IV

Just as the poll tax was part of the elaborate southern machinery designed to nullify the Fifteenth Amendment and prevent African-Americans from voting, the fantasy of "separate but equal" was constructed to defeat the Fourteenth Amendment's promise of equal protection under the law. As Congress was debating whether to end the poll tax, it also took up proposals "to prohibit discrimination in employment based on race, creed, color or ancestry."[46] Bills introduced in both chambers declared that the right to work and to seek work without discrimination "shall not be abridged by any State or by any instrumentality or any creature of any State."[47] Speaking in favor of the bill he had introduced, Representative Thomas Scanlon (D-PA) told his colleagues, "If there is any more vicious denial of American democracy than discrimination in jobs because of a man's race, creed, or color, I cannot imagine what it is. . . . Discrimination because a man is a Negro, a Jew, a Catholic, or because his ancestors came from another country" is a "gnawing evil" and "a slap in the face to every decent American who believes in American fair play."[48]

> This is the time for the Congress of the United States to say to the people of America that their Government guarantees their right to jobs, regardless of their color, race, or their form of divine worship. This is the time to say to the world that we in America mean what we say when we tell them this is a land of opportunity in which a man can go as far as his ability can carry him. This is the way to show the people of the world that we practice what we preach.[49]

Hearings on the bill opened in the House Committee on Labor June 1, 1944, and continued as U.S. troops stormed ashore at Normandy, beginning the invasion that would destroy the Nazi regime and end World War II in Europe. The ugly contrast between imminent freedom abroad and enduring discrimination at home served as a powerful backdrop to the debates. "There are nearly 1,000,000 Negroes in the Army, Navy, and Marines," Scanlon said. "The men on Bataan were largely of Mexican origin from Arizona and New Mexico. The first heroes of our war were of many religions, colors, and national origins. . . . If our returning servicemen, who fought side by side with these heroes, are barred from jobs because of color, religion, or national origin, what a hollow thing our victory will be."[50] On February 20, 1945, the day after U.S. Marines landed at Iwo Jima, the House Committee recommended that the bill be passed, once again invoking the war. "When the war comes to a victorious end, and our men and women return to peacetime occupations from the battlefields, . . . there must be equal opportunity for all. The men who fought for economic freedoms for peoples throughout the world will not, and should not, be satisfied with anything less in our own country."[51] In March and April, while the Allies were liberating the concentration camps at Buchenwald, Bergen-Belsen, and Dachau, supporters of the bill pleaded with the House Committee on Rules to let it come to a vote. "The men and women serving in the armed forces are of all creeds, color and national origin," Representative Mary Norton (D-NJ) said.

> Their service to the country is not predicated on color or ancestry or anything else other than that they are good Americans. They are Americans fighting for a common objective—freedom, in the broadest sense of the word. We have repeated over and over again that this war is being fought to preserve freedom in our own country and to extend it to the peoples of the world. If we are honest, . . . there remains one way to prove it, and that is to end discrimination in our country.[52]

This is immediately recognizable as the language of the Creed as we now understand it. These views have been so thoroughly assimilated into American national identity that it is hard to imagine the argument against them. Yet many considered the bill dangerously radical and were so alarmed by its provisions that the sponsors considered it prudent to disavow the inflammatory suggestion that they meant to promote genuine equality. "This bill," Scanlon assured his colleagues, "has nothing to do with racial equality, or social equality. It simply says that all people must have an equal opportunity, according to their abilities, to work for their living regardless of their race, color, creed, national origin, or ancestry."[53] The House Committee on Labor repeated this insistence when it recommended that the bill be passed. "Let it be clearly understood this bill has for its purpose economic opportunity only. The opponents of this bill are attempting to confuse the issue by bringing up the question of social equality. We repeat, there is nothing in the bill concerned with anything other than economic equality."[54]

Assurances like these did not mollify the bill's opponents, who denounced it as un-American. Foremost, it represented an assault on property and the market, the twin pillars of laissez-faire. Representative Clark Fisher (D-TX) complained that the bill "is a departure from the traditional American system of free enterprise," which had historically allowed employers "to use their own sound judgment in selecting loyal and capable employees. It is through that system of competition and improvement that private enterprise has succeeded in America when it has failed in other countries." Any proposal that stripped businesses of this prerogative, Fisher warned, "smacks strongly of totalitarianism."[55] His southern colleague L. Mendel Rivers (D-SC) found the legislation contrary to "the American way of life," which demands that "no law should try to tell an employer whom he must hire."[56] A bill that strips a man of control of his business "will be destructive of initiative, destructive of progress, and would destroy forever any remaining vestige of democracy." Rivers said the bill "runs headlong into the fifth amendment to the Constitution," which guarantees that a man's property shall not be taken without due process. "By passage of this bill," he said, "you would in fact repeal the Constitution."[57] As much as we may now wish it otherwise, it is wrong to suggest that these arguments were not a faithful construction of American ideals as they were understood by millions of Americans. The fact that the construction ultimately did not prevail obviously does not, by itself, prove its illegitimacy. Indeed, responsible scholars continue to argue that antidiscrimination legislation is unconstitutional.[58]

Members of the Southern Caucus also argued that antidiscrimination legislation would not achieve its ostensible purpose. An exchange between Mississippi Congressman William Colmer and New Jersey's Mary Norton, the bill's principal sponsor, was especially revealing. "As you know," Colmer said, "I come from a section of the country that has quite a large Negro population. I am just wondering, as one who really feels kindly toward those people, . . . whether this type of legislation would not harm rather than help that class of people?"[59] "There will be a little difficulty in the beginning," Norton granted, "but, after all, is not this very much worthwhile? Do you believe in the objective we are setting for the world? . . . If we cannot solve the problem of freedom and justice for all, in our own country, it would be futile to attempt to influence the world."[60]

> COLMER: I know that a big majority of the white people in my section of the South feel kindly, and act accordingly, toward the Negro population.
> NORTON: What have they done for the Negroes in more than 200 years?
> COLMER: I fear you are not accurately advised as to that condition in the South. . . . We feed the colored people when they are hungry; we clothe them when they are naked; we provide medical attention when they are sick. We see to it that they do not suffer.[61]

Colmer's South was a bucolic idyll in which Jim Crow had finally solved the problem of racial conflict. It allowed the entire community to flourish together, in harmony and tranquility, so long as African-Americans and whites kept to their separate but equal spheres. All of this would disappear in an instant if the bill were to become law. The community would be engulfed in "strikes, riots, and violence," Representative Price Fisher of Texas predicted, leading to "racial prejudices and discrimination." The true victim would not be the white man but the Negro, "because it would retard his progress and would be calculated to foment racial feeling and bitterness against him."[62]

Once again, the southern construction of national identity prevailed. The antidiscrimination legislation was defeated—a state of play that would last for two more decades.

V

These legislative battles, while critical to the early struggle for civil rights, do not figure as prominently in modern memory as the 1954 Supreme

Court decision in *Brown v. Board of Education,* which struck down segregated public schools. The link between *Brown* and our current conception
of the Creed needs no elaboration; though scholars vigorously debate its
true legacy, *Brown* is widely seen as one of the great triumphs of the civil
rights era.[63] But once again, we are unfair to the historical record if we suppose that the southerners who defended segregated schools were motivated
by something other than the values of the American Creed as they understood them. The southern defense of segregation was thoroughly steeped
in the language of American ideals. One of the most prominent arguments
resurrected the (white) southern belief in an idealized community. In 1956
North Carolina Senator Sam Ervin wrote in *Look* magazine that southerners deplored *Brown* because it jeopardized "the harmonious race relations
now existing in the South."[64] The next year, Mike Wallace interviewed the
staunch segregationist Senator James Eastland of Mississippi, who offered
a classic defense of segregation. "It's a matter of choice," Eastland said, "by
both races."

> WALLACE: Are you suggesting the Negro . . .
> EASTLAND: I'm suggesting that the vast majority of Negroes want their own
> schools, their own hospitals, their own churches, their own restaurants. . . .
>
> WALLACE: Are you suggesting that the Negro in the south wants segregation?
> EASTLAND: I'm suggesting . . . oh, certainly.
> WALLACE: The Negro in the south wants segregation.
> EASTLAND: 99% yes.

Segregation had been a boon to African-Americans, Eastland insisted.
"Now the biggest business in my home is a Nigra insurance company. I
employ a Nigra in an executive capacity. . . . As I said, we have more Nigra
professional men, more businessmen, we have substantial Nigra cotton
planters. In fact, they have made more progress in the south than in the
north."[65]

But mostly, Eastland maintained, segregation was a matter for each state
to decide on its own:

> Well, what we are fighting for is a great principle and that is for each state to
> handle its own domestic affairs. If the North wants segregation, integration,

it's their affair—if New York wants it, it's their affair—under our system of government, the genius of the American system is control by the state of the domestic affairs of the states and we just want the right to handle it in our state for the best interest of all concerned and the way it is handled is endorsed by ninety-nine percent of the people of both races who live in peace and harmony and we have more peace and harmony than any section of the country. . . . We've worked out the system that is harmonious.[66]

Eastland's view was widely shared. The day after the decision in *Brown*, Senator Price Daniel of Texas warned it would be a disaster for both black and white:

I sincerely believe that the great majority of members of the Negro race in my State prefer to have their children go to separate schools and receive instruction from teachers of their race. I believe they wish to continue to enjoy the opportunities they have enjoyed in the past, under our separate school system. I do not believe they could enjoy as many advantages and as many opportunities if separate schools are abolished.[67]

In 1960 Senator Russell Long of Louisiana lamented that in colleges and universities "where whites predominate," African-Americans "have difficulty competing with the white students, and it would probably be better for them if they went to college among their own people."[68] "White men" who started law school "were probably better qualified . . . than the colored boys were when they entered law school." If they had to compete on equal terms, black students would probably not be able to graduate. Segregation was thus for their own good. In any case, "the colored people prefer to have their own teachers. They have pride in their race, and . . . every race should have pride in its own."[69]

The most comprehensive and succinct statement of the southern position on segregation, at least in Congress, was the "Southern Manifesto," the famous statement condemning the Supreme Court decision in *Brown* that was introduced into the congressional record in March 1956 by Georgia Senator Walter George on behalf of nineteen senators and seventy-seven representatives.[70] Styled a "Declaration of Constitutional Principles," it is a ringing tribute to the values of the Creed. The decision in *Brown*, the manifesto warned, was "now bearing the fruit always produced when men substitute naked power for established law." The Court had ignored "the inescapable lesson of history," recognized by the Founders and enshrined in the Constitution, "that no man or group of men can be safely entrusted with unlimited power." The Founders had drafted the Constitution "in order to secure the fundamentals of government against the dangers of popular passion or the personal predilections of public office holders."[71]

Time and again, "separate but equal" had been upheld by the Supreme Court and left in place by Congress. Over many years it had become "a part of the life of the people of many of the States and confirmed their habits, traditions, and way of life. It is founded on elemental humanity and commonsense."[72] Now the Court had thrown all this into disarray. In deciding as it had, the Court threatened the very foundation of democracy, "undertaking to legislate, in derogation of the authority of Congress, and to encroach upon the reserved rights of the States and the people." The result of this "unwarranted exercise of power by the Court, contrary to the Constitution," was "chaos and confusion in the States principally affected. It is destroying the amicable relations between the white and Negro races that have been created through 90 years of patient effort by the good people of both races. It has planted hatred and suspicion where there has been heretofore friendship and understanding."[73]

In the end, the signers of the manifesto placed their faith in the people. "Even though we constitute a minority in the present Congress, we have full faith that a majority of the American people believe in the dual system of government which has enabled us to achieve our greatness and will in time demand that the reserved rights of the States and of the people be made secure against judicial usurpation."[74] Acting out of "the gravest concern for the explosive and dangerous condition created by this decision and inflamed by outside meddlers," the signers reaffirmed "our reliance on the Constitution as the fundamental law of the land"; decried "the Supreme Court's encroachment on the rights reserved to the States and to the people, contrary to established law, and to the Constitution"; commended "the motives of those States which have declared the intention to resist forced integration by any lawful means"; and appealed "to the States and people who are not directly affected by these decisions to consider the constitutional principles involved against the time when they too, on issues vital to them, may be the victims of judicial encroachment."[75]

This is creedal rhetoric at its very best. In its grandeur and sweep, it is every bit as faithful to the American Creed as the decision in *Brown* itself. Limited government under a written constitution, the rule of law, the defense of republicanism, the reverence for the Founders—it is nothing if not a statement of American identity.

The demands of a single volume prevent a comprehensive study of the rhetoric used to justify other dark chapters in American history. To my surprise, no such study exists. I strongly suspect, however, that the student who makes the attempt will discover that the sort of shifting creedal justifications mounted in opposition to the civil rights movement are hardly unique. There is every reason to suspect that treasured social arrangements will consistently be defended in the terms that provide people the most comfort: the malleable and pleasant sounding rhetoric of shared national values. This is certainly the conclusion of other scholars who have examined other discrete periods in American history. The historian Laura Scalia, for instance, studied the state constitutional debates over suffrage in the mid-nineteenth century and concluded that the political language of liberalism "helped rationalize various illiberal policies." Liberalism, she concluded, "is not always the language of greater empowerment and inclusion; it can be the language of exclusion as well."[76] The political scientist Robert Lieberman, in a study of the civil rights movement, found that "concepts such as 'liberty' or 'equality' might be invoked to support very different practices in different contexts by people who all the while believe themselves to be upholding a timeless and unchanging political tradition."[77]

Our common point is that while the words attached to national values are the same—"timeless and unchanging," as Lieberman put it—their meaning is constantly being constructed in the public square.[78] National identity is what we make it.

VI

Passionate attachment to the Creed and what it represents contains its own capacity for exclusion, hysteria, and repression. Anything thought to threaten the Creed is met with a fury infused with the same moral fire that people hold for the nation itself. This explains the excesses so often attributed to wartime. They are a reaction to the unbearable thought that the innocence, the perfection, the virtue of the United States will collapse and that our great national journey will come to an end. What many have seen as a habit of mind completely separate from the American character is nothing of the sort. It *is* the American character, or part of it. Our tendency toward demonization is as genuine as our commitment to tolerance; the appeal of vigilante justice is as true as faith in the rule of law. Both exist because of the morally charged but almost infinitely elastic vision of America captured by the Creed.

This explains why, throughout American history, the initial frenzies of wartime hysteria have borne a family resemblance. A perceived threat to the same Creed, expressed in the same language, will invariably summon pretty much the same response. Because so much is believed to be at stake, the danger is magnified in the public imagination. But scholars make an unfortunate mistake if they conclude that war is the independent variable in all this. America does not have one creed for peace and another for war. We have one Creed, in peace and war, and whenever it is threatened, the reaction—if unrestrained by other forces—will be much the same. It emerges from a sense of threat to a shared Creed, and not simply the clash of arms.

Finally, because the Creed is never repudiated, it never needs to be reclaimed in the popular mind. If society turns its back on illiberal policies—if anti-Catholicism and anti-Semitism fade into memory, if the right of habeas corpus is restored and internment ends—it is the triumph of our better angels in the march toward a more perfect Union. Policies may be reassessed, but the truths they implement, having suffered no loss of prestige, remain eternal. But if society does not dismantle these policies—if slavery and Jim Crow endure through waves of abolitionist and reformist sentiment—we retain an arsenal of rhetorical defenses with which to beat back any claim that the behavior is a betrayal of national values. The Creed is never traduced. All is as it ought to be. This would prove especially true the day in early September when "everything changed."

PART II

HISTORY MAKES NO SHARP TURNS

4

Race and Religion in National Identity

"IF THE SITUATION IS RACIAL AND RELIGIOUS, it is because the terrorists defined it that way—by race and religion."[1] To most Americans, that observation by a *Newsweek* reader in late 2001 made all the sense in the world. September 11, they thought, had obviously brought race and religion to the fore. Yet that association was not inevitable. One could also imagine September 11 as an occasion to examine the legacy of colonialism, the wisdom of American global adventures, or several other external factors that might have motivated homicidal behavior. Intellectuals on the left tried, at least at first, to frame the attacks that way, and post-9/11 debates would have looked very different had they succeeded. As a rule, however, that is not how most Americans view the world. They have long believed that human behavior can be understood by reference to race and religion, which helps explain why these characteristics, rather than class, so often mark the bounds of community membership.

But in coming to terms with a racial and religious "situation" in the United States, people do not begin with a blank slate. Consciously or not, they approach the task armed with certain understandings of what race and religion have come to mean in American life and how they shape our national values. They start, in other words, with an image of the way things *ought to be*. Race and religion in American life have been endlessly studied, but our interest is more particular: the relationship between race, religion, and the shared values of national identity.

I

In late 1994 Charles Murray was in the first-class cabin of a flight to Aspen, Colorado, sipping champagne and discussing his most recent book with a reporter for the *New York Times*. He knew full well the content was explosive. "Here was a case of stumbling onto a subject that had all the allure of the forbidden," he said, describing the material that he and his coauthor, the Harvard psychologist Richard Herrnstein, had relied on in their research. "Some of the things we read to do this work, we literally hide when we're on planes and trains. We're furtively peering at this stuff."[2] The "stuff" that caused Murray to fear public embarrassment was not pornography. It was research that, according to Murray and Herrnstein, established that African-Americans are genetically predisposed to have significantly lower IQs than whites and that the difference cannot be overcome by government-run social welfare programs. These programs were doomed to fail because the most significant predictor of "success and failure in the American economy" was "the genes that people inherit."[3]

Murray's fear, of course, was that he and Herrnstein would be denounced as racists. And they were. *The Bell Curve* was widely criticized in academia and much of the press.[4] Yet despite (or perhaps because of) the denunciations, the book was a runaway best seller. In the last three months of 1994, it sold 400,000 copies in the United States alone, making it the best-selling nonfiction book of the entire year.[5] It further solidified the reputation Murray had garnered with his previous book, *Losing Ground,* which had argued that social welfare programs cause more problems than they solve. In his book proposal for *Losing Ground,* Murray had asked rhetorically, "Why can a publisher sell it? Because a huge number of well-meaning whites fear that they are closet racists, and this book tells them they are not. It's going to make them feel better about things they already think but do not know how to say."[6] Like *The Bell Curve, Losing Ground* was a sensation.

Murray's accurate prediction that he and his work would be publicly attacked but privately welcomed—at least by "a huge number of well-meaning whites"—suggests an important truth about American racial attitudes at the end of the twentieth century. A public commitment to the idea that people ought not be judged by the color of their skin exists alongside a widely held private belief that racial and ethnic differences are not only deep and wide, but a perfectly sensible way to distinguish one group from another. The powerful stigma against giving voice to overtly racist sentiments is matched by an equally powerful conviction on the part of a great many people that racial differences are genuine and should be taken into account by policy makers. And as with so much in American life, we reached this state of affairs by engaging in an extended contest over the meaning and content of our shared national values.

Like many careers, Jim Crow's ended when it no longer served a social purpose. The decline of the southern cotton economy, the rise of northern industrialism with its almost insatiable demand for labor, and the slowing of immigration from Eastern Europe all combined in the first three quarters of the twentieth century to produce a massive shift in the African-American population from the rural South to the urban North. Between 1910 and 1970, six and a half million African-Americans headed north, four-fifths of them after 1940.[7] This led to a dramatic increase in African-Americans' wealth, as they traded low-paying employment in agriculture for better-paid jobs in manufacturing. It also led to far greater *concentration* of wealth in urban centers, which in turn increased the power, resources, and social standing of leading African-American institutions like the church, black universities, black newspapers, and reform organizations like the NAACP. The African-American community in major urban centers became an electoral bloc that politicians ignored at their peril. And as African-American fortunes rose, those of the southern planter elite declined. This was the community that most benefited from the social and legal control imposed by Jim Crow, and as cotton declined and the rural, agricultural South increasingly lagged behind the urban, industrial North, the political and cultural strength of this group began to ebb.[8]

Other events gave these developments added force. Beginning in the 1920s, the scientific and intellectual communities had thrown their considerable cultural weight into sustained attacks on the idea that some races were innately superior to others. Their arguments became even more compelling in the thirties and forties, as the horror of Nazism dramatically undermined support for racist ideologies. After the war, many prominent scholars began to question whether race was anything more than a social construction. Their views were regularly given a respectful hearing in the press.[9] Meanwhile, the valor of African-American troops in the war, along with the successful (but controversial) integration of the armed forces in 1948, not only put the lie to myths about the inherent superiority of white soldiers but created a strong argument for equal treatment at home. The Cold War contributed to this emerging consensus when the Soviet Union scored ideological points with uncommitted nations by using America's racial inequality as evidence of capitalism's essential hypocrisy. Jim Crow became an embarrassment in the contest between Western capitalism and Soviet communism. The Truman administration urged the Supreme Court several times to rule in favor of civil rights in order to blunt the Soviet argument.[10]

Still, all this merely made change *possible.* Many factors combined to loosen social and political restraints and diminish support for an increasingly archaic institution, creating space in the public square for a new conversation about national identity. They did not, however, make the success of that conversation inevitable. That last step required something more: a combination of trusted voices and enthusiastic followers throughout society who could translate these developments into a program for social and political change.[11] To be successful, this combination of elite leadership and grassroots support had to describe their program in the language of national identity. To preach beyond the choir, in other words, the civil rights narrative had to appeal to the timeless virtues of the American Creed. Civil rights had to be seen as bringing the country closer to its "true" condition. No one understood this better than Martin Luther King, who invoked the mythic power of the national commitment to equality. "I have a dream," King said, "that my four little children will one day live in a nation where they will not be judged by the color of their skin but by the content of their character."

Today, the logic of the civil rights movement has become common sense. But to suggest that this success was inevitable, simply a product of inexorable structural forces, does a terrible injustice not only to the men and women who led the struggle but to the reality of the historical record, which shows clearly that what today seems obvious was once hotly contested. The civil rights movement succeeded in reshaping national identity because it had the right leadership, with the right message, at the right moment.

II

As Jim Crow becomes less the painful recollection of personal experience and more the arid study of a distant past, it becomes all too easy to forget the magnitude of the change in national identity ushered in by the civil rights movement. But events occasionally permit revealing comparisons between then and now, as when a public official took the stage in Kansas in 2004 to denounce Jim Crow:

> Generations of African American citizens grew up and grew old under laws designed to demean them. Under the rule of Jim Crow, almost no detail of life escaped the supervision of cruel and petty men. . . . Segregation dulled the conscience of people who knew better. It fed the violence of people with malice in their hearts. And however it was defended, segregation could never be squared with the ideals of America.[12]

The occasion was the fiftieth anniversary of *Brown v. Board,* the decision that had prompted "massive resistance" throughout the South. Pronouncing a judgment that today is commonplace but that fifty years earlier was heresy across the region, and joined on the dais by the conservative Kansas congressional delegation, the speaker—President George W. Bush—condemned Jim Crow as "codified cruelty at the service of racism."[13]

Though the institutionalized racism of Jim Crow was largely confined to the South, racist beliefs hardly ended at the Mason-Dixon Line. In the 1940s, most white Americans nationwide believed that African-Americans were innately less intelligent than whites.[14] More than half also thought it right that whites be given preferential treatment in hiring. Roughly as many believed buses and streetcars should be segregated by race.[15] Nearly 70 percent believed African-American and white children should attend separate schools. Even late in the decade, as two careful students of the history have observed, "assertions of the innate inferiority of blacks were commonplace."[16] Into the late 1950s, nearly 100 percent of white Americans disapproved of interracial marriage, and nearly two-thirds said they could not vote for a "well qualified man for president [who] happened to be a Negro."[17] In the 1960s, when Congress passed the most important civil rights acts in U.S. history, 60 percent of white Americans agreed (and 40 percent agreed strongly) that whites had a right to keep blacks out of their neighborhoods. As late as 1963, nearly two-thirds of white Americans favored laws banning interracial marriage.[18]

Today, attachment to the raw racism of the Jim Crow era has all but disappeared. Public opinion polling provides some insight into the change: a sharp decline in the number of people who believe that African-Americans are inherently inferior to whites or that whites should be given preferential treatment in hiring; an equally dramatic rise in the percentage of people who support racially mixed marriages. But poll results cannot describe the sea change in the public behavior of most white Americans, which is better captured by the thousands of quotidian interactions among African-Americans, whites, and other minorities, that have become so routine as to escape all notice. Countless small gestures of tolerance and acceptance, repeated across the country every day, literally could not have happened fifty years ago but now are utterly unremarkable. No amount of consternation over the present state of affairs should blind us to the enormous differences between the norms that prevailed only a few decades ago and those that predominate today. We have the civil rights movement to thank for the elementary proposition that in the tussle and struggle that is life, the government may not add to a man's burdens simply because of his race or ethnic origin. Americans today do not simply believe this is so. They believe it *ought* to be so.

Yet only the willfully ignorant thinks race is now irrelevant in American life. By the end of the twentieth century, African-American adults were two and a half times as likely as whites to be unemployed. They were five times as likely to be underemployed, meaning that they were unable to find full-time work or worked at below-poverty-level wages. Young, well-educated African-Americans still earn substantially less than similarly situated whites. And the significant employment disparities between African-Americans and whites pale in comparison to their wealth disparities. Despite the emergence of a relatively secure African-American middle class, for every dollar of wealth held by white households, African-American households have less than ten cents. The disparity is so great that white households near the bottom of the income scale among whites still have greater wealth than African-American households near the top of the income scale among blacks.[19]

These income and wealth disparities have enormous consequences. One of the most important, but too easily overlooked, is the self-evident fact that money buys a healthier, safer environment. Consider food: Fast and processed food is cheaper but considerably less nourishing than the foods widely available in wealthier parts of town. The urban poor are thus far less likely to have a healthy diet. Poor communities are also apt to suffer from the effects of urban pollution and be more heavily exposed to environmental toxins. These communities are apt to receive fewer municipal services, including public transportation and police protection. Collectively, urban African-Americans tend to live in areas that are comprehensively less healthful than the areas populated by urban or suburban whites. As a result, African-Americans are far more likely to suffer from a host of medical conditions, including cancer, kidney disease, and diabetes. They are also more likely to suffer from high blood pressure and coronary heart disease. These conditions often go untreated or undertreated because of relative disparities in the kind and quality of available medical services. African-American life expectancy remains shorter than that of whites, beginning with much higher rates of infant mortality. As my former colleague Dorothy Roberts recently observed, "Black infants are almost three times more likely than white infants to die before their first birthday."[20]

In a nation in which equality is thought to be a pillar of national identity, the gross disparities between the lives of black and white Americans are simply remarkable. Yet these disparities do not speak for themselves. They acquire significance by the explanation we impart to them. What these differences are believed to prove, in other words, is subject to debate in the public square. And the explanation that has come to dominate, especially among white Americans, is that African-Americans have only themselves to blame. Society, so long as it is officially neutral, is blameless. Whites overwhelmingly believe discrimination is no longer a significant problem in society and strongly oppose any preferential treatment of African-Americans

to correct these disparities. Substantial majorities believe that when compared with whites, "blacks have equal or greater opportunity to get ahead
generally," "equal or greater educational opportunities," "equal or greater
job opportunities," and "equal or greater opportunity for promotion to su-
pervisory or managerial jobs."[21] How this came to pass, and what it means
for national identity, must be examined carefully.

III

Just at the moment when the civil rights movement achieved its greatest
success, when the cultural and political transformation in favor of equality
seemed to have passed a national tipping point, a different set of forces gained
momentum and created the space for a new conversation about national
identity. In June 1965 President Johnson gave the commencement address
at Howard University in Washington, D.C. He celebrated the great achievements in the struggle for civil rights and looked forward to the day when
he would sign the Voting Rights Act. But Johnson was in no mood to be
complacent. In his address, he announced the beginning of "the next and
the more profound stage of the battle for civil rights."[22]

> You do not take a person who, for years, has been hobbled by chains and
> liberate him, bring him up to the starting line of a race and then say, "you
> are free to compete with all the others," and still justly believe that you have
> been completely fair.

In order to be "completely fair," Johnson said, we must have "not just equality as a right and a theory, but equality as a fact and equality as a result."[23]

Did Johnson plan to use the power of the national government to eliminate all racial disparities? To achieve equality in employment, income, education, housing, health care, criminal justice, community safety, and the
countless other areas where equality existed only as a right and a theory, not
a fact or result? This was a Rubicon in American life that had never been
crossed. When the Johnson administration and the civil rights community
turned from "equality as a right" to "equality as a result," they encountered
an entirely different national scene.

Mass migration in the first three-quarters of the twentieth century did not simply transfer blacks to northern cities. By the millions, whites had abandoned the cities of the North and upper Midwest for the suburbs, many of them also migrating to the South and Southwest. In the 1960s the suburban population nationwide grew by a third while that of the central cities grew by only 1 percent. By 1980, 40 percent of the U.S. population lived in the suburbs, compared with only 28 percent in the central cities.[24] These urban transplants were steeped in the ideology and rhetoric of equality, which not only hastened the decline of Jim Crow by diluting its cultural and political base but also brought a new, meritocratic voice to the public square. Having fled the turmoil of the cities and having achieved the American Dream of home ownership and middle-class respectability, these newcomers were determined to protect their new paradise. This translated into a demand to leave the city to itself and protect their hard-won suburban idyll, especially its property values, tax base, and schools. They believed with all sincerity that these preferences had nothing to do with race, and everything to do with enjoying the fruits of individual effort.[25]

At the same time, the steep economic downturn of the mid-1970s, which hit the manufacturing and municipal sectors hardest, threatened to pit blacks against ethnic whites in a battle for smaller slices of a shrinking pie. Growing black neighborhoods had already collided with those of ethnic whites in many northern cities. Occasionally this tension erupted into ugly racial violence; economics took it to another level. Ethnic whites—the Italian, Polish, Czech, Latvian, and Irish workers who filled the factories, police departments, and municipal offices—could believe in all sincerity that their preferences were a matter of basic fairness, not racial discrimination. It wasn't right, they believed, that blacks should take "their" jobs simply because the South had once been discriminatory. Whatever equality meant, surely it didn't mean punishing a man because of the color of his skin.[26]

Once again, powerful structural forces had combined to create the *possibility* of change. Yet as before, demographic, economic, cultural, and political factors at work did not make change inevitable. Just as other forces had loosened the attachment to Jim Crow, these new forces challenged the movement toward "equality of results" and created the opportunity for a different conversation about national identity. But as before, the last step— the step that converted possibility into reality—required the combination of trusted voices and enthusiastic followers who could convert this conversation into a program for change. The narrative that took shape, from modest stirrings in the 1940s to growing importance in the sixties to national dominance in the eighties, was the narrative of the modern conservative movement.[27]

As with civil rights, the success of the conservative movement depended on the ability of elites to frame their program in the almost infinitely malleable language of national identity—to create a narrative that would appeal to the frustrated suburbanite and the angry ethnic white without harking back to the culturally discredited language of Jim Crow racism. Like the civil rights movement, conservatism had to cast its message as a corrective that would return the country to its core values. And while the civil rights movement had achieved this by developing a narrative about equality as guaranteed by an expansive state, conservatism did it by developing an equally comprehensive narrative about *individualism* secured by a *restrained* state. Like the civil rights movement, modern conservatism took hold because it had the right leadership, with the right message, at the right moment.

It began modestly. Conservative intellectuals had long viewed the New Deal and the growing welfare state with alarm. For many years they had warned of the dangers of "collectivism" and the peril to liberty posed by unrestrained government. But not until the social upheaval of the late 1960s and early 1970s did these arguments begin to make substantial headway. When the government insisted that children be bused across town, or from suburb to city, to integrate schools that had never been segregated by law, or when government demanded that African-American applicants be given preference over whites in bidding for contracts, applying for jobs, and seeking admission to schools—in short, when the government began to make good on its promise to seek "equality of results"—conservatives began to articulate an argument that wedded civil rights to the potent symbolic appeal of individualism and limited government. These arguments first appeared in the early 1970s in the leading conservative journals of the day. Then, in 1975, the sociologist Nathan Glazer published *Affirmative Discrimination: Ethnic Inequality and Public Policy,* which, as one scholar has recently noted, "laid the groundwork for the new conservative position on race."[28]

Glazer argued that the great moral success of the Civil Rights Act of 1964 had been to outlaw de jure discrimination and replace it with the laudatory precept that the Constitution was colorblind. According to Glazer, the quest for "equality of results" had led the government to stray from this ideal and favor one group over another. This ran afoul of the "first principle of a liberal society: that the individual and the individual's interests and good and welfare are the test of the good society."[29] The determination to favor African-Americans at the expense of whites who had personally done no wrong, even if undertaken with the best of intentions and solely to remedy past injustice, was contrary to "what was intended by the Constitution and the Civil Rights Act, and what most of the American people . . . believe."[30] The challenge, Glazer wrote, was "to work with the intellectual, judicial, and political institutions of the country to re-establish the simple and clear understanding that rights attach to the individual, not the group, and that public policy must be exercised without distinction of race, color, or national origin."[31]

The strategic elegance of the conservative argument was to appropriate the essential message of the civil rights movement—that no one should be judged by the color of her skin—and to graft it onto a conservative conception of the individual and the state. The civil rights movement, conservatives now argued, had been correct all along. Jim Crow had been a monstrosity, a perversion of American ideals. But once the state assured formal equality of opportunity—once it swept away the restrictive covenants and shady practices that had kept minorities out of certain neighborhoods; outlawed discriminatory practices in employment and voting; did away with the insidious fiction that separate was equal; and eliminated all formal distinctions based on race, color, or national origin—society could not be faulted for unequal results. People would always be inherently unequal, conservatives argued, in ways no government could alter. Not everyone had the same determination to overcome the obstacles strewn in one's path by the indifferent fates. A person's lot in life was a product of his or her own choices. That, said conservatives, has always been the guiding ethos of American individualism. These choices enable a person to take advantage of the opportunities a bountiful nation has laid before him. If he chose instead to engage in unproductive or socially irresponsible behavior, that was certainly not the government's fault. When the government got into the business of ensuring "equality of results," it partook of precisely the behavior condemned by the civil rights movement and strayed from this foundational ideal of American identity.[32]

This argument allowed conservatives to project civil rights through the prism of individualism and limited government, which in turn let them champion "equality as a right and a theory," without risking "equality as a fact and equality as a result." In the 1960s, Ronald Reagan had opposed the civil rights movement and the federal legislation it produced. But in 1982 he became the first U.S. president to address the Alabama State Legislature. "Only two blocks from where I stand," he said, "a courageous American named Martin Luther King organized a struggle for racial equality that led to historic changes in our society nationwide. The sacrifice that he made brings tears of sorrow, but the good that he did brings tears of salvation."[33] In 1987 Reagan spoke at Tuskegee University:

> In the 1950's and 1960's, great strides were made through political action. The legal sanctions of bigotry and discrimination were torn away, laws protecting the civil rights of all Americans were put in place, and racism was, in effect, outlawed. These great achievements did not come easy. They were the result of the struggle and commitment of generations and the outstanding leadership of individuals like Dr. Martin Luther King. The civil rights movement earned the respect and gratitude of all good and decent Americans, even some who may at first have had reservations about what was happening.[34]

Yet Reagan was an implacable foe of all affirmative steps by the federal government to achieve "equality of results," a position he often defended by invoking Martin Luther King as the advocate of a colorblind society. At a 1986 press conference he was asked about his position on civil rights by the reporter Helen Thomas:

> Q. Mr. President, in the sixties you opposed all civil rights legislation, but more recently you said that you were a part of the Martin Luther King revolution. If that is the case, why is your administration so bent on wiping out the flexible hiring goals for blacks, minorities, and women?
> A. Helen, we're not wanting to do that. . . . We want what I think Martin

Luther King asked for. We want a colorblind society. The ideal will be when we have achieved the moment when no one—or when nothing is done to or for anyone because of race, differences, or religion, or ethnic origin.[35]

The appeal of colorblind individualism, which some scholars have called laissez-faire racism,[36] has proven irresistible. In 1962 the conservative commentator James Kilpatrick defended Jim Crow and mocked the very suggestion that blacks and whites were equal. "*Here and now*," he wrote, with the emphasis all his own, "the Negro race, as a race, plainly is not equal to the white race; nor, for that matter, . . . has the Negro race *ever* been the cultural or intellectual equal of the white race, as a race."[37] By 1974, however, Kilpatrick had enthusiastically embraced the rhetoric of equality, provided that it meant nothing as revolutionary as "equality in fact." "If it is wrong to discriminate by reason of race or sex," he once lectured a supporter of affirmative action, "well, then, it is wrong to discriminate by reason of race or sex."[38]

The conservative understanding of equality, individualism, and limited government was consistently phrased in the timeless language of the American Creed. In a message to the Congress on Racial Equality, Reagan said Dr. King had "challenged" the nation "to make real the promise of America as a land of freedom, equality, opportunity, and brotherhood—a land of liberty and justice for all."[39] The president saluted those who had worked to create "a truly color-blind America where all people are judged by the content of their character, not the color of their skin. To them I say, never, never abandon the dream. Never forget that this is America, the land where dreams come true. And take heart—look how far we have come!"[40] On another occasion, Reagan said that "equal treatment and equality before the law . . . are the foundations on which a just and free society is built." Yet there are people, he warned, "who, in the name of equality, would have us practice discrimination."[41]

They have turned our civil rights laws on their head, claiming they mean exactly the opposite of what they say. These people tell us that the Government should enforce discrimination in favor of some groups through hiring quotas, under which people get or lose particular jobs or promotions solely because of their race or sex. . . . That's discrimination pure and simple and

is exactly what the civil rights laws were designed to stop. . . . Our administration has worked to return the civil rights laws to their original meaning—
to prevent discrimination against any and all Americans.[42]

In matters of race, the emphasis on radical individualism—the idea that
each person is alone responsible for his or her lot in life—has had the most
perverse consequence: It encourages the perpetuation of precisely the group
stereotypes that the civil rights movement opposed. If we exclude imper-
sonal social forces as a contributing explanation for unequal results—as
conservative ideology insists we must—then overrepresentation by certain groups in particular behavior (or even perceived overrepresentation)
reveals something fundamental and enduring *about that group*. Members
of a group who transcend the stereotype and succeed, apparently without
government assistance, not only are taken as proof of the power of individual effort but are readily accepted as equals in the post–civil rights era. *Of
course* African-Americans can reserve a table in this restaurant and a room
in this hotel, buy a home in this neighborhood, and enroll their children in
this school. Any other view has become almost literally unthinkable.

But this does nothing to dislodge the stereotype itself. Today, a large fraction of white Americans believe that African-Americans, as a group, are lazy,
indolent, inclined to violence, and looking for "government handouts."[43] A
substantial majority think African-Americans could be "just as well off as
whites" if only they would "try harder." Fewer than one in ten white Americans "disagree strongly" with this view.[44] An even larger fraction believe
"most blacks who receive money from welfare programs could get along
without it if they tried." Fewer than one in five Americans believe "blacks
have gotten less than they deserve" in society, and most white Americans
"believe that blacks are less hardworking than whites, that blacks are more
violent than whites, and that blacks are less intelligent than whites."[45] Explicit, race-based explanations for persistent disparities are shouted down
in the public square as a reversion to a discredited past. But the private belief happily endures, nourished by the certainty that there can be no other
explanation for patterns of inequality that have lasted for generations.[46] In
matters of race, there is a deep reservoir of ill will restrained by a powerful bulwark of social custom. Custom acts like an enormous dam, hold-

ing back the staggering weight of vitriol and prejudice. The surface seems placid, but serenity prevails only so long as the dam is secure.

Because race in the United States has been so long associated with the peculiar relationship between African-Americans and whites, and because the contemporary understanding of race owes so much to the civil rights movement, black-white relations have been the subject of much more study than relations between whites and other minorities. But what I have described is hardly confined to the African-American image in the white mind. Stereotypes are far too useful to be so easily cabined. They serve the not altogether salutary purpose of imposing order on what could otherwise be chaos. The judgment that members of a particular community, as a group, share characteristics that make them more (or less) friendly to me and my community not only helps me plan my affairs in a way likely to increase my sense of well-being, it also helps give my community structure and identity. "We" are the people who are not like "them," or so we like to believe. The creation of stereotypes is thus inevitable, as anthropologists and social psychologists have long pointed out.[47] The danger arises when these stereotypes lead us to act foolishly, as they regularly do. We then become imprisoned by our own constructions, living in fear of a mythical beast of our own making.

Moreover, scholars have long known that the tendency to endorse negative stereotypes about perceived outsiders is a general one. People who harbor the most negative attitudes about African-Americans, for instance, also tend to hold the dimmest view of Jews;[48] people who stereotype Jews also tend to stereotype Muslims.[49] The stereotypes are not the same, of course. Jews are thought to be grasping and money-minded, Muslims are murderous terrorists, and African-Americans are lazy and predisposed to crime. But the inclination to see the world in grossly distorted terms—to generalize about the threat posed by the many from the real or imagined behavior of a few—is the same.

IV

The modern understanding of race reveals all too well the power and manipulability of the Creed. The explicit racism of the Jim Crow era lost its grip when the civil rights movement successfully recast American identity to require at least a rhetorical commitment to universal equality, which in turn implied a more expansive understanding of civic virtue. The modern conservative movement succeeded when it subordinated "equality in fact and equality as a result" to individualism and limited government. American identity at the start of the twenty-first century—at least with respect to race—combined elements of both movements. From the civil rights movement we have the language of equality, which now forbids the endorsement of explicit racial categories. But modern conservatism has given that language its contemporary meaning: Equality means equal opportunity to succeed or fail. The government has no business favoring one group over another and must remain officially neutral in matters of race. If some group is overrepresented in one population or activity, the overrepresentation tells us something about the group or its "culture," and not about American society.

And just as the past half-century's debates over race have done much to give us our modern understanding of equality, individualism, and limited government, the simultaneous debates over religion have significantly shaped our understanding of religious liberty, diversity, tolerance, and community membership. The United States is an exceptionally religious place. Eight in ten Americans are certain there is a God. Forty percent attend religious services once a week or more, nearly three-quarters say they pray at least once a week, and nine in ten say they pray at least occasionally. One-third believes the Scriptures are the actual word of God, and more than two-thirds believe in the afterlife.[50] These numbers are even more striking when compared with the rest of the world. By almost every metric, the United States is substantially more religious than virtually all other developed nations. Nor is this a recent development. These percentages have remained stable for the past fifty years (with the exception of the fraction who believe the Scriptures are the literal word of God, which has declined steadily over that time).[51]

But this consistent religiosity masks profound changes over the past half-century in the role that religion plays in American life. The difference in the meaning of race during this period may be more obvious, but the transformation in the meaning of religion is more momentous. At midcentury, the sociologist Will Herberg could say with some justification that to be other than a Protestant, Catholic, or Jew in the United States was to be un-American. Herberg defined what he called "the American Way of Life" as "the common set of ideas, rituals, and symbols" that give the United States "its overarching sense of unity."[52] He struggled at some length to describe this shared philosophy. If it "had to be defined in one word," he wrote, "democracy would undoubtedly be the word, but democracy in a peculiarly American sense. On its political side it means the Constitution; on its economic side, 'free enterprise'; on its social side, an equalitarianism which is not only compatible with but indeed actually implies vigorous economic competition and high mobility."[53]

We immediately recognize Herberg's attempt (and sympathize with his difficulty) as an effort to distill the American Creed into words: to describe, as he put it, "the framework in terms of which the crucial values of American existence are couched."[54] But his distinctive contribution to the literature about "the American Way of Life" was to discern the Creed in the common religious practices and beliefs of Protestants, Catholics, and Jews. All believed in the fatherhood of God, the brotherhood of man, the virtue of American democracy, and the evil of godless communism. Herberg went even farther, maintaining that this philosophy was shared *only* by members of the Judeo-Christian tradition. To profess oneself "a Buddhist, a Muslim, or anything but a Protestant, Catholic, or Jew," he wrote, is to admit to "being foreign."[55]

Herberg could also point to the imposing cultural barriers that separated these three religious traditions and conclude, like others of his day, that the country was not one but three very distinct melting pots, each offering a separate path to assimilation into American society. He believed that religious identity had replaced ethnic attachments as the means by which the children and grandchildren of immigrants "found an identifiable place in American life."[56] "Increasingly," he wrote, "the great mass of Americans understand themselves and their place in society in terms of the religious community with which they are identified. And 'religious community' in this usage refers not so much to the particular denomination, ... but to the three great divisions, Catholics, Protestants, and Jews. America is ... the land of the 'triple melting pot,' for it is within these three religious communities that the process of ethnic and cultural integration so characteristic of American life takes place."[57]

When Herberg wrote, religious preference and political affiliation aligned and overlapped very differently from the way they do today. Conservative Protestants in the rural South were almost all Democrats, as were liberal Catholics and Jews in the urban North. Liberal mainline Protestants in the North and West were likely to be Republicans, as were a growing number of rural conservative Catholics in the Midwest. Moreover, throughout the 1950s and 1960s, religiosity implied nothing about political affiliation.[58] Liberals and conservatives were in the pews in equal numbers. One indication of this disconnection is that the Republican Dwight D. Eisenhower received as much support from Americans who attended religious services frequently as he did from those who never attended. In 2008, by contrast, 61 percent of those who attended religious services frequently supported the Republican candidate, John McCain, versus only 39 percent of those who never attended.[59]

Herberg would hardly recognize the American religious scene at the end of the twentieth century. To begin with, there has been a dramatic decline in denominationalism. Divisions within Protestantism, and between Protestantism and Catholicism, once had surpassing importance in American life. By 2000 denominational attachments had become less significant than at any other time in American history. As the borders between denominations have become more porous, there has been a dramatic increase in religious sorting.[60] Americans no longer feel confined to the religious tradition into which they were born. In great numbers, they change faiths, sometimes more than once. According to the sociologist Robert Putnam and the political scientist David Campbell, "roughly 35–40% of all Americans and 40–45% of white Americans have switched at some point away from their parents' religion."[61]

They also marry outside their faith. By the end of the first decade of the twenty-first century, about half of all married Americans had done so.[62] This contributes to the bridging of religious divides, as couples learn to reconcile their religious differences and raise their children in faiths other than those in which they were raised.[63] Americans also go through periods of greater and lesser religiosity, at times describing themselves as having no organized religion and at other times indicating a religious preference; at times attending religious services frequently and at other times rarely. This constant mixing and changing has dramatically reduced intra- and interreligious tensions. The political scientist and sociologist Alan Wolfe summed it up well: "If you cannot be sure today what your faith will be to-morrow—let alone the faith of the people your son or daughter bring home for the weekend—you had better not say anything too nasty about any of them."[64]

The United States has also become substantially more diverse. In 1965, for the first time in decades, the country reopened its doors to large num-bers of immigrants. Newcomers flooded in from India, Asia, the Middle East, and Latin America, bringing new religious traditions and symbols. Buddhists from Southeast Asia, Muslims from the Middle East, Hindus and Sikhs from India, along with many others, settled throughout the country. Many of the Catholic and Protestant immigrants of this period, particularly from Latin America and Africa, practiced their faith in dramati-cally different ways from European Christians. As always, the immigrant experience complicated the imagined simplicity of American life, changing both recent immigrants and those who arrived before. For the first time, their fondness for experimentation allowed Americans to participate in Eastern as well as Western religious traditions and exposed them to Chris-tian practices very different from their own.[65]

Finally, the very idea of having a religious preference has declined dra-matically. In the 1950s only a small number of Americans told pollsters they did not belong to any religious tradition. Today, however, in a much-commented-upon development, "none" is the fastest-growing religious de-nomination.[66] These people do not consider themselves atheists; atheism remains almost unheard of among Americans. Most tell pollsters they be-lieve in God, and many say that religion is important in their lives. But they claim no formal religious attachment. They may have had one earlier in their lives, and may return to one later. But by 2006, 17 percent of Ameri-cans had no religious preference, more than the number identifying them-selves as members of *any* mainline Protestant denomination.[67] Not only is the percentage of "nones" growing across society, it has already reached unprecedented levels within the youngest generation. Roughly one in four

Americans who reached adulthood in the 1990s and 2000s reported no religion, substantially more than the number who identified themselves as evangelical Protestants.[68] By the end of the century, Herberg's insistence that to be an American meant being nothing other than a Protestant, Catholic, or Jew had become laughable.

Taken together, these changes have completely transformed religion in American life. Americans now live in a more religiously integrated society than at any time in the past. They are more likely than ever to have shifted their religious preference or to have decided, at least temporarily, that they are not part of any religious tradition. In most parts of the country, they are virtually certain to know, work, associate with, or be related or married to people of a different faith. As a result, most Americans have adopted a live-and-let-live attitude about most other religious traditions. The sectarian animosity that characterized American life for so long has diminished substantially. Many Americans are not much troubled by the prospect that their children will marry outside their faith. They tend to feel equally warmly toward Jews, Catholics, and mainline Protestants, and only slightly less warmly towards evangelical Protestants and the nonreligious.[69] As for the role of religion in public life, most Americans not only tolerate but demand that God remain, at least to some degree, in the public square. Yet they have no desire to eliminate the religious diversity of American society and show little inclination to elevate one religious tradition above others. A 2002 survey showed that only 13 percent of Americans believed that "America's growing religious diversity" represented "a threat to individual religious beliefs," whereas three-quarters considered diversity "a source of strength and vitality to individual beliefs."[70] All in all, the United States has become an enviably tolerant place.

Except, of course, when it isn't.

V

This cheery account glosses over two things. First, it is conspicuously silent about the struggles that brought the nation to this state. Much of American history, recent and remote, is a tale of fractious contests over religious freedom. Any hint that we arrived at today's relatively tolerant idyll simply by stepping through a wardrobe and passing into another time is impossibly naïve. Yesterday's religious outsiders became today's insiders only by engaging in extended, often violent conflict at the gates of national membership.[71] Each new group has discovered for itself that membership is not bestowed but won. These battles have been among the most rancorous in American life—rancorous because they involve more than the meaning and priority to be given to shared values. Instead, they concern the more elemental question of whether a new (or newly suspect) group shares the values themselves, and may therefore legitimately claim a place at America's vast table.

Second, this account of religious tolerance and diversity at the close of the twentieth century overlooks the extent to which it remains a fable. Throughout this discussion, I have referred to the view of most Americans, and this majority has certainly achieved an enviable degree of open-mindedness. They are religious, as Americans have always been, and many are exceptionally devout, but they no longer believe that one religious tradition has a monopoly on truth or civic virtue. Will Herberg's narrow midcentury conception of "the American Way of Life" has been repudiated. But "most" is not all, and tens of millions of Americans still define membership in the American community by adherence to Judeo-Christian beliefs. In early 2002 the Pew Research Center for People and the Press, in conjunction with the Pew Forum on Religion and Public Life, asked this simple question: "All in all, do you think a person can be a good American if he or she does not believe in basic Judeo-Christian values?" One in six respondents said no.[72]

Who in American society is most apt to hold this view? Prominent among them are the people the sociologist Robert Wuthnow calls Christian Exclusivists.[73] Their worldview is built around a belief that their interpretation of Christianity provides the exclusive path to salvation, that the Bible is the actual word of God and must be taken literally, and that the teachings of other religions are simply false. Overwhelmingly, they reject the suggestion that all religions "basically teach the same thing."[74] They are suspicious of the increasing diversity in American society and inclined to worry about its baleful effects on American values. By substantial margins, they say "the United States was founded on Christian principles" and "has been strong because of its faith in God."[75] Half of Christian Exclusivists identify themselves as evangelical Protestants. Another 15 percent are Roman Catholic. More than half live in small towns or rural areas, and a third live in the suburbs. Only a small number say they live in an urban setting. They are concentrated in the South and Midwest. Most are women. Most attend religious services almost every week.[76]

Certainly it is wrong to suggest that all Christian Exclusivists reject the live-and-let-live attitude of so many other Americans. Here as anywhere, it is important to remind oneself that no group with tens of millions of members speaks with a single voice. But as a group, the Christian Exclusivists are much more likely than other Americans to endorse a narrow worldview and to be exquisitely skeptical of social and religious diversity. Along with a very small number of socially conservative Jews, they constitute a significant fraction of that much-commented-upon and much-maligned conservative social movement, the religious right.[77]

But the Christian Exclusivists are not alone in resisting diversity. There are many for whom the "Other" has always been a powerful source of menace and anxiety. These are the authoritarians, the psychologically brittle souls whose sense of well-being is deeply threatened by those whom they see as standing outside the moral order. As the Princeton political scientist Karen Stenner recently put it, they are animated "by a fundamental and overwhelming desire to establish and defend *some* collective order of oneness and sameness."[78] Because the terror they feel springs from whatever has been constructed as a threat to their sense of "oneness and sameness," their denunciations range over a wide cultural field, shifting as new demons emerge and old ones pass from the public square. Yesterday it may have been African-Americans, today it may be Muslims, and tomorrow the Chinese. Depending on how the demon has been constructed, their alarm may align with and amplify the concerns of the religious right, but their concerns are not religious per se. Their cries depend on no particular substantive issue but on an intolerance of perceived difference. As two scholars recently put it, "the readiness to derogate outgroups tends to be general."[79] Perhaps most important, though authoritarians are no more likely than others to perceive something as a threat, they distinguish themselves by the ferocity of their response once that perception has been aroused. Authoritarians, Professor Stenner observes, "are not especially inclined to perceive normative . . . threat, they are just *especially intolerant once they do*."[80]

VI

The history and sociology of the religious right has been told often and well. Recent scholarship has likewise plumbed the depths of the authoritarian state of mind. Neither body of literature needs to be reprised here; in a book about the making of national identity, we can confine ourselves to the two groups' political preference. To a great extent, the passionate attachments of both the religious right and the authoritarian personality now find their outlet in the positions of the Republican Party.

The prominence of the religious right within the Republican tent is old news; many have even called the GOP "God's Own Party" and have described it as having been "captured" by religious conservatives. The GOP has steadily moved to the right over the past several decades on the issues of greatest importance to religious conservatives and has often made a specific appeal to that constituency.[81] Similarly, members of the religious right are not only overwhelmingly Republican but ardently so. Religious conservatives are the party's most reliable supporters and represent a significant fraction of its constituency. In 2004 conservative evangelical Protestants voted more than 7:1 for Bush over Kerry and accounted for nearly 40 percent of his total votes. In 2008 they supported McCain over Obama by similar margins.[82] White evangelicals accounted for 50 percent of all voters in the 2012 Republican presidential primaries.[83]

No Republican candidate for national office can afford to alienate this constituency, a fact that has not escaped the religious right's attention. Gary Bauer, the Christian right leader who campaigned for the Republican nomination in 2000, once told the Christian Broadcasting Network that religious conservatives had "gone way beyond the point where we need a seat at the table. . . . We're in a position to offer others a seat at the table, because we really are the heart of the party."[84] Many have noted the convergence of the religious right and the Republican Party. The journalist and public intellectual Bill Moyers has been especially vocal about it. Speaking at Union Theological Seminary in 2005, Moyers charged that "the radical religious right has succeeded in taking over one of America's great political parties—the country is not yet a theocracy but the Republican Party is—and they are driving American politics."[85] But an alliance between the religious right and the Republican Party is not all that worries Moyers and others. It is also "the intensity, organization, and anger" the religious right has "brought to the public square." Their "virulent intolerance," Moyers said, "has become an unprecedented sectarian crusade for state power. . . . The radicals on the Christian right are the dominant force in the governing party."[86]

The shrill virulence of the religious right has recently been amplified by another important constituency. Just as the GOP has become the home for religious conservatives, it is increasingly the party of choice for authoritarians. In a development that seemed to begin in the early 1990s, scholars have detected "a coalitional reconfiguration of the parties, . . . with authoritarians increasingly gravitating toward the Republican Party and non-authoritarians increasingly gravitating toward the Democratic."[87] In tandem, authoritarians and religious conservatives have completely reshaped the Republican Party, dragging it far to the right and purging all but its most radical members. Reflecting on these developments, the veteran political observers Thomas Mann of the Brookings Institute and Norman Ornstein of the American Enterprise Institute recently described the party as "an insurgent outlier in American politics. It is ideologically extreme; scornful of compromise; unmoved by conventional understanding of facts, evidence and science; and dismissive of the legitimacy of its political opposition."[88] Moderate Republicans like former Nebraska Senator Chuck Hagel, once the party's "center of gravity," are now "virtually extinct."[89]

These moderates have joined the rising chorus of criticism aimed at the Republican Party. In an interview with the *Financial Times*, Hagel said the GOP "is captive to political movements that are very ideological, that are very narrow."[90] In a subsequent interview with *Foreign Policy* magazine, he said the Republican Party was "in the hands of . . . the extreme right more than ever before." Ronald Reagan, he said, "would be stunned by the party today. . . . If Nixon or Eisenhower were alive today, they would be run out of the party."[91] Mike Lofgren, who spent decades on Capitol Hill as a Republican staffer before resigning in 2011 in disgust at what the

GOP had become, thought it was "evident to clear-eyed observers that the Republican Party is becoming less and less like a traditional political party in a representative democracy and . . . more like an apocalyptic cult, or one of the intensely ideological authoritarian parties of 20th century Europe."[92] The party, Lofgren said, maintained a bitter hostility toward the demonic "Other"—meaning "anyone not likely to vote Republican."[93]

> Racial minorities. Immigrants. Muslims. Gays. Intellectuals. Basically, anyone who doesn't look, think, or talk like the GOP base. This must account, at least to some degree, for their extraordinarily vitriolic hatred of President Obama. . . . Among the GOP base, there is constant harping about somebody else, some "other," who is deliberately, assiduously and with malice aforethought subverting the Good, the True and the Beautiful: Subversives. Commies. Socialists. Ragheads. Secular humanists. Blacks. Fags. Feminazis. The list may change with the political needs of the moment, but they always seem to need a scapegoat to hate and fear.[94]

To understand how authoritarians and religious conservatives have joined hands in the present political climate, we need look no farther than the GOP attacks on President Obama. During the 2012 election cycle, Republican candidates and their surrogates collapsed the many criticisms of Obama into a catch-all complaint that he is simply "not an American," meaning that he does not believe in the values and traditions of American identity shared by the Republican faithful. Thus, at a Colorado fundraiser, Congressman Mike Coffman (R-CO) told supporters, "I don't know whether Barack Obama was born in the United States of America. I don't know that. But I do know this, that in his heart, he's not an American. He's just not an American." And John Sununu, the former Republican governor of New Hampshire and a spokesman for the Romney campaign, likewise said, "I wish this president would learn how to be an American." The explanation for this essential "foreignness" is deliberately left vague and members of the audience are free to attach themselves to any of the various reasons in circulation that explain why the president is not "one of us." Perhaps it is because he is Muslim; perhaps it is because he is foreign-born; perhaps it is because he was raised in a foreign culture; perhaps it is because he is a socialist and does not believe in the free market system. But for whatever reason, Obama is an outsider, a threat to the "true" American identity. (Coffman and Sununu later apologized for their comments.)[95]

Race and religion have followed different paths to arrive at complementary but not identical places in American life. On the surface, there is an appearance of religious and racial tolerance shared by the great majority. But closer study reveals dangerous cracks in the façade. With respect to race, the public norm is offset by private belief; there are certain things one may not say, even if a great many people believe them. The conviction is commonplace, at least among whites, that race matters a great deal in predicting a person's behavior, yet this cannot be said in public. With respect to religion, most Americans have learned to welcome a great variety of traditions as equally genuine. But many people nonetheless take a much narrower view, believing that community membership does not and should not extend to those who practice certain "foreign" religions. Because religion is openly discussed in the public square, those who endorse this view can speak directly, summoning the language and imagery of a Judeo-Christian heritage to justify their preferences. The indirectness that characterizes discussion about race is therefore often absent in discussion about religion.

This, at least in summary, was the state of play that fateful Tuesday morning when "the terrorists defined it . . . by race and religion."

5

The Punitive Turn

THE COLLAPSE OF JIM CROW AND THE mixed success of the civil rights movement did more than alter the meaning of equality, individualism, and the proper role of government in American life. It also corresponded with the rise of a very different national sentiment. Over the past fifty years, the United States has become an exceptionally punitive place, a change that has been abundantly documented.[1] Yet few have paid close attention to the relationship between the punitive turn in American life and the changing content of our national values. Through this transformation, the attachment to individualism has intensified as the idea of community has fractured. The notion of limited government has been turned on its head as the federal government has increasingly been called upon to keep society safe by separating "us" from "them."[2] And the idea of the rule of law has changed from a restraint *on* the state (in order to protect individual liberty) into a weapon *of* the state (in order to enable the state to identify, seize, imprison, and punish those who threaten a blameless "us").

It is critical to understand that the punitive turn is not simply about punishment or retribution. These are just the end products of a much more comprehensive transformation in American life that has dramatically changed the way things *ought to be*. This transformation manifests itself in the repeated staging of an elaborate performance that engages all elements of society. It begins with the very public creation of imagined monsters that are thought to imperil the American way of life, each of which summons a distinct response by the national government as it struggles to control the new demon. This leads to a set of rituals that leaders are expected to observe in the face of these newly imagined threats. These rituals signal to society that the nation is responding to the threat in the "right" way, a way that honors and reaffirms national values. With each repetition, these rituals have grown more firmly entrenched until finally they have become received wisdom, a lesson political leaders ignore at their peril.

I

When the United States emerged in 1945 from the nightmare of total war, there was a consensus, at least among cultural elites, that dangerous criminals were not so much born as made. Deviant behavior, the thinking went, was substantially caused by social and economic forces, not merely individual action. Crime was considered "merely a form of primitive social protest."[3] End the conditions that gave rise to the protest, and most criminal behavior would disappear.[4] For that reason, crime control was largely synonymous with social welfare, and it was foolish to imagine one without the other. "The war on poverty," Lyndon Johnson said in 1964, "is a war against crime and a war against disorder." Speaking about Barry Goldwater, his opponent in the upcoming election, Johnson said there was "something mighty wrong when a candidate for the highest office bemoans violence in the streets but votes against the war on poverty, votes against the Civil Rights Act, votes against major educational bills that come before him as a legislator."[5]

Like any expression of American identity that achieves widespread acceptance, postwar optimism cast itself in the elastic rhetoric of the Creed, stressing mutual obligation and civic duty in service of the common good. The welfare of the community was *everyone's* responsibility, and all shared in the blame when broad segments of the population remained poor, uneducated, unemployed, and therefore prone to criminality. As the magazine *Commonweal* put it in 1946, "It is vain to write about the particular motivation of an individual who succumbs and commits a crime. The general public maladies that lead or tempt to crime are everybody's fault to the degree that each could, with justly demanded effort, work against the general demoralizing conditions."[6] Because the chaos and decay that grew from these "demoralizing conditions" affected everyone, the entire community was obligated to become part of the solution, and to take what steps it could to achieve greater equality. Only then could the nation realize its lofty goals.

The turbulence of the mid-1960s sorely tested this philosophy. In July 1967, after two weeks of deadly rioting in Detroit and Newark, President Johnson established the National Advisory Commission on Civil Disorders, better known as the Kerner Commission. Its conclusions, released in 1968, were a sober indictment of American life cast in the creedal language of communitarianism and equality. "Our nation is moving toward two societies, one black, one white—separate and unequal."[7] Though it was the ghetto that erupted, the commission made clear that blame did not rest solely with the rioters; causes must be found elsewhere. "What white Americans have never fully understood but what the Negro can never forget is that white society is deeply implicated in the ghetto. White institutions created it, white institutions maintain it, and white society condones it." The country's "deepening racial division . . . threaten[ed] the future of every American." Failure to act would lead to "continuing polarization of the American community and, ultimately, the destruction of basic democratic values."[8]

Yet by the time the Kerner Commission issued its report, the optimism of postwar liberalism had already begun to collapse. For years, the liberal view had been under attack by conservative intellectuals who derided the entire New Deal philosophy as a dangerous assault on the free market system and the free will of the individual. Ayn Rand, author of *The Fountainhead* and *Atlas Shrugged,* mocked the very notion of a "common good" and ridiculed the suggestion that "everybody is responsible for everybody's welfare."[9] But it was not till Barry Goldwater's campaign for the presidency in 1964 that the conservative view of individualism and personal responsibility began to achieve wider circulation in the context of crime control.

"If it is entirely proper for the government to take away from some to give to others," Goldwater asked, "then won't some be led to believe that they can rightfully take from anyone who has more than they? No wonder law and order has broken down, mob violence has engulfed great American cities, and our wives feel unsafe in the streets."[10] Though Goldwater lost decisively, his message of "law and order" struck a chord. In 1965 the Johnson administration's approach to crime began to move away from its liberal origins. "The problem runs deep and will not yield easy and quick answers," Johnson said. "We must identify and eliminate the causes of criminal activity whether they be in the environment around us or in the nature of individual men. . . . Crime will not wait until we pull it up by the roots. We must arrest and reverse the trend toward lawlessness."[11]

The 1968 presidential campaign continued the trend that Goldwater and other vanguards of modern conservatism had set in motion. The Republican national platform that year called upon the country to "think anew about the relationship of man and his government [and] enlarge the opportunity and autonomy of the individual." On crime policy, the GOP insisted, "we must re-establish the principle that men are accountable for what they do, that criminals are responsible for their crimes, that while the youth's environment may help to explain the man's crime, it does not excuse that crime."[12] Presidential candidate Richard Nixon pressed hard for law and order. The "solution to the crime problem," he said, "is not the quadrupling of funds for any governmental war on poverty but more convictions." He mocked his Democratic opponent, Hubert Humphrey, as naïve. "Doubling the conviction rate in this country would do far more to cure crime in America than quadrupling the funds for Mr. Humphrey's war on poverty."[13]

Yet the liberal explanation for crime was not yet dead, and Nixon continued to acknowledge that civil order required social justice. He resolved the tension in his position by adjusting his message to fit his audience. As *Time* magazine observed two months before the election, Nixon "is in favor of 'order with progress' when he speaks in Westchester but for 'law and order' when he is in Houston or Charlotte, N.C."[14] A third-party candidate, Alabama Governor George Wallace, was considerably less nuanced. He scoffed at the suggestion that crime had anything to do with a person's upbringing. "If a criminal knocks you over the head on your way home from work, he will be out of jail before you're out of the hospital and the policeman who arrested him will be on trial. But some psychologist will say, well, he's not to blame, society's to blame. His father didn't take him to see the Pittsburgh Pirates when he was a little boy."[15]

Democratic politicians, meanwhile, also joined the movement away from postwar liberalism. The Democratic national platform in 1964 represented the last pure expression of the New Deal communitarian spirit. "America is One Nation, One People," it began. "The welfare, progress, security, and survival of each of us reside in the common good—the sharing of responsibilities as well as benefits by all our people."[16] The lengthy document made scant reference to crime except to emphasize its origin in social conditions. "We cannot and will not tolerate lawlessness. We can and will seek to eliminate its economic and social causes." To that end, the platform vowed to use the war on poverty to increase "educational and employment opportunities, turning juvenile delinquents into good citizens and tax-users into tax-payers."[17]

By 1968 the tone had changed and the Democrats began to employ a different creedal language. Though the party's platform that year never used the distinctly Republican phrase "law and order," it came close when it stressed the need "to strengthen the fabric of our society by making justice and equity the cornerstones of order" and "to uphold the rule of law by securing to all the people the natural rights that belong to them."[18] Elsewhere, the platform candidly acknowledged that "the fact and fear of crime are uppermost in the minds of Americans today. The entire nation is united in its concern over crime." Employing the ascendant language of individualism, the platform stressed that "anyone who breaks the law must be held accountable."[19] And acknowledging the increased role of the federal government in combatting crime, the platform boasted that the Johnson administration had fought "to prevent and combat youth crime," "added more personnel to strengthen the [FBI]," and secured passage of a gun control law that would take "a step toward putting the weapons of wanton violence beyond the reach of the criminal and irresponsible hands."[20] The Democrats promised to "increase the numbers, raise the pay, and improve the training of local police officers," and vowed to ensure that every metropolitan area had "quick, balanced, coordinated control forces, with ample manpower . . . to suppress rioting."[21]

Responding to the call for crime control, Vice President Humphrey insisted defiantly that his campaign would not "out-Nixon Nixon, and we're not going to out-Wallace Wallace. We're going to say it like it is." But his message echoed the Democratic platform, calling for more resources for police and courts while maintaining vaguely that order depended on "a policy not of repression but of liberation; a policy not in reaction to fear but in affirmation of hope."[22] In their concrete proposals, Democrats thus found themselves moving steadily closer to the Republicans. And though their rhetoric continued to link crime to social conditions, that link became increasingly abstract. Unsurprisingly, as the view by trusted messengers on the left and right began to converge, public opinion followed suit. By 1969, "81% of those polled believed that law and order had broken down, and the majority blamed 'Negroes who start riots' and 'communists.'"[23]

The trend continued throughout the 1970s, though the Republican leadership on the issue temporarily derailed in mid-decade after the Watergate scandal. But it was Ronald Reagan in the 1980s who most successfully aligned the conservative understanding of crime and risk with the rhetoric of the American Creed. Under Reagan, the communitarian sentiment of the early postwar years was decisively replaced with the language of individualism and personal responsibility. In his first major address on crime, Reagan attacked "the social thinkers of the fifties and sixties who discussed crime only in the context of disadvantaged childhoods and poverty-stricken neighborhoods."[24] Reagan charted another course. It is "abundantly clear," he said, "that much of our crime problem was provoked by a social philosophy that saw man as primarily a creature of his material environment. . . . Society, not the individual, they said, was at fault for criminal wrongdoing. We were to blame. Well, today, a new political consensus utterly rejects this point of view."[25]

For Reagan, crime had nothing to do with society and everything to do with individual responsibility. "Choosing a career in crime is not the result of poverty or of an unhappy childhood or of a misunderstood adolescence; it is the result of a conscious, willful choice made by some who consider themselves above the law."[26] And some people choose crime simply because they are evil. While men "are basically good," Reagan said when he presented his anticrime package, some are "prone to evil," some in fact "are very prone to evil," and "society has the right to be protected from them."[27] Victory in the war on crime would come only "when an attitude of mind and a change of heart takes place in America—when certain truths take hold again . . . truths like right and wrong matters; individuals are responsible for their actions; [and] retribution should be swift and sure for those who prey on the innocent."[28]

By the end of the decade, the Republican and Democratic positions on crime were nearly indistinguishable. The Democratic platform of 1988 abandoned the now heretical suggestion that crime could be caused by social conditions and pledged an aggressive role for the federal government in controlling lawlessness. The Democrats pledged to "wage total war on drugs" by appointing a national drug "czar" to coordinate "every arm of every agency of government at every federal, state and local level . . . to halt both the international supply and domestic demand for illegal drugs now ravaging our country." The federal government would increase its assistance to law enforcement, reinforce its commitment to crime victims, and "assume a leadership role in securing the safety of our neighborhoods and homes."[29] The Republican platform that year no longer found it necessary to assert the primacy of individual autonomy and personal responsibility at the expense of community obligation; that battle had long since been won. The GOP contented itself with a laundry list of accomplishments, such as appointing federal judges who were "sensitive to the rights of victims" and vastly increasing the number of drug arrests and convictions. The party looked forward to continued movement in this direction, including restoration of the federal death penalty, reform of the exclusionary rule "to prevent the release of guilty felons on technicalities," and passage of preventive detention statutes that would allow "courts to deny bail to those considered dangerous and likely to commit additional crimes."[30]

By 1992 the shift to the conservative perspective was essentially complete. The two parties vied for no greater distinction than to be the tougher on crime, a stance that by then implied little besides a more expansive federal role, stiffer penalties, and greater support for victims. Nothing illustrates the transformation better than the career of Bill Clinton. In 1980, after he lost his bid for reelection to a second term as Arkansas governor, Clinton resolved that he would never again permit a Republican to use crime to outflank him on the right. In the 1992 presidential campaign, Clinton made his stand in the case of Ricky Rector. Rector, who was mentally retarded, had shot himself in the head after shooting and killing a police officer, leaving himself partially lobotomized. He had been sentenced to die but by all accounts he was profoundly impaired. Before his execution, he left the pecan pie from his last meal, telling prison guards he was saving it for later. Clinton allowed the execution to go forward. A Democratic activist later told the *Houston Chronicle* that the execution "completely undermines" any Republican attempt to portray Clinton as "out of touch with [the] mainstream public." A New York political observer wrote: "He had someone put to death who had only part of a brain. You can't find them any tougher than that."[31]

II

One of the enduring features of the punitive turn has been the repeated creation of mythical monsters whose apocalyptic threat requires expanding the federal enforcement power. This is justified in creedal language of community welfare and individual responsibility. But it is not the entire community, as it was during the New Deal and Great Society. Paramount now is only a frightened fraction of the community—the fraction that imagines itself at risk. Because society is blameless, crime no longer demands a communal response. Instead, it demands that some parts of the community be protected from others, who are cast beyond the pale. At the same time, the process has evolved to demand certain very public rituals. The demon must be publicly denounced as the monster that he is. This public, ritualistic denunciation acts as the signal for a second ritual—the call to action.

Like the bat-shaped light beamed into the dark sky that summons Batman to save Gotham City, the ritual of creating a monster summons the government to rescue law-abiding citizens from this new peril. Congress holds public hearings where the threat is described in apocalyptic language. The media spread the image to an increasingly anxious nation. Laws are solemnly passed that give the executive branch greater power to locate, track, arrest, convict, and punish the monster. The process is repeated in the states as legislatures grant similar power to state and local law enforcement. Society bands together, each segment playing its part to demonstrate that the nation is united in its determination both to rid itself of danger *and* to do so in a way that honors each group's role, even those few naysayers who protest and warn against overreaction. The new powers that emerge are thus legitimate precisely because they have been collectively bestowed by a society that has been permitted to participate in the process.

An example of this elaborate process is the dramatic rise and fall of the juvenile "superpredator." Violent juvenile crime rose precipitously in the mid-1980s, triggering widespread alarm. Attention naturally focused on particularly vicious assaults, the most sensational of which occurred April 19, 1989. Trisha Meili, a twenty-eight-year-old investment banker, was jogging in Central Park when she was brutally attacked, beaten, raped, and left for dead. That evening, police arrested five African-American and Latino boys from East Harlem who had been part of a much larger group of youths making trouble—some of it menacing and violent—elsewhere in the park. When Meili was found unconscious the next day, police turned their attention to the five youths, four of whom eventually confessed to the attack.[32] The media coverage was ferocious. Page 1 of the April 21 *New York Daily News* read: "CENTRAL PARK HORROR: WOLF PACK'S PREY: Female jogger near dead after savage attack by roving gang."[33] On April 22 the *New York Post* gave the problem a name that immediately spread across the country. It was "wilding," referring to "packs of bloodthirsty teens from the tenements, bursting with boredom and rage" who "roam the streets getting kicks from an evening of ultra-violence."[34] *Post* columnist Pete Hamill painted a terrifying image:

> They were coming downtown from a world of crack, welfare, guns, knives, indifference and ignorance. They were coming from a land with no fathers. They were coming from the anarchic province of the poor. And driven by a collective fury, brimming with the rippling energies of youth, their minds teeming with the violent images of the streets and the movies, they had only one goal: to smash, hurt, rob, stomp, rape. The enemies were rich. The enemies were white.[35]

New York Mayor Ed Koch called the defendants "monsters."[36] Governor Mario Cuomo said the attacks brought "the ultimate shriek of alarm." Donald Trump took out ads in four of the city's newspapers demanding the return of the death penalty.[37] The nightly news ran portions of the defendants' taped confessions.[38] "The boys, all between 14 and 17 years old, were described by reporters and columnists alike as 'bloodthirsty,' 'animals,' 'savages' and 'human mutations.'"[39] Soon, stories across the country chronicled youth violence. In 1993 the *Chicago Tribune* warned of a "street gang menace" that plays by "rules of their own making."[40] In 1994 papers nationwide ran sensational stories about two Chicago preteen boys who dropped a five-year-old out of a fourteenth-story window.[41]

In 1995 the conservative criminal justice scholar James Q. Wilson wrote, "We are terrified by the prospect of innocent people being gunned down at random, without warning, and almost without motive, by youngsters who afterwards show us the blank, unremorseful face of a feral, pre-social being."[42] But it was Wilson's former student, the criminologist John DiIulio, who gets the credit for the "superpredator" moniker. In a much-cited article in the *Weekly Standard,* he expressed dismay at a "youth crime wave" of "horrific proportions from coast to coast."[43] These were not "normal" criminals, DiIulio said, but "hardened, remorseless" predators with "absolutely no respect for human life," more dangerous than the most vicious adult criminals, who would "make even the leaders of the Bloods and Crips . . . look tame by comparison."[44] To dispel all doubt, DiIulio assured us he was no timid naïf:

> I will still waltz backwards, notebook in hand and alone, into any adult maximum-security cellblock full of killers, rapists, and muggers. But a few years ago, I forswore research inside juvenile lock-ups. The buzz of impulsive violence, the vacant stares and smiles, and the remorseless eyes were at once too frightening and too depressing.[45]

As bad as matters had become, DiIulio insisted, they were about to get much worse. "What is really frightening everyone is not what's happening now but what's just around the corner—namely, a sharp increase in the number of super crime-prone young males." DiIulio foresaw "tens of thousands" of "juvenile super-predators," a tidal wave of violence and mayhem "that hasn't yet begun to crest."[46]

> They are perfectly capable of committing the most heinous acts of physical violence for the most trivial reasons. . . . They fear neither the stigma of arrest nor the pain of imprisonment. They live by the meanest code of the meanest streets, a code that reinforces rather than restrains their violent,

hair-trigger mentality. In prison or out, the things that super-predators get by their criminal behavior—sex, drugs, money—are their own immediate rewards. Nothing else matters to them. So for as long as their youthful energies hold out, they will do what comes "naturally": murder, rape, rob, assault, burglarize, deal deadly drugs, and get high.[47]

Fast on the heels of this article came the best-selling book *Body Count: Moral Poverty . . . and How to Win America's War Against Crime and Drugs*, cowritten by DiIulio, William Bennett, who had headed the Office of Drug Policy under the first President Bush, and John Walters, who had been Bennett's assistant and later became executive director of the Council on Crime in America.[48] The authors warned that "America is now home to thickening ranks of juvenile 'super-predators'—radically impulsive, brutally remorseless youngsters, including ever more pre-teenage boys, who murder, assault, rape, rob, burglarize, deal deadly drugs, join gun-toting gangs, and create communal disorders."[49]

To account for this new monster, DiIulio invoked "a conservative theory of the root causes of crime," which he labeled "moral poverty."[50] "Moral poverty is the poverty of being without loving, capable, responsible adults who teach you right from wrong. It is the poverty of being without parents and other authorities who habituate you to feel joy at others' joy, pain at others' pain, happiness when you do right, remorse when you do wrong. It is the poverty of growing up in the virtual absence of people who teach morality by their own everyday example and who insist that you follow suit."[51] Violent juvenile crime, in other words, had nothing to do with the ready availability of guns or crack cocaine, or with the collapse of inner-city infrastructures, economies, or support services. Society bore no responsibility for the social conditions that contributed to the breakdown of families, including the ravages caused by the war on drugs. In fact, violent juvenile crime had nothing to do with anything for which society could be even partially responsible. It was a matter of personal moral failure. Children "are most likely to become criminally depraved when they are morally deprived."[52]

Though widely attacked by other scholars, the idea of the superpredator proved irresistible to the popular and political imagination. Politicians and pundits enthusiastically embraced the idea that violent crime was caused by the offender's moral poverty, not society's amoral indifference or immoral neglect. Yet if it was *their* fault, it was nonetheless *our* crisis. The problem was foisted upon a blameless society that could only hope to manage and control it. And it was "a monster of a problem," the *Washington Times* warned. "The super-predator is upon us. The super-predator is a boy, a preteen and teen, who murders, rapes, robs, assaults, does and deals in deadly drugs, joins gangs with guns, terrorizes neighborhoods and sees no relationship between right and wrong. . . . These boys are not so much demoralized as unmoralized."[53] They are "far more dangerous" than "'normal' criminals."[54] In fact, they "may be the biggest, baddest generation of criminals any society has ever known."[55] The media wrung its hands in apocalyptic worry. A *Time* headline predicted "A Teenage Timebomb,"[56] and *U.S. News and World Report* fretted that "it may take an even greater bloodbath to force effective crime solutions to the top of the nation's agenda."[57] Susan Estrich wrote in *USA Today*, "The tsunami is coming."[58]

Thus the first stage of the ritual: The monster was publicly denounced. It was given a name and constructed as an apocalyptic threat to a frightened fraction of the community. Next came the all-important call to action. The superpredator produced a demand for radical remedies.[59] As one Chicago prosecutor put it, the juvenile criminal code "was written at a time when kids were knocking over outhouses, not killing people. We're looking at a whole new breed here." A Brooklyn district attorney said the juvenile laws "were written at a time when kids were throwing spitballs. . . . Now they're committing murders." And the chief prosecutor in San Diego lamented, "Our juvenile justice system was created at a time of more *Leave It to Beaver* type crimes, less sophisticated and not incredibly violent. But what we see now . . . is kids who are real predators."[60]

The tidal wave that could not be stopped—but might be controlled—triggered a call for tougher juvenile laws, to which legislatures and governors responded with gusto. Statutes "that had stressed 'rehabilitation' and 'the best interests of the child' were rewritten to emphasize 'punishment' and 'the protection of the public.'"[61] The American fondness for policy-by-sound-bite yielded up the catchy phrase "adult time for adult crime." Between 1990 and 1996, forty states amended their laws to allow more children to be prosecuted as adults. Later in the decade, some states amended their statutes a second time to permit even more such prosecutions.[62] In 1998 alone, 200,000 children were prosecuted as adults in the United States.[63] Asked whether it was really necessary to have a federal law that would allow thirteen-year-olds to be prosecuted as adults, Florida Congressman Bill McCollum insisted, "They're the predators out there. They're not children anymore. They're the most violent criminals on the face of the earth."[64]

The superpredator was a myth: The predicted explosion in juvenile crime never materialized. By the time DiIulio coined the term, juvenile crime rates had already begun to fall, and they continued to decline every year from 1994 to 2004. After modest increases in 2005 and 2006, the rates fell again, and the most recent data published by the Department of Justice place juvenile violent crime at lower levels than at any point throughout the 1990s.[65] In 2001 the surgeon general issued a massive report on juvenile violence that exhaustively surveyed the available data.[66] Addressing themselves to the idea of the superpredator, the authors concluded "there is no evidence that the young people involved in violence during the peak years of the early 1990s were more frequent or more vicious offenders than youth in earlier years."[67] What changed was not the offender but how society viewed and responded to him.

Meanwhile, scholars who promoted the idea of the superpredator admitted their mistake and expressed their regrets. DiIulio, for instance, while praying at Mass on Palm Sunday in 1996, experienced an "epiphany—a conversion of heart, a conversion of mind."[68] In a flash, he said, he suddenly understood that the solution for juvenile crime was treatment and prevention rather than incarceration and control. "God had given me a Rolodex, good will and a passion that was sometimes misdirected, and I knew that for the rest of my life I would work on prevention, on helping bring caring, responsible adults to wrap their arms around these kids."[69] In a commentary for the *Wall Street Journal* he complained of "Washington's dangerously deluded dogmas about crime, . . . including the belief that most juvenile criminals are violent 'super-predators' who can be stopped by the threat of long, hard prison terms."[70] When asked about his theory, all he could say was, "Thank God we were wrong."[71]

The juvenile superpredator has largely disappeared from the public imagination. Yet he left an indelible mark, and not simply in the legal damage he caused—statutory and jurisprudential wreckage that endures long after its ostensible justification has evaporated. The more important effect of the superpredator fiasco was to reinforce the performative ritual as a distinctive way of creating, understanding, and responding to a perceived crisis.[72] And so it was that when one beast vanished and another appeared, society "knew" what must be done.

Like the marauding teen, the serial sexual predator was a monster beyond comprehension or reform. "Chronic sexual predators have crossed an osmotic membrane," one prolific commentator has observed. "They can't step back to the other side—our side. And they don't want to. . . . We have but one choice. Call them monsters and isolate them."[73] "When it comes to the sexual sadist, psychiatric diagnoses won't protect us. Appeasement endangers us. Rehabilitation is a joke." The only safe solution is long-term incarceration; "no-parole life sentences for certain sex crimes . . . offer our only hope against an epidemic of sexual violence that threatens to pollute our society beyond the possibility of its own rehabilitation."[74]

A new monster was thus publicly denounced, given a name, and constructed as a threat to our very existence. Yet the sexual predator was imagined as even more dangerous than his juvenile predecessor. While the juvenile superpredator was a new "breed" of criminal, at least in theory he could, like any wild beast, be captured and imprisoned. But the sexual predator is more cunning and therefore more difficult to monitor and control.[75] He can look and act just like "us," and can freely stalk the malls, the schoolyards, and, worst of all, the Internet, luring impressionable children and lonely women with a façade of normalcy.[76] The juvenile superpredator is a savage beast, dangerous but containable, but the sexual predator is a fiend, devious and elusive.[77]

Like the "crisis" in juvenile crime, the perceived crisis of sexual predators produced a call to action, which included a dramatic increase in the federal government's power to track, convict, and imprison the new beast. In 1994 Congress passed the Jacob Wetterling Crimes Against Children and Sexually Violent Offender Registration Act, named for a child abducted in Minnesota in 1989. The law provided that federal money would be withheld from states that did not have sex-offender registration systems in place. All states now have them. Two years later Congress passed Megan's Law, named for a child killed by a repeat sex offender in New Jersey, which added the mandate that states establish community notification systems. Though these vary from state to state, they all require that sex offenders report their whereabouts to law enforcement.

Many of these statutes prohibit sex offenders from living within a specified distance of places where children might gather, including parks, schools, malls, skating rinks, and swimming pools. This new federal legislation displays a touching faith in the power of modern technology, believing it will permit constant surveillance of sex offenders. Speaking in support of the Sexual Offender Tracking and Identification Act of 1996, for instance, then-Senator Joe Biden (D-DE) said, "We now seek to build a system where all movements of sexually violent and child offenders can be tracked and we will go a long way toward the day when none of these predators will fall between the cracks."[78] A number of states and the federal government have passed legislation allowing for continued confinement of certain sex offenders even after they complete their sentences.[79]

The response to the imaginary sexual marauder has been no more grounded in reality than the response to the mythical juvenile superpredator. To begin with, and contrary to the image that haunts the popular imagination, the largest number of sex offenders—and the overwhelming majority of child abusers—are not strangers who leap from behind the bushes or prowl on the Internet but family members, friends, and acquaintances.[80] Tracking strangers who move from state to state or forcing sex offenders to announce their presence to the community may make good television but has little to do with sound policy. Also contrary to the accepted wisdom, the recidivism rates for sex offenders are actually quite low. Most studies show that about 3–5 percent of sex offenders are rearrested for a new sex offense within three years of their release, and even fewer are reconvicted. Indeed, compared with most other offenders, released sex offenders are far less likely to be arrested for *any* new offense.[81] Finally, reliably predicting that a particular person will reoffend is simply beyond the expertise of modern science. As one researcher put it, "clinical predictions of future dangerousness, including sexual recidivism, are notoriously subjective and prone to bias and are frequently wrong."[82] Still, none of this seems to matter. Far more important is that society has ritualistically joined forces to answer the call to action.

III

Imaginary monsters have a way of justifying real solutions. The conservative vision of the criminal as depraved beast has led modern society to burden itself with the Sisyphean task of controlling the uncontrollable. The problem is not crime itself, which has declined steadily over the past two decades, but the image of crime in the public mind. Because the monster does not walk the street so much as haunt the imagination, he casually shrugs off the pathetic attempts at social control repeatedly fired at him by an anxious state. Nothing in the state's arsenal can solve the problem of a mythical beast. Like dragons, he disappears only when people stop believing he exists.[83]

Having created these rituals, however, politicians and pundits find it hard to let them go. So the state is left with the challenge of feigning control, which requires ever more draconian systems of supervision and management, all with an eye to reassuring a frightened population that the monster, though still at large, can at least be kept at bay.[84] The result has been an almost limitless appetite for punishment and social control. The numbers, despite their familiarity, are still sobering: two million, three hundred thousand people in prison or jail as of 2009—more than every man, woman, and child in Detroit, San Francisco, and St. Paul combined.[85] We have both the largest prison population and the highest incarceration rate in the world, which has been accommodated by an astounding growth in prison capacity: In the last quarter of the twentieth century, the states opened new prisons at a rate of more than one a month.[86] As of 2008 more than forty-one thousand men and women in the United States were serving life sentences without the possibility of parole.[87] Another five million are on probation or parole—again, far more than in any other country in the world.[88] The racial impact of these numbers is even more dispiriting. African-Americans are eight times as likely to be incarcerated as whites. As of 2004 more than 12 percent of African-American men between the ages of twenty-five and twenty-nine were in custody. For undereducated young black men, the incarceration rates are astounding: In 2000 nearly one in five African-American men under forty-one who had not attended college was in prison or jail.[89]

The punitive turn has not only produced a great many more prisoners and prisons. It has also generated an enthusiasm for harsh confinement that was unthinkable only a few decades ago. American prisons have become stunningly cruel places, a trend best illustrated by the dramatic growth in supermax facilities. In 1984 only one American prison fit the description of a supermax—the federal prison at Marion, Illinois, after the lockdown imposed in 1983.[90] Twenty years later, there were supermax prisons in forty-four states holding approximately twenty-five thousand inmates.[91] The Federal Bureau of Prisons also operates a supermax at Florence, Colorado, that houses another eleven thousand inmates, including many convicted of terrorism-related offenses.[92]

Conditions at supermax prisons vary somewhat, but they all maintain strict isolation and unrelenting control.[93] These prisons have abandoned even the pretense that they are meant to rehabilitate or reform. They typically provide little or no programming, education, or counseling—nothing more than the barest constitutional minima.[94] Prisoners, who are routinely described as "the worst of the worst,"[95] spend nearly every minute of every day confined in a small cell made of concrete and steel. The criminologist Norval Morris once described the cells at Tamms, the Illinois supermax:

> Your cell measures ten feet by twelve feet. It is made of poured concrete with a steel door—no bars—just a lot of little holes, smaller than the tip of your finger, punched through it. You have a stainless steel toilet and sink built as a unit that would not be easy to destroy. There is a small window, high and narrow, that lets in a little outside light. There is a mirror made of polished metal, again tending to be indestructible. Your bunk or bed, or whatever you may call it, is also of poured concrete, an integral part of the cell, but you have a slim plastic foam mattress to put on it. At night, . . . the light cannot be turned off entirely; it unrestrainedly gives out a dim light, bright enough for the guards to peer in at you. There is a small trapdoor, low down on the steel door to your cell, through which your food can be pushed to you.[96]

Within this space, where prisoners spend on average more than twenty-three hours a day, they cannot see or touch another human being. Depending on their disciplinary status, they are allowed out of their cells for exercise one to five hours a week—never for more than an hour a day.[97] They cannot leave their cells unless they are first heavily shackled and manacled, and only when escorted by several guards wearing riot gear and armor. Exercise, like everything in their lives, is an entirely solitary affair. At Tamms, they are brought to a concrete cage somewhat larger than their cell, "with a small grating high in the corner of the roof through which you can see the sky." There is no exercise equipment, "but some prisoners are now allowed to have tough rubber handballs to throw against the walls of the yard."[98] The evidence is now overwhelming that long stints in solitary confinement can cause profound psychological damage. Many prisoners become disoriented, paranoid, and psychotic; for some, the damage is irreversible.[99]

Meanwhile, outside the prison walls, mass incarceration has been complemented by an elaborate system of social controls. Most felons lose their right to vote, in some cases for life, which makes them irrelevant to the electoral process.[100] The modern penal system frequently also restricts their right to serve on a jury,[101] to live within designated locations or in public housing,[102] to travel or assemble within certain portions of a community,[103] to participate in most social welfare programs,[104] to receive college or small business loans,[105] or to work in various professions.[106] The aggregate result of these policies is the near replication of the colonial state of "civil death," a condition in which a person is deprived of all political, civil, and legal rights, except those he may enjoy if and when he is prosecuted again.[107]

Many judges and communities have taken these steps still farther and have embraced shaming ceremonies. Certain categories of ex-offenders are publicly identified, obligated to announce themselves to their community or their victims, or made to wear distinctive clothing or brand themselves by certain activity. "Some municipalities, for example, publish offenders' names in newspapers or even on billboards, a disposition that is especially common for men convicted of soliciting prostitutes. Other jurisdictions broadcast the names of various types of offenders on community-access television channels. . . . Some judges order petty thieves to wear t-shirts announcing their crimes. Others achieve the same effect with brightly colored bracelets that read 'DUI Convict,' 'I Write Bad Checks,' and the like. One judge ordered a woman to wear a sign declaring 'I am a convicted child molester.'"[108] These penalties seem to be limited only by official imagination. "Some jurisdictions insist that offenders publicly debase themselves. They must stand in the local courthouse with a sign describing their offense," for example, or publicize their own convictions in a first-person narrative.[109]

"In Maryland, juvenile offenders must apologize on their hands and knees and are released from confinement only if they persuade their victims that their remorse is sincere."[110]

IV

This punitive turn could not have taken place without leaving its mark on the values and traditions that make up national identity. In particular, the idea of limited government has been turned upside down. When it comes to controlling risk and responding to threats, local, state, and national government are expected to join forces and aggressively deploy their considerable resources to detect, prevent, and punish wrongdoers.[111] The rule of law has also been redefined. What was once imagined as a set of rules that would *restrain* the state to protect the liberty of the entire community has been recast as a set of rules that would *unleash* the state in order to promote the security of some by restricting the liberty of others. The effect has been to fracture the community into "us"—the people who call upon the state for protection—and "them," the people against whom the state directs its power, which has fundamentally altered the meaning of civic virtue and community membership.

The American criminal justice system is one of the great growth industries of recent decades. Between 1982 and 2007, the last year for which data are available, employment in the nation's justice system—including courts, police, and corrections at the state, local, and federal levels—increased by 93 percent, to more than 2.5 million jobs. By contrast, at the end of 2011, *the entire U.S. manufacturing sector* employed fewer than 12 million people, down nearly 40 percent from a 1979 high of almost 19.5 million. The increase in employment has come with a massive rise in spending. In 2007 total expenditures in the justice system were a staggering $228 billion, an increase of 171 percent from 1982. The federal share of this total has increased nearly 300 percent. Yet the public continues to clamor for more money spent on crime control.[112]

Alongside this growth has been a dramatic increase in the federal government's role in law enforcement. For many years, law enforcement was considered a matter for state and local governments. This began to change slowly in the last quarter of the nineteenth century. It was not until the punitive turn, however, that Congress acquired its present taste for federal involvement in crime control. A study by the Department of Justice in the early 1980s put the total number of federal offenses at three thousand. By 1999 the number had increased to roughly four thousand, and by 2008, Congress had added another 10 percent, bringing the total to more than forty-four hundred. More than half the federal crimes currently on the books were enacted since 1970.[113]

These statistics, however, do not begin to capture the vastly increased role of the federal government in shaping the practice of law enforcement. Since the mid-1960s, the federal government has awarded tens of billions of dollars to state and local law enforcement agencies, typically on the condition the recipients reform their practices in the manner specified by the federal government. The Office of Justice Programs awarded more than $2.7 billion in federal grants for such reforms in fiscal year 2010 and another $2.3 billion in 2011. Every state in the Union receives money from this program.[114] In addition, Congress routinely conditions federal money on adoption by the states of specific criminal statutes or law enforcement practices. For instance, in addition to sex-offender notification and registration programs, Congress in 1998 threatened to withhold federal highway funds from any state that did not adopt tougher drunk driving laws.[115] On other occasions, Congress has used its funding power to shape the behavior of private actors. The Drug Free Workplace Act, for instance, passed in 1988, obligated an employer who had received a federal grant to maintain a drug-free work environment and to sanction any employee convicted of a drug offense.[116] When it comes to social control, the idea of limited government is an oxymoron.

To facilitate this change, cultural elites have gradually redefined the meaning of the rule of law. The classic understanding, dating at least to Aristotle, is that the rule of law is a bulwark against a tyrannical state, interposing itself between a potentially capricious sovereign for the protection of the individual.[117] This is certainly how it was thought of in the immediate postwar era, when the nation was still stung by its battle against totalitarianism. In 1950, for instance, President Truman presided over a ceremony to commemorate the laying of the cornerstone of the federal courts building in Washington, D.C. Speaking in the unmistakable language of the Creed, Truman described the rule of law in its traditional terms:

This new Nation was to be a democracy based on the concept of the rule of law. It was to be a society in which every man had rights—inalienable rights—rights which were not based on creed, or rank, or economic power, but on equality. . . . The founders of this country had a very clear conception of the corruptibility of power—of the innate danger in all human affairs of the selfish or arbitrary exercise of authority. To guard against this everpresent danger, they adopted the principle that there is a fundamental law—expressed in the Constitution, and particularly in the Bill of Rights—to which every exercise of power has to conform. The purpose of this fundamental law is to protect the rights of the individual.[118]

This understanding could not withstand the punitive turn. In the mid-1960s, as President Johnson began to tack away from postwar liberalism and move toward modern conservatism, he addressed the nation on the question of crime. "The Great Society," he said, "cannot become a reality unless we strike at the roots of crime" and bring it "under our control." The country must address "the slow killers—want, ignorance, and prejudice," for they were the conditions that destroyed a man's soul and led him to crime. This is a classic statement of postwar liberalism, the belief that man is essentially decent and law-abiding and that crime is caused by social ills.[119]

Yet Johnson also insisted that he would not allow lawlessness to prevail while the Great Society moved forward. To that end, he announced that he had signed legislation to create the Law Enforcement Assistance Administration, which "will give us the means to accelerate the fight against crime now." The LEAA (the forerunner to the Office of Justice Policy) marked a major shift in federal law enforcement policy. For the first time, it made substantial federal funds available to enhance and modernize law enforcement by providing state and local police with new training and equipment, thereby redressing a perceived imbalance between criminals and the forces of law and order. Describing this shift, Johnson said, "Because the anchor of society must be an abiding respect for law and order, it is appropriate that the Federal Government provide material aid *to resist crime and promote the rule of law on the local level.*"[120]

But Johnson also made it clear that his administration's commitment to crime control did not stop there. "I will not be satisfied," he vowed, "until every woman and child in this Nation can walk any street, enjoy any park, drive on any highway, and live in any community at any time of the day or night without fear of being harmed." He directed the attorney general "to prepare a legislative program" that would "strengthen the partnership of the Federal Government with our States and local communities in performing the first and most basic function of government—the preservation of law and order and the protection of every citizen." With these remarks, Johnson rhetorically linked the rule of law with law and order. As important, he linked the promotion of the rule of law with massive federal efforts to prevent crime and to prosecute and imprison lawbreakers, a role he described as "the first and most basic function of government." Though much in this speech traced its philosophical lineage to postwar liberalism, it was also Johnson's first signal of support for an entirely different conception of the rule of law.[121]

During the Reagan administration, this understanding of the rule of law accelerated dramatically. In 1982 President Reagan created a task force on victims of crime. In signing the executive order, he explained that the rule of law "represented the collective moral voice of a free society—a voice that articulates our shared beliefs about the rules of civilized behavior." But these beliefs, he warned, "lose their meaning" if we lavish all our attention on people who "choose in cruel and violent ways to defy the rule of law."[122] In 1983, speaking at the American Bar Association, Reagan recounted the law-and-order reforms of his administration but insisted, "We need another reform, assurance that the American people can walk the streets and sleep in their homes without being afraid. The rule of law represents the civil discourse of a free people. Crime is the uncivilized shout that threatens to drown out and ultimately silence the language of liberty. I believe the scales of criminal justice have tilted too far toward protecting criminals."[123] The next year, before the National Sheriff's Association, he said:

> So, may I say to all of you today what millions of Americans would say if they had the chance: Thank you for standing up for this nation's dream of personal freedom under the rule of law. Thank you for standing against those who would transform that dream into a nightmare of wrongdoing and lawlessness. And thank you for your service to your communities, to your country, and to the cause of law and justice.[124]

The transformation continued under Reagan's successor. In March 1991, addressing the Attorney General's Crime Summit, George H. W. Bush pressed Congress for new weapons against crime. Referring to American success in the first Gulf War, Bush said that the same "moral force and national will that freed Kuwait City from abuse can free America's cities from crime. As in the Gulf, our goal is to strengthen and preserve the rule of law. As in the Gulf, we need creative and strategic thinking to free our cities from crime." As he launched into his prepared remarks, Bush made clear that these two goals—strengthening the rule of law and freeing our cities from crime—were two sides of the same coin. His administration, he said, had "taken the lead in fighting organized crime, drug trafficking, and the deadly tide of violence that follows in their wake. We've made record increases in Federal prosecutors and agents. By 1992, we will be well on our way to more than doubling our Federal prison space, allowing us to use tough Federal laws to put violent offenders behind bars to stay. Asset forfeiture laws allow us to take the ill-gotten gains of drug kingpins and use them to put more cops on the streets and more prosecutors in court."[125]

Three weeks later, after Los Angeles police officers were videotaped assaulting Rodney King, Bush addressed the problem of police brutality at a news conference. Though he was "shocked" by King's beating, he nonetheless used the occasion to stress the new conception of the rule of law. It was at least as great a concern, he said, "that 83 police officers, just in the last 15 months, have lost their lives in the line of duty. They need the support of the court system, and they need the faith and the support of local citizens. Nothing is more important than defending a sense of national decency and promoting the rule of law."[126] Three months later, he returned to this theme in a national radio address: "The American people are tired of watching hoodlums walk, of seeing criminals mock our justice system with endless technicalities. They want to bring order to streets shaken by chaos and crime. Yet, for more than two years, Congress has failed to act on my proposals to fight crime and strengthen the rule of law."[127]

By the time Bill Clinton was elected in 1992, the idea of the rule of law as a sword rather than a shield had become accepted fact. In 1993 he described the crime bill he had sent to Congress:

> I support capital punishment. This legislation will reform procedures by limiting death-row inmates to a single habeas corpus appeal. . . . And it will provide the death penalty for some Federal offenses, including killing a

Federal law enforcement officer. As I said, this is just the beginning of our efforts to restore the rule of law on our streets.[128]

Restoring the rule of law, in short, now meant improving the machinery of law enforcement and had nothing to do with protecting the rights of the citizenry.

By the end of the twentieth century, the punitive turn had supplied a set of deeply embedded assumptions about the individual's proper relationship to the state. Conservative notions of personal responsibility had decisively displaced the New Deal philosophy of shared obligation. Just as some people are simply lazy (the argument goes) and should not escape the consequences of their indolence by blaming society for their poverty, others are simply evil and should not escape the consequences of their mayhem by blaming society for their lawlessness.[129] Society is no more responsible for their marauding than it is for the instinctive actions of an animal. Its obligation in the face of such evil is to marshal the combined resources of government to separate "us" from "them." It is by speaking to this belief that the myths of successive monsters give rise to public ritual. Cultural elites warn that a blameless society faces imminent destruction unless government comes to the rescue. Politicians respond to the beast they have created with the tools that have become most familiar—punishment and control. To meet the demand, limited government and the rule of law are turne on their heads to mean *expansive* government and rule *by* law. The community is split; civic virtue morphs from a sense of shared obligation to all into a frightened insistence that "we" are in no way responsible for "them." National identity is remade to meet the perceived demands of the day.

The punitive turn gave President Bush great latitude to fashion an exceptionally aggressive response to September 11. Yet precisely because it has been integrated into national identity, the rituals that have evolved as part of the punitive turn describe how things *ought to be*. To ignore these rituals risks violating important creedal limits. In time, events would make these limits clear, much to President Bush's regret.

PART III

PRESERVATION AND TRANSFORMATION

6

"A Fight for Our Principles"

BECAUSE NATIONAL IDENTITY IS MADE, IT MAY also be preserved. Not every sudden shock will be welcomed as an occasion to reshape shared national values. Indeed, a more common reaction will be to preserve them unchanged and to resist whatever pressures may be brought to bear to alter their meaning. If things are as they ought to be, the first goal is generally to keep it that way. So it was with the immediate reaction to September 11. The attacks were instantly constructed as an assault on the Creed itself, on the values that define what it means to be an American. Victory in the war on terror was quickly linked not just to success on the battlefield, but to fidelity to the shared principles of national identity as they had taken shape by the end of the twentieth century. Islamic terrorists were immediately constructed as the nation's newest demon (which summoned the rhetoric and rituals of the punitive turn), while Arab- and Muslim-Americans as a group were proudly celebrated as an integral part of the national community (which reflected the prevailing understanding of race and religion). Contrary to what is often suggested, the great story of the early response to that morning is not the extent to which the country lost its way and abandoned its identity but the extent to which it instantly resolved that it would not.

I

Much writing about the American reaction to September 11 paints a bleak picture. Commentators have assailed the instant recourse to Manichean thinking that divided the world into us and them, good and evil, right and wrong; the deliberate creation of moral opposites achieved by the cartoonish amplification of "our" benevolence and "their" barbarity; the jingoistic calls for national unity coupled with an intolerance of dissent; the manipulation of fear to drum up support for government policy; the invocation of God as America's exclusive ally.[1] From this enormous body of writing, the image emerges of a nation gone collectively mad. Readers might be excused if they concluded that September 11 ushered in a wave of violent repression and hysteria.

But that was never the case. To be sure, the world pictured by this criticism certainly existed. Nativism, authoritarianism, and ethnocentrism have always been powerful impulses in American life, and many people were immediately seduced by the siren song of a simpler world. Yet these brutish sentiments never achieved anywhere near the dominance imagined by their critics. The nation never came close to the single-minded nationalism of World War I, for instance, or approached the madness of McCarthyism. Within hours of the attacks, these impulses were met in the public square by an alternative narrative.

If there was a theme to this alternative view, it was surely this: In moments of crisis, the United States loses its moral bearings, needlessly sacrifices liberty for security, and engages in behavior that cannot be squared with its values. Eventually the nation regrets this course and makes amends, but not before great damage is done. It is the myth of deviation and redemption: A sudden and violent storm has the Ship of State tempest-toss'd by buffeting gales of savage hatred, until the seas finally calm and the nation can begin its long, difficult journey back to more familiar waters. This idea quickly became the cautionary tale for those inclined to criticize the Manichean impulse. "Here we go again," it cautioned. "This is what we always do."[2] And the fear that we would go astray was nearly universal. A CBS News/New York Times Poll taken less than two weeks after the attacks found that 68 percent of Americans believed that anti-Arab sentiment in the United States was on the rise, and almost all Americans—fully 90 percent—thought people in the United States would probably single out Arab-Americans, Muslims, and immigrants for unfair treatment. Half of all respondents considered this very likely.[3]

But paradoxically, the very act of saying "Here we go again" helped to spare the nation—at least at first—from precisely this fate. Almost from the beginning, the Manichean narrative of us and them was engaged in the public square by a narrative of tolerance and restraint, a narrative that *feared* a dim future based on a dark past. Before the sun had set on September 11, the historian David McCullough lamented that the attacks might produce "a curtailing, trimming up some—maybe even eviscerating of the open society as we know it."[4] Countless others echoed his fear. A fierce determination was born, evident within minutes of the attacks, that this time must be different and that the response to 9/11 must honor rather than betray shared values. This determination produced a powerful narrative about national identity designed to act as a bulwark against the very thing the myth predicted.

II

Some have condemned the speed with which President Bush pronounced the country at war. In his otherwise careful account of the language of the post–September 11 era, for instance, the sociologist Richard Jackson blames the Bush administration for having quickly "remade" the attacks "from acts of terrorism . . . to acts of war."[5] Admittedly, the president used this language early and often, beginning on September 12. After meeting with his national security team, he told reporters the attacks "were more than acts of terror. They were acts of war."[6] The next day, after a morning call with New York Mayor Rudolph Giuliani and Governor George Pataki, the president told reporters "that an act of war was declared on the United States of America."[7] Over the next few days his language grew increasingly ominous. On the fourteenth, speaking to the nation from the National Cathedral in Washington, he said, "War has been waged against us by stealth and deceit."[8] The following day, after another meeting with his national security team, he said, "We're at war. There has been an act of war declared upon America by terrorists, and we will respond accordingly." He encouraged people to "go about their business, . . . but with a heightened sense of awareness that a group of barbarians have declared war on the American people."[9]

But the suggestion that Bush led the charge to war is nonetheless unfair since it fails to appreciate the extent to which the president followed rather than led public sentiment, at least in this particular regard. Hours before Bush gave it a name, the conviction was commonplace that the attacks of September 11 were an act of war, and almost no other view found a voice in the public square. "This is obviously an act of war that has been committed on the United States," said Arizona Republican Senator John McCain on September 11. "Everybody said it all day," Peter Jennings of ABC News correctly observed. It was "a declaration of war, an act of war against the United States. Any number of politicians and commentators, us included, who were reminded that the last time there was an attack like this on the United States was Pearl Harbor."[10]

One careful study has found that on the day of the attacks, just on the three major television networks, "anchors, correspondents, and reporters . . . mentioned the term 'war' 57 times; 'Pearl Harbor' 41 times, and 'war zone' 11 times. In addition, experts, public officials, historians, and other sources used the term 'war' a total of 29 times and 'Pearl Harbor' 17 times."[11] A concerted effort by the Bush administration might conceivably have dampened the enthusiasm for war, and certainly the administration took no steps in that direction. Likewise, the fact that the attacks were spontaneously interpreted as an act of war does not relieve the administration of responsibility for the policies it subsequently pursued. These, however, are separate matters. In the very first instance, it is unfair to suggest the administration dragged the country onto a wartime footing. The country was already there.[12]

Interpreting the attacks as an act of war would prove exceptionally important. For one thing, it gave a great boost to the Manichean impulse to divide the world into us and them, since war has always been a fellow traveler of that sort of thinking. "This will be a monumental struggle of good versus evil," President Bush said September 12, "but good will prevail."[13] On September 16 he vowed "to rid the world of evildoers," and famously described the war on terror as a crusade. Repeatedly, he cast terrorists as the newest threat to the American way of life, and terrorism as America's moral opposite:

> This new enemy seeks to destroy our freedom and impose its views. We value life; the terrorists ruthlessly destroy it. We value education; the terror-

ists do not believe women should be educated, or should have health care, or should leave their homes. We value the right to speak our minds; for the terrorists, free expression can be grounds for execution. We respect people of all faiths and welcome the free practice of religion; our enemy wants to dictate how to think and how to worship, even to their fellow Muslims. . . . We wage a war to save civilization, itself.[14]

Yet many had already cast terrorists and terrorism in the same terms. Congressman Henry Hyde (R-IL), chairman of the House International Relations Committee, spoke on September 13 of a "war for civilization itself."[15] Former Tennessee Republican Senator and Majority Leader Howard Baker said the attacks were "not just on the United States but on civilized societies everywhere. It was a strike against those values that separate us from animals—compassion, tolerance, mercy."[16] Secretary of State Colin Powell denounced terrorism as "a scourge not only against the United States but against civilization."[17] The *San Francisco Chronicle* editorialized about "the civilized world's fight against barbarity," a view shared by countless other papers. Robert Caldwell, the editor of *Insight* magazine, echoed the sentiment: "In truth, this is a war between civilization and the barbarism on such hideous display Tuesday."[18]

The idea of being "at war" summons to mind a resolute purposefulness, a national determination to marshal the entire nation's resources toward a single goal for the duration of the conflict.[19] In its salutary form, it implies a shared sense of patriotic sacrifice. But just as often, it can be shaped into a mindless demand for conformity and an intolerance of dissent. Worse, it can produce a dangerous impulse to lash out at all who might be conflated with the enemy. This habit of mind was much on display after the attacks. In just eight weeks, the Arab, Muslim, and South Asian communities in this country reported more than one thousand separate bias incidents, including as many as nineteen murders. Mosques and temples were bombed, innocent people assaulted, homes and property vandalized and destroyed.[20] Instances of verbal harassment and intimidation were too numerous to count.

This is the behavior that has attracted the ire of so many critics. But the extent to which this behavior also prompted immediate condemnation has not been adequately appreciated. Instantly, observers denounced the hate crimes as "un-American" and contrary to the principles of national identity.

Remarkably similar articles and editorials appeared all over the country. They paid fulsome tribute to the idea of an immigrant nation, open and welcoming, with hearty nods to equality, dignity, and mutual respect. Because these stories were so similar, one stands in for the others, and warrants its reproduction nearly in full. This appeared in the *Milwaukee Journal Sentinel* on the first Monday after the attacks:

> If the lines of donors at area blood centers last week symbolized the better angels of our national character, some of the calls to the Milwaukee Islamic Center in the days after Tuesday's horror did not.
>
> The enemy is a small band of terrorists from the fringes of radical Islam. The enemy almost certainly includes a handful of sympathizers who provide shelter or other support for those terrorists. The enemy may include leaders of certain states that harbor terrorists.
>
> . . .
>
> But the enemy is not the Kuwaiti kid on her way to school on Milwaukee's east side. Nor is it the Palestinian owner of a suburban gas station. And it is not those who gather at the local mosque. The enemy is not marked by the color of his or her skin, by having a "foreign" name, by wearing certain clothes or by having an accent.
>
> The enemy can be identified by a specific set of beliefs that include visiting death on one's enemies in the name of God. But those ideas violate the tenets of true Islam, and the radicals who allegedly carried out Tuesday's attacks have as much in common with mainstream Islam as the followers of David Koresh had with Christianity.
>
> And those who call in threats to the Islamic Center and who jeer at Arab-American children have at least something in common with the Palestinians who cheered when they heard the news of the attacks on Tuesday. Both groups have revealed an ignorance and a callousness toward life that is unacceptable in a civilized society.
>
> Of course, Milwaukee did not have a monopoly on such frightening behavior last week; similar incidents—including an ugly rally in Chicago—occurred across the country, and Internet chat rooms were rife with racist and religious slurs. If the truth were told, the United States has often failed to live up to its vaunted tolerance. Ask the Japanese-Americans of World War II. Ask African-Americans, Hispanics, Asians, the Irish Catholics of 19th-century America. Ask any immigrant who has been told to "go back where you came from."
>
> But if this nation is to triumph in its war against international terrorism,

Americans finally must let go of those ideas and remember who the real enemy is—and that Arab-Americans and Muslims, some of whom will be counted as victims in Tuesday's attacks, are not.[21]

Similar sentiments appeared over and over. With great uniformity, observers and cultural elites cast the attacks as a challenge to our shared principles and made clear that "success" would be measured not just in terrorists killed or captured but by adherence to national values. "Our challenge as a free country," a *Washington Post* columnist wrote, "will be to deal with those responsible for these mass murders without losing our liberties."[22] Fury was perfectly understandable, editorialized the *Denver Post,* but rather than "indulge our natural rage over atrocious acts of terrorism, we Americans must show the world that we are made of finer stuff. Unlike the terrorists, we must neither attack the innocent nor foster racism."[23] Because "this is not about 'Christian' and 'Muslim,'" cautioned the *Dallas Morning News.* "It's not about 'American' and 'Arab.' Yes, those political overtones are present, but thinking in those terms drags untold numbers of innocents into the fray. This is about the vast majority of us being shocked and unsettled by a handful of lunatics poisoned by their own fanaticism."[24]

Though "the desire to strike back at real or imagined enemies is natural," wrote a *San Antonio Express-News* editorialist, "in our desire to defend ourselves against terrorists, Americans must not terrorize Arab-Americans and Middle Easterners who are living in the United States."[25] The *San Diego Tribune* asked, "At whom will our anger be directed? Our hope should be that it not be directed at other Americans of one nationality or one religion or another."[26] There must be no "scapegoating," wrote the *New York Daily News:* "That cautionary note has since been sounded by everyone from President Bush to Muhammad Ali. Not all Arabs are terrorists, and not all Muslims are enemies."[27] "Soon," the *San Francisco Chronicle* warned, "our collective shock will turn to anger and calls for retribution. You know it will. . . . You want to think better of our citizenry. . . . You want to tell people that, while outrage and resolve is perfectly understandable in the wake of such horror, making blanket condemnations of any ethnic or religious group goes against the principles of our democracy."[28]

In this spirit, writers universally condemned the hate crimes occurring nationwide as a betrayal of national identity, often linking this behavior to the lesson of history. "The senseless attacks are reminiscent of our nation's treatment of Japanese Americans after the attack on Pearl Harbor on Dec. 7, 1941," one editorialist wrote. "Hard-working, devoted U.S. citizens were routed from their homes and locked in internment camps simply because they were of Japanese descent. Now rage over the terrorist attacks is being manifested by some as an excuse to attack anyone who happens to look different."[29] "One of the clear and painful lessons that we learned in the aftermath of Pearl Harbor," wrote another, "is what a mistake it was to question the loyalty of Japanese-Americans and to use them as scapegoats to vent our national anger."[30] This view was widely shared and often repeated. "We reacted to Pearl Harbor by interning loyal Japanese living in the United States, an eternal disgrace to our sense of justice."[31] "That was the lingering shame of having locked up thousands of Americans of Japanese ancestry for no earthly reason other than racial paranoia."[32] "Even the sainted Abraham Lincoln was not immune to this kind of hasty, dangerous, bad judgment. He suspended the writ of habeas corpus during the Civil War."[33] "History provides us some valuable lessons," one writer said in summing up, "and the most valuable may be this: Anger is a powerful weapon. Let's use it carefully."[34]

Still, as widespread as this sentiment was, it is at least open to question whether it would have survived had it not been endorsed by the most important voice in America. As one student of American culture reminds us, even during moments of international quiet and domestic calm, the president of the United States "speaks with a resonance no other voice within this nation musters. The Speaker of the House is dwarfed by comparison, as is the Senate Leader. In the United States, majesty is all the president's."[35] And whatever rhetorical advantage the president may have when the earth is still, the advantage is multiplied many times over when the ground shakes beneath the nation's feet. An anxious nation immediately looks to the president for comfort and guidance. The president also enjoys a unique capacity to frame an issue and set the terms of debate, to identify the problem as well as the solution. In moments of crisis, it is the president who tells the nation what matters and what does not, defines the principles at stake, and weaves the crisis into the stories and myths we tell each other about who we are as Americans.[36]

At this pivotal moment, President Bush did not limit himself, as he might have, to a banal pronouncement that the attacks heralded a contest between right and wrong or good and evil. This would have left a dangerous opening for others to define the "good" in less tolerant terms. Instead, he repeatedly insisted that the true grievance of Islamic terrorists was the American Creed itself. On September 11, in his televised remarks to the nation, he said America had been targeted "because we're the brightest beacon for freedom and opportunity in the world." In his address to a joint session of Congress on September 20, he expanded on this theme. "They hate what we see right here in this chamber—a democratically elected government. Their leaders are self-appointed. They hate our freedoms—our freedom of religion, our freedom of speech, our freedom to vote and assemble and disagree with each other." On another occasion he said, "They can't stand what America stands for . . . a place where all religions can flourish."[37] In short, the president constructed September 11 as an attack on the values and traditions that define what it means to be an American—an attack on national identity.

This rhetoric has been endlessly criticized for instantly casting the United States as irreproachably blameless. But this complaint fails to give the president sufficient credit for the way he described and prioritized the malleable values of the Creed. At precisely the moment when the nation most needed a reaffirmation of its identity, the president defined it in the language of universal equality and the welcome diversity of an immigrant nation. Tolerance and respect for Muslims and Arab-Americans were quickly framed not only as the moral opposite of terrorism and therefore the condition the nation fought to defend but as the "true" expression of the American Creed. Over and over, the president stressed that while the nation was at war against a new demonic threat, Muslims and Arab-Americans were not the enemy, and that mutual respect and religious tolerance were indispensable elements of American identity.

Deliberately positioning himself at symbolically potent sites and timing his announcements for symbolically potent occasions, President Bush would repeat this message of inclusion nearly three dozen times between September 11 and the end of 2001. On September 13, during his conversation with Giuliani and Pataki, he said, "our nation must be mindful that there are thousands of Arab Americans who live in New York City who love their flag just as much as the three of us do. And we must be mindful that as we seek to win the war, that we treat Arab Americans and Muslims with the respect they deserve."[38] Four days later, at the Islamic Center in Washington, D.C., he said:

> The face of terror is not the true faith of Islam. That's not what Islam is all about. Islam is peace. These terrorists don't represent peace. They represent evil and war. . . . When we think of Islam, we think of a faith that brings comfort to a billion people around the world—billions of people find comfort and solace and peace—and that's made brothers and sisters out of every race—out of every race.[39]

In his address to a joint session of Congress on September 20, Bush said the terrorists "practice a fringe form of Islamic extremism that has been rejected by Muslim scholars and . . . perverts the peaceful teaching of Islam. . . . The terrorists were traitors to their own faith, trying, in effect, to hijack Islam itself. The enemy of America is not our many Muslim friends; it is not our many Arab friends. Our enemy is a radical network of terrorists and every government that supports them."[40] On December 17 he hosted a dinner at the White House to mark Eid al-Fitr, the Muslim holiday at the end of Ramadan. "This year," he said, "Eid is celebrated at the same time as Hanukkah and Advent. So it's a good time for people of these great faiths, Islam, Judaism, and Christianity, to remember how much we have in common."[41] He also condemned those who attacked American Muslims. "That's not the America I know," he said. "That's not the America I value." The perpetrators of hate crimes "don't represent the best of America. They represent the worst of humankind and they should be ashamed of that kind of behavior."[42]

Officials throughout the federal government followed the president's lead. On September 14 the House of Representatives passed a resolution condemning bigotry and violence against Arab-Americans, American Muslims, and South Asians, declaring that these communities "are a vital part of the Nation."[43] A bipartisan, ideologically diverse collection of representatives took to the House floor to speak in favor of equality and religious tolerance. Democratic Congressman Nick Rahall of West Virginia said that "Arab Americans, Muslim Americans, South Asian Americans are Americans first. They chose to come to this country in order to seek a better way of life for themselves and their families. They pay taxes. They vote. They donate to various charitable causes within their communities. They have become well respected, and . . . have contributed so much to our American way of life."[44] By contrast, the people who committed hate crimes against perceived Muslims or Arab-Americans were "yahoos who . . . pose as great a threat to our American society, to our freedoms, and to our way of life as those perpetrators of those heinous crimes against our country last Tuesday."[45]

Republican Congressman George Gekas of Pennsylvania added that the resolution was inspired by a desire to avoid "the insidious events that took place after Pearl Harbor with respect to the treatment of Japanese-American citizens."[46] The resolution had 116 cosponsors and passed without objection. The Senate concurred without amendment September 26.[47] "Don't be confused about who the enemy is," cautioned one Texas congressman. "The campaign against terrorism unites Americans of all faiths, backgrounds and political leanings. Tolerance, justice and liberty are core American values, and we need not—and will not—sacrifice them as we fight the scourge of terrorism. I'm glad the president has so clearly stated that America's campaign targets the evil terrorists who threaten the civilized world, not the Arab people or the religion of Islam."[48] Even Vice President Dick Cheney, who would soon become the most reviled man in the Bush administration, was at pains to say, "This is by no means a war on Islam."[49]

The importance of this elite messaging in shaping the early terms of the national debate cannot be overstated. A study published in 2003 examined the treatment of Muslims and Arab-Americans in four major newspapers widely available in the New York area—*USA Today*, the *New York Times*, the *New York Daily News*, and the *New York Post*—during the year before and the six months after September 11.[50] The findings were astounding. The *Times*, of course, is the most prominent liberal newspaper in the nation; *USA Today* is avowedly more centrist; the *Daily News* and the *Post* are more conservative. Yet in the six months after the attacks, all four papers became significantly more solicitous of the rights of Arab-Americans and Muslims. Precisely when and where rage might have been at its peak, "the debate on civil liberties and civil rights of American Muslims and Arabs was substantially tilted in favor of those who spoke out in support of American Muslims' and Arabs' freedoms."[51] To be sure, calls for curbing these groups' civil liberties also increased in the six months after 9/11, at least compared with the twelve months before the attacks, but these increases "paled in comparison to increases for the opposing viewpoint."[52]

Perhaps even more important, favorable coverage of Muslims and Arab-Americans was not confined to articles and commentary that touched on the liberty vs. security debate. In a development the authors called "surprising," "the depiction of American Muslims and Arab Americans in the news was more positive and less negative in the wake of the terrorist events of 9/11 than in the previous year."[53] Muslims and Arab-Americans were shown engaged in the familiar struggles and joys of daily life, which instantly made their lives more or less indistinguishable from that of the reader. Once again, the effect was dramatic. In the year before the attacks, only one in four articles about Muslims and Arab-Americans were generally positive or supportive, while nearly one in three were negative (the rest being neutral). But after 9/11, the numbers more than reversed: 43 percent were supportive and only 22 percent were negative.[54]

President Bush later explained that cooling the impulse to intolerance had been precisely his objective. Asked at an event in August 2004 whether the war on terror justified the use of internment camps, he answered, "We don't need intern camps. I mean, forget it."[55] Bush then explained why he had been so assiduous in his defense of Arab- and Muslim-Americans:

> Right after 9/11, I knew this was going to be an issue in our country. I knew that there would be people that say, "There goes a Muslim-looking person; therefore, that person might be viewed as a terrorist." I knew that was going to be a problem. That's why I went to a mosque, to send the signal, right after the attacks, that said let's uphold our values. . . . Religious people, people that go to mosques, you know, need to be—Americans need to be viewed as equally American as their neighbor. . . . Our fellow citizens need to treat people with respect.[56]

III

Some have suggested that the tolerance encouraged by President Bush and others went only so far and that American opinion would not abide the heretical suggestion that September 11 might have been motivated not by "their" fanaticism but by our policies in the Middle East. The writer Susan Sontag, for instance, was excoriated for a short piece she wrote for the *New Yorker* criticizing "the self-righteous drivel and outright deceptions being peddled by public figures and TV commentators."[57] "Where is the acknowledgment," she asked, "that this was not a 'cowardly' attack on 'civilization' or 'liberty' or 'humanity' or 'the free world' but an attack on the world's self-proclaimed super-power, undertaken as a consequence of specific American alliances and actions? . . . The unanimity of the sanctimonious, reality-concealing rhetoric spouted by American officials and media commentators in recent days seems, well, unworthy of a mature democracy."[58] Sontag's claim that September 11 was a response to "specific American alliances and actions" was, for many, a bridge too far. The conservative commentator Charles Krauthammer ridiculed her as "morally obtuse," and Andrew Sullivan announced the Sontag Award for "glib moral equivalence in the war on terror and visceral anti-Americanism."[59] It would take no particular effort to come up with additional examples: Gore Vidal, Noam Chomsky, Barbara Kingsolver, and others were also attacked for perceived anti-Americanism. Nor was this vitriol confined to conservatives. Jonathan Alter, the left-leaning *Newsweek* journalist, denounced the "mindless moral equivalency" of the "Blame America Firsters."[60]

But even here, the magnitude of the attack on dissent should be kept in perspective. Many of the writers who would have been most sensitive to a tsunami of jingoism found themselves pleasantly surprised at its relative absence. In October 2001 Alexander Cockburn, the longtime columnist for the *Nation*, took heart that he did not feel the "crackle" of "war fever" in the air. "To be honest about it," he wrote, "I've been somewhat heartened, far beyond what I would have dared hope in the immediate aftermath of the awful destruction. Take the pleas for tolerance and the visit of President W. Bush to mosques. Better than FDR, who didn't take long to herd the Japanese-Americans into internment camps."[61] Cockburn's *Nation* colleague Michael Massing later took this a step farther, noting with astonishment that even prominent mainstream writers were willing to point an accusing finger at U.S. foreign policy.[62]

Polling during this period confirms their curbstone impression. A Gallup/

USA Today poll taken in November asked respondents, "How much responsibility do you think the United States itself bears for the hatred that led to
the terrorist attacks—a large amount, a moderate amount, a small amount,
a tiny amount, or not at all?" Nearly half replied that the United States bore
at least a "moderate" amount of responsibility, including 44 percent of conservatives and 64 percent of liberals. Another quarter thought the United
States had to accept "at least some" responsibility. More people thought the
United States bore a large amount of responsibility than thought it bore
none at all.[63] Another poll in October asked whether the people of Muslim
countries have "legitimate complaints" about United States conduct in the
region. One-third said yes, one-third said no and one-third couldn't say.[64]
The evidence simply does not support the idea that Americans insisted the
nation was entirely innocent.[65]

Likewise, nothing I have written should be taken to minimize the darker
impulse that was also on display after September 11. Not long after the attacks, a Time/CNN poll found that nearly one-third of respondents favored
allowing the government "to hold Arabs who are U.S. citizens in camps
until it can be determined whether they have links to terrorist organizations."[66] In a Newsweek poll taken about the same time, a slightly higher
percentage thought it was sensible to "put Arabs and Arab-Americans in
this country under special surveillance," even though the question was
specifically worded to remind respondents of the internment of Japanese-
Americans during the Second World War.[67] Data like these should come as
no surprise. At moments like this, nationalism becomes Hyde to patriotism's Jekyll.

Any impulse that appeals to millions of Americans cannot be ignored.
Yet this impulse never occupied the field alone, as is too often imagined.
From the beginning, it was met and challenged by the narrative of tolerance
and religious liberty, which adorned itself in familiar tales about dignity,
universal equality, and shared membership in the national community.
And even more important, the most trusted voices throughout American
society were not neutral in this contest. From the outset, they sided overwhelmingly with the narrative of restraint. These people have always been
the high priests of the American Creed, the cultural arbiters and opinion

leaders who decide how our shared values and beliefs will be defined, prioritized, and reconciled. When these leaders are in agreement, something
approaching a national consensus is not far behind.

Nor is the bloodshed produced by the more virulent strain of the nationalist impulse inconsequential. The FBI recorded 481 anti-Islamic attacks in
2001, a dramatic increase over the previous year.[68] The violence of some of
these attacks was appalling. Sadly, this behavior is all too familiar in American history. In February 1919 a jury in Hammond, Indiana, acquitted the
killer of a foreign national who had proclaimed, "To hell with the United
States." They deliberated two minutes. In May of the same year, a man refused to stand for "The Star-Spangled Banner" at an event in Washington,
D.C. At the end of the song, an enraged sailor shot him in the back. The
assembled crowd cheered lustily. In 1920 a man in Waterbury, Connecticut, was sentenced to six months in jail for calling Lenin one of the "braini-
est" political leaders in the world.[69]

Such guardians of the national honor—both the avengers and the ap-
proving crowds and juries—have always been present in American society,
and every society of which I am aware. A sense of threat draws them to the
surface like worms in the rain. They are important to our story, but only
insofar as they represent a reservoir of ill will and a source of nationalist rage that elite messengers can put to dangerous use. The question is
whether they receive encouragement from society's trusted voices: Without
it, their sentiment flashes with great fury but soon exhausts itself. While
the violence they commit cannot be condoned, we must still bear several
things in mind. First, antireligious hate crimes are nothing new. In most
cases, as the religion scholar Diana Eck has observed, they go unnoticed
by the larger community.[70] After September 11, however, these attacks
were the subject of national condemnation at the highest levels, putting
this behavior into the spotlight. Second, even in the worst year—2001—the
number of anti-Islamic incidents paled next to the number of anti-Jewish
incidents, even though the number of Jews and Muslims in the country is
approximately the same.[71] Yet no one speaks of a crisis of anti-Semitism.
Third, the number of anti-Islamic attacks fell by approximately two-thirds
in 2002 and has remained at that level ever since. Meanwhile, anti-Jewish

attacks consistently outnumber anti-Islamic attacks by about six to one.[72] In short, though anti-Islamic *sentiment* has skyrocketed in the past decade, only rarely does this sentiment manifest itself in hate crimes.

In time, the Bush administration would be lambasted for its response to September 11. Bush became the first president in American history to endorse torture as government policy and developed a counterterror program that badly misjudged the limits of the punitive turn. But what he did wrong should not blind us to what he did right, and President Bush has not gotten the credit he deserves for his role in setting the earliest terms of the post-9/11 debate.[73] For that reason, it is important to recall remarks like those of Dr. James Zogby, the longtime and well-respected head of the Arab-American Anti-Discrimination Committee, who submitted comments to the United States Commission on Civil Rights in October 2001:

> The President took the lead in cautioning against this backlash and was joined by the Secretary of State, the Attorney General, and the Director of the FBI. Their repeated statements, I believe, helped to stem the wave of backlash. Also worthy of note were the actions of the U.S. Senate and House of Representatives who passed resolutions decrying hate crimes against Arab Americans and American Muslims. Individual Senators and Representatives also took immediate action to shine a light on this problem. . . . The constant repetition of this positive message on TV and radio and in print media has helped restrain the hands of the bigots. The hate has not gone away, but the hate crimes have been greatly reduced.[74]

The president's determination to cast September 11 as an attack on the Creed, along with his complementary determination to define the Creed in terms that celebrated tolerance and diversity, was an attempt to preserve national identity as it had taken shape before the attacks. Differentiating between Islam as a religion of peace and radical Islamists as apostates who had betrayed their religion reflected the shared understanding of national life captured by the punitive turn on the one hand and the dominant vision of race and religion on the other. The punitive turn had conditioned policy makers to imagine demons who threatened to destroy the United States and all it stood for, and to demand certain communal rituals that would ostensibly keep the country safe. At the same time, a fragile consensus had developed that a person should not be judged based on immutable characteristics or private religious beliefs. This consensus reflected the shared meaning of equality and religious liberty at the end of the twentieth century.

Yet Bush did not recognize that these understandings are not fixed and immutable but contested and constructed. With respect to the punitive turn, he did not appreciate the extent to which demonization is and must be a communal affair. With respect to equality and religious liberty, as well as the image of the American community, he did not foresee that while these ideas can be preserved, they can also be torn down. Still, all this was for another day. For now, the president considered it perfectly natural to tell Congress on September 20 that the nation was embroiled "in a fight for our principles, and our first responsibility is to live by them. No one should be singled out for unfair treatment or unkind words because of their ethnic background or religious faith."[75] Time would put these principles to the test.

7

"We Need to Bring the News to People"

IT WAS ALL WELL AND GOOD TO say that September 11 was an attack on the shared values and traditions that represent what it means to be an American. But this could not be the last word. Questions naturally arose about what these principles meant and demanded in the new day. And it was all well and good to say that American Muslims and Arabs were not the enemy. But pronouncing what people *were not* implied a willingness to say what they *were*, and to engage in the common if sometimes disreputable habit of imagining truths about the many from the behavior of the few. September 11 thus set in motion a national debate, which continues to this day, about the relationship between the Creed and Islam. Many of the most cherished values and traditions in American life have been dragged into this contest, which seems to grow uglier with time.

Immediately after September 11, the most common view, expressed over and over, echoed the president's insistence that Islam was "a religion of peace" and that Muslims in the United States were no less loyal—and no less affected by the attacks—than other Americans. The media ran countless profiles of Muslims engaged in the same struggles, enjoying the same pleasures, and enduring the same hardships as their neighbors. All this was meant to demonstrate not only that Muslims had successfully integrated into what Will Herberg called "the American Way of Life" but that they were "just like us." With the exception of a small but vocal minority on the far right, elites were united in the view that the violent radicalism of al Qaeda did not represent the American Muslim community. As this view was repeated, it became the shared perspective of the great majority of Americans.

The repetition of this message was undoubtedly motivated by a desire to avoid scapegoating. But it also reinforced the idea that Muslims in the United States were a distinct entity whose character could be ascertained by reference to their religion. It became perfectly natural to speak of American Muslims as though they shared some essential characteristic that somehow emanated from their "Muslim-ness." The very act of producing journalistic profiles of American Muslims made sense to people precisely because "they" were conceived as a group, and imagined to think and behave in some characteristic way *because of* their religion. This put the idea of the Muslim character in play in the public square and made it particularly important to win the battle to define and describe this Muslim-ness.

The initial image was unmistakably benign. This reflected both the consensus that existed before September 11 that no religion could claim a monopoly on virtue or truth, as well as the determination by cultural elites to preserve that understanding unchanged. Having embraced the idea that the war on terror was a referendum on American values, people came easily to the conclusion that those values should not succumb to the pressure of a post-9/11 world. The impulse to preserve rather than transform was palpable. But within months this benevolent conception began to come under sustained attack. Before the first anniversary of September 11 had passed, a much darker image of the Muslim character had begun to take hold within a significant minority of the population. As has happened throughout American history, proponents of this darker vision deployed the elastic language of the American Creed to transform the meaning and content of widely shared values—tolerance, religious liberty, and community membership—in a concerted effort to remake national identity. The past decade is the unfinished story of their mixed success.

I

Though no one could have imagined it on September 11, it now appears that the twelve months after the attacks represented a brief golden age of religious tolerance in the United States. Following the president's lead, cultural leaders across the political and ideological spectrum were more united, and more vocal, in support of religious diversity than at any other time in American history. Even the liberal heyday of the 1960s cannot match the dominant sentiment among the nation's most trusted voices immediately after September 11. To what extent it was sincere may be forever beyond our knowledge; certainly the speed with which some people abandoned it gives cause for doubt. Its potency while it lasted, however, is unmistakable.

Interfaith demonstrations of religious unity became a fixture on the national landscape. Rabbis gathered with priests and imams at Protestant churches and community centers, and together preached tolerance, respect, and brotherhood. As part of a series entitled "The Spirit of America," *Newsweek* collected inspirational remarks by religious leaders from around the world. Meditations from across the religious spectrum appeared alongside the anguished reactions of Muslim cultural leaders, including an imam from the Manhattan Islamic Center. The minister at a Manhattan church implored his congregation to "go out of your way in the days ahead to practice the second great commandment and love your Arab neighbors as yourself. Few outside the circle of those who lost loved ones in yesterday's tragedy are more surely its victims than are the millions of innocent Muslims whose God's name has been taken so savagely in vain."[1] *National Geographic* ran a long profile on Abraham, father of the great monotheistic faiths, Christianity, Judaism, and Islam. "On the highest religious level Abraham and his monotheism was a model for Jesus and his early Christian disciples and, much later, Muhammad and his Muslim followers. Today he still stands out as a unique spiritual figure, transcending the frontiers of great religions. . . . Jews, Christians, and Muslims still revere him as the patriarch."[2]

The journalist Anna Quindlen updated the familiar story of the immigrant nation. "There is a grudging fairness among the citizens of the United States," she wrote, "that eventually leads most to admit that, no matter what the English-only advocates try to suggest, the new immigrants are not so different from our own parents or grandparents." Quoting Studs Terkel, she continued, "The old neighborhood Ma-Pa stores are still around. They are not Italian or Jewish or Eastern European any more. Ma and

Pa are now Korean, Vietnamese, Iraqi, Jordanian, Latin American. They live in the store. They work seven days a week. Their kids are doing well in school. They're making it. Sound familiar?"³ Quindlen deftly redefined patriotism—the watchword of the new era—as the embrace of diversity: The patriotic American was the person who accepted the richness of ethnic, religious, racial, and cultural diversity; to reject it was to be un-American:

> Tolerance is the word used most often when this kind of coexistence succeeds, but tolerance is a vanilla-pudding word, standing for little more than . . . letting others live unremarked and unmolested. Pride seems excessive, given the American willingness to endlessly complain about them, them being whoever is new, different, unknown or currently under suspicion. But patriotism is partly taking pride in this unlikely ability to throw all of us together in a country that across its length and breadth is as different as a dozen countries, and still be able to call it by one name. . . . [It is] a mongrel nation that somehow, at times like this, has one spirit. Like many improbable ideas, when it actually works, it's a wonder.⁴

Journalists went to elaborate lengths to capture Muslims engaged in the most prosaic, most American pursuits. The *Charlotte Observer* profiled a troop of Muslim Girl Scouts; one wore a head scarf bearing the words "I Love Being a Muslim Girl Scout."⁵ *Newsweek* ran a picture of a Muslim father carrying his flag-waving children on his way to donate blood for the victims of 9/11.⁶ In the *New York Times,* Laurie Goodstein profiled a Muslim investment banker in Los Angeles who had hung a Christmas wreath made by his seven-year-old daughter on his front door and had raised a Christmas tree in his living room. He and countless others, the article declared, are part of the "overlooked silent majority of Muslims in America," who call themselves moderates but are better understood as "cultural Muslims, akin to the assimilated cultural Jews who identify as Jewish, eat gefilte fish and celebrate Passover, but are for the most part not observant and not affiliated with a synagogue."⁷

Like Christians "who make it to church only on Easter or Jews who attend services only on the High Holy Days," cultural Muslims do not view the world through the lens of their religion, Goodstein wrote. Yet they nonetheless consider themselves Muslim, no less than the secular Jew considers herself a Jew and the nonobservant Catholic believes himself a Christian. Like many other Americans, they may describe themselves as "spiritual but not religious."[8] "The Muslims that I associate with are mostly the way I am, which is secular," said one Muslim doctor and writer in New York. "I'm not into rituals, and I put more importance on deeds, on the work you do. And I can't get too excited about mosques, the group experience. I was a big fan of The Who, and I've gone to hear them, but that's about it as far as group events."[9] Like cultural Jews, these Muslims are not especially strict about religious rules. They pray periodically if at all, have a drink at a bar now and again; the women have been known to wear shorts in the summer. Millions of readers could instantly recognize themselves or their loved ones in this profile, which was undoubtedly the point. "We need to bring the news to people," one man said in yet another of the countless profiles, "to show them [the terror attacks are] not the way of Islam."[10]

II

People who speak in the public square often wonder whether anyone is listening. In retrospect, it is clear that the early consensus among the trusted voices in American life—what James Zogby called the "constant repetition of this positive message"—was exceptionally influential in shaping public opinion. Though polling about Islam and Muslims has become a staple of the post-9/11 era, anyone trying to divine trends from the data must approach the task with caution. Many companies conducted their polls only in the first weeks and months after September 11 and then repeated them rarely or not at all. Other polls began well into the decade and therefore miss the important first years. Many social scientists have conducted surveys about Islam in connection with particular research projects, but these have generally not been repeated. Other polls are obviously partisan attempts to influence policy by creating the appearance of public support for this or that view. Only a few polling companies have focused consistently and impartially on attitudes about Muslims or Islam throughout the entire period, and even there, some of their questions were worded in a way that masked important viewpoints.[11] In addition, some organizations reworded their questions partway through the period, compromising any comparison of the results before and after.

Yet even with these caveats, the polls permit some important conclusions. First, before September 11, American attitudes about Islam were a blank slate. For instance, in a survey conducted just a few days before the first World Trade Center bombing in 1993, pollsters asked respondents whether they had a favorable or unfavorable opinion of Islam, a question very similar to one asked by several polling organizations after September 11. Nearly six in ten respondents—by far the largest percentage—said they hadn't heard enough to say.[12] When asked what comes to mind "when you think of the religion called Islam," by far the most common response was "Nothing." Only 3 percent said violence or terrorism.[13] In another survey, conducted a few days after the first WTC bombing, more than half the respondents had no opinion on whether the Muslim population in the United States was growing too quickly.[14] In 1995 more than one in three respondents had no opinion on whether Muslims had a positive or negative effect on society, greater than the fraction who thought the effect was either positive or negative.[15] In 2000, three in four Americans said they had no contact with Muslims, while eight in ten said that "in recent years" they had not had an "in-depth" conversation about religion with a Muslim.[16]

Second, cultural elites were astoundingly successful at inscribing their post-9/11 message of tolerance, inclusion, and respect onto this blank slate. Immediately after September 11, the overwhelming majority of Americans told pollsters the attacks were the work of a "radical fringe" element whose actions were "a perversion of Islam."[17] Even more strikingly, these results did not differ greatly when broken down by age, income, party affiliation, ideology, or geography. People who identified themselves as Republicans were just as likely as Democrats or independents to call the terrorist attacks "a perversion" of Islam,[18] and were equally likely to attribute the attacks to a radical fringe.[19] More than eight in ten respondents believed that Muslim-Americans were as outraged as other Americans, and by more than two to one, Americans believed the attacks signaled not a clash of civilizations but a conflict between the United States and "a small, radical group."[20]

And in what is surely the most remarkable polling result of the entire post-9/11 era, in early October 2001, the fraction of people who had a favorable impression of Islam reached its historic peak. This finding is so striking as to bear some emphasis. Days after Islamic radicals committed the worst terror attack in U.S. history—an attack they explicitly tied to their religion—and in the midst of an anthrax scare that was widely (but wrongly) attributed by political leaders to other members of the same radical Islamic group, the national view of Islam was *more favorable* than ever before or since.[21] Nor was the public divided along ideological lines. Self-identified conservatives and Republicans both had favorable views of Islam. Indeed, conservatives were *more* likely to hold a favorable view than moderates. (This particular poll surveyed too few liberals to gauge their sentiments).[22]

Yet from this very tolerant beginning, matters have grown steadily darker—the third conclusion of the polling data. Figure 7.1 maps the response to one of the few questions that has been asked about Islam since 2001 without a change in the wording: "Would you say you have a generally favorable or unfavorable opinion of Islam?" The percentage of people with an unfavorable view has more than doubled, from a low of 24 percent in January 2002 to a high of 49 percent in August 2010. Meanwhile, the percentage of people who hold a favorable view has trended down steadily, from 47 percent in October 2001 to 37 percent in August 2010, the last time the question was asked. In other words, and contrary to what we might have expected, as the nation has moved farther from September 11, tens of millions of Americans have moved steadily toward a more negative view of Islam.

This is something of a mystery. The conventional wisdom about the American response to crisis is that we begin with repressive impulses and grow gradually more tolerant. But to this mystery we must add another. Look more closely at Figure 7.1, and particularly at the dramatic increase between October 2001 and January 2002 in the number of people who could not or would not say whether their view of Islam was favorable or unfavorable. In October, only about one in eight put themselves in the "don't know" category; three months later, the number had soared to one in three. Given the times, this change cannot be attributed to national indifference, as though people were paying attention in October but had lost interest

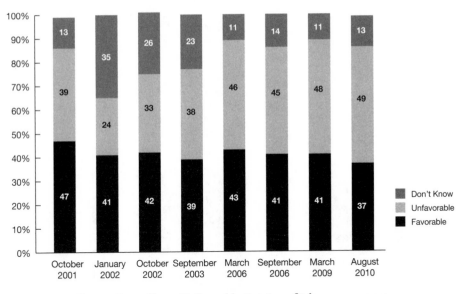

Fig. 7.1 Favorable vs. Unfavorable Opinion of Islam, 2001–2010

ninety days later. If that were the case, we would expect the number of people who didn't know to remain high, or to fluctuate randomly, but it doesn't. It peaked in January 2002 and then began to decline. By 2006 it had fallen to the low teens, where it remains. How can we explain both the growing animosity and the sudden surge and subsequent decline of the "don't knows"?

The answers are related, and they point to the last conclusion to be drawn from the polling data: the influence of elite, partisan cues on the public mind. As we can see from Figure 7.1, most of the increase in the "don't knows" between October 2001 and January 2002 came from a sharp *decrease* in the number of people who had an unfavorable view of Islam. To be sure, the number of people who viewed Islam favorably also declined somewhat, but the biggest increase in the "don't know" category came from people who switched their view of Islam from unfavorable to "don't know." Tens of millions of Americans either abandoned their unfavorable view of Islam or refused to admit it to pollsters. In either case, it strongly implies that expressing hostility to Islam per se had become culturally inappropriate. This development cannot plausibly be attributed to anything other than

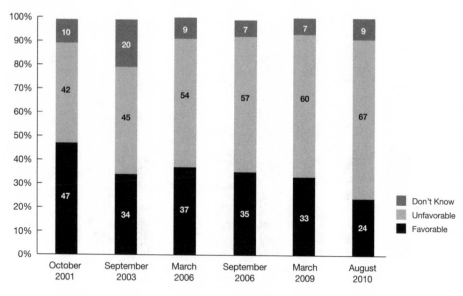

Fig. 7.2 Favorable vs. Unfavorable Opinion of Islam, Republicans

the bipartisan effort by cultural elites to shame expressions of anti-Islamic bigotry.

Yet the transformation was only partial. People did not change their opinion from unfavorable to *favorable*. Instead, they changed their opinion from unfavorable to *don't know*. The best interpretation appears to be that there was a period of immediate, almost reflexive expressions of tolerance (consistent with elite cues and the prevailing interpretation of national identity), quickly followed by widespread uncertainty. In a word, public opinion was in flux. Americans were trying to figure out where they stood. While a baldly intolerant view of Islam had become culturally unacceptable, many people were reluctant to embrace its opposite. People whose impulse had been hostile to Islam expressed no opinion as they waited for a culturally acceptable interpretation to emerge. It was not long in coming.

Look now at Figures 7.2, 7.3, and 7.4, which break down the results in Figure 7.1 by party identification. Here we have fewer data points, since the polling organization, ABC News, did not record the results by party identification for the polls taken in January and October 2002. Nonetheless, the trends are evident. Democrats have been fairly stable in their support

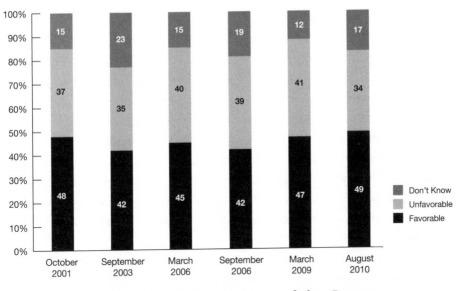

Fig. 7.3 Favorable vs. Unfavorable Opinion of Islam, Democrats

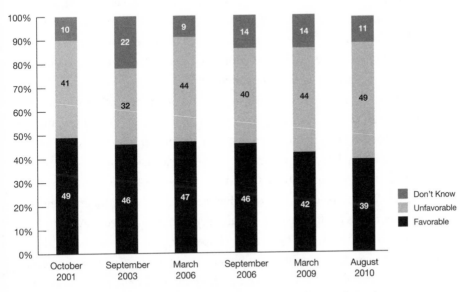

Fig. 7.4 Favorable vs. Unfavorable Opinion of Islam, Independents

for Islam. Republicans, however, have grown dramatically more hostile. In October 2001 a plurality of Republicans had a favorable view of Islam, a percentage almost identical to that of Democrats and independents. By August 2010 Republicans with an unfavorable view outnumbered those with a favorable view almost three to one. Independents have also become more hostile, though not nearly as much as Republicans. If we break down the numbers by political ideology rather than party identification (not pictured), we see much the same thing: Liberals and moderates remain fairly stable in their attitudes toward Islam, while conservatives have become appreciably more negative. Like the Republicans, conservatives with an unfavorable view in August 2010 outnumbered those with a favorable view by nearly three to one.[23]

Other polls capture the same partisan divide and, in some respects, paint an even grimmer picture. A 2010 poll conducted by Zogby International, for instance, found that an astounding 85 percent of Republicans had an unfavorable view of Muslims, compared with 34 percent of Democrats and 55 percent of independents.[24] Sixty percent of Republicans said Muslims tend to be "religious fanatics," and nearly as many disagreed with the statement "Islam teaches people to lead good and decent lives." Three-quarters agreed that "Islam teaches hate."[25] Perhaps most distressing, when asked whether they thought they knew enough about Muslims and Islam or whether they wanted to know more, fewer than three in ten Republicans wanted to know more, compared with more than two-thirds of the Democrats and more than half the independents.[26]

Before leaving these results, we should add one more piece of information. Though many more people have developed an unfavorable opinion of Islam, polling throughout the post-9/11 period continues to show, as it did before the attacks, that the majority of Americans do not know anyone who is Muslim, and only about a quarter say they are "close friends" with a Muslim.[27] When asked what most influenced their view of Muslims, one in three Americans (by far the largest number) point to the media. Another 10 percent say their view has been most shaped by their religion. Fewer than one in five based their opinion on personal experience. Those who attend church most frequently are far more likely than other Americans to say their views have been principally shaped by their religion, but far *less* likely to base that view on personal interaction with a Muslim.[28] In short, tens of millions of Americans have formed their view of Muslims from what they see on television, hear on the radio, read on the Internet, glean from the Bible, or gather from their church—in a word, from something other than personal contact. And for Republicans and conservatives, the view has grown decidedly more negative.

III

The explanation for this shift lies in the account of two steadily strengthening narratives. Though they differ in one important respect, they overlap and reinforce each other, appeal to complementary elements of the Republican base, and are often conflated. Together, they provide a coherent, thoroughgoing worldview. Most important, these narratives have achieved their success by deploying the emotionally potent language of the Creed to produce arguments that not only justify but compel a condemnation of Islam and American Muslims. As we have seen at other moments in American history, those who champion these narratives believe, with apparent sincerity, that they are defending the shared values of national identity from those who would destroy them.

The first narrative comes from the religious right. As many have noted, the religious right has created an extensive network to develop and disseminate its views—a network that includes publishing houses and magazines; television and radio programs broadcast over hundreds of Christian stations; a cluster of universities and seminaries; well-funded lobbying groups and think tanks; professionally maintained websites; and, of course, tens of thousands of churches and ministries.[29] Since September 11 this network has produced a mountain of commentary about Islam. Though the religious right is hardly monolithic and has never spoken with a single voice, the great majority of this material has denounced Islam, often in the most incendiary terms.[30]

The most familiar denunciations made the evening news. Franklin Graham, the son of the evangelical preacher Billy Graham, called Islam a "very evil and wicked religion." Jerry Falwell, the late founder of the Moral Majority, told 60 Minutes that "Muhammad was a terrorist." Jerry Vines, former president of the Southern Baptist Convention, described Muhammad as "a demon-obsessed pedophile." Pat Robertson said, "This is worse than the Nazis. Adolf Hitler was bad, but what the Muslims want to do to the Jews is worse."[31] But focusing attention on a few well-publicized remarks from conservative religious figures that cut the highest profile, and taking comfort from the denunciations their remarks elicited, creates a risk that we will overlook the great number of anti-Muslim polemics issued by the religious right since September 11.

At the risk of stating the obvious, the writing of the religious right appeals to a community for whom religion is a major part of their daily affairs. They pray more often than other Americans, are more apt to believe religion provides a solution to life's problems, and are more inclined to believe the Scriptures are the literal word of God.[32] For a group whose own behavior is so heavily shaped by religion and religious teaching, it is hardly surprising that they would think the same of others. Indeed, they believe that their religious beliefs open a window into the threat of radical Islam that is closed to secular Americans. "Secularists," Newt Gingrich once said, "can't understand the level of passion that a belief which is derived from an underlying religious form leads one to have, which is why, frankly, deeply believing Christians and Jewish Americans have a much better understanding of what's going on than do secular intellectuals in deracinated universities."[33] Muslims, they imagine, are as motivated by the example of Muhammad as Christians are by the example of Jesus Christ.[34] But there the similarity ends. "The greatest difference between Jesus Christ as God and Savior and Muhammad as prophet of Allah [is that] Jesus Christ shed his own blood . . . so that other people could come to God. Muhammad shed other people's blood so that his constituents could have political power. . . . No one questions the influence of both individuals, but the character of their influence is as different as the difference between peace and war."[35]

Christians may follow the example of Jesus as Muslims follow the example of Muhammad, but that does not make them brothers in faith, nor does it make their messages remotely the same. "The difference," noted one prolific author, "is that no Christian could credibly argue that Jesus, the prince of peace, taught violence. . . . But if Muhammad taught violence, if Muhammad taught a doctrine of required holy war against infidels, if Muhammad conflated religion and government, it will change mujahedin around the world not one bit to pretend otherwise."[36] Nor is it an answer to point out that Christians had their own bloodstained past. "This analogy is clearly false. Christians who have engaged in violence are betraying the explicit teachings and examples of Jesus Christ. On the other hand, Muslims who take upon themselves to destroy their alleged enemies in the name of God can rightly claim to be following the commands of God in the Qur'an and imitating their prophet as their role model."[37] To the religious right, a violent Christian betrays his faith, but a violent Muslim follows his.

Islam has long attracted the religious right's attention. One of the most widely consulted treatments before September 11 was *Answering Islam,* which describes what its authors Norman L. Geisler and Abdul Saleeb perceive as the doctrinal errors in Islam. Geisler is an extremely prolific Christian scholar, and Saleeb was raised a Muslim but converted to Christianity as an adult. Their book devotes little attention to the supposed connection between Islam and violence and acknowledges that Christians, Jews, and Muslims all worship the same God.[38] The literature appearing after September 11, however, takes a much darker turn. To begin with, most post-9/11 writers reject the suggestion that Muslims, Christians, and Jews all worship the same God. Allah, they insist, is a false god; some treatments deride Allah as nothing more than a pagan deity.[39] In addition, the writings after September 11 parse Islamic teachings in great detail in an effort to prove that Islam is an inherently violent religion whose adherents engage in murderous attacks on infidels as a matter of faith.

One of the most important of this genre is *Unveiling Islam,* by the brothers Ergun and Emir Caner, who hold prominent positions in different seminaries. Their book describes violent jihad and armed conflict as an "essential and indispensable tenet" of the Islamic faith. "War is not a sidebar of history for Islam; it is the main vehicle for religious expansion. It is the Muslim duty to bring world peace via the sword."[40] Far from apostates who betrayed their religion, the September 11 hijackers "knew the Koran quite well and followed the teachings of jihad to the letter."[41] The idea that Islam is inherently violent became far more common on the religious right after September 11. Even the authors of *Answering Islam* changed their tune. Whereas they once largely confined themselves to Islam's doctrinal flaws, the 2002 edition of their book includes an appendix, "Islam and Violence." A "religious foundation for violence," they claim, is "deeply embedded within the very worldview of Islam. . . . Such violence [goes] to the very roots of Islam, as found in the [Koran] and the actions and teachings of the prophet of Islam himself."[42]

Like a number of books about Islam from the religious right, *Unveiling Islam* was written by former Muslims who converted to Christianity. Such writers are thought to speak with particular authority. They know "the inside story," the truth hidden behind the veil, and their assessments carry more weight than those of a mere observer. And because they did not merely abandon Islam but embraced Christianity, they reaffirmed the moral superiority of their newly chosen community, which makes them especially prized. Richard Land, the president of the Ethics and Religious Liberty Commission of the Southern Baptist Convention, provided the Foreword to *Unveiling Islam*. The authors, Land wrote, "are trophies of God's grace—once devout followers of Allah, now of Jesus of Nazareth. . . . *Unveiling Islam* is exactly what its subtitle describes; it is an insider's look at Muslim life and beliefs. It is a bonus that this vivid analysis of Islam is by former insiders who are now Christians."[43]

This is a time-honored tradition in American demonology. Every student of the McCarthy era is familiar with Whittaker Chambers, the former communist who left the party and whose disclosures helped bring down Alger Hiss. Chambers's autobiography, *Witness,* is a classic of this genre.[44] A number of other former communists, many of whom became devout Catholics, figured prominently in House and Senate hearings about the threat of communist infiltration and testified as "experts" at the trials of American communists.[45] They were presumed to speak with particular authority about the true character of godless communism. Less well known are the many nineteenth-century books and pamphlets written by former nuns and priests who converted to Protestantism and wrote at great length about the depravity of the Catholic Church.[46] Even in a crowded field, there is always room for one more zealous convert.

IV

What difference does it make whether Islam is, according to the religious right, inherently violent? Why should anyone care that more than a billion

Muslims worldwide have erroneous views? National identity has long since come to accept that a person's religious beliefs are not the government's concern, and whatever Islam may teach and Muslims may believe is surely their own affair. Most Americans not only accept this philosophy but reject the idea that one religion is inherently superior to another. The claim that a good and virtuous life depends on which faith you choose is an anachronism in American life, and the complementary claim that religious liberty should be available only to white Protestants is anathema. That, at least, is the modern understanding of religious liberty. To overcome this, the narrative of the religious right must explain why non-Muslims should care what Muslims believe.

The core of this narrative, repeated again and again, is an insistence that Islam imposes an obligation on its followers to spread the faith, by sword if necessary, until Allah reigns supreme over the world. Sections of the Koran and Hadith (the narrations from the life of the Prophet that provide additional explanations of the Koran) are endlessly quoted to make this point. The authors of *Unveiling Islam,* for instance, observe, "Muhammad commanded in the Qur'an, 'Fight and slay the Pagans wherever you find them' (sura 9.5). This passage allows either of two interpretations: It is *descriptive,* explaining how Muhammad fought the pagan tribes. . . . Or it is *prescriptive,* demanding that believers carry on the fight until Allah is completely victorious. Followers of Muhammad have taken this message *prescriptively.*"[47] The Muslim "goal," writes another author, "is clear from the commands of the Qur'an and the Prophet, who told his followers that Allah had commanded him, 'to fight against the people until they testify that none has the right to be worshipped but Allah and that Muhammad is the messenger of Allah.'"[48] Americans should care what Muslims believe, in other words, because "the religion of Islam, as embraced by millions of radical Muslims," is a grave threat "not only to Christianity but to freedom of religion in general and to our very way of life as Americans."[49]

This is an exceptionally powerful argument, especially for those most prepared to believe that people conduct their lives based on religious teachings. The private religious preferences of a billion Muslims matter because Islam enjoins them to discriminate against—indeed, to "fight and slay"— those who do not share their faith and worldview. Islam, therefore, is not

simply a religion to be tolerated like any other but a threat to the liberties that all Americans hold dear. One measure of this argument's success is that white evangelical Protestants—the core of the religious right—
consistently distinguish themselves as among the most ardent opponents
of Islam. Nearly 60 percent believe that Islamic and American values are
fundamentally incompatible.[50]

Yet because the argument of the religious right trains its powerful guns
on Islam itself, it still struggles against the prevailing winds of national
identity. It demands that people accept what much of mainstream culture
rejects: that some religions pose a threat to religious liberty and so must
be suppressed. There is another conservative narrative, however, that does
not suffer this limitation. While the religious right attacks Islam, a more
sophisticated, and far more powerful, critique levels its objection only at
political Islam, or "Islamism."

The core of this second narrative is that Islamism is distinct from Islam.
Political Islam, as the name implies, is a *political* movement with distinctly
political objectives. It invokes Islam, but does so to achieve political goals.
Apart from this noteworthy difference, the two narratives are broadly similar. The main difference is that the second narrative (which we may call the
secular conservative argument) attributes the threat to the Islamist rather
than to Islam itself. Otherwise the two narratives are much the same. Like
the religious right, the secular conservatives claim that Islamists dream of
building "an inviolate wall around Islam, endowing it with something like
the sacrosanct status it enjoys in traditionally Muslim countries."[51] They
hope to raise Islam to an exalted status in American life, and throughout the West, by promoting Islamic rituals in the public square, securing
preferential treatment for Muslims in immigration policy, and preventing
any critical discussion of Islam. This "religionization of politics" is meant
to promote a political order "that is believed to emanate from the will of
Allah."[52] "What the Islamists are demanding, in short, is that the United
States take a giant step toward applying within its borders the strictures of
Islamic law (the *shari'a*) itself."[53]

How will the roughly six million Muslims in the United States convert
the country into an Islamic state? Here, both narratives deploy the elastic
language of the Creed, positioning themselves as defenders of national

values. Both argue that those who seek to impose Islamic law in the United States will opportunistically employ the tools most readily available. Because armed violence in the United States is apt to meet only limited success, Muslims (or Islamists) have developed a clever strategy of twisting the openness of American society against itself. Mindful that Americans have become exquisitely sensitive to the charge of religious bigotry, the argument goes, Muslims (Islamists) wield it as a weapon.

Under the guise of seeking equality, they aspire to preferential treatment; under the guise of challenging discrimination, they hope to avoid the even-handed application of the law; under the guise of protecting their religious freedom, they aim to abridge the freedom of others. In short, by invoking the law, they hope to subvert it; by claiming the protection of the Constitution, they hope to destroy it. They eschew violence only because it generally doesn't work and can backfire, but share the goals of their violent jihadist coreligionists. They practice "stealth jihad" (also known as cultural jihad or civilizational jihad). "Stealth jihadis," Newt Gingrich once explained, "use political, cultural, societal, religious, intellectual tools; violent jihadis use violence. But in fact they're both engaged in jihad and they're both seeking to impose the same end state, which is to replace Western civilization with . . . Sharia."[54] The difference is "not in doctrines or fundamental goals concerning Islamist governance," but in the tactics they employ.[55]

Both the secular conservative and religious narratives thus portray themselves not as threats to the Creed but as its champions. The denunciations by the religious right and secular conservatives are a defense of shared values: intolerance in the defense of tolerance.

An essential pillar of this argument, for both the religious right and the secular conservative, is that virtually everyone who claims to speak on behalf of the Muslim community in the United States is bent on imposing Islamic law and therefore part of the problem. The conservative Middle East scholar Daniel Pipes, for instance, has claimed that "extremists" control more than 80 percent of the mosques in the United States, as well as "schools, youth groups, community centers, political organizations, professional associations, and commercial enterprises," all of which "tend to share a militant outlook, hostile to the prevailing order in the United States and advocating its replacement with an Islamic one."[56] According to Pipes, "much if not everything about the conduct of these organizations points to their essential agreement with the 'conquer America' agenda."[57]

In his 2002 book *American Jihad: The Terrorists Living Among Us,* the journalist Steven Emerson made the same point.[58] Emerson argued that most Muslim advocacy organizations in the United States are part of "the terrorists' support network" and that their activities "support the agenda of radical Islamic ideology."[59] He singled out the American Muslim Council, the Council on American-Islamic Relations (CAIR), the Muslim Public Affairs Council, the American Muslim Alliance, and the Islamic Society of North America. The first four joined to form the American Muslim Political Coordination Council, whose endorsement Governor George Bush eagerly sought (and received) when he ran for president in 2000. The fifth, according to Emerson, is the largest Muslim organization in the country.[60]

V

The story of the American Creed in the decade following 9/11 is in large part an account of the increasing strength of the narratives advanced by the religious right and secular conservatives at the continued expense of the liberal narrative of tolerance, restraint, and respect. It is tempting to dismiss the right-wing narratives as products of the Obama era, as if anti-Muslim sentiment began only in 2008, but this reading is simply not supported by the evidence. From a very tolerant beginning, Republicans and conservatives have grown steadily more hostile to Islam as a religion and Muslims as its adherents—a trend that began long before Obama appeared on the national scene. And as the fortunes of these two narratives have improved, it is worth recalling that the stakes are the meaning and content of shared national values. Before tracing the fate of these narratives, however, it is important to recognize their long pedigree in American demonology.

Many have noted the similarity between twenty-first-century attacks on Islam and nineteenth-century attacks on Catholicism.[61] As one historian recently pointed out, Catholicism and Islam were often denounced together as the twin Antichrists, one rising in the East and the other in the West.[62] But for many years in this country, Catholicism was perceived as a far more serious threat. Popular and scholarly writers of the mid-nineteenth century never tired of demonstrating the incompatibility between Papism and American democracy. Catholicism, it was said, was not a religion but a political system inherently opposed to American institutions. Preserving the liberties of which Americans were so justly proud required keeping Catholics at bay. Tracts appeared with titles like *A Compilation of Startling Facts; or, Romanism against Republicanism; Liberty versus Romanism; The Temporal Powers of the Pope Dangerous to the Religious and Civil Liberties of the American Republic;* and *Protestantism; the Parent and Guardian of Civil and Religious Liberty.* Because these polemics invited accusations of religious bigotry, anti-Catholic writers went to great lengths to turn the accusation around, insisting that religious liberty for Catholics meant religious slavery for Protestants. Should Catholics gain a foothold in this country, warned one author, "All knees would bend, or be broken, before 'His Holiness' of Rome; all tongues would sing paeans to the tenant of the Vatican, or be plucked out by the roots; . . . emperors and kings, and, may be, presidents, would go a-toe-kissing . . . "[63]

When the suggestion was timidly advanced that bigotry aimed at the Roman Catholic Church could not be squared with the American tradition of religious liberty, nativists mocked the sentiment as hopelessly naïve about the sinister reality of papal intentions. An 1834 tract called *A Foreign Conspiracy against the Liberties of the United States* warned of a plot to flood the country with Catholic immigrants who were loyal only to the pope and ready to rise up at his command. The immense success of this jeremiad spurred the author to enlarge on the theme the following year. In a series of letters titled *Imminent Dangers to the Free Institutions of the United States through Foreign Immigration,* he pleaded with Americans to awaken "to the apprehension of the reality and extent of your danger."

Will you be longer deceived by the pensioned Jesuits, who having surrounded your press, are now using it all over the country to stifle the cries of danger? . . . Up! Up! I beseech you. Awake! To your posts! Let the tocsin sound from Maine to Louisiana. Fly to protect the vulnerable places of your Constitution and Laws. Place your guards; you will need them, and quickly too.—And first, shut your gates.

The author was Samuel Morse, storied inventor of the telegraph.[64]

That Catholics were more loyal to the pope than to the Constitution became an article of faith for many Americans. In this climate, even a whisper that a candidate was Catholic became a political liability. During the 1856 presidential campaign, the rumor circulated that the Republican candidate, John C. Fremont, was a Catholic and a Jesuit. Pamphlets suddenly appeared: *Fremont's Romanism Established; Colonel Fremont's Religious History: Papist or Protestant?* and *The Romish Intrigue: Fremont a Catholic.* The Republicans felt compelled to issue a rebuttal and quickly published *Colonel Fremont Not a Roman Catholic* in the hope of putting the matter to rest. In fact, Fremont was Episcopalian; the rumor apparently took hold because he had been married by a Catholic priest.[65]

This view of Catholicism would endure for more than a century. Well into the 1950s the foremost critic of Catholicism, Paul Blanshard, could write that the "Catholic problem . . . is not primarily a religious problem; it is an institutional and political problem."[66] Blanshard always insisted that "Catholicism as a theory of the relationship between man and God" was not his concern but that it was "political Catholicism as a world power" and the threat to American liberties posed by "the Vatican dictatorship" that worried him.[67] His books, always published to enthusiastic reviews, were wildly successful. One remained on the *New York Times* best-seller list for seven months.[68] His view of Catholicism survives today only among a tiny fraction of ultraconservative Protestants. But its successor, which substitutes Islam and Islamism for Catholicism, is alive and well.

8

"A War for the Survival of America"

SINCE THE 9/11 ATTACKS, THERE HAS NEVER been a moment when the anti-Islamic narrative was absent from the public square. Even in the immediate aftermath, when the overwhelming majority of cultural elites united behind a message of tolerance and restraint, one could uncover virtually the entire gamut of post-9/11 anti-Islamic tropes. Yet the anti-Islamic narrative has become immeasurably more potent over the past decade, and in 2012 has come to enjoy a prominence and acceptance that was almost unimaginable ten years earlier. The range of allowable opinion has shifted unmistakably: What was once denounced as hate-filled bigotry now passes for legitimate social commentary. In short, the change during the post-9/11 era is less in the narrative itself than in its reception.

Over that decade, those who demonize Islam have found their voice. As the political center has moved to the right, the rhetoric that marks the far extreme has grown darker and less nuanced, more alarmist and hysterical. The great majority of it is still couched in the symbols and language of the American Creed, but the message itself has become distinctly militaristic. For tens of millions of Americans, pronouncements of the sort repeated by President Bush again and again in the weeks and months after the attacks now provoke a toxic combination of derision and rage. These people have reached the state foretold and most feared immediately after September 11—not because of some blind, unthinking reaction to the attacks, but through a deliberate and very successful effort to make attacks on Islam perfectly compatible with the shared values of national identity.

How has this narrative spread, and why has it succeeded? An entire book could be devoted to the events that have been used over the past decade by champions of the anti-Islamic narrative to advance their cause in the public square. These incidents range from outbursts of venomous rage (like the vow by the Florida pastor Terry Jones to burn the Koran) to displays of eye-rolling pettiness (like the attack on the Miss USA contest for having the temerity to name a Muslim winner). But they also include occasions of momentous symbolic importance, like the 2006 congressional election of Keith Ellison (D-MN), who became the first Muslim elected to national office and who swore to "support and defend the Constitution of the United States against all enemies, foreign and domestic" with his hand on the Koran that once belonged to Thomas Jefferson. They include as well the 2009 speech in Cairo by President Obama, who declared, "let there be no doubt, Islam is a part of America," and vowed "to seek a new beginning between the United States and Muslims around the world."[1]

Some episodes, like the 2010 controversy surrounding the Cordoba House, the Islamic mosque and community center originally slated to be built near Ground Zero and quickly dubbed the "Ground Zero mosque," prompted thousands of articles and hours of commentary, part of it quite thoughtful but much of it incendiary and vicious.[2] A prominent member of the Tea Party and leader of the opposition to the project, for instance, wrote that "the animals of allah for whom any day is a great day for a massacre are drooling over the positive response that they are getting from New York City officials over a proposal to build a 13 story monument to the 9/11 Muslims who hijacked those 4 airliners. The monument would consist of a Mosque for the worship of the terrorists' monkey-god and a 'cultural center' to propagandize for the extermination of all things not approved by their cult."[3] Other developments, like the hearings conducted in 2011 and 2012 by Congressman Peter King (R-NY) into the risk of domestic radicalization, generated a great deal of consternation at first but have faded into irrelevance.

But we are not interested in tracing this arc for its own sake and can therefore approach the history more selectively. Our interest is in explaining how a narrative so fundamentally at odds with the dominant trends in national identity has achieved such success, especially against the powerful current of elite opinion.

I

The first and most important stage in the development of the anti-Islamic narrative was to distance itself from the expressions of tolerance that filled the public square immediately after 9/11. Many on the right quickly tired of this sentiment and grew visibly impatient with what they saw as pious but naïve tributes to the brotherhood of man. "Of course," Jay Nordlinger wrote in *National Review* a week after the attacks, "all the right-thinking people say much the same thing about cheering Arabs at the moment: 'They [the terrorists] are but a trifling faction, hardly representative of the population at large.' Everyone, suddenly, is George Gallup. Let's hope they are right. The press has held back—I know this for a fact—on reporting Arab and Muslim pleasure in the United States. Stories are being spiked in the name of unity. The press—major elements of it—are afraid of stirring backlash, of being accused of fomenting 'hate crimes.'"[4] The implication was that only the anti-Islamic right had the moral courage to resist the stultifying torpor of political correctness and to speak the truth.

Sentiments like these, which quickly became widespread within a number of right-wing journals and media outlets, were essential to the success of the anti-Islamic narrative. For one thing, they carved out a culturally acceptable space in the public square where people could metaphorically assemble and voice their dissent from the dominant message without fear of ridicule. This allowed elites to refine and spread their views, which gave the narrative the early opportunity to circulate and grow relatively undisturbed. Even more importantly, these early expressions of impatience and disgust with the dominant narrative attached themselves to the criticisms that social and religious conservatives have leveled at American society for many years. The insistence on "tolerance," for instance, was just the latest manifestation of a naïve multiculturalism that permitted foreigners to resist assimilation into the "American Way of Life." The search for alleged "root causes" of terrorism was simply the latest idiocy of the left, which reflexively blamed American society for all that was wrong with the world and refused to hold people accountable for their behavior. The refusal by cultural elites to call evil by its name slipped easily into the familiar attack on the moral relativism of secular society.

In short, a critical stage in the growth of the anti-Islamic narrative was to assure the faithful that this was fundamentally the same battle they had been waging for years—the battle against secularists, "the liberal media," the academics, the politically correct, and all the forces of modern society that threaten "true" American values. It is easy to overlook the significance of this familiarity. One tends to stop listening when the music all sounds the same. Yet this familiarity is itself important. The anti-Islamic narrative was able to spread, at least within a certain community, precisely because it *was* familiar—because it consistently built on and linked to tropes and arguments that have long been a part of the social and religious conservative critique of modern secular society in the United States.

But the growth of anti-Islamic narrative has required more than a recognizable message and a space in the public square to repeat it. It has also required messengers. The core of the narrative emanates from a small network of writers, activists, and journalists organized in think tanks, policy centers, and nonprofit organizations that have been funded by a group of conservative foundations, abetted by a cluster of like-minded Republican politicians, and given a national platform by sympathetic secular and religious media outlets. A number of writers have described this community at length, complete with its complicated interconnections. The most detailed account is that of the Center for American Progress in a book-length report entitled "Fear, Inc.: The Roots of the Islamophobia Network in America."[5]

These exposés have been unsparing in their criticism of the anti-Islamic narrative. Predictably, they cast their attack in the language of the Creed. The authors of "Fear, Inc.," for instance, write that the attacks on Islam "recall some of the darkest episodes in American history, in which religious, ethnic, and racial minorities were discriminated against and persecuted. From Catholics, Mormons, Japanese Americans, European immigrants, Jews, and African Americans, the story of America is one of struggle to achieve in practice our founding ideals. Unfortunately, American Muslims and Islam are the latest chapter in a long American struggle against scapegoating based on religion, race, or creed."[6] In general, however, these critiques ignore the extent to which the proponents of the anti-Islamic narrative likewise deploy creedal language to spread their message.

One of the key members of the anti-Islamic community, for instance, is a Florida-based nonprofit group called Act! For America, which bills itself as "the nation's largest national security movement" and says it is dedicated to "public policies that promote America's national security and the defense of American democratic values against the assault of radical Islam." "The warriors of radical Islam," they warn ominously, "are not only 'over there.' Tens of thousands of Islamic militants now reside in America, operating in sleeper cells. . . . Waiting. Preparing." They may not engage in violent jihad, but they "are committed to 'stealth jihad' or 'cultural jihad.' . . . The ultimate goal of both violent jihad and stealth jihad is the same: the advance and imposition of Islamic sharia law throughout the world. Only the means to the end is different." And in the coming battle, there is no room for political correctness. "Political correctness can be annoying, frustrating, even exasperating. In the struggle against the threat of radical Islam, political correctness will literally kill us."[7] Here in a few short lines is the familiar ("political correctness"), the new ("tens of thousands of Islamic militants" who seek to "advance and impos[e] . . . shari'a law"), and the creedal (at the expense of "American democratic values").

II

But no narrative of danger, no matter how familiar, will take hold unless people feel the threat is genuine. The most important anti-Islamic charge has always been the most provocative—that a significant (but unknown) number of Muslims in the United States were committed to creating an Islamic theocracy, and were working as a fifth column toward that very goal. Shortly after 9/11, this undoubtedly struck most people as exceptionally far-fetched. Cultural leaders were flooding the public square with precisely the opposite message, and just a few months earlier, Republican leaders had assiduously courted the Arab- and Muslim-American vote, making every effort to cast them as natural conservatives. Nor did it seem probable that Arab and Muslim advocacy groups were really subversive organizations in disguise, as the anti-Islamic champions consistently alleged. Scores of interest groups, including many within the religious right, have consciously adopted the model of civil rights organizations like the NAACP and have sought to advance their agendas in the public square through the same combination of public advocacy, litigation, and lobbying. Arab and Muslim groups seemed to be no different. Thus, after the anti-Islamic right developed a recognizable message, claimed a space in the public square, and cultivated a set of dedicated messengers, its next step was a demonstration that the threat to the Creed was not at all remote. With that project in mind, the narrative at first focused not on the United States but on Europe, especially after the al Qaeda–inspired bombings in Madrid in March 2004 and London in July 2005.

Conservatives used these attacks to illustrate how "Islamization" (sometimes also described as "Islamification") can happen in a secular Western democracy with a tiny Muslim population, and to underscore the risk that it can happen here unless all true Americans man the barricades. The London and Madrid bombings were quickly interpreted not simply as acts of violence but as part of a far more disturbing trend that was overtaking Europe. Books with titles like *Londonistan: How Britain Is Creating a Terror State Within; Eurabia: The Euro-Arab Axis;* and *While Europe Slept: How Radical Islam Is Destroying the West from Within* began to appear and were lovingly reviewed in the conservative press. *Londonistan* is representative of the genre.[8] Written by the British journalist Melanie Phillips, the book described what the author saw as the alarming increase in the influence of radical Islamists in Britain and lamented the embrace of jihadis by the British establishment. According to Phillips, the British cultural elite, blinded by multiculturalism and political correctness, had become the dupes of radical Islamists, playing into their hands by refusing to see Islam for the threat it is. "Britain," she later wrote, "has caved in to the key Islamist demand that no one should suggest that Islamic terrorism has anything to do with Islam."[9]

Phillips reserved particular scorn for the elites throughout British society—in government, the church, law enforcement, and academia—whose enthusiastic embrace of Islam and Islamists in the name of tolerance hastened the decline of British culture. In an article for *National Review,* she warned about "slippery Islamists and their apologists, who serve up a carefully sanitized version of Islam." Those who appease the Islamists, she said, fail to see that *"jihad* consists not only of terrorism but the 'soft *jihad'* of cultural infiltration, intimidation, and takeover." British authorities were "simply blind to the ruthless way in which the Islamists are exploiting Britain's chronic muddle of well-meaning tolerance and political correctness (backed up by the threat of more violence) to put Islam on a special—indeed, unique—footing within Britain." The result has been "the steady Islamization of British public space," supported by "a political, security, and judicial establishment that is failing to identify the stealthy and mind-bending game being played. It will not acknowledge the extremism within mainstream Islam. Defining 'extremism' narrowly as supporting violence against Britain, it makes the catastrophic mistake of treating the aim of Islamizing Britain as an eccentric but unthreatening position, and not one to be taken seriously."[10]

Given that she denounces them as apologists, dupes, and fellow travelers, we should not be surprised that most British authorities dismiss Phillips as an alarmist and a bigot. Muslims make up about 3 percent of the British population. Phillips takes their rebuff as proof of their idiocy or complicity. In the anti-Islamic press in this country, however, she was treated as a hero, and even rebuked for being too tame. "If anything," a reviewer in *Commentary* wrote, she had "understated the peril that the 'Londonistan' phenomenon poses to the U.S. and to Europe, both of which owe a profound debt to the British culture that is now in such disarray." It would be "hard to imagine a greater prize for the Islamists than the infiltration of the land that gave birth to liberty. Anyone who cares about Britain, or indeed about the survival of Judeo-Christian civilization, should read Melanie Phillips's brave and disturbing book."[11]

Because of the unique historic connections between Britain and the United States, the supposed Islamist threat to British culture has figured most prominently in the anti-Islamic literature. But much of Europe was likewise imagined to be at risk of "Islamization." In a lengthy article for *Commentary*, George Weigel, a senior fellow at a Washington, D.C., think tank, described the two "culture wars" raging in Europe. The first was merely "a sharper form of the red state/blue state divide in America: a war between the postmodern forces of moral relativism and the defenders of traditional moral conviction." The second was "the struggle to define the nature of civil society, the meaning of tolerance and pluralism, and the limits of multiculturalism."[12] Weigel warned that these two wars were closely linked: Secular hostility to Judeo-Christian institutions and traditions, coupled with a misguided attachment to multiculturalism, blinded mainstream politicians and elites to the threat posed by Islamic radicalism.

The result, he said, was the increasing "Islamification of Europe," the evidence of which was everywhere. "There are dozens of 'ungovernable' areas in France," Weigel claimed. "Muslim-dominated suburbs, mainly, where the writ of French law does not run and into which the French police do not go. Similar extraterritorial enclaves, in which *shari'a* law is enforced by local Muslim clerics, can be found in other European countries." Worse, European authorities turned a blind eye to Muslim practices "that range from the physically cruel (female circumcision) through the morally cruel (arranged and forced marriages) to the socially disruptive (remanding Muslim children back to radical madrassas) and the illegal ('honor' killings in cases of adultery and rape)." This indifference by European governments and cultural elites allowed shari'a to extend its tentacles ever deeper into European society, until events threatened to reach a tipping point and all would be lost. In the Swedish city of Malmö, Weigel wrote, "rapes, robberies, school-burnings, 'honor' killings, and anti-Semitic agitation got so out of hand that large numbers of native Swedes reportedly moved out." But instead of taking a firm stand against the Islamists, the Swedish government, according to Weigel, blamed the city's problems on "Swedish racism." "Sixty years after the end of World War II," he concluded, "the European instinct for appeasement is alive and well."[13]

The alarm over the predicted fate of Europe was a crucial stage in the gradual expansion of the anti-Islamic narrative. Repeated in scores of articles, it was offered as a clear illustration of what happens to Judeo-Christian institutions and Western democracies when the secular left is allowed to prevail, which has long been a potent argument within the right. Conservatives have been suspicious of Europe for years, considering it a haven of galloping secularism, indecent tolerance for all things untraditional, and runaway welfare states. Linking this suspicion to the rising tide of "Islamification" thus drew on firmly entrenched beliefs. What could one expect from a godless, socialist place like Europe but that it would become the Islamic radicals' willing prey? Accepting the downfall of Europe as a fait accompli made it that much more urgent that America be on its guard against anything that smacked of "appeasement."

Intensifying the argument about Europe is a simple demographic reality. For most Americans, Europe exists only as a remote symbol. In 2012, according to the State Department, fewer than four in ten Americans held a valid passport.[14] An even smaller percentage speak a foreign language. The great majority of Americans thus have no way to see for themselves whether Europe is riddled with "ungovernable" areas where the writ of Western law does not run and "honor killings" are commonplace. They cannot assess to what extent "Londonistan" is a reality. For them, Europe is only a "picture in the mind," which makes it especially subject to partisan manipulation. In addition, and perhaps most important, the critique of developments in Europe allowed anti-Islamic conservatives to link the violence of the Madrid and London bombings to the subversion of stealth jihad. Both represented a threat to democracy, but the latter was more dangerous for being hidden in plain sight, twisting and perverting the prized Western values of tolerance and religious liberty in order to foist an intolerant Islamism on an unsuspecting population. Europe allowed the anti-Islamic right to make the threat of stealth jihad real to an American audience.

III

Having identified the risk to Western democracies, and having linked the threat to fears already firmly embedded in conservative thought, it remained only to reiterate the narrative over and over in response to events. In this, the anti-Islamic right has been tireless. Each new incident was an opportunity to reinforce the message. Some of these were ridiculous, like the charge that Rima Fakih, who won the Miss USA contest in 2010, was an "extremist" with "deadly ties."[15] Others were simply false. A guest on Fox News, for instance, denounced the Cordoba House as an exercise in stealth jihad.[16] But other commentary reflected a far more thoughtful and ambitious attempt to build the narrative. When Nidal Malik Hasan shot and killed thirteen people and wounded many others at a Texas military base, *National Review* ran a lengthy article about the incident, in an effort to educate its readers about "what radical Islam is, . . . and how it turns American-born Muslims into jihadist time bombs."[17] Radical Islam, the author explained, "is less a religious movement than a revolutionary ideology . . . like Nazism and Communism." "Quintessentially totalitarian" in its outlook, its goal is nothing short of "worldwide Muslim rule," which has led to "the demonization of the West as a subhuman civilization that must be destroyed if Islam is to survive and triumph."[18] To achieve this goal, Islamists "must first destroy Western civilization—beginning with the United States, its most powerful protector." Violence is "an essential element" in this struggle, but "in the current state of Islamic weakness and American strength, the preferred tactics are proselytism, indoctrination, infiltration, and undermining American society from within . . . by exploiting the rights and freedoms our democratic system guarantees."[19]

A focus on the violence by someone like Hasan, therefore, was not only misguided but dangerous: It allowed "a vastly greater threat" to grow unmolested. This is the threat of stealth jihad, practiced by the many groups in American society that "claim to be independent and mainstream representatives of American Muslims" but in fact are "part of the same radical-Islamic construct."[20] This "fifth column" accounts "for much of the radicalization of American Islam over the last three decades." These groups were started by "committed cadres of professional revolutionaries" who "descended on America" in the early 1960s to "build an infrastructure for radical Islam." "Armed with their radical ideology and amply endowed with Saudi funds," they were the advance guard, forerunners of the Islamist leaders who today carry out the same agenda at organizations across the country.[21] With the help of steady and generous infusions of Saudi cash, these organizations have expanded and multiplied. "As a result, there is hardly a city of any size in America or Europe today that does not have a Saudi-controlled institution preaching extremism and spewing hatred against Western civilization, directly or indirectly advocating its destruction." Only in the context of "this vast subversive enterprise," the author explained, can one truly understand Hasan's homicidal violence.[22]

Articles like this one were noteworthy only for their length and level of detail. By 2009 the view it expressed had become entirely representative, repeated over and over in conservative journals in the right-wing media. Appearing on the *Glenn Beck Show,* for instance, the anti-Islamic author Robert Spencer repeated the charge that "all the major Muslim organizations in the United States" were linked to the Muslim Brotherhood. "These groups are . . . working in the United States to subvert the U.S. Constitution and, ultimately, to replace it with Islamic law. And we have to recognize that and recognize that that's a political agenda that free people need to fight and resist."[23]

Gone entirely were the suggestions that radical Islam represented a fringe perversion of Islam and that the great majority of American Muslims were as deeply appalled by the violence of September 11 as any other American. Much more common was Spencer's deliberate ambiguity, as when he claimed vaguely that while there were "innumerable Muslims in this country who are happy to live in a pluralistic society," there were also "untold numbers . . . who are working today to make the U.S., someday, into an Islamic state."[24] Even more typical was the sarcastic view expressed by the conservative radio host and author Mark Steyn. In his book *America Alone,* Steyn offered an updated version of an old joke: "A ten-dollar bill is in the center of the crossroads. To the north, there's Santa Claus. To the west, the Tooth Fairy. To the east, a radical Muslim. To the south, a moderate Muslim. Who reaches the bill first? Answer: the radical Muslim. All the others are mythical creatures."[25] Though Steyn allowed that the moderate Muslim was "not entirely fictional," he could not help noticing "that the most prominent 'moderate Muslims' would seem to be . . . apostate or ex-Muslims, like the feminist lesbian Canadian Irshad Manji. . . . It seems likely that the beliefs of [9/11 hijacker] Mohammed Atta are closer to the thinking of most Muslims than those of Ms. Manji are."[26]

IV

The latest stage in the growth of the anti-Islamic narrative has been an attempt to take the offensive, to act preemptively rather than to wait for the scourge of Islam to spread. The weapon of choice has been the invocation and manipulation of one of the most important values of national identity—the rule of law. Opponents of the imagined threat of "Islamization" have tried to create legal bulwarks against its deadly encroachment. The first such effort was in Oklahoma, which the local Republican Party proudly describes as "the reddest state in the country." In 2010 Oklahomans voted on a proposed state constitutional amendment that barred judges in state courts from relying on "the legal precepts of other nations or cultures." Courts were specifically instructed not to "consider international law or Sharia law," and could look to the law of other states in the United States only so long as "the law of the other state does not include Sharia law."[27]

The legislature entitled the proposal the "Save Our State Amendment," and its chief legislative sponsor described it as part of "a war for the survival of America."[28] The generally conservative Oklahoma City *Journal Record* denounced the proposal as "ill-conceived pandering to the ultra-right and ill-informed" that was motivated by "blatant anti-Muslim sentiment." Playing off the city's nickname, the *Journal Record* said that "passage of State Question 755 . . . would tell the world yet again that we're the Big Friendly—but only if you look, sound and believe exactly as we do."[29] But champions of the anti-Islamic narrative rallied its constituencies to support the proposal. Act! For America, for instance, purchased a number of one-minute radio ads that backed the measure and paid for 600,000 telephone calls to likely voters that featured the recorded voice of Jim Woolsey, the former director of the CIA and native Oklahoman, who also endorsed the proposal.[30] In the end, the measure was approved by 70 percent of the voters.

Almost immediately, however, it was enjoined from going into effect. A federal judge in Oklahoma City noted that the legislation targeted a particular religion, in violation of the First Amendment.[31] Oklahoma appealed to the Tenth Circuit Court of Appeals, which upheld the injunction, but not before an Oklahoma state legislator called for Congress to impeach the judge who had granted the injunction.[32] While the Tenth Circuit's decision was pending, Oklahoma's legislators, evidently undeterred by the court's decision, passed a statute that outlawed reliance on *any* international law but was careful not to single out shari'a. Still, the legislation's sponsor in the Oklahoma House of Representatives left no doubt that shari'a remained the focus. "This legislation," she explained, "reinforces and puts in statute the intent of SQ 755 and will prevent the documented creep of foreign and offensive laws being recognized by state and federal courts. . . . Basically, this will require that American courts rely on American law." The bill passed the House 76–3.[33]

The odds that shari'a will overrun Oklahoma are about the same as a polar bear wandering through a Texas picnic. During oral argument on the lawsuit, Oklahoma officials acknowledged they could not identify a single instance when a state judge had applied shari'a. Proponents described the legislation as "precautionary," and "a pre-emptive strike."[34] Oklahoma, however, was not an outlier but a trend setter. By the middle of 2012 more than forty bills or constitutional amendments designed to ban reliance on shari'a or international law had been introduced in two dozen states. In four states—Kansas, Louisiana, Arizona, and Tennessee—the legislation has been signed into law.[35] Similar provisions have become a fixture in state GOP platforms, some of which retain the original focus on shari'a. The 2012 Republican platform for the State of Washington, for instance, warns that "Sharia law . . . threaten[s] our sovereignty. Therefore, judges, state and local authorities must be barred from using foreign agendas, laws, and resolutions for the purposes of interpreting United States law."[36] The Minnesota GOP platform for 2012 declares, "The rule of Law in Minnesota is solely based on the United States and Minnesota Constitutions, not on international or Sharia law."[37]

National Republican leaders have climbed aboard the antishari'a bandwagon. At a speech to the American Enterprise Institute shortly after the Oklahoma legislature had sent its proposal to the voters, Newt Gingrich said he endorsed passage of "a federal law which says no court anywhere in the United States under any circumstance is allowed to consider Sharia as a replacement for American law."[38] He described shari'a as "a mortal threat to the survival of freedom in the United States and in the world as we know it. I think it's that straightforward and that real." Republican presidential candidate Michele Bachmann pledged to abide by the "Marriage Vow," written by a socially conservative advocacy group in Iowa. Among other things, the "Marriage Vow" called upon candidates to reject "Sharia Islam" as "a threat to Western human rights in general, and to American liberty in particular."[39] Herman Cain spoke of a "creeping attempt . . . to gradually ease Sharia law and the Muslim faith into our government," and promised he would not appoint a Muslim to be a federal judge or a member of his cabinet.[40]

The antishari'a movement has led to fierce denunciations, invariably couched in the elastic language of the Creed. The judge who enjoined the Oklahoma constitutional amendment, for instance, opened her decision with the pronouncement that her order "addresses issues that go to the very foundation of our country, our Constitution, and particularly, the Bill of Rights. Throughout the course of our country's history, the will of the 'majority' has on occasion conflicted with the constitutional rights of individuals, an occurrence which our founders foresaw and provided for through the Bill of Rights."[41] Yet it would be a grave mistake to dismiss the anti-Islamic narrative or the antishari'a legislation as "un-American." Defending the legislation, the prolific and vitriolic Robert Spencer insisted that in its "classic formulations," shari'a is inherently incompatible with Western and American political norms. "There is no school of Islamic jurisprudence that does not mandate stoning for adultery, amputation of the hand for theft, and the subjugation of women," Spencer writes.

And because shari'a is "political and supremacist," because it insists upon a society "in which non-Muslims do not enjoy equality of rights with Muslims," a legislative bulwark against it is absolutely essential if we are to "prevent this authoritarian and oppressive political and social system from eroding the freedoms we enjoy as Americans."[42] Obviously, Spencer writes, "no one wants to restrict individual Muslim religious practice, or even cares about it." Instead, the purpose of antishari'a laws is simply "to stop the political and supremacist aspects of Islam that infringe upon the rights and freedoms of non-Muslims. The Islamic state, as delineated by sharia, encroaches on the basic rights of non-Muslims. It would be a sad irony for non-Muslims to oppose anti-sharia and thereby abet their own subjugation."[43]

This is plainly creedal language. It is not intolerance and bigotry that motivates Spencer but a sincere attachment to tolerance and liberty, or so he insists. Opposition to shari'a is a defense of American values, not their betrayal. Those who are so misguided as to oppose this legislation merely "abet their own subjugation." One measure of how Spencer's views have been received appears in the comments that followed his article. "This could not be more clear," one reader noted. "Those who advocate Sharia Law are intent on using it to overthrow the Constitution of the United States. We know this because Sharia is wholly opposed to the liberties and freedoms protected by our Constitution. They know this whether they admit it or not. Therefore it is quite clear that those who advocate and promote Sharia in America are by default enemies of America. They are intent on overthrowing our form of government and replacing it with the slavery that is Shariah. Consequently we need to start treating them as the enemies that they are or perish at their hand. I see no middle ground here. Do You?" "Muslims who attack the anti Sharia Laws," another wrote, "will use their devious lawfare strategies to take us down from the inside IF we let them. Just think, we are now having to defend our own Constitution because of an assault by immigrants from a barbarian totalitarian cult!"

Another reader's comment demonstrates particularly well how the narrative of the anti-Islamic right unites familiar elements of the conservative critique of modern society and is worth quoting in its entirety:

Thank you, Mr. Spencer, for another important essay.

It is really quite simple: Sharia law is incompatible with the U.S. Constitution. Muslims who push for sharia law in the U.S., and their sympathizers, should be made to understand that this fact is not negotiable. Foreign born Muslims who, upon gaining citizenship, took an oath to support the U.S. Constitution. If such persons, then, engage in efforts to institute sharia law in the U.S., their oath becomes void and, according to the law, I believe that their citizenship can legally be removed.

Unfortunately, many "Progressives" and Socialists, such as those in the ACLU, have another agenda in foisting sharia law in the U.S. Once the Constitution and the laws that protect our freedoms are marginalized, ignored and made void, Socialist laws can be put in place. This is happening incredibly rapidly under Barack Obama.

States are right to legislate against sharia law. Once again, we see that honest Americans are put on the defensive against those who would remove our hard won freedoms. The muslim push (and the Socialist push) is real. In Britain, sharia courts, in just several years, have increased to where there are now well over one hundred.[44]

The problem, then, can be traced to collusion by progressives, socialists, the ACLU, and "foreign born Muslims," who "once again" threaten "our hard won freedoms," the proof of which is the more than one hundred "sharia courts" in Britain.

V

Before considering how this narrative has fared over the past decade, we must consider one last feature that has been key to its success. In one of the most important but unremarked developments of the post-9/11 era, the anti-Islamic narrative has collapsed the space in the public square between race and religion in national identity.

Immediately after September 11, Muslims and Arab-Americans were invariably linked, presented as partners at equal risk of overreaction. Gradually, however, this has changed. Largely without comment, race fell out of the discussion and attention fixed almost entirely on religion. Being Arab was relevant only insofar as it implied being Muslim, which is why so many articles were at such pains to point out that most Arabs in this country are Christian. It became important to stress that an Arab-American was likely to be Christian only because it became an error of some significance to be mistaken for a Muslim. Being a Muslim Arab was a problem that being a Christian Arab was thought to solve.

The changing significance of race appeared immediately in the polls. Right after September 11, polling organizations repeatedly probed American attitudes about both Muslims and Arabs, sometimes in a single question but most often separately. Early polls asked, for instance, whether the authorities should place Arab-Americans under "special surveillance" or whether, compared with other American citizens, Arab-Americans were more sympathetic to terrorists. Other polls asked respondents whether the terror attacks had made them "personally more suspicious" of Arabs. But by the first anniversary of 9/11, all of these questions had been permanently dropped. By the end of 2002 questions about attitudes toward Arab-Americans had all but disappeared from the polls.[45] Polling about Muslims and Islam, meanwhile, has not only continued but increased. Pollsters routinely ask whether Islam is a violent religion, not whether Arabs are a violent ethnic group.

Has race become irrelevant in post-9/11 debates? Quite the contrary, it plays a larger role than ever, but the rhetoric is couched in religious terms. To understand this, we must return to the role of race and religion in national identity.

By the end of the twentieth century, race and religion had taken different paths to reach complementary destinations. The view had become widespread (though far from universal) that the government should not play favorites with either race or religion and should not advance the interests of one group over another. Likewise, the conviction had taken hold that membership in the national community should not be made to turn on anything as accidental as race or as private as religion. The overlap in these two resting places led some observers to treat race and religion as essentially interchangeable, as when the *New York Times* disclosed Republican plans to attack President Obama in the 2012 presidential campaign based on his former relationship with the Reverend Jeremiah Wright, in an article entitled, "Race and Religion Rear Their Heads."[46]

But conflating race and religion does justice to neither. The two differ in key respects, and at the end of the twentieth century did not play remotely the same role in American life. As a result of our peculiar history, race is not *supposed* to matter, in the sense that people are strongly discouraged from declaring race as a basis for their public or private choices. To take only the most immediate example, no one is supposed to say they oppose President Obama merely because he is African-American. Yet only the willfully ignorant imagine that race is irrelevant. Racial stereotyping is pervasive, people routinely make private judgments based on race, and racial disparities have been an enduring feature of American life since long before the Founding. Race and ethnicity are constant facts that we know matter but pretend do not.

Religion, by contrast, *is* supposed to matter. God is a constant presence in the public square, and religiosity is openly encouraged. Our national motto and currency declare our trust in Him and our patriotic songs implore Him to shed His grace upon the nation. Every session of Congress begins, and every presidential address ends, with a call for His blessing. Few Americans deny a belief in God, and atheists are openly viewed with suspicion and hostility. Yet by the end of the twentieth century, in contrast to most of our nation's history, Americans had largely come to accept the religious diversity of American society. Most are no longer much troubled that others in their lives—from neighbors and friends to coworkers and children—have chosen to follow a different path to faith. As important, for most people, the personal bond and sense of like-mindedness formerly created by a shared commitment to a particular denomination has been replaced by the bond that forms from a shared social or political outlook. A conservative evangelical Protestant today is much more likely to share the worldview of a conservative Catholic than of a liberal mainline Protestant, despite differences in religious doctrine that were once thought irreconcilable. An urban, liberal Jew probably has more in common with his urban, liberal neighbor who identifies with no religious tradition than with his devout and conservative coreligionists in the suburbs.

In short, at the turn of the millennium, race and religion overlapped in the public square but supplied different stories about national identity. And it is precisely this fragile separation that has come under siege in the post-9/11 era. A great many Americans now endorse a new category—"Muslim-looking"—that has revitalized an attachment to the exclusionary aspects of American *religious* attitudes and merged them with the most odious aspects of American *racial* attitudes. This category combines the public belief that religion is a proper subject of comment with the private belief that people can be judged and sorted based on the way they look. President Bush warned of this outcome. "I knew that there would be people that say, 'There goes a Muslim-looking person; therefore, that person might be viewed as a terrorist.' I knew that was going to be a problem." Yet the category is nonsensical. Most of the world's Muslims live in Asia, and those in the United States hail from many places. The majority are from Pakistan, India, Bangladesh, Indonesia, and a number of countries in Africa. Contrary to what is widely imagined, most are not from the Middle East, and most Arabs in the United States are Christian. The U.S. census classifies Arabs as white.[47] A Muslim can no more be identified on sight than a Catholic. If the president were to suggest a need to protect "Catholic-looking" people, it is impossible that the comment would have passed unnoticed. The president's remark makes sense, in other words, only if we understand him to have conflated religious affiliation with identifiable racial features. The fact that no one apparently thought to question the president in this regard underscores that others understood it in precisely the same way.

Despite its incoherence, acceptance of this category is now widespread. During a 2012 Republican presidential primary debate on national security, former Senator Rick Santorum argued that the Transportation Security Administration should be allowed to target "the folks who are most likely to be committing" acts of terrorism. "Obviously," he continued, "Muslims would be someone you'd look at, absolutely."[48] In articles about the senator's remarks, the press referred to his position as advocating "racial profiling of Muslims," apparently with no sense of the incongruity.[49] Likewise, the best-selling author Sam Harris posted a blog entry on his website entitled "In Defense of Profiling," which concluded, "We should profile Muslims, or anyone who looks like he or she could conceivably be Muslim, and we should be honest about it."[50] Harris received a degree in philosophy from Stanford and a doctorate in neuroscience from UCLA. In addition to his writing, he is the CEO of Project Reason, a foundation "devoted to spreading scientific knowledge and secular values in society" in order "to encourage critical thinking and erode the influence of dogmatism, superstition, and bigotry in our world."[51] But he did not pause in his blog to describe what a Muslim "looks like."

It takes no great effort to assemble other examples. Not long after 9/11, an ABC News poll found that nearly half the respondents supported giving the police the discretionary power to stop anyone "who appears to be Arab or Muslim."[52] Neither the people who answered this question nor the social scientists who drafted it seemed daunted by the challenge of identifying people who "appear to be" Muslim. A website entitled "Abusive and Invasive Searches" is apparently devoted to assembling every available account of allegedly overbearing or misguided behavior by airport screeners.[53] "Isn't it time to admit that there are some people who are obviously harmless and others who are obviously suspicious?" the site's author asks. "Since one hundred percent of the people involved in terrorist attacks on airplanes have been Muslims, isn't that where all the attention should be focused?"[54] The idea that the country should vest police with discretionary power to seize anyone who "appears" Muslim, or "focus" its attention on Muslims

because they are among the "obviously suspicious" reflects the same increasingly reflexive conflation of race and religion.

For many people, the words "Islam" and "Muslim" summon more to
the mind's eye than a religion. They conjure a person with identifiable
features and predictable beliefs who can be expected to act in conformity
with this stereotype. Those who endorse this category have taken their willingness to trade in racial stereotypes and superimposed it onto their antipathy toward Islam as a religion and Muslims as its adherents. Modern racial
attitudes make it all but impossible to act on racial and ethnic stereotypes
or to express them as a basis of public policy: Race is not *supposed* to matter.
But because religion is considered a proper subject for public comment,
there are ample rhetorical resources available to construct a culturally acceptable critique of Islam as a threat to national identity. Racial and ethnic
stereotypes that once were restrained have been unleashed and legitimized
as part of a critique of religion, which has provided a powerful boost to the
anti-Islamic narrative.

VI

The relentless pounding by the anti-Islamic right has had a predictable
effect. As a whole, the American view of Islam has become modestly less
favorable. The shift among Republicans, however, has been much more
dramatic. And antipathy among the GOP rank and file extends well beyond
viewing Islam unfavorably. Under the pressure of a narrative that equates
opposition to Islam with the defense of national values, Republicans have
adopted increasingly nationalistic and menacing views. In November 2010
pollsters asked whether "the values of Islam" were "at odds with" American
values. Two-thirds of Republicans and two-thirds of Tea Party members
thought so, compared with only three in ten Democrats and slightly more
than four in ten independents.[55] Though the results also divided along religious, educational, and generational lines, no other difference was nearly
as large as the 37-point gap between Democrats and Republicans.[56] Other
polls have shown similar results. Pollsters asked early in 2011 whether
American Muslims wanted to establish shari'a law as "the law of the land"
in the United States. They repeated the question eight months later. Be-

tween the two polls, the percentage answering yes rose among all political groups, and among Republicans it climbed from 31 percent to 45 percent. Among Republicans who most trust Fox News as an information source, the yesses were nearly 60 percent.[57]

At the same time, there is growing evidence that, particularly among Republicans and the very religious, Muslims are simply the "Other," and that antipathy toward them does not depend on their behavior. In 2005 the Baylor Institute for Studies of Religion asked whether a Muslim should be allowed to teach in a high school. The question got at discrimination in its purest sense: It said nothing about the putative teacher except that she was a Muslim. Even so, 17 percent of those surveyed disapproved of allowing a Muslim to teach. The view was held by 22 percent of the respondents who attended church at least once a week and by 24 percent of respondents who supported George Bush in the 2004 election.[58]

Six years later, pollsters asked whether respondents would be comfortable with a Muslim teaching in an elementary school (as opposed to a high school). This time, more than four in ten said they would not.[59] But the topline results mask the partisan divide. Nearly two-thirds of Democrats and nearly six in ten independents said they would be comfortable with the idea, compared with fewer than half the Republicans. The poll found similar partisan divides for behavior that is not illegal or violent but simply marks a person as a Muslim. A majority of Republicans and six in ten Tea Party members said they would be uncomfortable at the sight of Muslim men kneeling to pray at an airport. Slightly smaller majorities of both groups would be uncomfortable with a Muslim woman wearing religious covering.[60]

Polls also consistently suggest that Republicans believe Islam is inherently violent. Unfortunately, no one question on this topic has been asked through the entire period. We should therefore confine our interpretations to broad sentiments at any one time rather than try to interpret trends over the past dozen years.[61] In early 2011, two polls showed that a majority of Republicans considered Islam more violent than other religions, compared with one in five Democrats and slightly more than one in four independents.[62] One pair of questions was especially revealing. The first was, "When people claim to be Christian and commit acts of violence in the name of Christianity, do you believe they are really Christian, or not?" The second was identical except it substituted "Muslim" and "Islam" for "Christian" and "Christianity." This is a particularly apt wording since it gets precisely at the religious right's argument that Christian violence is anomalous while Muslim violence is essential. The results confirmed the success of this message: Overwhelmingly, respondents saw violence by Christians as a betrayal of the religion but were almost evenly divided on violence by Muslims. Once again, however, the topline results mask the partisan division. Nearly six in ten evangelical Protestants said violence by Muslims was consistent with their religion, versus roughly four in ten mainline Protestants, Catholics, and African-American Protestants, and about one in three non-Christians.[63]

VII

The anti-Islamic narrative is undeniably potent and commands great support from tens of millions of Americans. It has become completely nonfalsifiable. Each new event is interpreted to confirm the narrative as true, and events that do not confirm the narrative are explained away or dismissed as aberrational. If the Council on American Islamic Relations (CAIR) protests about some act of anti-Islamic behavior, the charge is never taken at face value. Instead, it provides an opportunity to repeat the claim that CAIR and other Muslim advocacy groups are part of the radical Islamic agenda and that their preferred method is infiltration from within, which in turn leads to more articles about stealth jihad. Any complaint from CAIR, therefore, is not evidence of anti-Islamic sentiment but proof that radical Islam is hard at work and the threat remains grave.

Or the complaint by CAIR provides another occasion to air the charge that the Saudis have funded many of the mosques, community centers, and Islamic schools in this country, which in turn leads to a discussion of the "radicalization" of American Muslims indoctrinated by Saudi views. If anyone points out the infrequency of Muslim violence in the United States, the speaker is dismissed as an apologist or denounced as a fellow traveler who does not understand the true nature of the Islamist threat. Worse, she, like Europe's misguided elites, has been blinded by political correctness and fails to understand the opportunistic character of radical Islam. If this prompts a protest about the successful assimilation of "moderate Muslims" in the United States, conservatives respond that their complaint has never been with the elusive moderate, and then seek shelter in the vagueness of their charge, pointing out that "many," or "tens of thousands," or "millions of Muslims worldwide," or "a dangerous number" of Muslims in the United States are not so moderate. This in turn is accompanied by the charge that, if there are so many moderates, why don't they protest more loudly against Islamic terrorism, denounce Hezbollah or Hamas, or side with American policy regarding Israel?

Most important, if one protests that denunciations of Islam violate the cherished American commitment to tolerance and religious liberty, or that conservative attacks on Muslims are out of touch with the live-and-let-live attitude that has taken shape in American religious life, the answer—always at the ready—portrays the conservative as liberty's last champion. It is the Islamist, not the conservative, who threatens the Creed. It is the Islamist, not the conservative, who would expel Judeo-Christian institutions and values from the public square. It is the Islamist, not the conservative, who would sacrifice religious liberty to make one religion dominant, who threatens the Constitution and the rule of law, who seeks to transform national identity and remake American life in theocratic form. Such is the great malleability of the language of national identity. The champions of a particular social arrangement never place themselves outside the Creed. Instead, they contort the Creed to justify their position.

And yet the anti-Islamic narrative has taken on the stridency and belligerence of people who shout when they perceive that others have stopped listening. A careful review of the record since September 11 discloses a certain petulance and volubility, a sense that the rest of the country "doesn't get it," and is not paying attention to the looming apocalypse. Robert Spencer dedicated his book *Stealth Jihad* to "all those who recognize the danger of the stealth jihad and are ready to resist." One gets the feeling from reading his work, and so much of the anti-Islamic narrative, that he fears this camp numbers altogether too few. He says as much: "Most Americans regard the terror threat as one that necessarily involves guns and bombs. . . .

[But] stealth jihadists have already made significant inroads into American life. . . . And every day, they are advancing their agenda. . . . The stealth jihadists are working energetically to wear away the very fabric of American culture. It is happening right now, under our noses."[64]

Spencer is certainly right that most Americans do not sense an "energetic" effort on the part of less than 2 percent of the population to "wear away the very fabric of American culture," and do not detect "a full-scale effort to transform pluralistic societies into Islamic states, and to sweep away Western notions of legal equality, freedom of conscience, freedom of speech, and more."[65] In late 2010 Frank Gaffney, a former official in the Reagan White House and today one of the most energetic supporters of the anti-Islamic narrative, appeared on Fox News and chided the network for paying insufficient heed to the threat posed by stealth jihad.[66] His criticism speaks volumes. An Islamic threat so subtle that even Fox News does not pay it sufficient regard is not likely to stir the hearts and minds of mainstream America.

In the end, it seems the anti-Islamic narrative cannot overcome the more powerful countervailing force of the dominant trends in national identity. Most Americans have embraced the religious diversity of American life. They reject the theocratic dogmatism of the religious right and welcome the secular trends that make social conservatives profoundly uncomfortable. To be sure, a certain fraction of the population emphatically rejects these developments, and casts its opposition in the elastic language of national identity. This includes most prominently the religious right and the authoritarians who react so strongly to the "Other," whoever he may be at the moment. The anti-Islamic narrative has certainly won over this fraction, and the importance of that victory should not be minimized. But neither should it be overstated, as this is an increasingly isolated minority of the population.

The anti-Islamic right is thus a victim of its own success. By linking its narrative so closely to the conservative memes that have developed over the past several decades, the narrative attracts only the people who are predisposed to hear it. The conservative narrative has so far been unable to make the jump from the right wing to mainstream civil society. It is propagated by a nucleus of media outlets, think tanks, and nonprofit organizations, many of which receive funding from the same small pool of wealthy conservative donors.[67] A core group repeats the same message over and over, reinforcing one another but almost never preaching beyond the choir. One spokesperson for the narrative makes a guest appearance on another's radio program or television show; a second writes for a cluster of conservative journals, rehashing the same points; a third is asked to speak at a symposium sponsored by the first one's think tank.[68] This churning allows the narrative to maintain a certain visibility but confines it to a fairly isolated corner of the public square. The narrative thrives, in other words, but only within a very particular atmosphere. It dies once it steps outside the safety of its world.

This is perhaps best illustrated by the public humiliation of Congresswoman Michele Bachmann (R-MN), a darling of the anti-Islamic right, after she made the mistake of exposing the narrative to the mainstream air. In the summer of 2012 Bachmann and four congressional colleagues sent letters to the inspectors general at five federal offices (the Departments of State, Justice, Defense, and Homeland Security, as well as the Office of the Director of National Security). The letters expressed alarm about the possible infiltration and influence of the Muslim Brotherhood in the national government.[69] Each letter cited "The Muslim Brotherhood in America: A Course in Ten Parts," a report and training course prepared by the Center for Security Policy, a small think tank run by Frank Gaffney, the man who criticized Fox News for not taking stealth jihad seriously enough.[70] Making generous use of apocalyptic language and forecasting a dire threat to the Creed, "The Muslim Brotherhood" accused both the Bush and Obama administrations of placing Islamists in high office and warned ominously that "America faces in addition to the threat of violent jihad another, even more toxic danger—a stealthy and pre-violent form of warfare aimed at destroying our constitutional form of democratic government and free society. The Muslim Brotherhood is the prime mover behind this seditious campaign, which it calls 'civilizational jihad.'"[71]

Within the echo chamber of the anti-Islamic right, such charges have circulated for years. For that reason, the letter writers may not have expected the public condemnation they elicited, particularly among Republicans. One of the letters cast suspicion on Huma Abedin, an aide to Secretary of State Hillary Clinton. Arizona Senator John McCain took to the Senate floor to defend Abedin, describing her as "an intelligent, upstanding, hard-working, and loyal servant of our country and our government, who has devoted countless days of her life to advancing the ideals of the nation she loves and looking after its most precious interests."[72] In classic creedal language, McCain said that Abedin "represents what is best about America: the daughter of immigrants, who has risen to the highest levels of our government on the basis of her substantial personal merit and her abiding commitment to the American ideals that she embodies so fully."[73]

Turning to the allegations against Abedin, McCain was unsparing in his denunciation. "To say that the accusations" were "not substantiated by the evidence," McCain said, "is to be overly polite and diplomatic about it. . . . These allegations about Huma, and the report from which they are drawn, are nothing less than an unwarranted and unfounded attack on an honorable citizen, a dedicated American, and a loyal public servant. . . . These attacks on Huma have no logic, no basis, and no merit. And they need to stop now."[74] In closing, McCain excoriated Bachmann and the other signatories in the symbolically potent language of the Creed:

> Ultimately, what is at stake in this matter is larger even than the reputation of one person. This is about who we are as a nation, and who we aspire to be. What makes America exceptional among the countries of the world is that we are bound together as citizens not by blood or class, not by sect or ethnicity, but by a set of enduring, universal, and equal rights that are the foundation of our constitution, our laws, our citizenry, and our identity. When anyone, not least a member of Congress, launches specious and degrading attacks against fellow Americans on the basis of nothing more than fear of who they are and ignorance of what they stand for, it defames the spirit of our nation, and we all grow poorer because of it. Our reputations, our character, are the only things we leave behind when we depart this earth, and unjust attacks that malign the good name of a decent and honorable person is not only wrong; it is contrary to everything we hold dear as Americans.[75]

McCain's comments, though remarkable for their bluntness, were not the worst Bachmann received. Ed Rollins, her former campaign manager in her run for the presidency, published a piece for Fox News in which he attacked her for leveling charges that were "outrageous and false," "unsubstantiated," and "downright vicious." "The Republican Party," he said, "is going to become irrelevant if we become the party of intolerance and hate. . . . Shame on you, Michele! You should stand on the floor of the House and apologize to Huma Abedin and to Secretary Clinton and to the millions of hard-working, loyal, Muslim Americans for your wild and un-substantiated charges."[76] Other prominent Republicans joined in. Senator Scott Brown (R-MA) wrote that Bachmann's accusations were "out of line. This kind of rhetoric has no place in our public discourse." Senator Lindsey Graham (R-SC) called the charges "ridiculous."[77]

So long as the anti-Islamic narrative ties its fortunes to the larger critique made by social and religious conservatives, there is little reason to expect it will win mainstream support. For one thing, the demographics are against it. Support for the conservative narrative about Islam increases with age and religiosity, and the most enthusiastic supporters are the elderly, white, conservative Protestants who form the core of the Republican Party. Young people are consistently more receptive than other Americans to the secular trends in national life and show no impulse to roll them back. They are also considerably more hostile to the perceived dogmatism of the religious right, and far less likely to report that religion plays a prominent role in their lives. They are more likely to experiment with other religious tradi-tions and less likely to believe that one religion holds a monopoly on truth. Their profile, in other words, is almost diametrically opposite the profile of the religious and social conservative. Not unexpectedly, young people in the United States have proven most resistant to the anti-Islamic message. Indeed, the most recent polling data as of late summer 2012 indicate that young people between the ages of eighteen and twenty-nine had an over-whelmingly favorable view of Muslims.[78] This is not an auspicious sign for those who would spread the anti-Islamic message to a new generation.

In addition to the demographics, the conservative narrative faces a credibility gap. The ideological rigidity and extremism of the conservative media, while contributing to its enormous success, has also contained its growth. Recent polls show that conservatives tend to trust *only* Fox News and that moderates and liberals tend to trust *anyone but* Fox News. The par-tisan divide in this regard is enormous.[79] This means that narratives that depend on support from right-wing media, as the anti-Islamic narrative does, face particularly high hurdles as they try to jump from the margins to the mainstream.

Finally, there is some evidence, still tentative, that the shouting of the anti-Islamic right may have become counterproductive. The wave of anti-shari'a legislation, to take just one example, is beginning to recede. The Oklahoma Senate did not vote on the bill passed by the House and in 2012 allowed it to die in committee. Most of the bills in other states either did not make it out of committee or were withdrawn by their sponsors. These developments probably do not reflect any essential change in anti-Islamic sentiment. Instead, the determination to strip all reference to shari'a in order to avoid the drafting sin of overspecificity appears to have created the greater crime of overgenerality. International business groups have correctly pointed out that business contracts routinely refer to foreign law, and an international corporation that cannot apply international law in Oklahoma will surely take its business to another state. In addition, the legislation could be interpreted to ban the application of Jewish or Catholic law, which has led to protests from other religious leaders. Eventually, the realization that the law *cannot* be changed transforms itself into the belief that it *ought not* be changed. "Is" becomes "ought."

This is not to suggest that things cannot grow worse, that the anti-Islamic narrative is inherently incompatible with national identity, or that the narrative is inconsistent with the "true" meaning of America. I make no such claim. Things can certainly change—under the right circumstances, they can change very quickly—and the anti-Islamic narrative is no more "un-American" than the anti-Catholic narrative that dominated American religious life for centuries. I claim only that, at least for now, the anti-Islamic narrative may have spent itself. Because of the group to which it appeals, the language it adopts, and the way it has constructed the threat, its particular vision of national identity has limits that it may not be able to overcome. To be sure, if the United States is cursed to suffer another major attack by Islamic militants, the conservative narrative will, at least for a time, find new followers. If that should happen, people will discover that much of the heavy lifting has already been done and that a creedal justification for an attack on Islam is readily available in the public square. The narrative could then make the jump to the mainstream organs of civil society. But that is not our moment, and perhaps it is not our fate.

9

"Think the Unthinkable"

The danger that the United States will lose its soul in the coming fight against terrorism is virtually nonexistent.
—*Robert Kagan and William Kristol,* Weekly Standard,
September 24, 2001

The warrant would limit the torture to nonlethal means, such as sterile needles, being inserted beneath the nails to cause excruciating pain without endangering life.
—*Alan Dershowitz, "Want to Torture? Get a Warrant."*
San Francisco Chronicle, *January 22, 2002*

BECAUSE SEPTEMBER 11 HAD BEEN cast as an attack on the shared values and traditions of national identity, protecting and preserving these principles became the raison d'être for the war on terror. But just how strong was this attachment? What would happen when the nation faced a concrete test of its commitments? The test came sooner than anyone expected.

I

Just as the attacks were immediately interpreted as an act of war, they were quickly cast as a particular *type* of war. The Holy Grail of America's newest war quickly became more and better "intelligence." By the evening of September 11, commentators were stumbling over the language, searching for just the right adjective to describe the magnitude of the intelligence failure that must have happened in order for such an attack to take place. Peter Jennings of ABC News called it "a desperate failure of intelligence in both the human and technical area."[1] The *Washington Post* described it as "a massive intelligence breakdown."[2] The *Los Angeles Times* called it "an intelligence failure of colossal proportions."[3] *Newsday* bemoaned the "incredible failure of our intelligence system."[4] Leon Panetta, the former chief of staff for President Clinton and later the director of the CIA and the secretary of defense for President Obama, said it "was clearly a colossal failure of our intelligence community."[5] Vice President Dick Cheney's ominous warning on September 16 that the war on terror would take the United States to "the dark side," working "in the shadows, in the intelligence world," simply provided official confirmation of what the nation expected.[6]

Obtaining this intelligence promised to be no small challenge. "The enemy is in many places," Secretary of State Colin Powell warned. "The enemy is not looking to be found. The enemy is hidden. The enemy is very often right here within our own country."[7] Such sentiments were endlessly repeated; we recognize them as part of the ritual of naming a new demon. Our adversary was "shadowy and elusive," "capable of continually reinventing itself," shape-shifters "who can run and hide almost everywhere," "turning up in Hamburg, Amsterdam, Delray Beach, and Jersey City," and "creating battle zones potentially anywhere."[8] "They travel light and move fast."[9] Terrorists were supposedly segregated into highly disciplined cells that were nearly impossible to penetrate. Disrupting one cell would do nothing to disturb the others because each operated independently, "blending in locally, earning money at simple jobs," planning and preparing until they were "activated" by an unknown, unseen mastermind.[10]

As difficult as the challenge was thought to be, the need and urgency were believed to be even greater. Beginning the afternoon of September 11 and continuing without pause for months, virtually every organ that could claim a role in shaping American thought reported endlessly on what might come next. The coverage was ubiquitous. Every major paper in the country, every news magazine, every radio and television program that addressed itself to serious questions of the day, and every think tank or nongovernmental organization with even a remote connection to national security joined in trying to predict when and where the next shoe would drop. Experts with terrifying portfolios assured us that bin Laden and his operatives had acquired, or were close to acquiring, nuclear, chemical, radiological, or biological weapons. From the paper of record to the chaos of the blogosphere, the nation fixated on the unknowable world of future terror.

In one early account, bin Laden had reached an agreement with "organized crime figures in Chechnya" to pay $30 million in cash and two tons of opium in exchange for twenty nuclear warheads, which he planned to convert into "suitcase nukes." In late September, the *New York Times* warned that the nation was "woefully unprepared to deal with bioterrorism." The likelihood is growing, the *Times* predicted, that "some rogue state or terrorist group will successfully deploy germ weapons."[11] The next day, *Time* magazine said "the idea that weapons of mass destruction might be trained on the U.S.—not by such rogue nations as Iraq but by rogues like Osama bin Laden—suddenly seems a lot less unthinkable. Ordinary Americans are waking up in the middle of the night with nightmares about poisoned water supplies and miniature nuclear weapons set off in city streets."[12] October opened with a statement by Richard Butler, the former chairman of the U.N. Special Commission overseeing the inspection of Iraq's weapons of mass destruction, who warned that "a nuclear terrorist threat from bin Laden, by way of the Russian criminal underground, is a reality."[13]

One reason for Americans' nightmares was the sensationalistic coverage by the national press. The public was bombarded with talk of biological and chemical warfare. Nearly every news program explored the issue in great detail, always focusing on the most frightening aspects. David Ensor, a correspondent for CNN, said that agents made from anthrax "produce fever, stomach pain, then, a horrific death."[14] ABC's *Good Morning America* opened its coverage of biological and chemical weapons with a warning by Diane Sawyer that parents might want their children to leave the room. Then she asked, "Should you buy a gas mask?"[15] The same day, biological terrorism was apparently NBC News's theme for the day. Reports on *Today*, *Nightly News with Tom Brokaw*, *Dateline NBC*, and the MSNBC and CNBC cable networks all devoted themselves to the story.[16]

Analysts worried over the security of smallpox stores and nuclear arsenals in Russia, and of power plants and water supplies in the American heartland.[17] Interactive graphics let anxious readers chart contamination zones, infection rates, and mortality tables. The *New York Times* reported that New Yorkers were stocking up on ciprofloxacin, or cipro, an antibiotic used to treat anthrax. A pharmacist on the Upper East Side said he couldn't keep it in stock: One nervous customer bought one thousand tablets. In an observation that could not have calmed many nerves, one expert pointed out that the drug was probably useless, since "once you're showing signs it's probably too late."[18] Still, the run on cipro continued. A nurse from an infectious disease practice in Washington said her group was inundated with calls from doctors and patients. Government officials were repeatedly asked whether they could promise that every man, woman, and child in America would be vaccinated. Many Americans also began "to stock up on gas masks, handguns and bottled water." The CBS program *48 Hours* said gas masks were "flying off the shelves."[19]

The anthrax attacks began in late September.[20] Suspicion at the highest levels of government immediately focused on al Qaeda or Iraq. The FBI issued what the *New York Times* called "a stark and urgent alert" that the United States could be attacked within days, the first time any government agency had warned of an attack within a specific period.[21] In October, House Minority Leader Dick Gephardt (D-MO), emerging from a meeting with the president, was asked whether al Qaeda was behind the anthrax attacks. "I don't think there's a way to prove that," he said, "but I think we all suspect that."[22] Vice President Cheney said the nation should act on that suspicion.[23] By November the *Boston Globe* reported that senior law enforcement officials were leaning toward the conclusion that the anthrax was produced in the United States either by someone sympathetic to al Qaeda's goals or by a "sleeper" agent connected to al Qaeda who acted on a prearranged signal. One official said that was "very much in keeping with the cell structure" of al Qaeda. An FBI profiler analyzed three of the letters sent with the envelopes of anthrax powder and concluded they were written by someone for whom English was a second language. "It's 60–40 that it's connected to September 11," one official concluded.[24]

To be sure, some commentators went to heroic lengths to dampen the hysteria. Kenan Malik, writing in the London-based *New Statesman*, pointed out that "the terrorist with a suitcase full of plague bugs or anthrax" was "a mythical creation, the aim of which is to make palatable draconian and illiberal measures—from the demolition of civil liberties at home to the prosecution of war abroad."[25] But such voices were in a distinct minority, and Malik was not writing for an American audience. Even when the press acknowledged that experts were divided on the risk posed by chemical weapons or bioterror, it often sided with the experts who voiced the greatest alarm. In an article titled "Unmasking Bioterror," *Newsweek* scoffed at the idea that this was "just a frustrating standoff among experts." "Those with the deepest firsthand knowledge of bugs-and-gas take the threat the most seriously."[26] The article then quoted a former "leader in America's bioweapons program," who believed that "unless something is done," a bioattack by al Qaeda was "highly likely."[27]

In the same issue, *Newsweek* reported that "intelligence officials" believed al Qaeda had already obtained the material to manufacture a "dirty bomb" or "radiological dispersion device," which "consists of conventional explosives wrapped in a shroud of radioactive material that creates fallout when the bomb explodes."[28] Just two days earlier, the *Economist*—by no means part of the alarmist press—had warned that radiological weapons that "could easily be stashed in a truck, or even a suitcase" could spread contamination "over a wide area."[29] At his first prime-time news conference after 9/11, President Bush was asked what Americans were "supposed to look for and report to the police or to the FBI." "Well," he answered, "if you find a person that you've never seen before getting in a crop duster that doesn't belong to you—report it."[30]

Pollsters quickly began to probe the depth of American fear. In a survey taken in October 2001, with a follow-up in March 2002, 86 percent of respondents reported they were very or somewhat concerned that the United States would suffer another attack, while 84 percent were very or somewhat concerned the attack would come from biological or chemical weapons. More than two-thirds reported being very or somewhat concerned that they, a friend, or a relative would be "the victim of a future terrorist attack in the United States."[31] The odds that an individual American would be victimized by an act of terror are almost incalculably small. The finding that nearly seven in ten Americans believed that they or someone close to them would be the victim of a terrorist attack speaks volumes about the fear that pervaded American society.

It was in this desperate period that the idea of torture first appeared in the national debate.

II

The earliest suggestions were oblique. Speakers danced around the subject as though the word were obscene. In late October the *Wall Street Journal* ran a piece by the historian Jay Winik. Recounting the case of Abdul Hakim Murad, an al Qaeda operative tortured in the Philippines, Winik wondered "what would have happened if Murad had been in American custody."[32] Though the United States had to balance security and liberty, it also had to weigh the risk posed by "a largely hidden enemy, potentially armed with bioweapons—anthrax, plague, even smallpox—and perhaps a radiological bomb." Our security depended on the ability to extract information: "a lead about a terrorist cell; a confession from a captured bin Laden associate; one small lead could potentially save thousands or hundreds of thousands of lives—perhaps millions."[33] Winik did not follow the implication of what he had laid out, opting instead for what he perceived as the "lesson" of history—wartime illiberality poses no threat to national identity because "when our nation is again secure, so too will be our principles."[34]

Shortly after Winik's article, Senator Bob Graham (D-FL), the chairman of the Senate Intelligence Committee, told reporters about a dinner he had recently attended with U.S. intelligence officials. The conversation, Graham said, had turned to the Muslim uprising on the Philippine island of Mindanao after the Spanish-American War. On one occasion, American soldiers captured a group of Muslim insurgents. As Graham reported it, they killed part of the group with "bullets dipped into the fat of pigs," wrapped them in funeral shrouds made of pigskin, and "buried them face down so they could not see Mecca. Then they poured the entrails of the pigs over them." The other insurgents were forced to watch and then allowed to escape. "And that," Graham said, "was the end of the insurrection on Mindanao."[35] Though Graham said he disapproved of these methods and "personally would advise" against the use of torture by U.S. intelligence agencies, "there are a lot of people putting ideas like that forward."[36] In lieu of torture, he said, interrogators might need to exploit other vulnerabilities, "including families, relatives, [or] religious beliefs." Still, Graham insisted, it was all just talk.[37]

Events seemed to crowd the country closer and closer to the precipice. The FBI had arrested hundreds of Muslim men in the United States, and agents were interrogating them about possible al Qaeda connections. In late October unnamed FBI agents complained to *Washington Post* reporter Walter Pincus that four suspects held in New York had refused to talk. The four included Zacarias Moussaoui, who was detained before 9/11 in Minnesota "after he sought lessons on how to fly commercial jetliners but not how to take off or land them." Also on the list were two Indian nationals "traveling with false passports who were detained the day after the World Trade Center and Pentagon attacks with box cutters, hair dye and $5,000 in cash" as well as "a former Boston cabdriver with alleged links to al Qaeda."[38]

According to the FBI, all the blandishments traditionally used to loosen the tongues of suspects had come to naught, and the FBI was growing frustrated. "We are known for humanitarian treatment, so basically we are stuck," complained one agent. "Usually there is some incentive, some angle to play, what you can do for them. But it could get to that spot where we could go to pressure . . . where we won't have a choice, and we are probably getting there."[39] The Bureau was reportedly considering "drugs or pressure tactics, such as those employed occasionally by Israeli interrogators." Agents were also apparently thinking about transferring the men to a third country that was not so squeamish about torture.[40]

The *Post* story, reprinted around the country, electrified the torture debate. Torture was no longer an abstract proposal. The four suspects who had been arrested under suspicious circumstances were instantly labeled terrorists. Their guilt was a foregone conclusion, their intelligence value assumed. An editorial in the *Omaha World* lamented that the four were "withholding vital information. They are not ordinary criminals; rather, they are fanatically committed to bin Laden and his twisted interpretation of Islam. Their reward, they appear to believe, won't be in this world but in the next. The problems for a criminal interrogation are obvious."[41] The question presented itself: Should they be tortured?

Overwhelmingly, the answer was no. National identity, even at this extraordinary moment, could not accept the idea of torture. Fox News, reliably conservative and immensely popular, took up the question immediately after the *Post* article appeared. Fox anchor Jon Scott interviewed Eric Haney, a founding member of the army special operations unit, Delta Force. Scott asked whether "maybe a little strong arm tactic might be useful to get some info we need?" "It doesn't work," Haney answered. "Doesn't produce the information that you need to gain from the people and it's always counterproductive."[42] Four days later, Scott interviewed Larry Johnson, a former CIA officer and deputy director of the State Department Office of Counterterrorism from 1989 to 1993. Scott asked specifically about Jaweed Azmath and Ayub Khan, the two suspects arrested in Texas with box cutters and cash. Johnson found their silence "disconcerting" but insisted that "torture is not the best way to get information." The United States, he said, doesn't have "to lower ourselves to the level of committing torture."[43]

Bill O'Reilly, the influential Fox News host, also interviewed Haney. He asked what Haney would do if the four suspects were in his custody. Haney's response was telling: Some people just won't talk. "They're rare and they're few," but they exist, and no interrogation technique works on all prisoners all the time.[44] The admission that some information was simply beyond an interrogator's capacity to extract, though self-evident in a pre-9/11 world, would eventually become heretical, an admission of failure that American policy makers could not abide. At the time, however, it was still uncontroversial. Rounding out the interview, O'Reilly linked torture to American exceptionalism, pointing out that "other countries use torture, and they take eyes out and they maim and they use electricity and all of that. But the United States, even in a terror war, will not do any of that?" "No, sir," Haney answered. "We absolutely will not. And there are several reasons. There's the legal reason, there's the moral reason, and there's the tactical reason. All you get from the man is what he thinks that you want to hear, just so you'll stop. So in essence what you've done is you've slowed your process down."[45]

National Public Radio weighed in shortly after. Neal Conan, the host of the afternoon program *Talk of the Nation*, interviewed Robert Litt, a former Justice Department official, and David Cole, a prominent civil rights attorney and scholar from Georgetown University Law School.[46] (Litt later became general counsel for the Office of the Director of National Intelligence under the Obama administration.) Conan started the show with the mistaken prediction that "torture will probably never become a legal tool," but he wondered whether it could be justified in certain circumstances. Litt thought the proverbial ticking time bomb raised a difficult question but quickly added that none of the people currently in custody presented such a situation—"certainly nobody responsible is suggesting that"—and that the United States should never "have any laws or practices in this country that legally authorize the use of torture."[47] Cole was more emphatic. No country in the world, Cole said, authorizes torture as a legitimate form of interrogation, "and I don't think we should be the first." A caller from San Diego took Litt and Cole to task, arguing that suspects who were not cooperating "obviously . . . have something to hide."[48] To his credit, Cole provided the answer that seems obvious in retrospect but was uniformly missed at the time. Silence often has an innocent explanation, he said, and what the FBI had characterized as stubborn silence could also be complete ignorance.[49]

Editorial pages and columnists across the country condemned the FBI for floating the idea of torture as government policy. Clarence Page, the liberal syndicated columnist for the *Chicago Tribune*, wrote a widely distributed piece that played on President Bush's well-publicized contention that terrorists "hate our freedoms." "Sometimes," Page said, "we Americans don't like our freedoms very much, either."[50] Detecting this spirit in the FBI's frustration, he warned against the fleeting satisfaction of expedience. A nation "pays a heavy moral price whenever it sacrifices its highest principles of human rights, even temporarily. Like a one-night sinner, we may get what we want [but] . . . we'll also have a good reason to hate ourselves in the morning."[51] The columnist Rekha Basu said the FBI was apparently considering "exactly the kind of violations that groups like Human Rights Watch and Amnesty International chastise other countries for. Our own rejection of those barbaric practices has given America the right to criticize regimes that engage in them. . . . This is so fundamentally un-American I can't believe we're even discussing it."[52] The editorial board of the *Houston Chronicle* said, "This sounds distressingly like the FBI flirting with the use of torture on suspects in its custody." While Americans were "understandably eager, even desperate" to bring bin Laden to justice, "if the government is asking for the public's blessing to use physical torture to wring information and confessions out of even a suspected international terrorist, the public must withhold it."[53]

Shortly after the *Post* article appeared, a reporter with the *Las Vegas Review-Journal* asked the Nevada congressional delegation for its views on torture. Republicans and Democrats alike opposed it, in essentially identical language. "This nation has to stand for something," said Democratic congresswoman Shelley Berkley. Republican Congressman Jim Gibbons said the American people would not tolerate torture. "I think there may be other means that are more humane."[54] Nevada's two senators agreed. Republican John Ensign said that although another terror attack was just a matter of time, he could not support using torture to obtain information that could prevent those attacks. "This is the United States," he said. "The FBI can't do that." Democrat Harry Reid flatly rejected the idea of torturing suspects to gather information. "I'm not for any kind of physical abuse."[55]

Letters to the editor echoed these themes, articulating their objections in the creedal language of American exceptionalism. Responding to the FBI's suggestion, a reader in Maryland wrote, "If the Taliban did this, we would be howling at their lack of civilization. If democracy and respect for life and people are our hallmarks, then there is no place for such tactics. . . . I reject the use of physical torture or similar methods of physical coercion to obtain information, even information needed to defend ourselves. It demeans us." Another reader in Washington said the FBI proposal

> sends the message that our freedoms and rights, guaranteed by the Constitution, count only when they do not get in the way: Racial profiling is a crime, unless it helps catch criminals; torture is a crime, unless it works; privacy rights are guaranteed, until they hinder law enforcement. Our Constitution establishes fairly black and white guidelines for when the rest of the world gets gray. Allegiance to that document's rules of law—especially when allegiance requires discipline—makes us free. Let us not allow the terrorists to break our discipline.[56]

Not all were hostile to torture. On the CNN news program *Crossfire*, Maurice Sonnenberg, the former vice chairman of the National Committee on

Terrorism, said the United States should not adopt torture as an investigative tool, but the host, Tucker Carlson, quipped, "Torture is bad. Keep in mind, some things are worse. And under certain circumstances, it may be the lesser of two evils. Because some things are pretty evil."[57] And on November 5, 2001, *Newsweek* columnist Jonathan Alter wrote an important article titled "Time to Think About Torture." "In this autumn of anger," he mused, "even a liberal can find his thoughts turning to . . . torture."[58] Nothing as uncivilized as "cattle prods or rubber hoses, at least not here in the United States, but *something* . . . " Pondering the FBI's dilemma, Alter wondered whether suspects could be subjected to "psychological torture, like tapes of dying rabbits or high decibel rap. . . . Or deportation to Saudi Arabia, the land of beheadings."[59] In the end, Alter cast his lot with American exceptionalism. "We can't legalize physical torture; it's contrary to American values." But what *were* those values in his "autumn of anger"? Alter had no answer, apart from the dark hint that "we need to keep an open mind."[60]

Alter's column was the first explicit suggestion in the post-9/11 world that alleged terrorists should be tortured. His proposal was immediately denounced. Alexander Cockburn in the *Nation* and Alisa Solomon in the *Village Voice* both mocked the suggestion that torture was somehow more palatable when it was outsourced.[61] On *The McLaughlin Group,* a weekly televised roundtable of prominent journalists who opine on the issues of the day, the conservative columnist Tony Blankley of the *Washington Times* arched an eyebrow at the idea. "If we were to make the decision that [torture] needed to be done, then we oughtn't to slough it off on anybody else and we ought to do it ourselves."[62] The *New York Times* was characteristically oblique in its criticism. "In many quarters," the *Times* sniffed, " . . . Jonathan Alter is considered a liberal," as if to make plain that no true liberal would have come up with such a proposal. But Alter later noted that he had been approached by "people who might be described as being on the left whispering, 'I agree with you.'" What he failed to grasp is that these people believed they had to whisper precisely because they understood that Alter's sentiment was at odds with American national identity, much as one would have to whisper support for the Klan.[63]

Without question, however, the most important of the elite critiques came from the federal government. Even before the *Post* article appeared, Attorney General John Ashcroft was interviewed on the television news program *Nightline,* where Ted Koppel asked whether the FBI might subject people "to any stressful interrogation."[64] Ashcroft was unequivocal.

> We don't want anyone to be subjected to interrogation that would violate their rights. And I mean by that, we don't want to extort any kind of confession. We don't believe extorted confessions are reliable. We think that when you force someone . . . they're likely to tell you something that's not true. Things that aren't true aren't valuable to us. We don't engage in those kinds of practices. As a matter of fact, if I were to learn that so—those kinds of practice had been undertaken—and I have had no report of that—I would be very distressed, and I would take action. . . . We'll not be driven to abandon our freedoms by those who would seek to destroy them.[65]

After the *Post* article, Ashcroft and the FBI immediately repudiated the unnamed agents who suggested that "pressure tactics" were under consideration.[66] At a moment when the federal government was the most trusted voice in American society, torture was not an option.

III

Alter's suggestion that "American values" allowed the United States to dispatch a presumptively innocent prisoner to another country for torture but prevented it from doing the deed itself was intellectually and morally bankrupt. But three days after Alter's article, a considerably more sophisticated thinker floated a new proposal. On November 8 the *Los Angeles Times* published an opinion piece by the Harvard law professor Alan Dershowitz titled "Is There a Torturous Road to Justice?"[67] It was the first post-9/11 attempt at what many thought could not be done, and what many others believed should not be tried: to reconcile torture with American values.

Unlike Alter, Dershowitz framed his position in the alluring language of the rule of law. Because society is inherently violent and rage a natural reaction, Dershowitz believed we must recognize and accept that torture will inevitably occur, regardless of whether it is right. Rather than leave the practice to the hidden recesses of the interrogation chamber, Dershowitz thought it better to acknowledge it and bring it into the open. He proposed authorizing judges to issue a "torture warrant" in the so-called ticking time bomb scenario. With this, he subtly shifted the argument. His certainty that torture would happen meant the question others refused to ask—does a liberal democracy torture?—was irrelevant. Human nature had already provided the answer. The issue was not so much *accepting* torture as *controlling* it. It was forced on us by our enemy, unbidden, and it is a measure of our commitment to humanity and the rule of law that we struggle to make it less savage. With this sleight of hand, what was yesterday inconceivable to a liberal democracy was today defended as a demonstration of liberal virtue.[68]

Dershowitz may have seemed an unlikely champion of legally regulated torture. He proudly regards himself as a civil libertarian. His personal website lists the many national and international organizations that have honored him as a champion of justice, and scores of media outlets have solicited his views on criminal justice issues of the day. He is also an extraordinarily prolific public intellectual, churning out books, articles, and commentary at an astonishing pace. Yet his status as a liberal icon undoubtedly contributed to the appeal of his proposal. Social scientists have long known that when prominent figures take positions contrary to their expected bias—when a prosecutor supports additional rights for criminal defendants, a prison warden condemns the war on crime, or a senior Republican publicly supports a Democratic candidate—the public attaches particular significance to their views. When Alan Dershowitz said torture could be reconciled with American values, people listened.

Dershowitz vigorously pressed his proposal in interviews, editorials, speeches, and appearances across the country. At an event in St. Louis, he was originally scheduled to promote his book about the contested 2000 presidential election but abruptly changed course. "I'm not in the mood to start being critical of the legitimacy of the president at a time like this," he said.[69] The next day, interviewed by a reporter for the *Los Angeles Times*, he said, "The events of Sept. 11 require us to imagine the unimaginable and think the unthinkable."[70] But, he added, linking his ideas to the potent symbol of constitutionalism, "we also have to use common sense and constitutional values." In January he promoted the idea on *60 Minutes* and the

Today Show, and wrote a piece for the *San Francisco Chronicle* in which he suggested that torture, if allowed by a judge, should involve sterilized needles inserted under a prisoner's fingernails.[71] This got people's attention.

Later in 2002, when a reporter for *Salon* asked whether it would be possible to devise a technique that was perhaps less painful, Dershowitz replied that he didn't want to minimize pain—he wanted "maximal pain, minimal lethality." He said he "didn't want to write about testicles, but that's what a lot of people use."[72] Many of these opinion pieces were reprinted in other papers, which considerably increased their visibility. Writers generally do not draft the headlines that accompany their columns, and the ones given to Dershowitz's proposal were sometimes revealing. The *Los Angeles Times,* for instance, titled his piece "A Torturous Road to Justice," but in Newark, New Jersey, it ran as "Torture in Service of Justice," and in Ontario it was "Can There Be a More Torturous Road to Justice?"[73]

Also in 2002, Dershowitz repeated his proposal in his book *Why Terrorism Works.* His call for torture warrants was by now familiar, and the book added little to his earlier argument. More revealing was his view of terror, especially Islamic terrorism. Terrorism works, he wrote, "because its perpetrators believe that by murdering innocent civilians they will succeed in attracting the attention of the world to their perceived grievances."[74] Since that is what they want, society must not give it to them. "We must commit ourselves *never to try to understand or eliminate its alleged root causes,* but rather to place it beyond the pale of dialogue and negotiation." These are not people with whom you can negotiate, Dershowitz said; instead, "they are like cunning beasts of prey: we cannot reason with them, but we can—if we work at it—outsmart them, set traps for them, cage them, or kill them. The difference is, of course, that they are much smarter than the most cunning of beasts. Indeed, we must operate on the assumption that they are as smart as we are, but more determined, more single-minded, more ruthless, and less constrained by morality, decency, and legality." In a few quick strokes, Dershowitz captured the essence of the mythical sub- and superhuman demon—less than human, but so much more.[75] Yet he underscored that "our" response must respect national identity and the American Creed and be "constrained by morality, decency, and legality."[76]

In certain respects, Dershowitz's proposal has a long pedigree in American law. When American society cannot agree on whether particular behavior should be allowed—and when strong claims can be made on both sides—the law frequently allows the behavior but limits its exercise with complicated regulations. The hope is that these rules will restrict the practice to its least controversial core. Abortion and the death penalty are obvious examples. Broad consensus cannot be reached on when and whether the government should be allowed to execute a prisoner, or when and whether a woman should be allowed to terminate a pregnancy, so the law permits the behavior but limits its use by a combination of substantive rules (for example, no death penalty for juveniles), and procedural hurdles (parental notification statutes). Dershowitz's proposal is in this vein. He would bar torture in all cases but the so-called ticking bomb, and subject the practice to careful regulation. The difference, however, is that until he offered his proposal, no one in American society had suggested that torture be made legal.[77]

As for his claim that torture was inevitable, and therefore a proper subject for regulation, there was a time in American history when one could have made remarkably similar arguments about lynching. When the honor of Southern Womanhood has been brutally defiled, one might have said, who could doubt that a lynching would occur? Who could see lynching as anything other than a natural response to a threat that strikes at the very fabric of society? Yet it is admittedly a savage practice, regrettable in a civilized society. Far better that it be banned in all but those limited circumstances when it is strictly necessary, and then only if a magistrate issues a "lynching warrant." The proponent of this policy could say, quite sincerely, that he was "normatively opposed" to lynching but acutely aware of its likelihood under certain conditions. If today this idea seems inconceivable, it is worth recalling that it was not always so, and that the idea of a "torture warrant" would once have been met with the same incredulous stare. Such is how American identity can change, unless that change is vigorously resisted.[78]

Dershowitz was widely condemned for his views, which were taken as support for torture. The condemnations, universally cast in the language of the Creed, reflected a determination to preserve rather than alter national identity. Writing in the conservative *Washington Times*, for instance,

Jed Babbin, a former deputy undersecretary of defense in the first Bush administration, said, "The war has changed so much in all of us, but it still shocks me to find myself on Alan Dershowitz's left, on any subject."[79] Likening Dershowitz to Torquemada, the infamous torturer of the Spanish Inquisition, Babbin expressed amazement that anyone would propose something as sadistic as needles beneath the nails. "Why stop there? Why not thumbscrews, the lash and the hundred other ways we can inflict pain without killing? One reason, and one reason only. We are Americans, and we will not torture people, even to save lives. This is one of the things that distinguishes us from our enemy."[80]

This was unfair. To call Dershowitz a supporter of torture simply distorts the record. In his innumerable appearances and articles, he always made clear that he considered torture abhorrent and that he was "normatively opposed" to it.[81] His point was that it is inevitable, at least under certain circumstances, and therefore—precisely because it *is* abhorrent—a proper subject for government regulation. He was not even an enthusiastic supporter of his own proposal; in an interview after his book appeared he described himself as "ambivalent" and only "moderately" in favor of it. Mostly, he said, he wanted to start a debate.[82] In that, he was undoubtedly successful.

Other critiques, however, were more thoughtful than Babbin's. Many expressed the fear that torture is a virus, and once introduced into the body of the law it would spread and multiply. Intelligence officers would find new occasions for its use that were close enough to the ticking bomb. As the circle of what is "close enough" grew steadily larger, the practice would become regularized and the exceptional would become routine. In that way, as conservative icon William F. Buckley put it in *National Review,* "torture breaks the spiritual back of the law." Far better, therefore, to insist that it remain illegal and to trust that in genuinely extraordinary circumstances— should they ever arise—the officer who tortured would not be punished.[83] But these criticisms obscure what is for our purposes a more important point about the struggle over national identity. Dershowitz's contribution marked a critical development in the national debate because it purported to reconcile American values with "un-American" behavior. He told us that a liberal democracy *can* torture without losing its soul. The challenge was simply one of implementation and administration. And just as important, the vigorous condemnation elicited by his proposals, even when the need was imagined to be at its greatest, demonstrated the strength of both the pre-9/11 consensus against torture and the broad commitment that 9/11 not be permitted to lead the nation astray.

IV

One part of the early national debate was especially useful to those who resisted the idea of torture as government policy. After 9/11, trusted voices throughout society had rushed to embrace the lofty ideals of a liberal democracy. The war on terror was interpreted as a challenge to the Creed, and the terrorists as the American's doppelgänger. At his first prime-time news conference after the attacks, President Bush asked rhetorically how he responds "when I see that in some Islamic countries there is vitriolic hatred for America? I'll tell you how I respond: I'm amazed. I'm amazed that there's such misunderstanding of what our country is about that people would hate us. I am—like most Americans, I just can't believe it because I know how good we are."[84] The proof that "we" were good and "they" were evil was everywhere, including in the use of torture. Far from attempting to reconcile torture with the Creed, trusted voices were using it to illustrate American superiority to her new enemies.

Stories began to appear describing torture by the Taliban, al Qaeda, and Saddam Hussein. Typical was the profile of Rahima Ghafoori, which appeared in the *Dallas Morning News* and the *Fort Worth Star-Telegram*. Ghafoori was an Afghan widow who had fled the Taliban, immigrated to the United States, and settled in Fort Worth. In her home country she had endured unimaginable misery. Her husband had been killed by the Soviets. Her youngest child had starved to death. Two sons had been killed by rocket attacks during the long civil war that followed the Soviet withdrawal. But it was the Taliban who finally made her flee to America. They "are the cruelest of them all," she said, for their atrocities were committed in the name of Islam. She could not stop thinking about a woman who briefly lifted her burqa as she bought food. "The minute she did, the religious policeman hit her from behind."[85] Life under the Taliban was a constant struggle. For nine months, she and what remained of her family lived next door to a torture chamber. The Taliban pulled up cables that anchored telephone poles into the ground and used them to beat prisoners. "The wailing and crying was so sad—I could not stand it. It came in the middle of the night, and all day long." The Taliban tortured them for information about hidden weapons and scattered enemy forces. "All day and all night, I heard the cries of men being beaten," she said. "I could not stand it so I moved out of there."[86] But life in the United States was different, she said, beaming as she described "the love that Texans have shown." At a refugee camp in Pakistan, "some people bad-mouthed the United States." But when she arrived, she found that "this is a land of laws. You don't need to lie." Ms. Ghafoori's only wish was that she could "bring each of the Taliban here and show them how nice Americans are."[87]

In a story about torture survivors living in the United States, the *Detroit Free Press* profiled Fatima Hassan, an Iraqi refugee in Dearborn, Michigan, who fled Saddam Hussein's regime after "Hussein's police officers" tortured and killed her husband. Many Iraqi refugees, the paper reported, lived in fear "that Hussein's police force is here [in the U.S.]." Refugees "take apart smoke detectors to look for spy cameras and check under tables for wiretaps."[88] Many torture survivors needed daily therapy to deal with the memory of the brutality they endured. Hassan, who has advanced degrees in nursing and English literature, had taken a job as a counselor for other victims. "I want them to go out, go shopping, go study," she said. "They need to see all the beautiful sights in the world."[89]

National Review also turned an early eye to Iraq, "an absolute totalitarian dictatorship completely controlled by one man and his immediate and extended family and a few close associates who use murder, torture, and blackmail to suppress all opposition and disagreement."[90] If, as the author suspected, Iraq was behind the attacks of 9/11, the United States should invade forthwith. He did not foresee a protracted struggle. "Small U.S. forces combined with a popular uprising by the Iraqi people can take Iraq away from Saddam in a matter of days."[91] Meanwhile, Fox News began a series designed to "introduce" the public to "the new America's most wanted," and "expose their faces of hate." Indiscriminately mixing members of al Qaeda and Hezbollah, the Shia militant group in Lebanon, Fox profiled

Imad Fayez Mugniyah, "the ultimate faceless terrorist." American intelligence officials said he was "guilty of several crimes," including "the kidnap, torture, and killing" in Lebanon of a CIA station chief and a U.S. marine in the 1980s.[92]

In October 2001 a federal judge in New York sentenced four al Qaeda operatives to life in prison for their role in the 1998 bombing of the American embassies in Dar es Salaam, Tanzania, and Nairobi, Kenya. The *Christian Science Monitor* called the trial "a triumph for the rule of law" that revealed "the depth, complexity, and international reach of Al Qaeda long before September 11."[93] At trial, prosecutors had introduced an al Qaeda training manual seized during a raid in Manchester, England, which "reads like a 'how to' guidebook for the embassy bombings and the Sept. 11 attacks." Among other things, the manual "gives explicit instructions on how to assassinate adversaries, build bombs, torture prisoners, and escape undetected after an operation."[94] A week later, *Newsweek* described the training manual as a "slick, thoughtful—and a highly unsettling guide to assassination and mass murder." Many of its chapters used "extended citations from the Quran, the Muslim holy book, to justify espionage [as well as] the torture and even killing of hostages."[95]

Such stories were typical exercises in demonization that played a powerful role in shaping the early course of post-9/11 thought. They etched impenetrable boundaries between America and her newest enemies. Americans lived in "a land of laws," where no one had to fear "the religious policeman," or "check under tables for wiretaps." Women enjoyed the same rights as men. Torture was unthinkable, even when used to uncover enemy forces and their hidden weapons. Afghans, by contrast, cowered under the yoke of the Taliban, "the cruelest of them all." Iraqis lived in perpetual fear of torture at the hands of "Hussein's police force," and al Qaeda devoted chapters of its hate-filled training manual to the use of torture.[96]

In the thick of this period, a wide array of pollsters began to pose a question that had never before been asked of the American public: Did they support torture as official government policy? Torture polls have since become a staple of post-9/11 discourse. Some are careful attempts by social scientists to gauge public opinion. Others are thinly disguised attempts by partisan organizations to gin up support for particular policies by creating the appearance of a consensus. These polls must be read with great care. Yet it is worth recalling that before 9/11, the entire enterprise would have been inconceivable.

On October 5 and 6, 2001, Gallup, CNN, and *USA Today* conducted the first post-9/11 poll on torture. If the United States "thought it was necessary to combat terrorism," would respondents be willing for the government to "torture known terrorists if [the terrorists] know details about future terrorist attacks in the U.S.?" In a classic glass-half-full-or-half-empty moment, 45 percent of Americans supported torture under these circumstances, 53 percent opposed it, and 2 percent had no opinion.[97] Under one view, the poll revealed an astonishing degree of support for a policy that only three weeks earlier had been unthinkable. Many commentators read the results that way, and in light of the great emphasis placed on national values, there is much to be said for this reading.[98] Yet given the unprecedented level of fear gripping American society at that moment (the polling started the day after the public announcement that a person had been poisoned by anthrax, and ended immediately after he died) perhaps the more noteworthy fact is that over half the population still opposed torture. To put the point in perspective, most polls consistently show that approximately 70 percent of Americans support capital punishment, regardless of the level of threat present in society. People were substantially more willing to kill a convicted terrorist for one murder he had already committed than to torture him for information the government believed "was necessary" to prevent mass murder in the future.

That fewer than half the respondents supported torture is even more significant given the way the question was worded. Social scientists have long known that polling data are extremely sensitive to variations in wording.[99] Here the wording was critical. Respondents were asked to assume that the person to be tortured was a "known terrorist," that he knew "details about future terrorist attacks in the U.S.," and that the federal government had concluded his torture "was necessary." This phrasing invited people to imagine the worst-case scenario, and it signaled that the most trusted voice in American society at that moment—that of the federal government—had already concluded torture was congenial to American values. Yet support was still below 50 percent. The following month, the *Christian Science Monitor* phrased the question somewhat differently, asking respondents whether they could "envision a scenario in the war against terrorism in which [they] would support . . . [the] torture of suspects held in the U.S. or abroad." While the threat environment was essentially the same, this question did not direct respondents to assume the prisoner was a known terrorist with information about future attacks whose torture had been determined necessary by the government. Support for torture dropped significantly. Only 32 percent favored it, 66 percent opposed it, and 2 percent had no opinion.[100] Then, in March 2002, when the sense of threat had diminished modestly, Fox News asked respondents if they could support torture "to obtain information that would protect the United States from a terrorist attack" and save "innocent lives." Even when it was framed this way, fewer than one in four people supported torture, and nearly two-thirds opposed it.[101]

V

Several things are striking about this first phase of the torture debate. Most obvious is that torture remained one of the important markers that distinguished an honorable America from a savage enemy. As a symbol of savagery, it could not have a legitimate purpose. It was simply wrong, even as an ostensible tool for gathering intelligence. In addition, it could not be parsed. The mere word signaled all that needed to be said. Though everyone understood that tyrannical regimes could devise different techniques, no one speculated whether this technique or that constituted torture. Torture was considered an undifferentiated and unmitigated evil and writers did not pause to ask whether particular techniques rose to the level of torture. Finally, opposition to it was not a partisan affair, at least not at the elite level. The political left and right were equal in their condemnation. If any pattern can be detected, it is that prominent conservatives were more opposed to torture than their liberal counterparts like *Newsweek*'s Alter. Opposition to torture was an American value, not a political position.[102]

Dershowitz's proposal was hardly the last word in the torture debate, and his plan for "torture warrants" went nowhere. But he raised the important question of how society should respond to the ticking bomb and purported to show that the response could include torture and still be compatible with American values. This opened the door for discussion of the many subsidiary issues that eventually became part of the torture debate, including, among others, whether the ticking bomb actually exists, whether torture "works," and whether it produces intelligence that could not have been secured by other means. An article in *Playboy* neatly captured the transition: "The chief problem with the idea of torture is that while it's an efficient way to degrade human beings, silence dissent and create martyrs, it sucks as an investigative tool."[103]

Yet the national conversation still retained an academic, hypothetical quality. In a debate on the *Today* show in January 2002, Nadine Strossen, then the president of the ACLU, chided Dershowitz, her former professor, for doing what law professors do—conjuring wild hypotheticals to stimulate discussion. Dershowitz protested that the ticking bomb could happen, but after Attorney General Ashcroft insisted that the FBI would not torture prisoners, there was a sense that torture could be taken up at a distance, ruminated over in classrooms, batted around on talk shows, and groused about in bars. Jim Murphy, the executive producer of *Evening News with Dan Rather,* said the program would address the topic only if the network were "presented with real evidence that torture is being used or being considered." Until then, he said, "it's like the conversation you or I would have at dinner: 'I wonder if we should torture?'"[104]

Because the debate remained hypothetical, Americans were not called upon to integrate torture into their conception of national identity. If a woman is asked whether she would kill an innocent child if she knew that doing so would cure cancer, she knows the question is purely hypothetical. Though it might make an interesting parlor game, it does not force her to consider what kind of society would be willing to make that choice, or how that society differs from her own. Context matters, and so long as Americans could believe torture was something practiced by other countries, the Creed was not called into question.

The past—or what we contrive it to be—has a comforting way of conforming to our expectations. We imagine it to have unfolded a certain way and thereby to hold familiar lessons. Then, when we attempt to reconstruct it, we discover it fits neatly into the mold we imagined. In that way, history reassures us that it is not so complex or inscrutable. A decade after 9/11, some people are reassured by the belief that society must have embraced torture under the disorienting strain of apocalyptic threat—reflexively, organically, a spontaneous combustion that could not be stopped. Thus reassured, we are apt to forgive ourselves, since no one is to blame.

But this interpretation is not borne out by the record. During the period of greatest perceived danger—at a time when much of America believed itself to be under a more dire threat than at any other time in her existence, and when intelligence alone held out the alluring promise of security restored—Americans *did not* embrace torture. The determination to preserve rather than transform national identity triumphed—at least for a time.

"Can You Think of Anything More Un-American?"

All nationalists have the power of not seeing resemblances between similar sets of facts. . . . Actions are held to be good or bad, not on their own merits, but according to who does them, and there is almost no kind of outrage—torture, the use of hostages, forced labour, mass deportations, imprisonment without trial, forgery, assassination, the bombing of civilians—which does not change its moral colour when it is committed by "our" side. . . . The nationalist not only does not disapprove of atrocities committed by his own side, but he has a remarkable capacity for not even hearing about them.

—*George Orwell, "Notes on Nationalism" (1945)*

I

BY 2003 THE TORTURE DEBATE HAD STALLED. The federal government, at least outwardly, remained opposed to coercive interrogations. Torture continued to be a marker separating "us" from "them," and resistance to it remained a potent symbol of American exceptionalism. On the day after Christmas 2002, the *Washington Post* reported that U.S. interrogators were using "stress and duress" techniques during interrogations overseas and that prisoners who did not respond to questioning could be sent to third countries for further interrogations. But the Bush administration repeated its insistence that it did not condone torture, and the disclosures passed largely unnoticed. At the time, there were other issues associated with the metaphorical war on terror and the impending war in Iraq that demanded attention, and torture fell out of the public debate. After the Fox News poll in March 2002 that showed widespread opposition to torture, national polling organizations all but ignored the issue for two years.[1]

Yet while the debate died down, torture as an idea in popular culture remained very much alive. If anything, it grew more visible: 2002 ushered in an unprecedented era of torture as entertainment. The most commented-upon development was the wildly popular Fox television series *24*, in which agent Jack Bauer of the fictional Counter Terrorist Unit tortured a new prisoner nearly every week, always to brilliant effect. In the course of one season (that is, a single cinematic day), Bauer tortured his brother, shot his boss, and executed a prisoner, all in the name of gathering lifesaving intelligence. Websites called for him to be elected president, *Entertainment Weekly* placed him on their list of the coolest pop heroes of all time, and the show ran for eight years.[2]

A number of observers have asked how and whether *24*, with its relentless normalization of torture, affected American culture.[3] The Heritage Foundation, a conservative think tank, hosted an event entitled "*24* and America's Image in Fighting Terrorism: Fact, Fiction, or Does It Matter?" Rush Limbaugh moderated and Michael Chertoff, the secretary of homeland security, was a panelist.[4] Though the change is surely not attributable to *24* alone, the show certainly marked a turning point in the cultural portrayal of torture. Even in the most punitive moments of the last quarter of the twentieth century, torture was invariably presented in popular culture as a tool used by the demonic "Other" against the (usually) American hero. After 9/11, it became part of the American hero's arsenal. Before, the cultural message was that America would prevail despite torture. Today, the message is just as often that America will prevail *because of* torture.[5]

Early in 2004, however, the sickening pictures from the Abu Ghraib prison transformed the torture debate from idle speculation about "what if" to angry recrimination about "what now." At first, some hoped the scandal would be confined to a single prison and a single military unit. But gruesome details came to light throughout 2004 and 2005 about prisoners who had been humiliated, beaten, and killed by American interrogators and guards all over the world. The United States eventually opened more than two hundred investigations into prisoner abuse.[6] By early 2005, 108 prisoners had died in U.S. custody in Iraq and Afghanistan. Twenty-eight of these cases were investigated by the military as suspected or confirmed homicides.[7]

Some of what came to light during this period was horrific. According to army documents, for instance, two prisoners killed at Bagram Air Base in Afghanistan had been chained to the ceiling and kicked and beaten over several days. A U.S. soldier admitted striking one prisoner thirty-seven times, "destroying his leg muscle tissue with repeated unlawful knee strikes."[8] Three other interrogators participated in the assault on one of the prisoners with "kicks to the groin and leg, shoving or slamming him into walls/table, forcing the detainee to maintain painful, contorted body positions during interviews and forcing water into his mouth until he could not breathe."[9] One of the prisoners had been captured by Afghan militiamen, who stopped him at a checkpoint near Khost. They turned him over to the United States, where he was beaten so severely that, even if he had survived, doctors determined he would have lost both his legs.[10] Yet by the time the interrogators finished, most of them were convinced the detainee was innocent.[11]

To the rest of the world, the prisoner abuse scandal may be the most important symbol to emerge from the war on terror. Iconic images of naked prisoners stacked atop each other like cords of wood, or of a hooded prisoner standing with his arms outstretched with electrical wires clipped to his fingertips, have done more damage to the United States than most Americans will ever understand. Yet paradoxically, despite its domestic importance at the time and its continuing impact abroad, the abuse scandal probably will not have a significant impact on national identity. Because the abuse of prisoners was instantly denounced by elites in the United States, it did not change the "pictures in the mind" about what was and was not consistent with shared national values. No one tried to defend or justify the behavior in the language of the Creed, which meant it could not be interpreted as a legitimate expression of national identity.

To be sure, some in the conservative media tried to minimize the seriousness of the abuse. Rush Limbaugh infamously dismissed the treatment at Abu Ghraib prison as no worse than fraternity antics.[12] But sentiments like these were more than offset by the official position of the Bush administration, which insisted the behavior was not only an inexcusable assault on personal dignity, it was in many cases criminal. "The American people were horrified by the abuse of detainees at Abu Ghraib prison in Iraq," President Bush said in the summer of 2004. "These acts were wrong. They were inconsistent with our policies and our values as a Nation."[13]

Instead of disagreement over the meaning of the scandal, controversy focused on the extent to which responsibility reached back across the oceans to those senior officials within the Bush administration who created the conditions that allowed the brutality to occur. This question has never been resolved and probably never will be, for it requires consensus about whether senior officials should be held responsible for the unintended but readily foreseeable consequences of their policies. But the fact that attention focused on the question of blame confirms that the behavior was considered indefensible. No one suggested, in other words, that this was how things *ought to be*.

II

The same cannot be said, however, about the "black site" and "enhanced" interrogation program, the controversial CIA operation employed from 2002 to 2006. Beginning in April 2002, the CIA began to detain people at secret prisons around the world, called black sites, where they were held incommunicado and subjected to what were euphemistically known as enhanced interrogations. Officially, the operation ended in September 2006, when the Bush administration transferred the prisoners from CIA to military custody and closed the black sites. In contrast to the official stance against prisoner abuse, the Bush administration vigorously defended the black site and enhanced interrogation program as precisely how things ought to be in post–September 11 America. When President Obama scuttled the program in early 2009, conservatives denounced him and intensified their support for the program, using Obama's decision as part of their attack on his presidency. Routinely, they cast their criticism not simply in the pragmatic language of national security but in the far more potent language of national values.

The effect of these efforts has been to legitimize torture in the public square. For the first time in U.S. history, Americans now have ready access to a creedal argument by the federal government in defense of state-sanctioned torture. The result has been sobering. Just as opinions about Islam have grown more negative as we move farther from September 11, opinions about torture have grown more positive. In late 2001 and early 2002, when the perceived threat was at its peak and the demand for immediate intelligence was palpable, only a small fraction of the population supported the idea of torture as government policy. A decade later, the proportion had swelled to more than half the population. Within some segments of society, support for torture is overwhelming. And those who are most apt to endorse torture are the same people who are most apt to demonize Islam: self-identified conservatives and Republicans.

The history of the enhanced interrogation program—so far as it is known—has been told many times and only the barest summary is needed here.[14] In late March 2002 a combined team of FBI, CIA, and Pakistani intelligence agents arrested Abu Zubaydah at a home in Pakistan. The United States then believed Zubaydah was a high-ranking member of al Qaeda, a view it later admitted was mistaken. Initial interrogations by the FBI at a black site in Thailand did not produce the intelligence expected from a person of Zubaydah's supposed importance. The interrogation was transferred from the FBI to psychologists under contract with the CIA, who wanted to subject Zubaydah to enhanced interrogations. CIA agents on site worried that these methods were illegal, so they sought guidance from Washington. In July senior officials at the National Security Council gave conditional authority for the interrogations to proceed.[15] Days later, lawyers with the Office of Legal Counsel in the Department of Justice issued two memos giving more definitive approval. The first memo provided an interpretation of the domestic and international laws against torture, while the second applied this interpretation to the interrogation plan for Zubaydah. The lawyers concluded that all the enhanced techniques proposed by the CIA were legal.

Zubaydah later described a portion of his interrogation:[16]

> About two or three months after I arrived in this place, the interrogation began again, but with more intensity than before. Then the real torturing

started. Two black wooden boxes were brought into the room outside my cell. One was tall, slightly higher than me and narrow. . . . The other was shorter, perhaps only 1 m[eter] in height. I was taken out of my cell and one of the interrogators wrapped a towel around my neck, then they used it to swing me around and smash me repeatedly against the hard walls of the room. I was also repeatedly slapped in the face. . . .

After the beating I was then placed in the small box. They placed a cloth or cover over the box to cut out all light and restrict my air supply. As it was not high enough even to sit upright, I had to crouch down. It was very difficult because of my wounds. . . . It was always cold in the room, but when the cover was placed over the box it made it hot and sweaty inside. The wound on my leg began to open and started to bleed. I don't know how long I remained in the small box. I think I may have slept or maybe fainted.

These were a few hours of an interrogation that lasted for months. The paragraphs are taken from an account given by Zubaydah to the International Red Cross several years after he had been transferred out of CIA custody. As the Red Cross pointed out, his description is remarkably similar to the accounts independently provided by other CIA prisoners, all of whom had been isolated from each other.[17] In this snippet, Zubaydah described several techniques authorized by the Department of Justice and employed by the CIA contractors, including "walling," "cramped confinement," "stress position," "facial slap," and "environmental manipulation." He was also subjected to "wall standing," which involved suspending prisoners from hooks in the ceiling for hours at a time, and "sleep deprivation," which meant keeping prisoners awake for eleven consecutive days (later reduced to seven) by, among other things, dousing them with cold water.[18] The interrogation technique that would attract the most attention, however, was waterboarding, which Zubaydah also described:

I was then dragged from the small box . . . and put on what looked like a hospital bed, and strapped down very tightly with belts. A black cloth was then placed over my face and the interrogators . . . pour[ed] water on the cloth so that I could not breathe. After a few minutes the cloth was removed and the bed was rotated into an upright position. . . . I vomited. The bed was then again lowered to a horizontal position and the same torture carried out again with the black cloth over my face and water poured . . . from a bottle. On this occasion my head was in a more backward, downwards position and the water was poured on for a longer time. I struggled against the straps,

trying to breathe but it was hopeless. I thought I was going to die. I lost
control of my urine. Since that time I still lose control of my urine when
under stress.[19]

The United States claims Zubaydah was the only prisoner who was subjected to all of the enhanced techniques. In August 2002 he was water-
boarded eighty-three times. (Full disclosure: Zubaydah is my client. His
account to the Red Cross predates my involvement as his lawyer.)

The enhanced interrogation program came to light in 2004 after someone
leaked one of the Office of Legal Counsel memos to the *Washington Post*.
Promptly dubbed "the torture memo," this document concluded that interrogations were legal unless they inflicted "excruciating and agonizing"
pain, "equivalent in intensity to the pain accompanying serious physical
injury, such as organ failure, impairment of bodily function, or even death."
Mere mental suffering does not amount to torture unless it produces "significant psychological harm of significant duration, *e.g.*, lasting for months
or even years."[20] And even if an interrogator committed an act constitut-
ing torture, he would still be immune from prosecution if he acted at the
direction of the president, who had the unilateral and inherent authority
to order any interrogation technique that he believed was necessary. Upon
its release, the torture memo was widely denounced. Harold Koh, then the
dean of the Yale Law School and later a senior official in the Obama State
Department, called it "perhaps the most clearly erroneous legal opinion I
have ever read."[21] His view was widely shared. In December 2004 the Bush
administration adopted a new legal standard. The Department of Justice
was careful to say, however, that the new memo would not force a change
in practice because none of the enhanced techniques employed by the CIA
ran afoul of either the original or the new standard.[22]

Congress began to respond to this controversy in 2005, when Senator
John McCain (R-AZ), a former prisoner of war who had been tortured in
Vietnam, introduced legislation that would confine military interrogators
to noncoercive techniques and rein in the CIA.[23] Summoning the lesson
of American exceptionalism, Senator McCain said that it was irrelevant
whether al Qaeda or rogue states might abuse or torture their prisoners;

"what differentiates us, the United States of America, from other countries is the fact that we do not."[24] The White House sent a bluntly worded warning to Capitol Hill that the president would veto any bill that included McCain's amendments and dispatched Vice President Cheney to urge him to abandon his position.[25] When these clumsy attempts failed, Senate Majority Leader Bill Frist (R-TN), acting on instructions from the White House, tried to cut off further debate. When that also failed, he scuttled further consideration of the bill until after Congress's summer recess.[26]

In October 2005 McCain reintroduced his proposed amendments and the White House renewed its veto threat. Editorial pages from every corner of the country came out in support of the Arizona senator, all of them rich in the language and symbols of the Creed.[27] "For anyone who reveres the Founding Fathers or gets misty-eyed during the show that opens a visit to the National Constitution Center," the *Philadelphia Inquirer* said, support for the McCain amendments "should be a slam dunk. How could America not adhere to its ideals, no matter the threat posed by terrorism, and still be a beacon of democracy?"[28] "As Americans," the *Modesto Bee* added, "we don't want people tortured in our name. It runs against our grain; it's written into our Bill of Rights. It's what makes us different. That's why it is so very difficult to understand the president's objection to [McCain's] bill."[29] "The American people," said the *Dallas Morning News,* "want their warriors, including those in the clandestine services, to wage the war on Islamist terrorism as fiercely and as effectively as they can. But in so doing, we can never lose the honor, decency and basic humanity that separate us from the cutthroats we fight."[30] "This should be simple," concluded the *Des Moines Register.*[31]

The McCain amendments passed the Senate by a vote of 90–9.[32] The president renewed his threat to use the first veto of his administration to scuttle the legislation. The White House complained that the language endorsed by this overwhelming majority of the Senate, including forty-six Republicans, would "restrict the President's authority." The *New York Times* observed dryly, "Yes, exactly."[33] In December the president relented and signed the McCain amendments into law. Yet this was not the end of the matter. In a signing statement, President Bush reserved the right to construe the McCain amendments "in a manner consistent with the constitutional authority of the President . . . as Commander in Chief and consistent with the constitutional limitations on the judicial power."[34] According to a senior administration official, the signing statement signaled the administration's intention to use "harsher methods" as it saw fit, notwithstanding the language of the statute.[35] As important, the Department of Justice had already drafted secret memos concluding that the enhanced techniques did not violate the McCain amendments.[36] So far as the Bush administration was concerned, the new law changed nothing.

These machinations took their toll on the president's popularity. In the first five months of 2004, support for the Bush administration's war on terror fell from 70 percent to 50 percent, and in November 2005, during the fight over the McCain amendments, it fell below 50 percent for the first time. When the amendments were so much in the news and had received such enthusiastic and bipartisan backing by politicians and opinion makers, support for torture fell to post-9/11 lows. In late 2005 respondents agreed almost four to one that U.S. troops or government officials had tortured prisoners in Iraq and elsewhere, and 64 percent said that the use of torture against people suspected of involvement in terrorism was "unacceptable."[37]

III

There matters stood until September 2006, when President Bush, in a nationally televised speech, acknowledged the black site and enhanced interrogation program for the first time. Three months earlier, the Supreme Court had struck down the administration's military commission system for trying detainees at Guantánamo Bay because it had not been authorized by Congress. In his speech, the president announced that the CIA prisoners had been transferred to Guantánamo and pressed Congress to pass legislation that would authorize a new military commission system so these prisoners could be prosecuted. He began his remarks by reminding the nation of the day we "awoke to a nightmare attack" that forced us into "an unprecedented war against an enemy unlike any we had fought before."[38] In this new war, he said, nothing is more important than intelligence, and "the most important source of information on where the terrorists are hiding and what they are planning is the terrorists, themselves." This intelligence "cannot be found any other place. And our security depends on getting this kind of information."[39] To meet this challenge, he said, the CIA had developed the black site program, where prisoners could be detained and interrogated in secret facilities around the world.

The president then turned to the enhanced interrogation techniques. "These procedures," he insisted, "were designed to be safe, to comply with our laws, our Constitution, and our treaty obligations." Referring to the controversial torture memo, he said the Department of Justice had "reviewed the authorized methods extensively and determined them to be lawful." The president could not describe the methods publicly but insisted they "were tough, and they were safe, and lawful, and necessary."[40] In fact, he said, "Were it not for this program, our intelligence community believes that al Qaeda and its allies would have succeeded in launching another attack against the American homeland. By giving us information about terrorist plans we could not get anywhere else, this program has saved innocent lives." Yet he added: "I want to be absolutely clear with our people and the world. The United States does not torture. It's against our laws, and it's against our values. I have not authorized it, and I will not authorize it."[41]

At the same time, the Office of the Director of National Intelligence released an extended defense of the enhanced interrogation program. Like Bush's speech, the DNI report began with the reminder that September 11 had ushered in "a struggle against an elusive enemy," who works "in the shadows, relying on secrecy and the element of surprise to maximize" the devastation of its attacks. To meet the demands of the day, the CIA had designed a new interrogation program that was "safe, effective, and legal."[42] The Agency had obtained guidance from the Department of Justice that none of its new procedures violated the laws prohibiting torture—another reference to the torture memo. In addition, the Agency had developed "safeguards" that its agents would follow in every interrogation. Each enhanced technique had to be approved in advance, with no deviations permitted. All interrogations would be monitored by observers, who could end an interrogation if they believed anything unauthorized was taking place. The DNI said the entire program was meant "to ensure that intelligence is collected in a manner that does not violate the US Constitution, any US statute, or US treaty obligations."[43]

Thus by late 2006 the Bush administration had traveled full circle.

Shortly after September 11, no one in the federal government openly favored torture, and Attorney General Ashcroft had publicly denounced coercive interrogations, warning that any FBI agent who employed them would be disciplined. In 2002 the administration secretly drafted memos allowing it to subject prisoners to enhanced interrogations. In 2004, in the midst of the prisoner abuse scandal, the most controversial of these memos came to light. In the harsh criticism that followed the memo's release, the administration adopted a new standard but insisted it would not change CIA practices. Throughout 2005, the administration fought aggressively to prevent Congress from reining in the CIA. And when that failed, the president quietly issued a signing statement that reserved the right to ignore the law.

Then, under pressure in 2006, the administration acknowledged the black site and enhanced interrogation program. Indeed, it went farther, arguing strenuously that enhanced interrogations had prevented an al Qaeda attack inside the United States. Yet it insisted that the program was not remotely the same as torture and was in all respects compatible with American values. In the continuing struggle to construct national identity, the importance of this public embrace cannot be overstated: The administration's determination to defend publicly rather than deny disingenuously marked a critical turning point in the debate. It began the process of integrating torture into national identity, a process that continues to this day.

The Bush administration's decision to defend the enhanced interrogations immediately elevated their status in the public square. More important, it was the first extended attempt by the federal government to integrate torture into national identity by making it appear congenial to shared values. Yet the rapidly declining fortunes of the Bush administration after 2006, combined with the fact that the Republican standard bearer in the 2008 election was John McCain, made it difficult for this defense to gain traction. McCain had spearheaded the drive to restrain interrogators, and the law he championed was universally known by his name. The Democratic candidate, Barack Obama, also opposed the enhanced techniques. This meant that throughout the campaign, the "pictures in the mind, placed there by television news, newspapers, magazines, and discussions" almost uniformly opposed the CIA special interrogation program. It is hardly surprising that the techniques remained unpopular for the duration of the Bush presidency.

IV

On January 22, 2009, President Obama issued an executive order that ended the enhanced interrogation program and ordered CIA operatives to forgo coercive interrogations. Polls showed substantial support for his move. An ABC/Washington Post poll in January 2009 showed that 58 percent of respondents supported a ban on torture "no matter what the circumstances." A Gallup/USA Today poll taken in January and February found that nearly three in four respondents favored a ban on coercive interrogations. Even when the question was framed to maximize support for torture—as in a January Fox News poll that asked whether, "in extreme circumstances," the CIA should be allowed to use "enhanced interrogation techniques, or even torture, to obtain information from prisoners that might protect the United States from terrorist attacks"—more people opposed it than supported it. (From this experience, Fox quickly learned not to use the word "torture" in its polling. In April 2009 it conducted another poll that asked whether the CIA should be allowed to use "harsh interrogation techniques . . . to obtain information from prisoners that might protect the United States from terrorist attacks." When the question was framed that way, 52 percent of respondents thought the interrogations should be allowed.)[44]

But the decision to end the enhanced interrogation program summoned the right wing to action. The issue could now be reframed from whether the Bush administration was correct to start the program to whether the Obama administration was correct to end it. Among the earliest and most vocal critics was former Vice President Cheney, who denounced Obama's decision as "recklessness cloaked in righteousness." In a 2009 speech to the American Enterprise Institute, Cheney said that he remained "a strong proponent of our enhanced interrogation program." These techniques, he said, "were used on hardened terrorists" and only "after other efforts failed. They were legal, essential, justified, successful, and the right thing to do. The intelligence officers who questioned the terrorists can be proud of their work and proud of the results, because they prevented the violent death of thousands, if not hundreds of thousands, of innocent people. . . . And to call this a program of torture is to libel the dedicated professionals who have saved American lives, and to cast terrorists and murderers as innocent victims."[45]

The most comprehensive attack on Obama's decision, however, came from Marc Thiessen, who had written President Bush's 2006 speech defending the CIA program. In 2010 Thiessen published a three hundred–page broadside, the gist of which is captured in the title: *Courting Disaster: How the CIA Kept America Safe and How Barack Obama Is Inviting the Next Attack.*[46] "In shutting down the CIA program," Thiessen wrote, "Obama eliminated our nation's most important tool to prevent the terrorists from striking America." He called the decision among "the most dangerous and irresponsible acts an American president has ever committed in a time of war." According to Thiessen, whose expertise is as a speechwriter and journalist, "Barack Obama arguably did more damage to America's national security . . . than any president in American history."[47]

Still, while the partisan attack on President Obama was undoubtedly an important part of the attempt to transform national identity, it alone would not have been sufficient to change the meaning and content of national values. A national policy is not likely to carry the day if the only argument to commend it is that the other guy wants something different. It was therefore essential to cast the support for torture in the elastic language of the American Creed, and the alternative as a threat to the Creed. Indeed, it is probably fair to say that a national policy that cannot be framed in terms of the Creed will never secure widespread support.[48] To that end, partisans have developed elaborate arguments that purport to show how torture, as practiced by the United States, is perfectly compatible with "what the United States is all about at our core."

V

Two arguments in defense of torture have come to dominate the field. They differ only at the first step, and both invariably end up at the same place: as ringing tributes to the shared values of national identity. The first and more intellectually honest argument accepts that some prisoners in U.S. custody were tortured. Rather than try to suggest that suspending a prisoner naked for hours at a time from hooks in the ceiling while periodically dousing him with cold water is somehow humane, the people in this camp accept that what the United States did was torture. In their most candid moments, they even express deep qualms about the use of these techniques, in terms whose sincerity we have no reason to doubt. It was, they maintain, a necessary evil—no less evil because it was necessary, but no less necessary because it was evil.[49] But the great majority of people who support the Bush administration's program cannot take this first step. Because they cannot accept that the United States would torture anyone, they insist that "enhanced interrogations" were not torture.

Apart from this opening difference, the two arguments proceed on the same course to conclude that torture as practiced by the United States is fully consistent with the best of American values. Invariably, the defense begins where it has begun ever since Alan Dershowitz proposed torture warrants in 2001, with the ticking time bomb. One is directed to assume that an interrogation is under way and that thousands of lives, "if not hundreds of thousands," as Richard Cheney said, hang in the balance. The prisoner, whose guilt is certain, knows how to defuse the threat but refuses to speak. Time is impossibly short. What was a reasonable person to do? The conservative economist Thomas Sowell, writing in the magazine *Human Events*, put it this way: "If a captured terrorist knows where a nuclear bomb has been planted in some American city, and when it is timed to go off, are millions of Americans to be allowed to be incinerated because we have become too squeamish to get that information out of him by whatever means are necessary? What a price to pay for moral exhibitionism or political grandstanding!"[50] In some versions, the answer was made even more irresistible: One was directed to assume that torture alone will secure the information. Enhanced interrogations, Cheney reminded us, were used only after other efforts had failed. The purpose of creating this scenario, of course, was to build a rhetorical prison from which there could be no escape. The terms were meant to permit only one responsible answer. Any other response would seem impossibly naïve and therefore morally illegitimate.

Once confined to this rhetorical box, many listeners understandably agreed that, so long as the terms of the hypothetical remained fixed, torture indeed seemed the only available recourse. At this, the triumphant interlocutor would adopt the position attributed to George Bernard Shaw: Now we are just haggling about the price. Having established that torture *could be* justified in some cases, it remained only to establish what those cases were. This is where the ideals of national identity came in. Advocates of torture insist that the United States, as a mark of its values, had restricted the use of torture in ways that continue to demonstrate American exceptionalism. First, unlike torture as "they" practiced it, the United States tortured only when absolutely necessary. Our motives were as pure as the nation itself. Unlike the barbarians we faced, we tortured only to gather lifesaving intelligence, and not simply to gratify our sadistic nature. While "they" tortured for any reason or no reason—simply because they were savages—"we" tortured only because "they" had forced us into an impossible dilemma: Either torture or allow innocent men, women, and children to be slaughtered. In short, we tortured *because* we were civilized; they because they were not. We were motivated and constrained by our values, which continued to distinguish "us" from "them."

We see this thinking in the remarks of former CIA agent and frequent Fox News guest Wayne Simmons. Recall that shortly after September 11, Fox News had invited Eric Haney to its programs. Haney, the retired founder of the elite army special operations unit, Delta Force, had emphatically rejected all "strong arm tactics" and cautioned that some prisoners just don't respond to interrogation.[51] But after the Bush administration had embraced "strong arm tactics," Haney made no additional appearances on Fox. Instead, Fox came to rely on the much more colorful Simmons, who was asked in one interview whether torture should ever be used by American personnel to get information. "What I can tell you," he answered, "is we're not going to slice someone's arm open and dump salt in the wound. That's preposterous, we don't do that."[52] On the other hand, "am I going to make someone very, very uncomfortable? I'm absolutely going to do that, especially if I know that the intel is time-sensitive. That's what it comes down to. If . . . I know that somebody's planted some bombs in Manhattan and we have 24 hours to find them, you can bet that 99.99 percent of Americans would tell me to do whatever I had to find those bombs."[53]

When asked whether making someone "very, very uncomfortable" might constitute torture, Simmons was more explicit. "Listen," he said, "waterboarding is acceptable; hooding is acceptable; putting people in freezers, quite frankly, until they're very uncomfortable is acceptable. What I consider torture . . . is if we're lopping off heads, if we're cutting off digits, if we're using hammers on fingers like the enemy does to our people, but no one seems to care about that."[54] Asked if he could think of anything more un-American than torture, Simmons quickly agreed that it "is reprehensible in any manner, way, shape, or form." But using "interrogation tactics" like those applied by the United States in order to get information to protect against another attack was quite different.[55]

In addition, because of both the nature of the war on terror and the nature of terrorists, any sovereign would be justified in doing much more than the United States had done. "Let's put it right on the table," Simmons once said. "These are sub-humans. These are very, very smart sub-humans. Their sole goal in life is to kill us, to kill the West, to kill your children, to take us down."[56] "And I might add, once these barbarians against humanity have decided to become terrorists, their lives as they know it is over. All bets are off against these guys."[57] "I lived with these animals," he said on another occasion. "This is a sub-human species of somehow a deviation of the human, of the true human. They care for nothing. They kill everything in their path. . . . I lived with them. I ate with them. I slept with them. I drank with them. I have watched them slice the throats of human beings two feet from me, pull their eyes out, cut their fingers out."[58] Simmons's view, though perhaps more dramatically put, is typical among those who defend torture. As the conservative commentator Charles Krauthammer put it, "Anyone who blows up a car bomb in a market deserves to spend the rest of his life roasting on a spit over an open fire. But we don't do that because we do not descend to the level of our enemy. We don't do that because, unlike him, we are civilized. Even though terrorists are entitled to no humane treatment, we give it to them because it is in our nature as a moral and humane people."[59]

Even though the United States was morally authorized to do much more than it had done, it acted with deliberate and appropriate restraint, or so the argument goes. Unlike "their" torture, which was meant only to prolong a prisoner's agony before he was killed in some gruesome fashion, every technique employed by the United States had been carefully and exhaustively vetted. Because we are dedicated to the rule of law, every method, whether applied in isolation or in combination, had been carefully studied by a small army of elite lawyers to ensure compliance with both domestic and international law. Because we are humane, every interrogation was supervised and monitored by psychologists and medical personnel to ensure that the prisoner was in no real danger. And because we are committed to the dignity of the individual, no interrogation went farther than was absolutely necessary. There would be no greater assault on human dignity than circumstances required.

This defense often entailed a gross distortion of the "enhanced" techniques. "My definition of torture is simple," declared a writer in *Human Events*. "It involves physical or mental abuse that leaves lasting scars. Cutting off fingers, toes, limbs—that would be torture. Forcing prisoners to play Russian roulette—that would be torture. Sticking hot pokers in the eyes of prisoners—that would be torture. But a few seconds of dripping water on a prisoner's face? That's not torture to me."[60] On *60 Minutes*, Jose Rodriguez, the former head of the CIA Clandestine Services and the agent in charge of the black site and enhanced interrogation program, said the CIA merely made some prisoners "uncomfortable for a few days."[61]

And when the interrogators were done, the prisoners were given the best American care—far beyond what they deserved and far better than they received in their home countries. Speaking on the Senate floor in February 2009, Senator James Inhofe (R-OK) expressed a common sentiment on the right when he said of the prison at Guantánamo, "I can say without any doubt in my mind that I have never seen a prison where people are cared for better than they are there. There is one medical practitioner for every two detainees who are down there. The medical facilities even do colonoscopies for anyone over 50, if they want them. None of these detainees would ever have treatment like that back in their country of origin. The food they are getting is better than they have ever had before. So it is not true they are being abused."[62] In any other country, the argument goes, their fate would be far worse. As Fox News's Bill O'Reilly put it, "every nation in the world does 30 times worse than we do."[63]

Finally, because we are a nation of laws, if an interrogator ever broke the rules—and supporters of torture admit that such things happened occasionally—there were consequences. "Isolated individuals here and there may abuse their authority and violate existing laws and policies by their treatment of prisoners," Sowell wrote in *Human Events*, "but the point is that these are in fact violations."[64] In other countries, torture was an entirely lawless affair. Torturers were encouraged to be ingenious in their cruelty, the better to instill terror. In the United States, by contrast, transgressors were subjected to national scorn and referred for investigation by their own colleagues. "Stupid things," Jose Rodriguez said, "were done by people who had no authority. . . . And we found out about it and we self-reported."[65] Inquiries exposed wrongdoing at the microscopic level. Charges were leveled and juries empaneled, convictions returned and sentences imposed. If convictions could not be obtained, discipline was meted out, careers were ended. The rule of law prevailed.

At this point in the defense, the infamous torture memo assumes particular importance. In a country that routinely confuses "legal" with "morally legitimate," the torture memo provides an important source of public legitimacy. Its turgid, heavily footnoted prose is precisely the sort of almost impenetrable gibberish that many associate with erudition. The memo *looks like* impressive legal reasoning, just as a blackboard covered with equations and esoteric symbols *looks like* higher mathematical reasoning, even though to a trained eye it may be nonsense. The great majority of people will never read the memo itself, any more than they would read the empirical evidence on the economic effect of deficit spending. Instead, they will rely on the judgment of others whom they trust, who use the memo to support one view or another. "I have read the memo about waterboarding," Karl Rove told Sean Hannity on Fox News, "and [determined that the enhanced techniques] are not torture. And so did a lot of lawyers who have great expertise in these issues, and the Justice Department and the Defense Department and the State Department."[66] It is not particularly important whether the memo is "right" or "wrong" as a matter of law, or whether it represents good or bad legal reasoning. Its contribution to the debate is symbolic: For a great many people, it symbolizes fidelity to the rule of law.

This contribution should not be underestimated. It permits those who support torture to deploy national values against claims of the sort lodged by the National Religious Campaign Against Torture. "Torture is a moral issue," the campaign declares. "Torture violates the basic dignity of the human person that all religions, in their highest ideals, hold dear [and] contradicts our nation's most cherished ideals. . . . Nothing less is at stake in the torture abuse crisis than the soul of our nation. What does it signify if torture is condemned in word but allowed in deed?"[67] But thanks to the torture memo, supporters of the enhanced interrogations say that they too condemn torture and heartily agree that it "contradicts our nation's most cherished ideals." If the Department of Justice Office of Legal Counsel had concluded from the outset that the program were illegal, the Bush administration probably would not have gone forward. But because the Justice Department concluded that the program was lawful in every respect, its supporters could plausibly argue that it was harmonious with one of the most potent American values. And when the torture memo is combined with all the other restraints built into the process, many people have no difficulty at all reconciling torture to the demands of the American Creed.

The defense of the enhanced interrogation program trades in the most transparent euphemism. Yet it is precisely this euphemism—the idea that what something *is* depends on what we call it—that permits torture advocates to maintain a distance between "us" and "them," and thereby reaffirm that the war on terror continues to celebrate what makes America special.[68] *They* torture; *we* apply "enhanced interrogation." The difference between the two has become something more than mere words. Embedded within this distinction is an entire story that a great many people have come to believe in an effort to make wretched behavior congenial to national values. *They* inflict gratuitous pain because they are savages; *we* seek lifesaving information to protect the innocent. *They* show no restraint or respect; *we* remain within the law and make every effort to preserve even a terrorist's dignity. When they tire of their torture, they murder their prisoners with ruthless cruelty; our "enhanced interrogations" last only as long as they must, and afterward we treat our prisoners to a far better life than they would enjoy in their own land. For those who support "enhanced interrogations," *their* torture conjures up mental pictures that can never be confused or conflated with *our* torture. An entire world can be made to fit within the imaginary space that lies between "us" and "them." Within that space is where national identity is made.

VI

This attempt to remake national identity in order to rationalize torture has been remarkably successful. To begin with, it has dramatically transformed the language. A research team at Harvard uncovered striking differences in how waterboarding (and similar techniques that simulate drowning) had been described by the press in the years before and after September 11. For roughly seventy years before 9/11, major papers in the United States almost invariably said or implied that these methods were torture.[69] After September 11, and particularly after 2004, when the Bush administration's use of the technique became known, the language changed dramatically. In nearly three hundred articles published between 2002 and 2008, the *New York Times*, the *Los Angeles Times*, the *Wall Street Journal*, and *USA Today* said or implied that waterboarding was torture only four times. Rather than call it torture, as they had for so many years, the papers adopted a variety of euphemisms, including "harsh," "controversial," "aggressive," and "co-ercive." Yet the same papers, before and after September 11, consistently described waterboarding as torture *when it was practiced by other countries.*[70]

As the language of torture has changed, so too has the range of socially acceptable opinion, which has always been a reliable way to map the outer limits of national identity. In 1997, the CIA declassified the infamous *Kubark Counterintelligence Interrogation Manual*, a Cold War–era training guide that has been called the "bible of interrogation."[71] The enhanced interrogations used after September 11 ultimately trace their lineage to the techniques described in the *Kubark Manual*, which distilled years of postwar, government-funded research regarding the psychology of human coercion into lessons for Agency interrogators.[72] The CIA released the manual, as well as a successor written for its operatives in Latin America, in response to a Freedom of Information Act request filed by journalists with the *Baltimore Sun*.[73]

Upon their release, the manuals were met with universal condemnation, invariably expressed in the language of the Creed. The *Houston Chronicle,* struggling for an explanation, concluded that the CIA "could spread such insane doctrine only if its leaders and agents had completely forgotten the traditional American values they were sworn to uphold and protect— freedom, democracy, justice, human rights and other stuff like that. Americans can only hope that the foggy Cold War atmosphere inside the CIA has dissipated enough for the intelligence agency to behave in a more civilized and humane manner."[74] "It is appalling," the *Pittsburgh Post-Gazette* said, "that such a manual was produced by a democratic nation with a fierce devotion to civil rights and liberties. It goes beyond irony to perversity that it was done in the name of freedom. God only knows how many people—real and imagined Communists—paid in blood."[75] The *St. Louis Post-Dispatch* lamented that the manuals represented "another sad chapter in the CIA's checkered history."[76] Nor did the CIA defend its former practices. "Physical abuse or other degrading treatment" had been rejected by the Agency "not only because it is wrong, but because it has historically proven to be ineffective."[77] A Pentagon spokesman said, in the passive voice familiar to bureaucracies everywhere, that "many mistakes were made," but he insisted that "nobody in the department now endorses" the old methods.[78]

Today, torture is no longer outside the range of acceptable opinion. Less than a year after President Obama ended the CIA program, in a special election to fill the Senate seat made available by the death of Massachusetts Senator Ted Kennedy, Scott Brown, the eventual winner, vigorously defended the enhanced techniques. "If there is a time bomb situation and they know of a person who in fact has information, it should be up to the president to determine what tools he wants to use to gather information," including waterboarding. Brown insisted that the enhanced techniques should not be confused with torture. "I'm a military attorney," he said, "so I understand the law on this very important issue. I believe it's not torture."[79]

Indeed, for some audiences, a *failure* to support the enhanced techniques comes close to apostasy. During the 2012 primary campaign, nearly every Republican candidate endorsed these techniques, including waterboarding: Mitt Romney ("I do not support torture, but I do support enhanced interrogation techniques to learn from terrorists what we need to learn to keep the bombs from going off"); Michele Bachmann ("If I were president, I

would be willing to use waterboarding. I think it was very effective");
Herman Cain ("I don't see it as torture. I see it as an enhanced interrogation
technique"); Rick Perry ("I am for using the techniques, not torture, but
using those techniques that we know will extract the information to save
young American lives. And I will be for it until I die"); Rick Santorum
("Some of this information that . . . led to Osama bin Laden actually came
from these enhanced interrogation techniques").[80]

Nor should any Republican candidate fear that support for torture will
cost him votes among the rank and file. The most recent poll on this matter, taken in August 2011 by the Pew Research Center for People and the
Press, shows that more than seven in ten Republicans think torture is often
or sometimes justified "in order to gain important information"; only 13
percent take the position that torture is never acceptable. The numbers for
self-identified conservatives are similar. Moreover, support for torture is
not confined to Republicans and conservatives. The same poll found that
more than half the independents and nearly half the Democrats believe
torture is often or sometimes justified, while less than a third considered
it completely off limits.[81] Compared with the results of an identical poll in
2004, support for torture has increased dramatically, and across the board.
Though Republicans and conservatives are the most enthusiastic supporters, they are by no means alone.[82]

Put another way, many more people now are willing to accept torture
than to attack Islam. Both narratives marshal the rhetoric of the American
Creed, yet the anti-Islamic narrative is consigned to a small corner of the
public square. The explanation for this difference lies in the relationship
between the two narratives and the dominant trends in national identity.
Whereas the attack on Islam runs counter to these trends by embracing a
narrow and brittle conception of religious liberty, the support for torture
has aligned itself with both the punitive turn in American life and the prevailing understanding of race and religion.

Rather than taking aim at an entire community, the torture narrative
targets only the demonized "Other," and only for his threatening behavior; society is supposedly indifferent to his race and religion. It is purely
coincidental that the people tortured have all been Muslims. If a person
becomes a target for torture, the argument goes, it is only because of what

he *did* (or threatens to do) and not because of his skin color or beliefs. The same explanation is routinely given to account for the overrepresentation of African-Americans in the criminal justice system: Society is blameless, and the fact that blacks fill American prisons has nothing to do with their race and everything to do with their behavior. It tells us something about them, not about us. Finally, the torture narrative deploys the rule of law in its modern sense, as a weapon of the state that protects *us* from *them*, rather than a restraint *on* the state that guarantees individual liberty. Viewed in its entirety, the torture narrative succeeds for the same reason the anti-Islamic narrative struggles.

Still, this alignment with the prevailing understanding of national values is incomplete. We are, after all, talking about torture. Regardless of whether the narrative attaches itself opportunistically to certain aspects of American life whose standing has risen in the postwar decades, we are still left with the objection that torture involves the violent and often grotesque coercion of presumptively innocent human beings, which mocks whatever attachment we profess to human dignity and the sanctity of life. Torture is barbaric, and no amount of name-changing and pin-dancing can make it otherwise. This objection will limit the appeal of the torture narrative. The only question is how much.

The defense of torture that now echoes through the public square was unheard of fifteen years ago. But this alone does not render it illegitimate. The millions who accept this defense do not think they have abandoned American values. In fact they are quite confident they have not, just as those who defended Jim Crow were confident that their positions represented the very best of American ideals. And our certainty in this regard is in no way diminished by the knowledge that the facts brought forward in defense of torture have never been entirely true and are often demonstrably false. Defenders of torture have yet to show either its necessity or utility. There is no evidence that information obtained by torture could not have been obtained by lawful, noncoercive means, and a great deal of evidence to the contrary.[83]

There is also no evidence that American interrogators ever confronted, let alone confined themselves to, the so-called ticking time bomb scenario. Torture was never as limited as its defenders suggest; the legal vetting was never as evenhanded; the medical supervision never as scrupulous; the political oversight never as rigorous. Far more people were harmed than should have been; fewer misdeeds were condemned than might have been. But when all is said and done, the defense of torture is like many American myths—not entirely true, often false, but not entirely a lie, and in that way able to provide people with much needed comfort in an uncertain world. It is a new myth, born of the post-9/11 era: the myth of how America can torture without betraying its values. Many today accept the myth while some do not. And if it is allowed to become conventional wisdom—if it becomes simply another tale we tell our children and ourselves about what it means to be an American—we will have made torture a cherished part of our national identity.

11

"Must We Sell Our Birthright?"

THE WELCOME INSISTENCE BY President Bush that Muslims and Arab-Americans were "us" was only half of his administration's response to September 11. The second half, of course, was the complementary insistence that Islamist terrorists were "them," the newest and most dangerous threat to confront the United States. The country was united in its resolution to rid itself of this new menace, but to do so in a way that preserved rather than transformed national identity. In this case, the national attachment was not to equality, religious liberty, and an expansive concept of community membership (the values most implicated in the initial response to Islam), or to individual dignity (the value at stake in the first phase of the torture debate), but to limited government and the rule of law—at least, as those values had come to be defined and understood by the end of the twentieth century. The failure by the Bush administration to recognize this attachment would prove the president's undoing.

To put it simply, the Bush administration ignored the rituals and symbolic limits of the punitive turn. As I have stressed, the punitive turn is not just about punishment. It has also imparted a characteristic way to understand and respond to perceived threats. In this response, the nation reaffirms its values by *collectively* naming and describing a new demon and acting jointly to charge the government with purging the demon from society. The entire process is a shared national exercise in symbolic reassurance, a communal project meant to acknowledge the common verities of national identity as they are pressed into service to preserve and protect a portion of the community. The punitive turn, in other words, is not simply an exercise in harshness and retribution but a celebration of shared values.

And that is where the administration went awry. The most prominent objection to the Bush administration's prosecution of the war on terror was not as much to the policies themselves as to the way those policies were pursued and implemented. Certainly many took issue with what the administration did in its approach to counterterror policy. But at least outside the torture debate, the objection that gained the most traction and had the most symbolic appeal was that the administration was arrogating to itself powers that it could not legitimately claim. The administration thus betrayed the idea that the punitive turn had become a communal affair. Society as a whole—the executive, Congress, the judiciary, and civil society—needed to participate in the demonization in order to give it legitimacy and validate the results.

By excluding other members of the community and insisting on unilateral power, the Bush administration badly misjudged both the lesson of the punitive turn in American life (thinking it was just about harshness) and, more important, the nation's willingness to accept a reconfiguration of its values after September 11. In contrast to their approach to Islam, the president and his advisers tried to use the war on terror as an occasion to radically reinterpret shared values. They were seen as putting themselves above the law, and they paid dearly.

I

September 11 was hardly the country's first encounter with Islamic terror. But for the great majority of Americans, the difference between those earlier encounters and the enormity and immediacy of 9/11 was the difference between watching a car crash on television and being hit by a truck on the highway. The collective process of naming the new demon began immediately. As others have observed, the division between "us" and "them" is accomplished through a mental reimagining, a form of psychic self-defense. Boundaries of community membership are redrawn and hardened, gerrymandered to exclude those believed to threaten the community, who are quickly remade into something more beast than man.[1] So it was with past monsters we have created, and so it was with the Islamic terrorist.

Within hours of the attacks, a dual image of the terrorist enemy began to take shape. On the one hand, he was less than human. He was, as scores of observers immediately pronounced, "vermin," "a beast," "a cancer," "a disease that must be eradicated," "a barbarian" who had renounced the conventions of the civilized world.[2] A "zealot" and "fanatic," he was the distillation of "pure evil," bent on the destruction of America and her institutions, a goal for which he labored tirelessly, living like an animal "on the hunted margin of mankind." His cruelty set him apart "from the values that define civilization itself."[3] He recognized no ties to civilized society and was eager to sacrifice himself in the slaughter of innocents. Whatever kindness we extended to him was because we are benevolent and humane, not because he was deserving. Yet the Islamic terrorist was also more than human. Though he was everywhere, he was invisible; anyone might be a terrorist, and all terrorists were the same. At special camps and schools, he was immersed in "a cultlike atmosphere designed to break waverers and forge implacable hatreds."[4] He trained his mind and body "in the dark arts," learning not only how to kill but how to disappear.[5] Even if you managed to capture him, he had rare skills that allowed him to resist all conventional interrogations. No ordinary jail could hold him. He was not like mortal men.[6]

Constructions like this are nothing new. Americans have often drawn the "Other" in apocalyptic and paradoxical terms, simultaneously attacking them as subhuman and mythologizing them as superhuman. Early in the Second World War, the myth of a superhuman Japanese fighter became so entrenched that the Roosevelt administration turned to the media to help debunk it before it could damage American morale. The historian John Dower traces the rapid appearance of this myth to the Japanese military's stunning and unexpected success in the first months after Pearl Harbor. By March 1942 "a new creature roamed the fertile fields of the Anglo-American imagination: the Japanese superman. The superman came from land, sea, and air, as well as from the nightmares of the Westerners."[7]

The Cold War produced a similar creature. The communist was quickly endowed with a fanaticism that defied comprehension. In her masterful summary of McCarthyism, the historian Ellen Schrecker notes that "like the Japanese during World War II, Communists during the Cold War were both subhuman and superhuman. They were inferior beings who were at the same time uniquely powerful."[8] The federal judge who presided over a 1949 trial of Communist Party members later told Schrecker that throughout the proceedings he never allowed himself to lock eyes with the defendants' supporters in the gallery. Communists, he explained, had mastered the art of mind control.[9] In the 1970s and 1980s, Western security agencies deliberately created a popular myth about the terrorist Ilich Ramírez Sánchez (a.k.a. "Carlos the Jackal") as "a kind of super-terrorist of exceptional cunning and skills who was personally involved in virtually every major terrorist incident in western Europe at this time." Later investigations revealed Sánchez as a bungler who benefited from good fortune and official incompetence.[10]

Yet if the nature of the construction is familiar, there is another aspect to this demonization that is less frequently observed but even more important to any study of national identity: the critical role played by the American Creed. Contrary to what is sometimes supposed, the Creed is never set on some imaginary shelf until the danger passes. Quite the opposite: It is revered with new intensity, cherished with the zeal of someone who has suddenly awakened to the realization that it cannot be taken for granted. Shortly after September 11, pollsters asked people to list the things they were "very proud" of in American life. The fraction of people who identified "the way democracy works" soared dramatically, registering a larger increase compared with the results of a similar question in 1996 (both in real and percentage terms) than any other choice, including the military.[11] Some even maintain that the very *purpose* of demonization by a liberal democracy is to reaffirm society's core values, and that demonization appears precisely when those values are believed to be at risk. The community finds comfort in the knowledge that its principles are not only intact but as strong and resolute as ever, and that it stands united behind values worth preserving and defending. Within this newly configured village, the Creed becomes especially prized and loudly celebrated.

In this spirit, President Bush repeatedly cast the values of national identity as the ideal for which the war on terror was waged. With respect to Islam, he and his administration commendably defined those values expansively, at least initially encouraging a significant level of national acceptance and tolerance. But when it came to counterterror policy, the Bush administration undertook a remarkably bold attempt to reconfigure the values of national identity. Though demonization has a long history in this country, the post-1960s era of the punitive turn in American life has produced a distinctive national response to perceived demons and the supposedly apocalyptic threat they pose. This response has now been fully integrated into the Creed. So far as national identity is concerned, there is a right way and a wrong way to respond to grave threats. The Bush administration got it very wrong.

II

The idea that the administration would launch a principled response to an unprincipled assault tapped into the potent symbolic force of American values—of moral righteousness and legal restraint in the service of an honorable defense. This placed it on hallowed ground in American memory. References to Pearl Harbor and the virtue of the American role in World War II were immediate and ubiquitous.[12] But what would a principled response look like? We now know what it meant to the Bush administration: domestic surveillance and infiltration of mosques and Muslim communities; military commissions created by the executive branch instead of regularly constituted military or civilian courts; extralegal detentions at Guantánamo Bay and elsewhere; wiretapping without authorization; enhanced interrogations at black sites around the world; renditions to third countries with well-deserved reputations for torture; and the expanded government powers accompanying the USA Patriot Act.

Though the policies set in motion by the Bush administration ranged across a wide field, they were united by a common set of assumptions held by the administration's key policy makers. The first and perhaps most important was that September 11 was not a crime but an act of war that should be confronted with all the vigor and resources of a wartime nation. The second was that the risk facing the nation was uniquely grave. The third was that nothing short of perfect intelligence could save the country from further disaster. "Intelligence," the 2002 National Security Strategy warned, "is our first line of defense against terrorists and the threat posed by hostile states."[13] If we examine the Bush administration's response to September 11 from the perspective of a person who genuinely believed these propositions to be true, all that follows becomes at least understandable. Whatever criticisms one may fairly level against the Bush administration, inconsistency is not among them.

We also know how most of these initiatives were defended and justified. The Bush administration developed an interconnected set of arguments whose ultimate purpose was to allow it to prosecute the war on terror unilaterally, anywhere in the world, unrestrained by the other branches of government and unobserved by the public. The centerpiece of this defense was the contention that the president's inherent authority as commander in chief permitted him to disregard other provisions of the Constitution and the Bill of Rights, the express will of Congress, and the clear language of statutes and international treaties. On the strength of this argument, the Department of Justice insisted that the president could order enhanced interrogations, notwithstanding statutes and treaties that outlawed torture. This argument also stood behind the department's conclusion that the National Security Agency could eavesdrop on electronic communications without warrants, despite a statute forbidding precisely that. It was also the basis for the contention that the military could deploy inside the United States, a power the Bush administration claimed but never invoked. As Supreme Court Justice Robert Jackson said of a similar claim advanced by the Truman administration, power of this sort "either has no beginning or it has no end."[14]

But the claim of the commander in chief's inherent power was only one arrow in a well-stocked quiver. The Bush administration advanced a host of hyperlegalistic arguments to justify its policies. It insisted that the prisoners at Guantánamo could not challenge their detention in court because the naval base was on Cuban territory, even though the United States had exercised undisputed control over the base for nearly a century. The prisoners in black sites could not challenge their detention because the United States refused to confirm or deny they were being held, or give them access to a court, and insisted the Constitution did not extend to aliens in U.S. custody overseas. Private citizens could not discover whether their conversations were monitored because the information was classified and exempt from disclosure; companies that "rendered" prisoners to third countries or otherwise helped in the war on terror were shielded from accountability by the "state secrets" doctrine, which allowed the administration to place material off limits to the litigants and thereby force the court to dismiss the lawsuit; government officials who designed or implemented the policies were immune from suit. On several occasions the administration directed executive branch officials not to comply with congressional requests for information. And if Congress passed legislation that tried to alter the administration's behavior, the president could issue a "signing statement" reaffirming his inherent authority to ignore Congress and interpret the law as he saw fit.

To say that these policies and their associated defenses were controversial does not remotely do the matter justice. Whole forests have been sacrificed to produce the paper on which this controversy has played out. The available record includes scores of congressional hearings and inquiries, hundreds of books and reports, thousands of scholarly articles, and tens of thousands of news stories in print and on television, radio, and the Internet. Though the administration never lacked for defenders, the largest part of this mountain of material is sharply critical of its actions. And unlike the attacks on Islam, the criticism emanated not from a small cluster of voices concentrated at one part of the ideological spectrum but from almost all corners of the public square. Special interest groups and nongovernmental organizations were relentless in their criticism and repeatedly mobilized their members against various policies. Libertarian and conservative think tanks like the Cato and Rutherford Institutes, bipartisan organizations like the Constitution Project, an army of liberal policy centers, religious, civic, and military groups, and thousands of academics across the country and around the world inveighed against various aspects of the post-9/11 world. Professional groups like the American Bar Association, the American Medical Association, and the American Psychological Association took official positions against one or more post-9/11 policies. Editorial pages and television newsrooms eventually joined these forces to castigate the president and his inner circle.

Sometimes a broad array of voices came together to protest a particular policy or support a certain position. For example, scores of domestic and international organizations, thousands of academics, diplomats, politicians, and military specialists, and more than four hundred members of the British Parliament came together to file thirty-seven "friend of the court" briefs in the U.S. Supreme Court in support of Salim Hamdan, Osama bin Laden's former driver, in his successful challenge to the Bush administration's military commission system in 2006.[15] Just as often, however, groups stayed within their organizational lanes. Physicians for Human Rights and the American Medical Association, for example, were more dismayed about the role of medical and mental health professionals in coercive interrogations than by the abuse of presidential signing statements, which incurred the particular ire of the American Bar Association.[16]

But with time, as the single-minded philosophy of the Bush administration became clearer, the differences among the criticisms and critics became less prominent. As more and more policies became known, a consensus emerged that the administration had gone too far. Gradually, a master narrative took shape: The administration was bent on a power grab, in the service of which it consistently and unapologetically engaged in behavior that betrayed the very principles for which the war was being waged. The administration, it was said, treated the rule of law like a presidential plaything and scoffed at the idea of limited government. Most of the elements of this narrative, which were invariably expressed in the language of the Creed, were clearly discernible within weeks of September 11, even before many of the administration's policies had come into view. Though the narrative became stronger and more complete with time, apart from the very first days after the attack, it is impossible to point to a moment when it was not present in the public square. It grew by assimilating new and apparently unrelated events into its ambit, like the war in Iraq and the disastrous response to Hurricane Katrina. By 2006 it had become the albatross hung from the president's neck, an ever-present reminder of his ill deeds that accompanied him wherever he went. By 2008 it was the symbol of a presidency run amok.

All the customary caveats apply when considering this trend. As with any dominant intellectual current, it is certainly possible to identify countercurrents. The ascendance of the narrative was not uninterrupted: Its fortunes waxed and waned with passing events. But over the longer sweep, the trend is unmistakable. By any measure—public opinion polling, the mobilization of civil society, stiffening bipartisan political opposition, or electoral outcomes—the lesson of counterterror policy during the Bush years, just like the early response to Islam and torture, is not how much the country lost its way but how firmly it resolved not to. Certainly the executive branch lost its way, at least so far as much of the public was concerned. But what the administration did must not be confused with what the country embraced. The policies of the Bush administration triggered a heated debate about the meaning and content of some of the most revered symbols in American life. To an extent that has not been adequately appreciated, the debate ended in November 2008 with the country's ringing pronouncement that the policies were a betrayal of the very principles for which the war was ostensibly waged. By prosecuting the war on terror as it did, the Bush administration lost the battle to remake national identity.

III

The germ of the master narrative, expressed repeatedly in the hours and days after the attacks, was the widespread fear that September 11 would cost the country its soul. On September 20, 2001—the day the president vowed to "give law enforcement . . . additional tools" in order "to track down terror here at home"[17]—more than 150 groups joined with more than three hundred law professors and forty computer scientists to create the In Defense of Freedom Coalition.[18] The list of organizations was striking for its diversity. Groups dedicated to preserving and protecting the rights of Arab-Americans and Muslims joined with conservative groups like the American Conservative Union and the Eagle Forum. Civil liberties groups of the political left were matched by libertarian groups like the Citizens Committee for the Right to Keep and Bear Arms. Religious organizations on the list included CatholicVote.org, which would endorse Rick Santorum for president in 2012, the Progressive Jewish Alliance, and the Baptist Joint Committee for Religious Liberty.[19] In the language of the Creed, the coalition called for calm. We must not "erode the liberties and freedoms that are at the core of the American way of life." Government must remain accountable. National policies must be "consistent with the Constitution." The country must "resist efforts to target people because of their race, religion, ethnic background or appearance, including immigrants in general, Arab Americans and Muslims."[20]

Many of the coalition's concerns echoed the abstract appeals to American values heard in the immediate aftermath of September 11. But what began as an abstract plea quickly became concrete. The administration's first worry was that an unknown number of would-be terrorists or their sympathizers had disappeared into the vast anonymity of American society. Many of its initial policies were directed toward finding these needles in the national haystack. The federal government began to arrest foreign nationals who were considered possible threats. On September 28 Attorney General Ashcroft announced that 480 people had been detained in this sweep. A month later, the number was nearly 1,000, after which the Department of Justice announced that it would no longer release a running total.[21] Some of the people taken into custody were released in relatively short order, but most were held without bond and put through secret immigration proceedings. The government refused to release their names, their locations, or the reasons for their detention.[22] Building on these detentions, the government announced in November 2001 that it would conduct voluntary interviews of approximately 5,000 Arab and Muslim men who "fit the criteria of persons who might have knowledge of foreign-based terrorists." It eventually interviewed about 2,300 people. Fewer than 20 were taken into custody, and only 3 were arrested on criminal charges. None was charged with or convicted of a terrorist offense.[23]

The great majority of the country had no great objection to the detentions and interviews per se. The idea that additional terrorists or al Qaeda members might be at large did not seem far-fetched (especially since the administration repeatedly insisted it was true), and a concerted effort to find them did not strike most people as unwarranted. An ABC/Washington Post poll taken in November 2001 found that 86 percent of Americans believed the detentions were justified.[24] Moreover, in a nation of nearly 300 million people with a Muslim population of roughly 5 million, the fact that the federal government detained about 1,000 people and interviewed several thousand others demonstrated at the very least an acute sensitivity to the lesson of

history. The Bush administration seemed determined to avoid anything remotely like the internment of the Japanese during the Second World War,
and even the most skeptical observer would have to acknowledge that the
targeted arrest and detention of 1,000 people, all of whom were at least in
technical violation of their immigration status, bears not even a glancing
relationship to the mass roundup of more than 120,000 innocent men,
women, and children of Japanese descent. The criticism that resonated was
not of the detentions themselves but of their unprecedented secrecy.

"Secret detention of uncharged individuals," wrote the *Milwaukee Journal
Sentinel*, "is one of the offenses for which American officials and human
rights groups properly pillory other countries." The *Journal* said the secrecy
would "eat away at the very freedoms and constitutional principles America
fights to protect."[25] Appeals to the shared values of American identity became commonplace. An editorial in *USA Today* said, "This isn't supposed
to be a country in which the government can secretly imprison people.
Such practices were among the reasons the colonists rebelled against the
British."[26] In an editorial titled "An Un-American Secrecy," the *Los Angeles
Times* insisted that the attacks, "awful as they were, do not call for the Bush
administration to dismiss constitutional protections."[27] "Secret arrests and
secret detention are police state tactics," warned the *St. Petersburg Times*,
"and for America to resort to them—as federal authorities have already
done on a massive scale in the Sept. 11 investigation—is a victory for our
enemies."[28] The administration was clearly taken aback by these criticisms.
But having cast the war on terror as a referendum on national values, it
might have anticipated that its policies would be measured by their fidelity
to these ideals.

At the U.S. Mayors Conference in October, Attorney General Ashcroft
told his audience, "Terrorists live in the shadows, under the cover of darkness. We will shine the light of justice on them."[29] But when called upon to
shine the light of disclosure on the shadowy detentions of his department,
he said, "I will not share valuable intelligence with our enemies. We might
as well mail this list to the Osama bin Laden al-Qaeda network as release
it."[30] Later that month, the Center for National Security Studies, eventually
joined by thirty-six other organizations, filed a request under the Freedom
of Information Act asking the government to disclose the names of all peo-

ple arrested or detained in connection with the September 11 investigation, as well as their current locations. The FBI denied the request.[31] While the request was pending, a group of Democratic senators and representatives sent Attorney General Ashcroft a letter seeking the same information. They also agreed to meet with Ashcroft in a secure setting in the event some of the requested information was classified. Ashcroft did not respond.[32] Senator Patrick Leahy (D-VT), the chairman of the Senate Judiciary Committee and a signatory of the first letter, sent a follow-up letter that repeated the request. Leahy scribbled a note to his former colleague at the bottom of the page: "General—*Many* people are concerned about this and I do need an answer." Again, no response.[33]

Concerns continued to mount as the weeks passed. In October a notice appeared in the Federal Register. With little fanfare, the attorney general had unilaterally decreed that the executive branch could eavesdrop on conversations between lawyers and their clients in federal custody. Senator Leahy said he was "deeply troubled by what appears to be an executive effort to exercise new powers without judicial scrutiny or statutory authorization."[34] Note that Leahy expressed no particular concern that attorney-client conversations would be monitored. He objected to the suggestion that it would be done by executive fiat, "without judicial scrutiny or statutory authorization." The objection, in other words, was to the administration's failure to include the community in its response to the new demon, which was a betrayal of the rituals of the punitive turn. This would quickly become the complaint at the heart of the master narrative. The conservative *Chicago Tribune,* for instance, which had endorsed President Bush in the 2000 elections, asked in an editorial, "Must We Sell Our Birthright for Security?" Like others, the editor detected an emerging pattern to the administration's behavior, which is how a narrative takes shape. Taking issue with both the secret detentions and the rule allowing the FBI to monitor attorney-client conversations, the *Tribune* concluded, "What is remarkable about each of these expansions of government power is that they have been put through with only the most meager public discussion and debate."[35]

While the immigration detentions and interviews were taking place, Attorney General Ashcroft delivered the Bush administration's proposed antiterrorism package to Congress. This package would culminate in the USA

Patriot Act, one of the most controversial (and misunderstood) elements of the administration's response to September 11. The debate over this law provides a revealing demonstration of how the administration's approach to counterterror policy outran the limits of the punitive turn. To begin with, Congress clearly did not object to giving the administration greater investigative and enforcement power; for decades, that has been an essential part of the punitive turn, and perhaps its most enduring legacy. The Senate Judiciary Committee under Senator Leahy's leadership had drafted legislation that would have given the executive branch additional powers even before the president's proposal arrived. Some provisions in the Senate version gave the administration power it had not sought in its own proposal. According to a careful account written by Beryl Howell, who was then Senator Leahy's general counsel and would later be appointed to the federal bench, only about a third of the final bill was included in the administration's initial draft.[36] In addition, a number of legislators complained that the administration had not gone far enough. Senator Joe Biden (D-DE), for instance, lamented Bush's failure to seek such "common sense tools" as a blanket exception that would have excused all good faith violations of the Fourth Amendment in terrorism-related crimes.[37] In short, support for the punitive turn was bipartisan.

The most noteworthy aspect of the administration's proposal was not that it sought new powers (which Congress was eager to grant) but that it wanted to conduct surveillance, collect and share information, and detain aliens largely without judicial oversight.[38] The Leahy draft, by contrast, provided for additional executive power but would have subjected that authority to review by the courts. Leahy's proposal, in other words, was more consistent with the rituals and limits of the punitive turn because it engaged all three branches of government in the response to the new demon. Yet the administration protested bitterly against these proposed restraints, insisting that anything other than unilateral authority would imperil national security.[39]

The administration and its allies embarked on a campaign to pressure Congressional Democrats into accepting the administration's demands. Attorney General Ashcroft warned ominously that "the American people do not have the luxury of unlimited time. . . . Every day that passes with outdated statutes . . . is a day that terrorists have a competitive advantage. Until the Congress makes these changes, we are fighting an unnecessarily uphill battle."[40] "Talk will not prevent terrorism," he said on another occasion. "We need to have action by the Congress." Congressional Republicans also took up the cudgel. Senate Minority Leader Trent Lott (R-MS) warned that if another attack occurred, Democrats would have to explain why they failed to give law enforcement "the additional tools that are needed to . . . find these terrorists and avoid plots that may be in place."[41] This campaign, however, only contributed to the growing master narrative. The *New York Times* attacked Ashcroft for taking umbrage at the legislative process and for his "scurrilous" suggestion that allowing a coequal branch of government to do its job would endanger national security.[42]

In the end, House and Senate Democrats forced the administration to accept a number of compromises, leaving it with considerably less unilateral power than it had sought but considerably more than it had before September 11. Yet after the president signed the USA Patriot Act into law, the Justice Department inexplicably described it as a near-total victory for the administration.[43] By creating the mistaken impression that the bill was entirely the administration's handiwork, this immodesty served to relieve Congress of responsibility for the final product. Taking credit for someone else's work is risky business, since it leaves no one to share the blame if things go awry. Ultimately, the act substantially expanded the government's authority to conduct surveillance of people in the United States and to collect and share information about them. It also enlarged the government's power to prosecute speech and association that was said to provide "material support" to terrorist groups,[44] and granted the federal government a number of powers that a Republican Congress had denied to President Clinton after the Oklahoma City bombing in 1995.[45]

Civil liberties groups have been unsparing in their criticism of the act, which struck a chord throughout the country. In early 2002 the City and County of Denver passed the first resolution objecting to the USA Patriot Act. Denver's resolution came on the heels of disclosures that local police had begun maintaining files on peaceful protesters, just as those who objected to the act had feared.[46] "WHEREAS," the resolution stated, in the excessively formal tone of American lawmaking, "the provisions of the USA

PATRIOT Act expand the authority of the federal government to detain and investigate citizens and non-citizens and engage in electronic surveillance of citizens and non-citizens; and WHEREAS, many people throughout communities across the nation, including Denver, are concerned that certain provisions in the USA PATRIOT Act threaten civil rights and liberties guaranteed under the United States Constitution," the City resolved that

> every person has the right to be free from unreasonable search and seizure, arrests may not be made without establishing reasonable suspicion or probable cause that a crime has been committed or is about to be committed, every person has a right to equal protection under the law and the right not to be deprived of life, liberty or property without due process of law, and every person has the right to free speech and freedom of association under the First Amendment of the United States Constitution.[47]

Denver directed that "no information about political, religious or social views, associations, or activities should be collected unless the information relates to criminal activity and the subject is suspected of criminal activity," and that "no law enforcement or other city agency may profile or discriminate against any person on the basis of race, ethnicity, national origin, age, sex, sexual orientation, or religion."[48] By the end of 2002, twenty other municipalities had passed similar resolutions, and another 216 were passed in 2003, including statewide resolutions in Alaska, Hawaii, and Vermont. By 2008 the number had grown to more than 400, with resolutions passed in some of the largest cities in the country.[49] Significantly, however, because the administration claimed the bill as its own, the bulk of the criticism was directed at the Bush administration rather than at Congress or the government as a whole.

By the time the president signed the USA Patriot Act, the master narrative was fixed. Events would only make it more prominent. In mid-November 2001 the president announced plans to try suspected terrorists in specially created military commissions rather than in a regularly constituted military or civilian court. Once again, the administration bypassed Congress entirely, which would eventually be the grounds on which the Supreme Court would rule the commissions unconstitutional.[50] As originally contemplated, the commissions contained none of the protections Americans have long associated with a fair trial, including the presumption of innocence and the right to silence; William Safire dismissed them as "kangaroo courts."[51] And in the gathering battle for national identity, the administration did itself no favors when it dispatched Attorney General Ashcroft to the Senate Judiciary Committee to explain the tribunals, the secret detentions, and the determination to monitor attorney-client conversations.

Ashcroft tried to defend the policies in the language of the punitive turn, insisting that the initiatives had been "carefully drawn to target a narrow class of individuals—terrorists."[52] But this response revealed the limits of the administration's understanding. The punitive turn is not just about punishment or retribution, and Ashcroft made no attempt to justify or defend the radical departures from past practice, including the administration's attachment to secrecy, hostility to public oversight, and determination to bypass Congress and the courts. Instead, he took the opportunity to issue his now infamous warning: "To those who scare peace-loving people with phantoms of lost liberty, my message is this: Your tactics only aid terrorists for they erode our national unity and diminish our resolve. They give ammunition to America's enemies and pause to America's friends. They encourage people of good will to remain silent in the face of evil."[53] Symbolically, Ashcroft and the administration were now setting themselves *against* the community. Instead of allowing demonization to be a communal affair, Ashcroft attacked those who wanted to participate, apparently out of a fear that their participation would dilute the administration's response. This was a dangerous betrayal of the rituals of the punitive turn. His remarks were not well received and encouraged the growing fear that the administration should not be given too much authority. "It is difficult to trust the attorney general to wield power responsibly," *Newsday* said, "when legitimate questions about the administration's unilateral decisions on military tribunals, secret detentions and monitoring attorney-client conversations are met with holier-than-thou disdain."[54]

Another important milestone in the creation of the master narrative arrived in late 2001 and early 2002, as groups began to take their objections to court. The Center for National Security Studies, which had sought the names of people in secret immigration detention, brought its request to the federal court in Washington, D.C. Other groups, including a number of newspapers, sued under the First Amendment to force the government to open the immigration proceedings to the public. Again, the objection was not to the detentions themselves but to the way they had been shielded from public scrutiny. In the end, this litigation met with mixed results. The lower court in Washington ordered the government to disclose information, but the appellate court reversed; a federal court in Michigan ordered the government to open its proceedings, but one in New Jersey disagreed.[55] The larger significance of the litigation, however, was in the determination to enlist the judiciary in the national debate. Because Americans have come to view the law as a surrogate for moral legitimacy, conflating what is lawful with what is good, courts often play an outsize role in any debate over national values. Judicial decisions become ammunition that partisans can use to advance arguments about national identity.[56] When the federal appellate court in Michigan held that the hearings must be open (with the alliterative creedal warning that "democracies die behind closed doors"), the *New York Times* called the decision "the most powerful rebuke yet to the Bush administration's policy of flouting the Bill of Rights in the name of national security."[57]

IV

In formulating its counterterror policy, the administration's first objective was to locate would-be terrorists inside the United States. Its second was to interrogate those who were captured abroad. Its detention policy— the most familiar symbol of which is the prison at Guantánamo—would eventually become one of the most controversial aspects of the response to September 11 and a major impetus to the master narrative. Once again, however, the administration's downfall was not to hold prisoners but to ignore the limits of the punitive turn by excluding the community from the demonization process.

The administration correctly expected that military operations would lead to the capture of people who might have knowledge of terrorist operations. The United States military has detained and interrogated enemy prisoners for centuries, and nothing about September 11 called this accumulated expertise into question. But as we now know, the Bush administration abandoned past practices by determining unilaterally that the prisoners were not entitled to protection under the Geneva Conventions and that their status as "unlawful enemy combatants" had been conclusively established by the president himself, with no legal process apart from his say-so and no involvement by Congress or the courts. The administration also decided that prisoners could be interrogated using any method the administration saw fit to employ, again without congressional participation and without charges or judicial review. The cumulative effect was twofold: to place post-9/11 prisoners completely beyond the law and to exclude the entire community from any role in the detention process. Taken together, the Bush administration's detention policy was an unprecedented assault on the limits of the punitive turn.[58]

The first prisoners arrived at Guantánamo in January 2002. Though the prison was immediately controversial, especially overseas, there were initial hopes that the detentions would be confined to foreign nationals seized on the battlefield. These hopes were quickly dashed. In April 2002 the administration transferred Yaser Hamdi, a U.S. citizen, from Guantánamo to a naval brig in Norfolk, Virginia. Like the prisoners in Cuba, Hamdi was designated an enemy combatant and held without charges in solitary, incommunicado detention. Hamdi had been captured in Afghanistan. But any thought that Guantánamo-style detentions, even of U.S. citizens, would at least be limited to people captured on the battlefield ended when the United States arrested José Padilla, another U.S. citizen, as he stepped from a plane at O'Hare Airport in Chicago. He was held in New York as a "material witness." Lawyers were appointed on his behalf, but before they could seek his release, the United States designated him an enemy combatant and whisked him to a military brig in South Carolina. All contact with the outside world was cut off. Even the lawyers who had represented him in New York were no longer allowed to communicate with him. Hamdi was later transferred to the same prison as Padilla and held under the same brutal conditions. The two men were completely isolated, both from each other and from all other human contact apart from interrogators.

Hamdi, Padilla, and a group of prisoners at Guantánamo challenged their detentions in federal court. In June 2004 the Supreme Court dealt a blow to the administration's detention policy, holding that both the citizen in the United States and the foreign national at Guantánamo could challenge their detention in federal court. These were exceedingly important decisions, less for the relatively little they would eventually accomplish for the prisoners themselves than for their contribution to the thickening narrative about the abuse of presidential power and the importance of the rule of law. The cases—*Hamdi v. Rumsfeld, Rumsfeld v. Padilla,* and *Rasul v. Bush*—marked the Court's first foray into the post-9/11 debate. (Full disclosure: I was counsel of record in *Rasul v. Bush* throughout the litigation.) In a nation that confuses legal authority with moral sanction, the pronouncements by the Supreme Court gave a powerful boost to the master narrative, rendering an invaluable symbolic judgment that the administration had overstepped its bounds by trying to create prisons beyond the law.

In the unmistakable language of the American Creed, newspapers across the country heralded the decisions as an important check on the administration. "The king is dead," wrote the *Buffalo News.* "So said the U.S. Supreme Court this week in knocking down the Bush Administration's monarchist pretensions."[59] The *Milwaukee Journal Sentinel* said, "American citizens who are distrustful of unchecked government power—and we should all be members of that club—have reason to cheer."[60] "This week courage and good sense graced the U.S. Supreme Court," the *Pittsburgh Post-Gazette* wrote, "and the justices said enough is enough."[61] The *Boston Globe* said the rulings "struck decisively at Bush Administration assertions of sweeping power over combat detainees . . . [and] kept the Bill of Rights from being a collateral victim of the war on terror."[62] "At last," the *Ft. Lauderdale Sun-Sentinel* pronounced, "President Bush is being taught some valuable lessons about the limits of his power by the U.S. Supreme Court."[63] And the *Los Angeles Times,* in an editorial titled "It's Called Democracy," wrote, "It is hard to see what is left of American freedom if the government has the authority to make anyone on its soil—citizen or non-citizen—disappear and then rule that no one can do anything about it."[64] It bears repeating that the objection most often expressed in these and many other venues was not to the detentions themselves but to the idea that they be based only on the president's say-so, which had placed the detentions beyond the reach authorized by the punitive turn.[65]

V

The master narrative gathered force throughout 2004 but was not nearly potent enough to derail Bush's reelection campaign. Most Americans continued to support the administration's approach to terrorism, though the numbers had fallen precipitously from the level of support Bush had enjoyed in 2001 and 2002. Polling conducted by ABC and the *Washington Post*, for instance, showed that support for the president's handling of the war on terror declined from a 92 percent approval rate in October 2001 to a pre–2004 election low of 50 percent in June 2004. A CBS/New York Times poll likewise traced a steady decline from 90 percent in December 2001 to a preelection low of 51 percent in July 2004.[66] But Massachusetts Senator John Kerry made little attempt to capitalize on Bush's handling of the war on terror, arguing only that Bush had not gone far enough in the campaign against al Qaeda and preferring to focus on the war in Iraq. This was a miscalculation in at least two respects. First, public opinion did not turn heavily against the war in Iraq until after the election.[67] Second, Kerry's position on al Qaeda fell flat: Most people found it unlikely that he would be more aggressive than Bush. Indeed, the voters who ranked terrorism as their most important concern—and there were a great many—voted overwhelmingly for Bush.[68] By effectively conceding that issue, Kerry gave up where it may have mattered most.

But events continued to give the master narrative added strength. In late 2005 the *New York Times* revealed that shortly after September 11, President Bush had signed a secret executive order that authorized the National Security Agency to wiretap electronic devices without a warrant, including devices owned or used by U.S. citizens, despite a federal law that made such surveillance a crime.[69] As with other initiatives, the administration defended the program by insisting that the president had an inherent power to bypass Congress and ignore existing laws. The outcry was predictable and immediate, prompting what one writer called "a bipartisan revolt on Capitol Hill."[70] Republicans and Democrats alike demanded an explanation and called for hearings. Democratic Senators Harry Reid (D-NV), John D. Rockefeller (D-WV), and Patrick Leahy (D-VT) sent a letter to the president asking for information about the program. Senator Arlen Specter (R-PA), who had replaced Leahy as chairman of the Judiciary Committee, thought there was "no doubt" that the NSA program was "inappropriate." Conservative Senator Lindsey Graham (R-SC), a strong supporter of the war on terror and a respected authority on military justice, also called for a congressional review and worried that "we cannot set aside the rule of law in a time of war." House Democrats began to murmur about impeachment. "There is no question that the U.S. Congress has impeached Presidents for lesser offenses," Congressman John Lewis (D-GA) said.[71]

Denunciations echoed beyond the beltway. "President Bush believes that whatever he thinks is necessary must be lawful," wrote Chicago law professor Geoffrey Stone in the *Chicago Tribune*, "whether it be domestic surveillance by NSA, or torture, or denying the Guantanamo Bay detainees the protections of the Geneva Conventions. Bush is a man of faith, not a man of law. That is a problem."[72] The *Philadelphia Daily News*, asking whether the administration had "finally gone too far," insisted, "The blowback from this betrayal of our Constitution has to be harsh and unforgiving."[73] *USA Today* said the program revealed "an inexcusable lack of respect for the two other branches of government, for the rule of law, and for the individual liberties that our divided form of government was designed to protect," and wondered why the administration had shown "such blatant disregard for the restraints on presidential power that the Founding Fathers imposed."[74] And the *St. Petersburg Times*, uniting the many abuses of the Bush administration, said:

> This is part of an imperial presidency that has emerged under Bush since the 9/11 terrorist attacks. On the authority of the executive branch alone, the administration has imprisoned people for years without charge, captured suspects and put them in secret overseas prisons, and engaged in interrogation techniques that violate domestic law and international treaties. Now the New York Times report on more spying reveals that the dictates of the Fourth Amendment, requiring a showing of probable cause before someone's privacy can be invaded, have been set aside upon the president's sole say-so.[75]

The NSA controversy intensified in January 2006, when the public learned that in 2002 the administration had resisted a proposal by Senator Mike DeWine (R-OH) to grant it greater statutory power to monitor electronic communications. At the time, the White House told Congress that DeWine's proposal was unnecessary and possibly unconstitutional. Yet even as the administration was publicly eschewing the offer by Congress to provide it with greater statutory power, it was secretly engaging in precisely the conduct it said was unnecessary and possibly illegal. When asked to account for this, administration officials explained they had wanted to avoid any public debate about wiretapping in 2002 for fear that it would lead to disclosure of the NSA program. This explanation was not well received. Senator Leahy said that if the administration "really believed the current law is too burdensome, the Bush administration should have asked Congress to change it, but they did not." An ACLU attorney accused the administration of "remarkable duplicity."[76]

The wiretapping debate shows once again that Congress was more than willing to give the president greater power to monitor electronic conversations. After the scandal broke, bills were introduced in both the House and Senate that gave the president very nearly the same authority he had claimed under the secret program. New legislation, passed by Congress and signed by the president in July 2008, gave the attorney general broad authority to target and monitor international electronic conversations.[77] In other words, the objection that resonated was not to the conduct per se but to the president's determination to act unilaterally, which was widely interpreted as a betrayal of national values. By lying to Congress and acting in secret, the administration suffered another self-inflicted wound. And by continuing to ignore the limits and rituals of the punitive turn, the administration fueled the growing narrative. In a widely reported speech a month after the NSA program was disclosed, former Vice President Al Gore warned that "America's Constitution is in grave danger."[78] Speaking the unmistakable language of the Creed and interrupted by repeated ovations, he said, "The American values we hold most dear have been placed at serious risk by the unprecedented claims of the administration to a truly breathtaking expansion of executive power." Gore linked the NSA program to other elements of the Bush administration's response to September 11 and denounced them all as "part of a larger pattern of seeming indifference to the Constitution."[79]

VI

The disclosure of the wiretapping program in December 2005 was followed in early 2006 by Charles Savage's lengthy article in the *Boston Globe* on the president's use of signing statements. "President Bush," Savage reported, "has quietly claimed the authority to disobey more than 750 laws enacted since he took office."[80] In more than five years, the president had not vetoed a single piece of legislation, a record unmatched by any president in American history. "Instead," Savage wrote, "he has signed every bill that reached his desk, often inviting the legislation's sponsors to signing ceremonies at which he lavishes praise upon their work."[81] But when the cameras were gone and the celebration had ended, his administration quietly filed statements that set out his interpretation of the law, reserving the right to ignore provisions with which he disagreed. As of early 2006 Bush had appended such statements to more than one in ten bills, including some of the most controversial.[82]

Savage's article, which earned him a Pulitzer Prize, set off another firestorm. One after another, commentators attacked the administration for mocking the rule of law and resisting legitimate restraints on presidential power. "Few if any principles are more fundamental to our way of life as Americans," the *Milwaukee Journal Sentinel* said, "than the notion that no one is above the law. It is this very principle—the requirement that all of us without exception must obey the law—that makes social order possible and prevents our country from sliding into anarchy and ruin."[83] "King George picks and chooses the laws he'll obey," read the headline in the *Lewiston (Idaho) Morning Tribune.* "Eventually, this president will be impeached—by history. Future generations of Americans will marvel at how we survived the reign of the King George the Worst."[84] "The arrogance is mind-boggling," wrote the *Philadelphia Daily News.* "Bush has taken unprecedented powers for himself, using the war on terror to justify his imperium. The tyrant is the child of Pride, said Socrates, and we are coming much too close to tyranny."[85]

This criticism came from voices large and small. "The unchecked power of this presidency," wrote the daily in Waco, Texas, "has weakened the constitutional order on which the American way of life depends."[86] The paper quoted with approval a recently released report from the libertarian Cato

Institute, which it accurately described as "generally a durable friend of Republicans." Looking ahead to the 2006 midterm elections, the paper said "the question must be asked: Is this a nation governed by men empowered by a political hold on the three branches of government? Or is this a nation of laws?"[87] Even fellow Republicans were alarmed. Senator Specter called for hearings, warning that if the president's "blatant encroachments" were tolerated, "there may as well soon not be a Congress. What's the point of having a statute if the president can cherry-pick what he likes and what he doesn't like?"[88] The *Roanoke Times* complained that the Bush administration "continues to thumb its nose at the very notion of accountability."[89]

Observers tied this latest controversy to earlier excesses, reinforcing the idea of a united narrative. The signing statement scandal was "yet another case of the Bush Administration's relentless push to expand the power of the executive at the expense of the other two branches of government," wrote the *Seattle-Post Intelligencer*.[90] "It's official," the *Buffalo News* said. "The Bush Administration has no conception of the meaning of civil rights in America, especially rights that might interfere with its ability to do what it wants when it wants and to whom it wants."[91] The paper was reacting to a statement by the administration, shortly after Savage's article came out, that journalists who published classified information would be prosecuted. "This comes from the same administration that believes the president can, among other things: Hold certain prisoners indefinitely without giving them access to the courts; authorize wiretaps with no warrant required; secretly collect telephone records of millions of Americans; [and] selectively decide which parts of laws it will follow."[92] "NSA spying," said the *Roanoke Times*, no less than locking up American citizens indefinitely "simply by declaring them enemy combatants" and asserting the authority "to ignore or subvert the intent of Congress," all presented the same fundamental issue: "whether the president alone will decide the limits of presidential authority."[93]

VII

By the middle of 2006 the master narrative was firmly in place. Hundreds of diverse groups had joined to create this narrative, which they advanced in the unmistakable language of national identity. Bush's policies, they said, were un-American, an assault on American values, a threat to "what the United States is all about at our core." Unlike the conservative anti-Islam narrative, the master narrative about the Bush administration had spread throughout the public square. And the most prominent complaint was fought on what may be the oldest and most sacred ground in American life, the original creedal value. The president, it seems, had mistaken himself for a king.

One measure of the robustness of this criticism is in the resurgence of an epithet popularized nearly three decades earlier by the historian Arthur Schlesinger, Jr.: George Bush, it was said, had revived the imperial presidency. The expression, which also became the title of a book by Schlesinger about the Nixon presidency, was originally meant to describe the rise of executive power at the expense of the legislature, particularly in foreign affairs.[94] Years after his book was published, Schlesinger concluded that the imperial presidency had died with the Clinton impeachment, an assessment that others shared.[95] In the decade before September 11, the *New York Times,* the *Los Angeles Times,* the *Chicago Tribune,* and the *Washington Post* made scant reference to the concept except to note its increasing irrelevance.

But in the seven-plus years from September 11, 2001, to January 20, 2009, when Obama replaced Bush in the Oval Office, the same papers referred to the imperial presidency more than 200 times, largely in indictments of the Bush administration and its policies. One enterprising historian conducted a Google search for "Bush imperial presidency" in early 2009 and discovered 150,000 web entries, most of them hostile to the administration.[96] "We are seeing a return to the imperial presidency," Darrell West, a presidential scholar at Brown University, told the *Chicago Tribune.*[97] His view was widely shared.

The expression found its way into a slew of books, articles, and government reports and ultimately became the most common indictment of the Bush presidency. The political scientist Peter Irons wrote a book titled *War Powers: How the Imperial Presidency Hijacked the Constitution.*[98] Charles Savage expanded on his account of Bush's signing statements in *Takeover: The Return of the Imperial Presidency and the Subversion of American Democracy.*[99]

The Bar Association for the City of New York published a two-volume edited work entitled *The Imperial Presidency and the Consequences of 9/11: Lawyers React to the Global War on Terrorism.*[100] Gene Healy of the Cato Institute wrote articles with telling titles like "The Imperial Presidency and the War on Terror" and "Learning to Love the Imperial Presidency: How Conservatives Made Peace with Executive Power."[101] Reflections on the imperial presidency continued well after Bush had left office.

All of this writing appealed to the American attachment to limited government and its close cousin, the fear of centralized authority. Over and over, the literature struck the same chords: By claiming an inherent and unreviewable executive power, the president had betrayed the design envisioned by the Founders and enshrined in the Constitution and had created a system better suited to a monarchy than a democracy. The Majority Staff of the House Judiciary Committee, in a book-length report to Congressman John Conyers (D-MI) entitled *Reining in the Imperial Presidency: Lessons and Recommendations Relating to the Presidency of George W. Bush,* warned that the vision of the commander in chief embraced by the Bush administration "could render the rest of the Constitution null, eviscerating the separation of powers structure designed to limit Executive power, and trampling the Bill of Rights."[102] The "ambitious reach of the Bush Administration's imperial vision" and "the audacity with which it was pursued" were "unprecedented in our Nation's history." Yet the "imperial impulse" was a familiar one. "The Founders had ready examples from their own era, beginning with King George III of England."[103] This complaint was not confined to Democrats. The conservative activist Grover Norquist, who had played such a prominent role in bringing Muslims and Arab-Americans into the Republican tent in the 2000 elections, said, "If you interpret the Constitution's saying that the president is commander in chief to mean that the president can do anything he wants and can ignore the laws[,] you don't have a constitution: you have a king."[104]

The master narrative about the Bush administration did not spread evenly across the nation, like a winter storm that gradually blankets the countryside. But it penetrated a steadily widening set of cultural and political circles as the post-9/11 policies became known. What began with a nucleus of activists and litigators spread to an increasingly bipartisan group of think tanks, special interest groups, and nongovernmental organizations, which relied on their members to share and spread their concerns. In time, the narrative expanded to professional organizations and academia, which have their own networks and channels by which they publicize their views. Each revelation seemed to enlarge the universe of people convinced by the master narrative. And as the narrative grew, these groups could amplify their voices by engaging the support of an increasingly large and sympathetic corps of editorial boards, journalists, and television newsrooms.[105]

It is also important that we not ignore the many voices that rose in defense of the Bush administration. Fox News and the editorial pages of the *Wall Street Journal* could usually be counted on to back the president's positions and mock his critics. Other journals also proved themselves generally reliable supporters, including *National Review* and the *Weekly Standard,* as did the enormously popular conservative radio talk show hosts, beginning with Rush Limbaugh and including Glenn Beck, Bill O'Reilly, Sean Hannity, and others. The administration was never at a loss for friendly coverage.

But these defenses were notably tepid. *National Review,* for instance, frequently attacked lawyers who enlisted the courts in the struggle to restrain the president, an approach the *Review* derisively dubbed "lawfare."[106] Recourse to the law, however, is firmly entrenched in national identity, and these attacks only served to underscore the Bush administration's intent to operate without regard to the public rituals that are integral to the punitive turn. Attacks on the lawyers thus tended to encourage rather than weaken the master narrative. The "lawfare" sideshow reached its nadir when an official in the Bush administration publicly questioned the loyalty of defense attorneys representing Guantánamo prisoners. Some of these attorneys were partners in the most prestigious law firms in the country. The backlash was so severe that even Attorney General Alberto Gonzales was roused to defend the so-called Guantánamo Bar Association, and the Bush official resigned in disgrace.[107]

To be sure, the right could have attacked the master narrative for its attachment to remote and ill-defined symbols. It could have pointed out, for instance, that the average American probably had not taken the time to parse the debates over the inherent power of the president in order to de-

cide whether Article II of the Constitution gave President Bush the constitutional duty to ignore the will of Congress when the latter encroached on
an executive prerogative. Still less likely was it that she worked through the
complicated questions of statutory interpretation and constitutional law to
arrive at a judgment about, for instance, whether the federal courts should
have jurisdiction over the prisoners at Guantánamo, whether presidential
signing statements violate the Separation of Powers doctrine, or whether
the war on terror triggered an inherent power that authorized the president
to conduct warrantless wiretaps. It is even less likely that she was moved to
undertake these inquiries because she was personally affected by any of
these policies. In most cases she undoubtedly responded to these matters
on a symbolic level, which is the level at which national identity operates.
But attacking the master narrative for relying on remote symbols would be
to attack the very language of national identity, and the right could not level
this charge without silencing its own voice.

For most Americans, the idea of the rule of law or limited government
(or equality, or liberty, or individualism) summons to mind an image of the
way America *ought to be*. America *ought to be* a land of limited government;
it *ought to be* a place where the rule of law prevails—regardless of what
those expressions mean in practice. Just as important, it *ought to be* a place
where certain rituals are observed before anyone is cast beyond the pale.
It is this sentiment, this potent symbolic meaning, that President Bush
betrayed. By placing his actions beyond congressional restraint or judicial
review, by adopting such a cavalier attitude toward the law, by being so inor-
dinately attached to secrecy, by being indifferent to accusations of imperial
pretensions, he ran afoul of the symbolic limits that define contemporary
American life. As a historian once said of Adlai Stevenson, Bush "exceeded
the perimeters of respectable opinion."[108] It hardly takes a constitutional
law scholar to appreciate the virtue (if not the precise meaning) of "checks
and balances," one of those creedal expressions, like "liberty and justice
for all," whose symbolic importance we accept without serious reflection.
These are rhetorical positions that no one in American life dares to attack.

To be sure, the thesis of this book is that national identity is malleable
and will change as society gradually redefines the meaning and content
of its shared values. Nothing I have said should be taken to mean that the

vision propounded by the Bush administration is *inherently* incompatible with American ideals or that national identity *cannot* be reshaped in the way the Bush administration attempted. The inescapable lesson of American history is that national identity can be made into something grotesque as well as something magnificent. As George Bernard Shaw reminded us, "Democracy is a device that ensures we shall be governed no better than we deserve." But having constructed September 11 as a referendum on the Creed, President Bush should have realized the extent to which people would attach themselves to its rituals. Nothing in the punitive turn suggested that the public would accept an executive who could ignore the will of the other branches of government as he saw fit.

Yet the fact that the attachment to these values is symbolic is nonetheless a matter of exceptional importance. As events since September 11 have repeatedly shown, symbolic attachments are the easiest to manipulate.

12

The Paradox of the Obama Era

I

BARACK OBAMA BEGAN HIS TERM backed by an apparent national consensus that his predecessor had badly misplayed his hand. By ignoring the rituals and limits of the punitive turn, the Bush administration had tried in its response to 9/11 to transform rather than preserve national identity, giving rise to a potent narrative about the rule of law and limited government. This narrative had grown by assimilating new developments as they arose. The fiasco in Iraq and the disastrous response to Hurricane Katrina, for instance, contributed to the view that the Bush team was so blinded by its ideology that it was unprepared for the reality of events. Senator Slade Gordon (R-WA) lamented that Hurricane Katrina showed "we have not heeded the lessons of 9/11."[1] In the same way, the administration's decision to replace a number of U.S. attorneys around the country with candidates who were less qualified lawyers but more committed conservatives reinforced the conviction that within the administration, the law took second place to ideology.[2] All of these complaints fused with the master narrative about the Bush administration; each revealed the danger and hubris of unchecked presidential power. Bush left office with the lowest presidential approval rating in modern history.[3]

The tendency of the narrative to embrace new developments was captured perfectly by the *Los Angeles Times* when it endorsed Obama over John

McCain shortly before the 2008 election. The *Times* criticized the Bush administration as much for its response to September 11 as for its reaction to the worsening economy, all of which it expressed in the language of the Creed:

> In both cases, the pattern is the same. Ineptitude led to crisis; crisis then became the argument for the radical expansion of executive power. The administration insisted that it exercise its new authority with a minimum of scrutiny by Congress, the courts or the public.
>
> In the so-called war on terror, that has meant the abdication of our most basic American principles. We have forfeited privacy and honor—the administration has monitored phones and e-mails without warrants and has secreted prisoners in foreign lands, arguing that they deserved none of our protections even while in our custody. As a nation, we have stooped to torture . . . and refused to recognize one of our most basic Anglo-American notions, the principle of habeas corpus. . . . We have held prisoners in detention without trial, without charge, without end. In so doing, we have antagonized the world and debased America's moral authority to lead.
>
> The same administration responsible for these catastrophes has over the last month nationalized the largest source of funding for mortgages and the largest insurance company on the planet. And it proposed to intervene even more dramatically in the nation's economy by having the Treasury Department—with no court, congressional or public oversight—relieve financial institutions of the troubled mortgages and related securities that have locked up the lending system.[4]

President Bush, the paper concluded, "has transformed the balance of power in our government. We are seeing the erection of an imperial presidency, immune from oversight when it fights terrorists and when it rescues banks."[5]

The Democrats poured into office in a landslide. In addition to carrying the traditional battleground states of Ohio, Florida, and Indiana, Obama even made inroads into the South, capturing Virginia and North Carolina. North Carolina had not voted for a Democrat in a presidential election since 1976, and Virginia not since 1964.[6] Democrats picked up twenty-one seats in the House and eight in the Senate, leaving them with substantial majorities in both chambers.[7] The defeat once again prompted pundits to predict the demise of the GOP. Writing in *Time* magazine in the spring of 2009, Michael Grunwald observed that "Republicans have the desperate aura of an endangered species." The journalist Joe Rothstein thought they might "decline into permanent minority status." More sensibly, the *New York Times* commentator David Brooks predicted the party would "veer right in the years ahead, and suffer more defeats" before reforming itself along more centrist lines.[8]

During the campaign, Obama had promised to correct the abuses of the Bush administration's war on terror. He vowed to end torture, reform rendition, restrict the use of the state secrets privilege, restore the dominant role of civilian courts as the preferred venue for terrorism prosecutions, and close the prison at Guantánamo.[9] Far from being controversial, many of these positions had long been mainstream. The Bush Justice Department had prosecuted hundreds of terrorists in civilian courts, and the president had long said he wanted to close Guantánamo. Secretary of State Condoleezza Rice and Secretary of Defense Robert Gates joined the call to close Guantánamo in 2007, and in early 2008 Admiral Mike Mullen, chairman of the Joint Chiefs of Staff, called for the prison to be closed as soon as possible.[10] At a gathering at the University of Georgia in March 2008, five former secretaries of state—Henry Kissinger, James Baker, Warren Christopher, Madeleine Albright, and Colin Powell—agreed that the next president should move quickly to close the prison. Baker said that Guantánamo "gives us a very, very bad name, not just internationally." Powell said he hoped the new president would close Guantánamo "immediately."[11]

Though it would be wrong to suggest that Congress as a whole ever joined the attack on Guantánamo, the Democrats certainly did, casting their complaint in the language of the Creed. In June 2007, 145 representatives—144 of them Democrats—sent a letter to President Bush urging him to close the prison. "Holding prisoners for an indefinite period of time, without charging them with a crime, goes against our values, ideals and principles as a nation governed by the rule of law." Calling the prison a "liability of our own creation," the representatives said the facility was "defeating our effort to ensure that the principles of freedom, justice and human rights are spread throughout the world."[12] In December 2007 Congress passed the National Defense Authorization Act of 2008, which provided funding for defense operations. One provision argued that the administration should end the indefinite detentions at Guantánamo and "to the maximum extent possible" replace them with lawful prosecutions. In another provision, Congress urged that prisoners who had been cleared for transfer or release be repatriated in short order, and that operations at the prison "be carried out in a way that upholds the national interest and core values of the American people."[13] Campaign promises by Senators McCain, Clinton, and Obama to close the camp provoked no particular public outcry.

On January 22, 2009, President Obama began to act on this apparent national consensus. After meeting with a group of retired generals, many of whom had long opposed the Bush detention policies, he signed an executive order directing that the prison at Guantánamo be shut within a year (part of the trio of orders that also ended the CIA enhanced interrogation program and permanently closed the black sites). Noting the "significant concerns" raised by the facility "both within the United States and internationally," Obama said it "would further the national security and foreign policy interests of the United States and the interests of justice" to close the base.[14]

Polls suggested considerable support for the president's order. A CNN poll in January found that a majority of Americans favored closing Guantánamo. An ABC/Washington Post poll taken the same month asked whether President Obama should continue holding prisoners at Guantánamo or "find another way to deal with these terrorism suspects." Fifty-three percent said he should "find another way," and most of those believed the "other way" should be prosecution in federal court.[15] A Gallup/USA Today poll during the same period found that one in three Americans considered it "very important" that the president keep his promise to close Guantánamo, and another 24 percent thought it was "somewhat" important. In an Associated Press/Roper poll, an astounding 49 percent said that closing the prison should be the new president's "top priority" or an "important priority," which suggests that the worsening economy had not yet eclipsed concern over the Bush administration's response to 9/11. Only 22 percent thought that the prison should not be closed. In February 2009 only 39 percent of respondents told pollsters in an ABC/Washington Post poll that they disapproved of Obama's decision to close the base. In May 2009 a Gallup/USA Today poll found that only 17 percent of respondents would be "upset" if the president were to close the prison in a year, compared with more than half when a similar question was asked in July 2007.[16]

Yet by 2010 this apparently broad national consensus had all but disappeared. Politicians and pollsters now confidently claimed to know what Americans *really* wanted. In polls taken since early 2010, respondents have consistently opposed closing Guantánamo, sometimes by large margins.[17] Similar numbers have voiced support for trying alleged terrorists in a military commission rather than in a civilian court.[18] The Obama administration, meanwhile, was attacked as out of touch with the popular will, deaf to danger, and more concerned with the rights of foreign terrorists than with the safety of innocent Americans. And the shift over detentions is merely representative. Policies that once excited anxiety and protest are now completely ignored. The Patriot Act, for instance, is renewed every four years with overwhelming bipartisan support, and since Obama's victory no city in the country has passed a resolution against it. The Obama administration invokes the state secrets doctrine to block litigation in much the same way as its predecessor, yet protest over the lack of accountability and judicial oversight has virtually disappeared. Muslim communities continue to be targets for infiltration and surveillance with almost no public reaction.[19] Thousands of New York police officers were treated to a training video that traded in the most vicious anti-Islamic tropes.[20] The story excited little comment and fell from the news cycle within days.

At the same time, a demand has emerged for policies that are considerably more aggressive than anything proposed by the Bush administration. As of mid-2012, for instance, legislation is in place that effectively bars transfers from Guantánamo to the United States or elsewhere; compels military custody for foreign nationals suspected of terrorism unless the president certifies that civilian custody is in the national interest; and authorizes indefinite military detention without trial "until the end of the hostilities."[21] Nothing like this was enacted—or would likely have been acceptable—under the Bush administration, which released more than five hundred prisoners from Guantánamo without objection by Republicans in Congress and tried hundreds of terrorism suspects in federal court. In 2007 the great majority of House Democrats complained that indefinite detention without trial "goes against our values, ideals, and principles as a nation governed by the rule of law." Precious few Democrats were inclined to express such a view in 2012.

II

Such dramatic reversals cry out for an explanation. The obvious candidate—a resurgent threat that reset the emergency clock—can be quickly set aside. The official consensus of the intelligence community is that al Qaeda has been substantially weakened. As one expert recently concluded, the organization—which never commanded widespread support in the Muslim world—is badly damaged and has not even been a player in the protest movements that swept the region. Even before bin Laden's death, its decimated leadership was barely able to communicate with its few remaining foot soldiers, let alone conceive and execute significant attacks against the United States.[22] Material taken from bin Laden's compound revealed "a beleaguered movement, a battered movement, and a leader" who realized he was "losing control."[23]

In the national security assessment of 2009, Dennis Blair, then the director of national intelligence for the Obama administration, reported that the threat of terrorism was no longer the greatest risk facing the United States, a position he repeated in 2010.[24] His successor, James Clapper, said in 2011 that while terrorism "will remain at the forefront of our national security threats," al Qaeda "continues to be damaged" by U.S. counterterrorism efforts. In addition, "the loss of experienced personnel" has forced al Qaeda to turn to "smaller, simpler" plots, if only "to demonstrate its continued relevance to the global jihad."[25] In 2012 Clapper was more explicit about the organization's "diminishing . . . operational importance." He said it was the consensus of the intelligence community that al Qaeda, increasingly fragmented and lacking a charismatic leader, would henceforth play little more than a "symbolic" role.[26] John Brennan, the assistant to the president for homeland security and counterterrorism, described al Qaeda in April 2012 as "a shadow of its former self. . . . They're struggling to attract new recruits. Morale is low, with intelligence indicating that some members are giving up and returning home. . . . In short, al-Qa'ida is losing, badly."[27]

Some new terrorist groups have attached themselves to al Qaeda's name to play on its notoriety. In the United States, these groups are often described as "franchises," or "affiliates" of al Qaeda. The implication, sometimes stated explicitly, is that the organization continues to extend its deadly tentacles into new corners of the Muslim world. But this was never true, even at al Qaeda's peak, and is certainly not true now—a fact that is slowly entering into the mainstream press.[28] The first and most prominent of these organizations, al Qaeda in Iraq, was always outside bin Laden's control. He even took the exceptional step of publicly condemning the sectarian attacks on innocent Muslims orchestrated by al Qaeda Iraq's former leader Abu Musab al-Zarqawi. His rebuke fell on deaf ears. After Zarqawi's death in 2006, al Qaeda Iraq became "splintered and decentralized."[29] In 2008 CIA Director Michael Hayden said the group had been virtually defeated. The 2009 National Intelligence Assessment pointed to its "continued decline," and the 2012 National Security Assessment said the group was focused on challenging the government in Baghdad rather than on transnational terrorism.[30]

The other group that looms large in the public imagination, al Qaeda in the Arabian Peninsula or AQAP, has inspired a number of violent attacks by U.S. citizens (including the unsuccessful attempt by Faisal Shahzad to blow up a crude car bomb at Times Square in New York in May 2010, and the rampage by U.S. Army officer Nidal Malik Hasan, who shot and killed thirteen people and wounded more than two dozen in November 2009 at a Texas military base). But AQAP contains no more than three hundred members and perhaps as few as fifty. The Combatting Terrorism Center at West Point called the group "a marginal player at best."[31] Most of its fighters are inexperienced and semiliterate, neither coordinated by nor under the control of al Qaeda's core remnants, and their key objectives have always been local.[32] Their only hope for broader relevance is American overreaction. "An overly expansive or impatient targeting campaign," the West Point center said, "represents one of the few scenarios in which AQAP could begin to meaningfully draw broad support from a Yemeni populace enraged by the constant threat of U.S. air power."[33]

Finally, the long-awaited explosion of "homegrown" terrorism has failed to materialize. In 2009 the number of American Muslims charged with violent terrorist plots spiked unexpectedly, to nearly fifty. Included in this tally was the November shooting by Major Hasan. The year's violence prompted a great deal of anxious and irresponsible commentary. Fox News called homegrown Islamic terrorism "the biggest challenge America's security officials have ever faced,"[34] and the Christian Broadcasting Network, citing unnamed "terrorism experts," said "the rise of homegrown terrorism has left the U.S. more vulnerable to attack than at any time since 9/11."[35] But attacks by American Muslims declined considerably in 2010 and again in 2011. In 2011, twenty Muslims were charged with planning or conducting a violent terrorist act. Of these, only one actually carried out an attack, firing shots at military buildings in Northern Virginia. No one was injured.[36]

The twenty charges in 2011 bring the total number of Muslim-Americans charged since September 11 to 193—fewer than 20 per year, a vanishingly small number compared with the level of violence in the United States. In 2010, the last year for which numbers are available, the FBI reported nearly thirteen thousand homicides in the United States.[37] And in the majority of the Muslim-American terrorist incidents since September 11, the plot was disrupted early; the FBI often knew of the suspect practically from the start of the planning and played a prominent role in shaping the course of his plot. Allegations of entrapment have been lodged, to be resolved by the courts. In some of the cases, the FBI learned of the suspect and his designs from family members, suggesting at the very least a willingness to cooperate with authorities. In any event, there was never a risk of harm to the public.[38] In many of the "homegrown" cases, moreover, the defendants were not recruited by al Qaeda or any other terrorist organization. The best evidence is that they had been radicalized by the way the United States had conducted itself in Afghanistan and Iraq and had sought out radical groups.[39] The importance of this distinction is too often overlooked. Had al Qaeda successfully recruited these people, one might be more alarmed about the organization's viability and capacity to extend itself into the United States. Finally, the number of Muslim-Americans indicted for material support of terrorism has declined dramatically, from twenty-seven in 2010 to eight in 2011, continuing a downward trend that has been fairly steady since 2001.[40]

Furthermore, cases of Muslim-American terrorism are not only fewer but also a good deal less serious than those involving right-wing extremists. According to the FBI, approximately two-thirds of the terrorist acts in the United States from 1980 to 2001 were conducted by non-Islamic American extremists. From 2002 to 2005, the fraction increased to 95 percent.[41] In 2009 the Southern Poverty Law Center released a study of seventy-five terrorist plots orchestrated by right-wing groups in the United States since the 1995 Oklahoma City bombing. (They updated the study with accounts of twenty-two additional plots two years later.) The conspiracies, many of which were carried out, were extraordinarily violent. As the center reports, "These have included plans to bomb government buildings, banks, refineries, utilities, clinics, synagogues, mosques, memorials and bridges; to assassinate police officers, judges, politicians, civil rights figures and others; to rob banks, armored cars and other criminals; and to amass illegal machine guns, missiles, explosives and biological and chemical weapons. Each of these plots aimed to make changes in America through the use of political violence. Most contemplated the deaths of large numbers of people—in one case, as many as 30,000, or 10 times the number murdered on Sept. 11, 2001."[42]

Nor can the first and most significant attempted act of terrorism during the Obama administration (homegrown or otherwise) account for the apparent reversal in the national mood. On Christmas Day 2009, Abdul Farouk Abdulmutallab tried to bring down an international flight by igniting explosives sewn into his clothing. By that time, however, the apparent consensus of 2008 and early 2009 had already evaporated. The reaction to Abdulmutallab's attempt demonstrates convincingly how the narrative now demanded policies that were *more aggressive* than those pursued by President Bush. When the Obama administration arrested and charged Abdulmutallab in federal court, the partisan outcry was immediate and vitriolic. To *National Review,* bringing him into the criminal justice system was "brazen self-sabotage."[43] Pundits and politicians demanded to know why he had been read his *Miranda* warnings and prosecuted "like a common criminal." Fox News, which attacked the decision almost every day for more than a month, likened it to "Mirandizing Germans we captured on the battlefield in World War Two."[44] Polls quickly revealed substantial support for subjecting Abdulmutallab to enhanced interrogations, including waterboarding, even though he had confessed and cooperated with his interrogators. Respondents also demanded trial by military commission.[45]

Yet the Obama administration's response had been precisely the same as its predecessor's. In December 2001, when the anthrax scare was near its peak and the threat of another terrorist attack hung over the country like a shroud, Richard Reid tried to bring down an international flight by igniting the same type of explosives concealed in his shoe. He was prosecuted in civilian court, convicted, and sentenced to life in prison. Even though President Bush had already announced plans to try terrorism suspects in military commissions, no one suggested that this should be Reid's fate. On the contrary, conservative commentators looked forward to his prosecution in civilian court. Stephen Schwartz, for instance, wrote in the *Weekly Standard* that Reid's prosecution in federal court would "make it possible to trace, identify, and shut down Islamic extremist recruiting networks with which [he] had contact in the United States and Britain."[46]

So the riddle remains: The Bush administration ended with its approach to September 11 widely considered a betrayal of American values. Obama won in a landslide and Democrats comfortably controlled both chambers of Congress. The executive orders issued by Obama not only had wide support but in many cases reflected positions that political and cultural leaders, including President Bush and the most senior members of his cabinet, had taken for years. The near-universal assessment of the intelligence community is that al Qaeda is little more than a "symbolic" threat, "a shadow of its former self." Yet the call to reform policies adopted by the Bush administration has all but disappeared. Worse, commentators have demanded, and lawmakers have endorsed, positions that are far more draconian than anything proposed under Bush. Substantial majorities favor these more aggressive positions and now widely support programs that were rejected when the threat environment was far more serious. Like the worsening perception of Islam and Muslims and the growing support for torture, why has the American countenance grown so much darker as the outlook has grown so much brighter?

Accounting for this turn of events is especially important since it is contrary to one of the most important tales Americans tell themselves as they construct their national identity, what I have called the myth of deviation and redemption. In this account, the nation veers off course at the onset of a military emergency but gradually steers back to a peacetime norm once the threat recedes. It was the fear of precisely this response that acted as such a powerful restraint on the Bush administration. The idea received its most prominent endorsement in May 2009 when President Obama, in his only major speech on national security, contrasted his approach with that of his predecessor.[47] Speaking at the National Archives in the unmistakable language of the Creed, and invoking the great symbolic power of the Constitution, the Declaration of Independence, and the Bill of Rights, Obama said that the Bush administration "went off course" when it made "a series of hasty decisions" that "established an *ad hoc* legal approach for fighting terrorism . . . that failed to rely on our legal traditions and time-tested institutions, and that failed to use our values as a compass."[48] To correct these mistakes, Obama said, he had made "dramatic changes" that represented "a new direction from the last eight years," and that his approach to terrorism, unlike that of the previous administration, was faithful to "our most fundamental values . . . [to] liberty and justice in this country." These changes, he said, would once again make the United States "a light that shines for all who seek freedom, fairness, equality, and dignity around the world" and permit the country to resume its timeless "journey . . . 'to form a more perfect Union.'"[49]

Events since Obama's election have been exceedingly unkind to this myth. The metaphor of deviation and redemption cannot explain a sudden return to the repressive wilderness just when it seemed the country had recovered its moral bearings. Nor can it account for an apparent determination to dive deeper into the wilds after the threat has substantially diminished.

III

How do we account for the paradox of the Obama era? One explanation that leaps to mind—partisanship—is certainly part of the answer. In 2011 a profile of Senator Mitch McConnell (R-KY) in the *Atlantic* credited him with conceiving and implementing the strategy of delay and obstruction that frustrated the Obama administration and played such a singular role in the Republican resurgence in 2010. McConnell, the profile said, struggled at first to find an issue that might stick with the public. "But in February [2009], he settled on opposing Obama's plan to close the terrorist-detention center at Guantánamo Bay. . . . The campaign was not orchestrated from some smoke-filled room but on the Senate floor itself. Most mornings, McConnell would give a speech of just a minute or two laying out the day's message about Guantánamo (often the same one). His phraseology would be picked up by other Republican lawmakers and FOX News, and echo around the blogosphere. He gave 25 such speeches."[50]

Though this makes for a nice story, it is pure fancy. The suggestion that Fox News "picked up" a message that McConnell (or any other politician) did not begin to spread until February is simply wrong. It was Fox that led the attack, pummeling the president from the very day he issued his executive orders. The theme, repeated over and over, was that Obama had not learned the lesson of 9/11 and was determined to tear down the protections that had kept the country safe for the past seven and a half years. This was condensed into a single sentence: Obama thinks we're not at war. On January 22 Bill O'Reilly reported that Obama's executive orders were part of a deliberate attempt to dismantle "the whole anti-terror apparatus" created by the Bush administration. His guest that evening, the conservative commentator Laura Ingraham, immediately agreed and struck the chords that Fox News would repeat for months: "Shutting down the military tribunals, . . . closing Gitmo by 2010, and of course doing away with harsh interrogation methods, I think you can make a pretty compelling case that our country's less safe today" than it was seventy-two hours earlier, before Obama took office.[51]

The following day, Sean Hannity said, "It took the new president almost no time whatsoever to take a strategy that has kept us safe and turn[] it on its head." Then he asked his guest, Karl Rove, "Are we headed to a pre-9/11 mentality?" "No," Rove answered, "we're already there. . . . They don't recognize we're in a war. You—in a war, you do not take tools that are working and stop using them and say we'll—get back to you in four months, six months, eight months, a year and tell you what we're going to do to replace this valuable tool which has helped keep America safe."[52] On January 26 Hannity began to profile some of the "high value" prisoners at Guantánamo, promising to introduce "a different Gitmo detainee each and every night, and asking just where on our shores that President Obama thinks these terrorists should call home."[53] Between January 22 and February 1, Fox News attacked the decision to close Guantánamo every day, on two and sometimes three different programs each evening, as well as its Sunday morning program.[54] A dedicated follower of Fox News, of which there are millions, would have seen the president mocked, ridiculed, and condemned for his executive orders dozens of times before Senator McConnell ever spoke up.

What began January 22 did not end for months. Though the pace slackened somewhat, on most days at least one Fox News program attacked the president for his national security policies.[55] Nor was Fox alone. On January 29 the *Wall Street Journal* published an opinion piece by John Yoo, the author of the infamous torture memo, denouncing Obama for "returning America to the failed law enforcement approach to fighting terrorism that prevailed before September 11." Though he accepted that Obama's executive orders had been well received by the left—"gone are the cries of an imperial presidency"—he lamented that Obama had ended "the tough interrogation of high level operatives" that had done so much to keep the nation safe. Such recklessness, Yoo wrote, "may have opened the door to further terrorist attacks on U.S. soil by shattering some of the nation's most critical defenses."[56] In launching this attack, the conservative press assiduously ignored the fact that President Bush and most of his senior advisers had agreed that Guantánamo should be closed and had already closed the black sites. Instead, the right dismissed Obama's executive orders as pandering to what Rush Limbaugh called "the far-left fringe kook base" of the Democratic Party.[57] The stable, centrist middle, it implied, could never support such a preposterous policy.

This attack on Obama's nascent counterterror policy was no doubt abetted by the rising anti-Islamic narrative, which by the time of Obama's election had become a potent force among Republicans. The Republican claim that Obama was a Muslim, though false, fit hand in glove with the attempt to rouse the right to action in order to paralyze Obama's presidency. It is hard to imagine a more potent attack than to charge one's opponent as not merely sympathetic to but a coreligionist of America's newest demon.

In partisan terms it was not important that the charge was untrue. The measure of a political attack is not its truth but its success. And this particular attack has been stunningly successful.

In late 2008 and early 2009, the Pew Organization asked people whether they "happen to know what Barack Obama's religion is." Nearly half of all respondents said he was a Christian, and another third said they didn't know. Only 12 percent said they thought he was a Muslim. Though Republicans were more likely to say he was a Muslim, the difference was fairly modest. Republicans, like everyone else, overwhelmingly reported either that Obama was a Christian or that they didn't know. By July 2010 the number of Republicans who thought he was a Muslim had skyrocketed to 31 percent, and those who thought he was a Christian had fallen to just over one in four, a drop of about 20 percentage points.[58]

This falsehood has proven remarkably durable. During the 2012 presidential primary season, roughly half the likely Republican voters in Mississippi and Alabama (an admittedly hyperpartisan group) said Obama was a Muslim.[59] And until President Obama released a copy of his birth certificate, similar numbers did not believe he was a U.S. citizen. Polls in April 2011 showed that one in four Americans, and a plurality of all Republicans, thought the president was foreign born. (After he released his birth certificate, only 3 percent clung to this fiction.)[60]

Partisanship no doubt partly explains the paradox of the Obama era, but it cannot be the whole answer. If the partisan ravings of Fox News and the rest of the conservative media were enough to shape public opinion, Barack Obama would never have been elected in the first place. Far more must be at work to account for the reversal in the national security narrative. For that, we must return to the lesson of the punitive turn. As I have shown, the essence of the punitive turn is the shared determination to *jointly* create a monster and *collectively* respond to the construction by dramatically expanding the executive branch's power to track, seize, and imprison the new demon in order to protect "us" from "them." It is a communal exercise. The Bush administration outran the limits of this sentiment by claiming an inherent power to ignore Congress, bypass the courts, and exclude the public. This placed it at odds with the dominant trends in national identity and led to a powerful creedal attack on Bush's imperial pretensions.

But the Obama administration has disavowed this claim to inherent power and relies instead on the power granted to it by Congress. The administration does not claim a unilateral power to ignore the will of Congress, nor has it notably used signing statements to reserve a right to disregard Congress's handiwork. The distinction is mostly symbolic, since the administration does not suggest that eschewing an inherent authority has led to a reduction in its power. But as I have stressed, national identity operates on a symbolic level, and limiting itself in this way has not only quieted the fear of an imperial presidency but has more closely aligned the administration's approach with the rituals and limits of the punitive turn, and therefore with the dominant currents of national identity. The Obama administration is doing precisely what presidents have done for decades, working in partnership with the other branches of government and the organs of civil society to denounce and pursue the monster in our midst by expanding the power of the executive branch. Unlike Bush, Obama thus acts with national identity rather than against it, and therefore encounters far less symbolic resistance (at least to his counterterror policy).

The legal scholar and civil rights lawyer David Cole has described this difference between Obama and Bush as a commitment to "the rule of law," and believes it marks "the essence of the distinction" between the two.[61] But Cole is only invoking a rhetorical trope about national identity: The Bush administration never conceded that it was behaving lawlessly. A better way to understand the difference between the two administrations is to recognize that the Obama administration generally tries to honor the rituals and limits of the punitive turn by eschewing unilateral power and working collaboratively with Congress and civil society to purge the nation of its newest demon. Yet it shows no inclination to end the punitive turn, or even arrest its growth.

Nothing demonstrates this better than the recent debate over the reauthorization of some of the controversial provisions of the Patriot Act, which were set to expire in mid-2011. Congressional and administration figures urged reauthorization in the unmistakable language of the punitive turn that has long been a staple of crime-control debates. Attorney General Eric Holder and Director of National Intelligence James Clapper, for instance, wrote a joint letter to Congress saying, "In the current threat environment, it is imperative that our intelligence and law enforcement agencies have the tools they need to protect our national security."[62] They did not expand on what "the current threat environment" was, and Holder and Clapper were careful not to contradict the consensus view of the intelligence community that the threat from al Qaeda is dramatically weakened. But this is precisely the sort of language the executive branch has used for years as it prepares to answer the demand to purge the community of a new demon, saying, in essence: "There is a monster among us, and we need you (Congress) to give us more power so we can track, capture, and imprison it for a very long time."

Acting on the administration's request, Congress played its traditional role. Senate Majority Leader Harry Reid (D-NV) warned, in words that could easily have come from former Attorney General John Ashcroft, that if the Patriot Act were allowed to expire, "we would be giving terrorists the opportunity to plot attacks against our country, undetected." Reid took the unusual step of criticizing freshman Senator Rand Paul (R-KY) for holding up the legislation. Paul, a strong libertarian and the son of libertarian Congressman Ron Paul (R-TX), had blocked the reauthorization because he felt the bill went too far in its encroachments on personal liberty, a concern Democrats had raised during the Bush administration. This time, however, the Democrat Reid warned that the Republican Paul was "threatening to take away the best tools we have for stopping" terrorists.[63] After Congress reauthorized them, Senate Republican leader Mitch McConnell said the extended provisions "have kept us safe for nearly a decade and Americans today should be relieved and reassured to know that these programs will continue." When the president signed the bill, he called the Patriot Act "an important tool for us to continue dealing with an ongoing terrorist threat."[64] The entire exercise was a communal triumph of the punitive turn.

But Obama's attachment to the punitive turn is not simply rhetorical. The entire counterterror philosophy of the Obama administration bears the unmistakable stamp of the punitive turn. For instance, though Bush and Obama both view terrorism as primarily an intelligence challenge, the Bush administration placed great faith in human intelligence (information gathered from people, including captured prisoners), which is what led it into the Serbonian Bog of black sites, enhanced interrogations, and extraordinary renditions. The Obama administration, by contrast, leans far more heavily on signals intelligence (information gathered by high-tech monitoring and surveillance). As the journalists Dana Priest and William Arkin have described, the Obama administration has overseen an enormous expansion in the size, power, and reach of the national security state, which is the new face of the military-industrial complex. Corporations and consultancies large and small now feed the federal government's insatiable hunger for perfect intelligence. The total budget for this expenditure has made national security the greatest growth industry of the twenty-first century.[65] At the same time, the Obama administration has vested the National Security Agency with the power and resources that will eventually enable it to monitor and store nearly every electronic transmission in the world, including cell phones, email, credit cards, ATM withdrawals, and all the other ways people leave behind a virtual footprint in the digital world.[66]

Some people have expressed alarm at this turn of events. In truth, however, these developments simply accelerate and extend the trends that have long been part of the punitive turn. For years, the branches of government have joined forces to harness the power of modern technology in an effort to track, monitor, and capture whatever demon is thought to threaten American civilization. In the end, there is no difference between the attempts to locate and keep track of every would-be sexual predator and every putative terrorist; conditioned by the punitive turn, most Americans now imagine both efforts as a perfectly salutary use of federal power. In addition, Americans have long since grown accustomed to sacrificing some measure of digital privacy as the price for participation in the modern world. They may understand at some barely conscious level that their email is neither private nor secure and that their credit card transactions are used to create a consumer profile, which is then sold to other businesses. Yet they assume—rightly or wrongly—that all this will be put to harmless use, leading to nothing more sinister than an unwanted pop-up in their inbox. As a result, the assiduous effort by the Obama administration to build a national security state, as well as its attachment to vast data-mining operations, does not strike most Americans as contrary to the way things ought to be.

Likewise, the Bush administration favored the muscular projection of American force worldwide, which led to a prominent and highly visible presence with tens of thousands of troops on the ground in Iraq and Afghanistan and sprawling American military bases throughout the region. The Obama administration, by contrast, favors a much smaller American footprint and much closer collaboration with local governments over a wider area of the globe. Obama has ended major military activity in Iraq and substantially reduced the American military presence in Afghanistan but has quietly expanded American counterterrorism operations elsewhere in the world. Smaller contingents of American forces now cooperate with local governments, which shoulder a larger share of the burden and have principal responsibility for any detentions that may occur. The United States provides funding, training, intelligence, and technical assistance to local partners like the governments of Tanzania, Uganda, Somalia, and Kenya, but ordinarily does not displace local authority.[67] As a result, these operations tend to resemble the low-intensity military operations conducted by the U.S. military and CIA around the world throughout the Cold War, and to which the American public has long since become indifferent.

To be sure, there is one respect in which Obama's approach to counterterror betrays the communal limits and rituals of the punitive turn. He has dramatically expanded the use of drone strikes by unmanned aerial vehicles (UAVs) and claims the right to launch strikes at targets wherever the need may arise, far from any combat zone. By late 2012 drones had replaced bombing campaigns and ground troops as the most visible weapon in the ever-evolving war on terror. In developing this policy, the Obama administration has excluded the entire community from the demonization process. Applying undisclosed criteria, the administration adds alleged militants to a "kill list" with no involvement by other branches of government, even when a U.S. citizen is placed on the list and killed by an American strike. The community learns of a citizen's death at the hands of his government only if it appears in the press.[68] Yet because the narrative about counterterror that was so prominent during the Bush administration has all but disappeared, even this objection is fairly tepid; Americans support the drone policy in large numbers.

IV

There is a third factor that helps account for the collapse of the anti-Bush narrative. In addition to attacks by the right and the administration's alignment with the punitive turn, no small amount of blame must fall on the president himself. Despite the consensus of the intelligence community about al Qaeda's severely debilitated state, the most prominent players within Obama's administration continue to champion what one scholar has dubbed the "terrorism narrative."[69] This is the idea that transnational terrorism in general, and al Qaeda in particular, represent an existential threat to the United States, which justifies the exceptional measures of wartime. Notwithstanding cosmetic rhetorical changes—the administration, for instance, no longer speaks of a war on terror—President Obama continues to insist the country faces a "persistent and evolving terrorist threat" and has warned ominously "that organizations like al Qaeda are in the process of trying to secure a nuclear weapon." He has vowed to be "unrelenting, unwavering, and unyielding" in the struggle "to defeat, disrupt, and dismantle al Qaeda and its allies." Secretary of State Hillary Clinton has said that "trans-national non-state networks" represent a more serious threat to U.S. security than a nuclear Iran or North Korea. And Attorney General Holder says that the threat of homegrown terrorism—a threat he has described as "real," "different," and "constant"—is what "keeps me up at night."[70]

Yet just as important as what Obama has said is what he has failed to say. In a deeply divided federal government, with entrenched institutional forces that frustrate even the most dedicated efforts at reform, the president's best weapon could be the power to set the agenda and frame the terms of debate, to define how an issue should be understood and received by the public, and to place it within the universe of national concerns. This is why President Bush's defense of Islam immediately after September 11 was so potent. The president, more than anyone else, constructs national identity by telling the country how the Creed should reveal itself. It is a weapon of unmatched significance.[71]

And it is this weapon that President Obama has largely left unused. In the first four years of his presidency, he made precisely one speech on national security. Almost without exception, he remained silent as events unfolded, passing up one opportunity after another to influence the debate in the public square. In his first ninety days in office, when he was the most popular man in the country and Fox News was assiduously attacking him as reckless and irresponsible, virtually the entire Obama administration remained silent on national security and counterterrorism policy. The administration made no attempt even to repeat, let alone develop or encourage, the narrative about national identity that had been so potent under Bush. Of course, the president was preoccupied with health care reform and the collapsing economy, issues that also generated fierce opposition. No suggestion is made that he ignored pressing matters. But when an issue acquires symbolic significance, as counterterrorism clearly had, its potency transcends the particular topic under discussion. Instead, the topic stands in for a larger cluster of ideas. "Softness" on Guantánamo, for example, symbolizes a broader weakness on national security. The particular issue wreaks havoc far beyond its bounds.

The president's silence was deafening. In late 2009, when Attorney General Holder announced that the alleged 9/11 conspirators held at Guantánamo would be prosecuted in federal court, it touched off an intense backlash. The *Wall Street Journal* said Holder "has invited grave and needless security risks by tempting jihadists the world over to strike Manhattan while the trial is in session."[72] Charles Krauthammer said the "trial will be a security nightmare and a terror threat to New York—what better propaganda-by-deed than blowing up the entire court room, making [Khalid Sheik Mohammed] a martyr and making the judge, jury and spectators into fresh victims?"[73] Republican Representative Peter King of New York attacked the decision as "not only misguided but extremely dangerous,"[74] and Lamar Smith of Texas, the highest-ranking Republican on the House Judiciary Committee, accused the administration of placing "the rights of terrorists over the rights of Americans to be safe and secure."[75]

Human Events thought an attack on the trial itself unlikely. "Smart terrorists—and it is critically important that we realize the degree of sophistication and cunning many of these men possess—are not going to attack the trial or prison in order to break the defendants out." Instead, they will target "schools, hospitals, and churches that they will take down and hold hostage for release of their compatriots. . . . If you live in a town where school children are held hostage, raped and murdered, perhaps in Westchester Country, New Jersey, or Long Island, or another more remote location, ask yourself, are you . . . personally willing to accept the risk?"[76] None of these commentators explained why, if al Qaeda was still capable of launching such an attack, it had thus far opted to restrain itself.

But the most noteworthy aspect of this debate was the complete absence of the president. The decision to bring the trial to the United States had been announced by the attorney general, and he alone was left to defend it. President Obama made no effort to justify Holder's announcement or explain why reliance on the criminal justice system demonstrated superior fidelity to the Creed. By choosing not to participate in the public square, he all but guaranteed the outcome. In the end, the Obama administration reversed itself; in April 2010 Attorney General Holder announced that the 9/11 defendants would be tried at Guantánamo before military commissions. This solidified the view that the original announcement had been misguided and emboldened the right.[77]

Presidential silence on national security has been the norm rather than the exception. In 2009 a federal grand jury in the Southern District of New York indicted Ahmed Ghailani for his role in the 1998 al Qaeda bombings of the United States embassies in Nairobi, Kenya, and Dar es Salaam, Tanzania.[78] The explosions killed nearly three hundred people, including more than two hundred civilians.[79] Four of Ghailani's coconspirators were captured shortly after the bombings, long before the attacks of September 11. They had been brought to New York by the FBI, where they were prosecuted in the Southern District, convicted, and sentenced to life in prison.[80] Ghailani, however, was not arrested until 2004, in Pakistan.[81] Rather than bring him to the United States to face prosecution, the CIA detained him at undisclosed black sites, where he was subjected to the Bush administration's enhanced interrogations. The administration transferred him to Guantánamo in 2006 and later brought him to the United States for trial.[82]

Ghailani was the first (and so far, the only) CIA and Guantánamo detainee to be tried in civilian court.[83] Before the trial, Judge Lewis Kaplan ruled that an important prosecution witness could not testify because the government had learned the man's identity from Ghailani, and the prosecution conceded that everything Ghailani had said during his interrogation had been coerced and involuntary.[84] After five days of deliberations, the jury acquitted Ghailani of all counts but one, convicting him of conspiracy to destroy government buildings and property.[85] The verdict was immediately denounced by conservatives, who attacked the Obama administration for its reckless decision to expose the country to the risk of an adverse outcome. Senator McConnell said that he, "like most Americans, wondered why we would even take the chance" of trying Ghailani in a civilian court.[86] Liz Cheney, the daughter of the former vice president and a member of the advocacy group Keep America Safe, found it inexcusable to be "roll[ing] the dice in a time of war."[87] Jennifer Rubin, writing in *Commentary* magazine, called the trial "part of a stunt by the Obama administration."[88] Conservatives also lamented the trial's failure to send an unambiguous signal of the community's outrage, as if only a conviction on every count could possibly satisfy the American people. Peter King, the chairman of the House Homeland Security Subcommittee, called the verdict "a total miscarriage of justice."[89] That Ghailani was sentenced to spend the rest of his life in prison drew far less comment on the right.

As the Ghailani debate unfolded, the president was again conspicuously absent. To be sure, some outside the administration quite properly pointed out that the function of a trial is "to guarantee fairness, not convictions."[90] Amy Davidson wrote in the *New Yorker* that "our legal system is not a machine for producing the maximum number of convictions, regardless of the law."[91] Others ventured that the United States had only itself to blame for the Ghailani verdict. Focusing on the impact of Judge Kaplan's pretrial ruling, the Center for Constitutional Rights said, "If anyone is unsatisfied with Ghailani's acquittal on 284 counts, they should blame the CIA agents who tortured him."[92] Some criticized the previous administration for mishandling the case at an earlier stage.[93] These are all creedal arguments, of course, and would have had more impact had they come from the administration. But the Obama administration made almost no attempt to defend the course of events, and the president was completely silent. The voices defending Ghailani's prosecution were thus drowned out by a chorus of angry indignation that Obama had "rolled the dice."[94]

What accounts for the administration's embrace of the terrorism narrative and refusal to defend its campaign positions? It is too early to render a verdict, but history may provide some insight. Presidential timidity in this domain is hardly unprecedented. Recent scholarship has shown convincingly that partisan politics—particularly attacks on Democrats from the right—helped sustain the Cold War long after the Soviet Union had ceased to pose any realistic threat and forced the United States into positions at home and abroad that, while they may have made sense from a political perspective, certainly were not justified by the demands of national security.[95] When the Truman administration capitulated to the anticommunist frothing of the far right, the journalist David Halberstam described the outcome in terms that apply equally well today:

> Rather than combat the charges of softness on communism and subversion, the Truman Administration, sure that it was the lesser of two evils, moved to expropriate the issue. . . . So the issue was legitimized; rather than being the property of the far right, which the centrist Republicans tolerated for obvious political benefits, it had even been picked up by the incumbent Democratic party.[96]

Regardless of the motivation, the effect on the public discourse is the same. The Obama administration has reinforced the narrative advanced by the Bush administration: that terrorism remains an existential threat requiring extraordinary measures by the national government. This brings the hyperbolic rhetoric of the extreme right closer to the political center and makes it more apt to become part of any political compromise. Many would say that as a purely political calculation, the president has been rewarded for his choices, since his movement to the right has largely silenced Republican criticism on this issue. Fox News has even conducted a poll that asks whether the Obama administration owes the Bush administration an apology for having adopted so many of its predecessor's policies after having attacked them during the campaign. To no one's surprise, the results split on partisan lines: Republicans said yes, Democrats no; independents were evenly divided.[97]

V

All of these factors—partisanship by the right, silence and capitulation by the president, and compatibility with the prevailing winds of national identity—help explain why the national security narrative has turned so decisively since President Obama took office. Yet they are merely evidence of the more fundamental explanation for the change in the national mood. If the American public had been firmly attached to the narrative that prevailed at the end of the Bush administration, it seems unlikely that these factors, alone or in combination, could have uprooted them so quickly. This suggests the most important explanation for the paradox of the Obama era: that creedal attachments to remote national controversies are symbolic and easily dislodged, and therefore exquisitely subject to elite manipulation.

As I have indicated, most Americans see national issues as remote and beyond their control. This applies especially to national security, where the details of the debate are often deliberately shrouded in secrecy and thought to be beyond the ken of all but a few esoteric specialists. For these issues, the American public is particularly at the mercy of its trusted elites.[98] Are the prisoners at Guantánamo innocent men, wrongly detained and horribly mistreated, or coddled terrorists committed to destruction and mayhem? Can they be put on trial in federal court, or would they overwhelm our courts and disappear into the shadows? Is the Patriot Act a dangerous encroachment on the lives and liberties of innocent people, or the only thing that has saved the United States from disaster? Most Americans cannot answer these questions for themselves, and necessarily look for guidance to those they trust.

This was brought home to me on September 11, 2010. I was speaking at an event marking the ninth anniversary of the attacks, and the sponsors had asked me to talk about the state of civil liberties in a post-9/11 world. The audience was self-selected to be interested in this question and therefore more likely than the average American to be informed about it. During the event, a member of the audience complained that the American people

had been "duped" by "the media" into believing "lies" about the risk of another terror attack. The idea of a manipulative media and a gullible public
is a common complaint on both the left and right. So I decided to conduct
an experiment. I asked how many people had an opinion—favorable or
unfavorable—about the Patriot Act. Every hand went up. Then I asked how
many people had actually *read* the act. Two or three hands. Directing myself to the scores of people who had formed an opinion without reading
the act, I asked what they had relied upon to reach their conclusions. The
answers varied, of course, but they all began with some version of, "People
say . . . " I have since repeated this experiment several times with a variety
of audiences, including my ideologically diverse classes at Northwestern
University Law School, and have always gotten the same results.[99]

This was precisely what I expected. People cannot readily get hold of the
text of a law or proposed legislation (though the Internet makes that much
easier than it used to be) and cannot easily understand the sometimes esoteric legislative language. Even if they could, who has time to read it? The
Patriot Act is hundreds of pages long and cross-references a number of
other laws. And even if they had the time and could penetrate the typically
turgid legislative prose, their investigation would be just beginning. Much
of what one needs to know to evaluate a law does not appear in its text. How
does the law affect other priorities? How does it shift resources? What part
of a legislative agenda does it leave undone? What compromises and horse-
trading went into the bill, and what will they lead to? These and countless
other questions are almost always impossible to answer from the text of the
law itself. Many people devote much of their professional careers to these
issues, and it would be foolish to demand that the casual observer approach
the matter the same way.

Quite understandably, the members of my audience had relied on
sources they trusted to inform their view of the act. For some, it was a position paper drafted by an organization like the ACLU or the Cato Institute.
For others, it was a prominent commentator or journalist who had written
about the act in a newspaper, magazine, or blog they considered reliable.
For still others, it was a "national security expert" who had appeared on a
television or radio program that they trusted to provide unbiased information about current events. The people in my makeshift experiment seemed to

be thoughtful and intelligent consumers of information. They did not consider themselves gullible, nor did they believe that they had been duped. All of them believed the sources they had relied upon were trustworthy.

But as we have seen with attitudes about Islam and torture, because remote attachments exist only as "a series of pictures in the mind," they can be dislodged by changing the pictures. The manipulability of public sentiment has often been on display in the post-9/11 era, especially when the "pictures in the mind" have been in flux. In November 2001, for instance, shortly after President Bush announced plans to convene military tribunals, an ABC/Washington Post poll asked the following question:

> George W. Bush favors the use of special military tribunals. Knowing Bush's position, what do you think—should non-U.S. citizens who are charged with terrorism be put on trial in the regular U.S. criminal court system or in a special military tribunal?

When framed that way—conducting the survey shortly after the president's announcement, specifically directing the respondent to take the president's view into consideration, and stressing that the defendants were "non-U.S. citizens"—the pollsters put a set of pictures into play that substantially increased the likelihood that the public would support military commissions. And it did, by more than 2:1.[100]

Yet only two weeks later, a CBS/New York Times poll asked this question:

> In the past, the United States has tried suspected terrorists in criminal court, requiring a jury, a unanimous verdict, and a civilian judge. Do you think this is the right way to deal with suspected terrorists involved in attacks against the United States, or not?

This framing puts an entirely different set of pictures in respondents' minds. It specifically directs the listener to some of the most hallowed features of American justice, including "a jury, a unanimous verdict, and a civilian judge," and asks whether these features are "right." The respondent cannot reject a civilian trial unless she is prepared to say that settled elements long associated with the rule of law are "wrong." This framing tilts the scale heavily in favor of civilian prosecution. The survey also does not mention that the military commission has been reserved for noncitizens, nor does it invoke the president's support for commissions. Under these very different circumstances, the public preferred trials in a regular court by a substantial margin.[101] Thus, when the pictures are unsettled, public opinion is particularly susceptible to elite guidance (or manipulation, depending on one's perspective), which only underscores the need to participate in the public square. Yet at this moment the Obama administration went inexplicably silent, with predictable results.

Obama's election and early actions "called [his] opponents to action." But because the Obama administration did not rise to the challenge—because it refused to engage the battle in the public square and defend its policy preferences with the same vigor its opponents used in attacking them (indeed, it largely embraced the "terrorism narrative")—the "pictures in the mind, placed there by television news, newspapers, magazines, and discussions" all sent the signal that the narrative that had taken shape in opposition to the Bush administration was not true to national identity. That narrative quickly collapsed and was replaced by a different one, which has led to far more aggressive positions without regard to the threat environment.

To recognize that creedal attachments are often symbolic—that they can be fleeting, ephemeral, and easily manipulated—is emphatically not the same as suggesting that they are insincere. The narrative that overwhelmed the Bush administration is not demonstrably more "true" to American identity than the very different narrative that prevailed at the end of 2012. I have my preference (there is no point denying one's biases), and the fact that both narratives claim to speak for national identity does not mean that both are equally faithful to the facts. A narrative may be wrong, at least to the extent that its assertions are subject to empirical proof. But to say that a narrative is mistaken is a far cry from dismissing it as illegitimate. In any event, assertions that are subject to empirical proof in this arena are few, and cannot be counted on to settle these debates. The relevant question—perhaps the only question—is not whether a view is "genuine" or "wrong" but whether it gains sufficient currency in the public square that it becomes entrenched, a matter of received wisdom beyond credible criticism. When that happens, that narrative becomes—by the unassailable power of the American Creed—the way things ought to be.

13

All Will Be as It Ought to Be

I

SO WHAT CHANGED WHEN EVERYTHING changed? It is certainly wrong to say that September 11 changed American values. At one level, our ideals have not changed for centuries and are not likely to change soon. We will always worship the same words and phrases—"liberty," "equality," the "rule of law," "limited government," "individualism," and "community." They may be the only constants in American life, connecting us to an imagined past and guiding us into an unknown future. We change only what these words represent—the meaning we assign to them, the space we give them in the public square, and the stories we tell that give them substance. It is how we make and remake our national identity.

This process creates endless and inevitable contest. One person's vindication of national values can be another's betrayal. Both will deploy the elastic language of the American Creed, invoke the legitimating symbols and myths of the American experience, and believe in their hearts that their vision alone represents all that is worth preserving in national life. When one of these views triumphs, when it marks the outermost limits of acceptable opinion, the American habit of converting "is" to "ought" will once again work its magic. All will be right with the world; national identity will be new again.

When we have achieved this new condition—when Jim Crow is replaced by civil rights, when the communal orientation of the New Deal is supplanted by the individualism of modern conservatism—we look back with wonder at what we now see as a benighted past. Imbued with the conviction that American life progresses inexorably to higher planes, we imagine that we stand on the shoulders of those who came before us and pity them that they could not see the vision of national life that is so clear to us. But it is only because the twists and turns of history have left us to face our foundational ideals from a new perspective that we see them so differently than our ancestors did. The light is different, and so too the shape of the surrounding landscape. Mountains that loomed large in their world have shriveled to insignificance in ours; crevices and gorges that divide us into warring camps were easily bridged in theirs. The constellations look very different from where we stand today than from where they stood yesterday. And the direction they took to reach the more perfect union was as true to the American ideal as the path we follow today.[1]

These insights may finally let us put to rest the idea that September 11 "changed everything." The attacks reinvigorated our continuing national debate about the meaning of shared values by giving rise to a new set of narratives. These narratives fall on a continuum that reflects their relationship to the dominant trends in national identity. At one extreme, the anti-Islamic narrative has reawakened an impulse to cinch the bonds of community membership more tightly and to define membership's boundaries in terms of a mythologized Judeo-Christian heritage. There is nothing new in this sentiment: It is modern only in the postwar willingness to include Jews and Judaism inside the magic circle. As before, the impulse is imagined not as a threat to the Creed but as the only thing that protects it from ruin.

But if the impulse is familiar, it nonetheless faces a different struggle for dominance in the public square than did its predecessors. We are not remotely the same country that spawned the anti-Catholic virulence of the Know Nothing Party in the 1830s, or that cast a wary eye on the Democratic presidential candidate Al Smith a century later and looked askance at John F. Kennedy a quarter-century after that. We have come a long way from the day in 1915 when a Georgia mob lynched the Jewish manufacturer Leo Frank in an insensate spasm of anti-Semitism. For the great majority of Americans, and the overwhelming majority of young people, those days are happily forgotten, irrelevant to the demands of daily life. Acceptance of religious diversity has become not only the "is" but the "ought" of the American experience.

For most Americans, the anti-Islamic narrative partakes far too much of this horrid past. As imagined by the religious right, the problem with Islam is the religion itself: It is inherently violent, inherently totalitarian, and inherently hostile to American values. The secular conservative variant of this narrative is only marginally less offensive: It deliberately blurs the distinction between "good" and "bad" Muslims by insisting that most Muslims who advocate on behalf of their coreligionists in the public square are in fact committed to the "Islamification" of America. Any good works are simply a form of stealth jihad. In decisive respects, therefore, the anti-Islamic narrative struggles against the heavy weight of majority opinion.

Because the purveyors of this narrative have attached themselves to tropes that stir the hearts and fire the imaginations of only a small minority of Americans—primarily religious and social conservatives and their authoritarian fellow travelers in the Republican Party—they have so far been unable to extend their reach beyond this group. Within this sector of society, they have been extraordinarily successful. But in the decade since September 11, animosity to Islam has devolved into yet another of those quintessentially American issues that divide liberals and moderates from conservatives; Democrats and independents from Republicans; young from old; and blue from red.

Occupying a somewhat less fragile position in American life is the new embrace of torture. As with Islam, since 9/11 the American view of torture has followed a steady descent into darkness. The torture narrative deploys the language of the Creed to justify the practice as strictly necessary, morally appropriate, legally sanctioned, and carefully regulated. Fortified by this creedal blessing, millions of Americans have embraced actions that a dozen years ago would have been unthinkable. The result is the satisfying belief that pouring water up a man's nose and down his throat to induce the sensation of imminent drowning is not only something other than what it is but something entirely consistent with American ideals. And as with Islam, the pit into which we have descended has grown blacker as the threat has receded. Nowhere is the myth of deviation and redemp-

tion more obviously untrue than in the torture debate. Moreover, and unlike with the anti-Islamic narrative, the torture narrative has aligned itself
more thoroughly with the dominant directions in national identity. This
has broadened its appeal to include millions of Americans who are aghast
at the attack on Islam.

At the other end of the continuum lies counterterror. Here, the objections that derailed the Bush administration have been swept aside. Having
learned the lesson of its predecessor, the Obama administration carefully
observes the limits and rituals of the punitive turn. The counter-terror debate now follows a well-trod path, the evidence of so many fevered hunts
for earlier demons: The administration warns of disaster and seeks new or
renewed tools; Congress complies; civil society applauds or objects. The
public, reassured that everything has gotten back to normal, ignores the
entire affair. The result is a set of policies that transforms the content of
shared national values not by reversing their meaning but by carrying them
to places they had not gone before. Today's counter-terror policies do not
break the rules of national identity; they merely extend their limits.

II

This assessment of the state of play a dozen years after 9/11 is incomplete unless we also recognize it as provisional. Americans may convert *is*
to *ought,* but only a romantic believes the *is* will always be. It is too early to
tell which of the various narratives now competing for a place in the public
square will eventually prove victorious. Still, we owe it to ourselves to haz-
ard a few predictions.

The anti-Islamic narrative may be the first to collapse. It is at odds with
the prevailing understanding of national identity, holds little appeal to the
young, and relies heavily on a media outlet that is distrusted by precisely
those it most needs to persuade. At the same time, the major constituencies for this narrative have no natural attachment to it. Authoritarians are
animated not by innate hostility to Islam but by a sense of threat to some
imagined communal identity. As a new demon is constructed—and a new
demon is always around the corner—the authoritarians will cleave off and
direct their considerable venom at the new threat to the moral order. Like-

wise, there is nothing inherent in the religious right that compels antipathy to Islam. The history of anti-Catholicism in this country provides ample proof that fundamentalist Protestants can reimagine the Antichrist. It also bears repeating that immediately after the attacks, the most prominent and most conservative evangelical Christian ever to hold high office in this country—George W. Bush—went to great lengths to insist that Islam was entirely compatible with the Judeo-Christian tradition, an insistence that had a powerful, if temporary, effect on public opinion. And let us not forget the very successful Republican courtship of Muslim- and Arab-Americans in the 2000 election. It was only a long decade ago that Grover Norquist described Muslims as natural conservatives.

What of the torture narrative? Like much of the Bush administration's response to September 11, torture was meant to be a secret affair, unapproved by Congress, unreviewed by the judiciary, and unknown to the public. But if torture were made a communal affair, I do not doubt that most Americans would find it entirely compatible with American values. If torture were championed by the president, taken up by Congress, and supported by prominent elements of civil society as a vital solution to the "crisis" of Islamic terrorism, all of which culminated in legislation that bore the stamp of the democratic process (and helpfully gave torture some other name), I suspect it would be quickly welcomed by the majority of the American public. In that way, national identity would bring torture within its capacious reach.

Is there reason to believe this may come to pass? Not long before the 2012 presidential election, Charlie Savage of the *New York Times* reported that the national security team assembled to advise Mitt Romney had recommended a return to coercive interrogations. Savage obtained a copy of an internal campaign memo entitled "Interrogation Techniques." The memo urged Romney, if elected, to "rescind and replace President Obama's executive order" that ended the CIA program and resume the use of "enhanced interrogation techniques against high-value detainees that are safe, legal and effective in generating intelligence to save American lives."[2] According to Savage, many of Romney's advisers in this area were part of the Bush administration's national security team. For his part, President Obama has always been steadfastly opposed to the enhanced techniques, saying in no uncertain terms that they were torture and that he would not authorize their use.[3] The nation may have decided the torture narrative's immediate fate last November.

Should we be optimistic about the fate of counterterror policy? There are indications that the punitive turn may have run its course. Capital punishment has always been a reliable barometer of the punitive impulse, and both the number of people sentenced to die and the number of death row inmates executed have been falling for more than a decade. In 2011, forty-three inmates were executed nationwide (compared with a high of ninety-eight in 1999), and substantially fewer than one hundred were sentenced to die (compared with more than three hundred each in 1995 and 1996).[4] A number of states have recently repealed their death penalty statutes, and the governor of Oregon has declared a moratorium on executions. New York's highest court struck down that state's death penalty statute, and the legislature has not passed a replacement. Leaders in other prominent capital punishment states, including the Republican chief justice of the California Supreme Court, have urged repeal of the death penalty in their respective domains.

Nor is this trend confined to the death penalty. Violent crime rates have been falling for decades, and in 2010, for the first time since 1972, the total number of people in custody in the United States actually declined (though only slightly).[5] Prison populations will probably continue to shrink. Violent crime is a young man's game, and the cohort of young males is growing at a substantially slower rate than the rest of the population.[6] Prison is extraordinarily expensive, and a number of states, facing fierce budgetary constraints, have taken steps to reduce the number of people incarcerated. Several have actually closed unused or underused prisons.[7]

It is tempting to craft from these few data points an argument that predicts a gradual softening of the punitive sentiment, and thus an end to post-9/11 policies like indefinite detention without trial. But such a prediction would be premature at best. The punitive turn supplies an orienting philosophy toward deviant behavior and risk, as well as a set of rituals and policy proscriptions that enable society to engage in the communal process of casting the demon beyond the pale. Perhaps this way of thinking will someday become discredited in the United States. But nothing in recent events suggests that this day is at hand. It seems more likely that at least some of the favorable developments in the criminal justice system are taking place because "common criminals" are no longer seen as the worst of the worst. The run-of-the-mill criminal defendant, in other words, may be the unintended beneficiary of the new insistence that Islamic terrorists are the greatest threat the country has ever faced, allowing others to improve by comparison.

This is precisely the language used by politicians who want to prosecute accused terrorists in military commissions rather than regular criminal courts. Senator Lindsey Graham (R-SC) described the 9/11 conspirators as "warriors bent on our destruction," not remotely comparable to "a guy who robbed a liquor store." His colleague Mitch McConnell (R-KY) thought it was preposterous to treat alleged terrorists as "somehow on the same level as a convenience store stick-up man," and Senator Saxby Chambliss (R-GA) insisted that Congress had a duty to make sure that the prisoners at Guantánamo—people "who get up every day thinking of ways to kill and harm Americans"—"are never subjected to the process that is developed in [federal] courts for average, ordinary criminals." The war on terror has led us to reimagine the criminal justice system as something that was never intended for genuine evil but for the softer souls of "ordinary criminals."[8]

More important, it would require extraordinary political courage for any national leader to "stand . . . athwart history, yelling Stop, at a time when no one is inclined to do so," as conservative icon William F. Buckley once said. Both parties understand that no politician has ever been punished for participating in communal demonization, a lesson the Obama administration quickly took to heart. It may be that the bell will toll on the punitive turn for some, but not for the Islamic terrorist.

Still, if we cannot tell which of these narratives will supply the content of shared national values in the years to come, if we cannot say which will provide the stories we tell ourselves about what it means to be an American, we can confidently predict *how* it will happen. Partisans will summon the soaring imagery of freedom and equality, of liberty and the rule of law, of individual sacrifice for the common good. In time, one set of narratives will collapse and another will prevail. The old words will again take on new meaning. As before, we will foresee an endless future in the timeless language of the American Creed. All will be new again. All will be as it ought to be.

NOTES

Chapter 1: "What the United States Is All About at Our Core"

1. Commission on Presidential Debates, The Second Gore-Bush Presidential Debate, October 11, 2000, transcript available at http://www.debates.org/index.php?page=october-11-2000 -debate-transcript. A CBS News poll taken the day before the debate had Gore a 1-point favorite over Bush, within the poll's margin of error. See "CBS Poll: Gore and Bush ThisClose," October 10, 2000, available at http://www.cbsnews.com/stories/2000/10/10/politics/main 239924.shtml?tag=cbsContent;contentMain. Bush apparently felt no fear that making a particular appeal to Arab and Muslim voters would cost him within his traditional constituency.
2. Commission on Presidential Debates, Second Gore-Bush Presidential Debate.
3. Ibid.
4. Ibid.
5. Ibid.
6. Ibid.
7. Grover Norquist, "'Natural Conservatives' Muslims Deliver for the GOP," *American Spectator,* June 2001. For other accounts of Norquist's role in the courtship of the Muslim vote, see, e.g., Paul Starobin, "Crescent Conflict," *National Journal,* November 19, 2005.
8. Bonior's bill, H.R. 2121, The Secret Evidence Repeal Act of 2000, was originally introduced June 10, 1999, and reported out of the House Judiciary Committee on October 17, 2000. The text of the bill is available at http://thomas.loc.gov/cgi-bin/query/z?c106:h2121:. Bonior reintroduced the bill, H.R. 1266, The Secret Evidence Repeal Act of 2001, March 28, 2001. On April 19 it was referred to the Judiciary Committee, where it died. The text is available at http://thomas.loc.gov/cgi-bin/query/z?c107:h1266:. H.R. 2121 had 128 cosponsors; H.R. 1266 had 100. Both bills included the following congressional findings:

    1. No person physically present in the United States, including its outlying possessions, should be deprived of liberty based on evidence kept secret from that person, including information classified for national security reasons.
    2. Removal from the United States can separate a person from the person's family, may expose the person to persecution and torture, and amounts to a severe deprivation of liberty.
    3. Use of secret evidence in immigration proceedings deprives the alien of due process

rights guaranteed under the United States Constitution and undermines our adversarial system, which relies on cross-examination as an engine of truth-seeking.

Abraham introduced his bill, S. 3139, Secret Evidence Repeal Act of 2000, September 28, 2000. It was referred to the Senate Judiciary Committee, where it died. Abraham's bill had four cosponsors. The text is available at http://thomas.loc.gov/cgi-bin/query/z?c106:S.3139:.

9. See Gallup News Service, "Racial Profiling Is Seen as Widespread, Particularly Among Young Black Men," December 9, 1999, available at http://www.gallup.com/poll/3421/Racial -Profiling-Seen-Widespread-Particularly-Among-Young-Black-Men.aspx.

10. "Governor George W. Bush's Record of Inclusion" is quoted in ACLU Letter to President Bush on Use of Secret Evidence in Immigration Proceedings, June 13, 2001, available at http://www.aclu.org/immigrants-rights/letter-president-bush-use-secret-evidence-immigra tion-proceedings.

11. The census data are available in a report prepared by the U.S. Census Bureau entitled "The Arab Population: 2000," December 2003, available at http://www.census.gov/prod/2003 pubs/c2kbr-23.pdf.

12. For an account of the meeting in Dearborn, see Niraj Warikoo, "Bush Chats with Arab Americans on Issues," *Detroit Free Press,* October 6, 2000; Jake Tapper, "Setback for Arab-Americans," Salon.com, available at http://archive.salon.com/politics/feature/2001/09/17/muslims/.

13. Nora Boustany, "One Man, Making a Difference," *Washington Post,* August 2, 2000.

14. "American Muslim PAC Endorses George W. Bush for President," October 23, 2000, available at http://ampolitics.ghazali.net/html/ampcc_endorses.html.

15. American Muslim Council, "Election 2000," October 23, 2000, quoting Dr. Yahya Basha.

16. Norquist, "'Natural Conservatives'"; Alexander Rose, "How Did Muslims Vote in 2000?" *Middle East Quarterly,* Summer 2001, 13–27. According to the American Muslim Association, which tracks political participation by Muslims in the United States, about 700 Muslims stood for office nationwide in 2000, of whom 152 were elected to state and local office, including 92 in Texas alone. Cited in Rose, "How Did Muslims Vote?"

17. Ralph Z. Hallow, "Muslim Turnout for Bush Fuels Hope; GOP Reaches Out on Core Values," *Washington Times,* January 24, 2001.

18. George W. Bush, Address Before a Joint Session of Congress, February 27, 2001, available at http://www.presidency.ucsb.edu/ws/index.php?pid=29643.

19. Ibid.; Attorney General John Ashcroft, News Conference, March 1, 2001, available at http:// www.justice.gov/archive/ag/speeches/2001/030101racialprofconf.htm.

20. Senator Hatch's remarks were made at a hearing to consider S-989, the End Racial Profiling Act of 2001, August 1, 2001, and are available at http://www.gpo.gov/fdsys/pkg/CHRG -107shrg80475/pdf/CHRG-107shrg80475.pdf.

21. Tapper, "Setback for Arab-Americans." For reflections on the importance of the Muslim vote in the 2012 presidential elections, see Farid Senzai, "Engaging American Muslims: Emerging Trends and Attitudes," Institute for Social Policy and Understanding, April 2012, available at http://ispu.org/pdfs/ISPU%20Report_Political%20Participation_Senzai_WEB.pdf.

22. Jane Mayer, *The Dark Side: The Inside Story of How the War on Terror Turned into a War on American Ideals* (New York: Doubleday, 2008).

23. Jimmy Carter, "Dallas, Texas, Remarks at a Dallas County Democratic Committee Voter Registration Rally," July 21, 1980, available online at Gerhard Peters and John T. Woolley, The American Presidency Project, http://www.presidency.ucsb.edu/ws/?pid=44784.

24. Quoted in Mark Silk, "Notes on the Judeo-Christian Tradition in America," *American Quarterly* 36, no. 1 (1984), 65–85.

25. Stephen Prothero, Introduction to *A Nation of Religions: The Politics of Pluralism in Multi-*

Religious America, ed. Stephen Prothero (Chapel Hill: University of North Carolina Press, 2006), 2.

26. Henry Kissinger, *White House Years* (Boston: Little, Brown, 1979), 54.

Chapter 2: "The Ceaseless Striving to Live Out Our True Creed"

Epigraph. "The Target," *The Wire,* HBO, June 2, 2002. According to David Simon, the creator of the *The Wire,* the Snot Boogie story is true. See David Simon, *Homicide: A Year of Killing in the Streets* (New York: Houghton Mifflin, 1991), 540–541.

1. Theodore J. Lowi, *The End of Liberalism: The Second Republic of the United States* (New York: W. W. Norton, 2009), xi.

2. See "The Generation Gap and the 2012 Election: Section 4: Views of the Nation," Pew Research Center for the People and the Press, http://www.people-press.org/2011/11/03/section-4-views-of-the-nation/.

3. These particular results are from the General Social Survey, 1996, questions 810 and 813, and may be viewed at http://www.thearda.com/Archive/Files/Codebooks/GSS1996_CB.asp#V810.

4. See, e.g., Will Herberg, *Protestant, Catholic, Jew: An Essay in American Religious Sociology* (1955; Chicago: University of Chicago Press, 1983), 74.

5. For discussion of the widespread empirical support for these values when they are stated in the most general terms, see, e.g., Andrew Kohut and Bruce Stokes, *America Against the World: How We Are Different and Why We Are Disliked* (New York: Times Books, 2011); Donald Devine, *The Political Culture of the United States: The Influence of Member Values on Regime Maintenance* (New York: Little, Brown, 1972); Herbert McClosky and John R. Zaller, *The American Ethos: Public Attitudes Toward Capitalism and Democracy* (Cambridge: Harvard University Press, 1984); Samuel Huntington, *American Politics: The Promise of Disharmony* (New York: Simon and Schuster, 1981).

6. Quoted in Huntington, *American Politics,* 25.

7. See Gunnar Myrdal, Richard Sterner, and Arnold Rose, *An American Dilemma: The Negro Problem and Modern Democracy* (New York: Harper and Row, 1944). In place of "American Creed," Herbert McClosky and John R. Zaller use "American ethos," though they mean the same thing. McClosky and Zaller, *American Ethos.* Other writers have tried to be a little more precise and have used the idea of an American "political culture." See Devine, *Political Culture of the United States.* Devine observes "that the United States has had a high degree of consensus on fundamental political values at the community and regime levels. This political consensus is conceived as having had an important shaping influence upon the content of its public policy, upon the maintenance of its democratic regime, and upon the persistence of its community"; ibid., 33. Devine conceives political culture as the sum of these shared political values and their expression throughout all levels of society in the form of widely observed rules, norms, and patterns of behavior; ibid., 4–43.

8. Though they may have given it different names, the authorities who have described aspects of the Creed over the many years—Crèvecœur, Tocqueville, Bryce, Hartz, Hofstadter, Bell, Rossiter, Boorstin, Bercovitch, Schlesinger, Bellah, Lipset, Huntington, McClosky, Zaller, and many others—are a veritable who's who of American social and political thought.

9. Myrdal, *American Dilemma,* 4.

10. Huntington, *American Politics,* 14.

11. Samuel Huntington, *Who Are We? The Challenges to America's National Identity* (New York: Simon and Schuster, 2004). For an earlier stage of Huntington's thinking in this field, see

Samuel Huntington, "The Erosion of American National Interests," *Foreign Affairs* 76 (1997), 28–49.

12. Arthur M. Schlesinger, Jr., *The Disuniting of America: Reflections on a Multicultural Society* (New York: W. W. Norton, 1998), 147.

13. Seymour Martin Lipset, *American Exceptionalism: A Double-Edged Sword* (New York: W. W. Norton, 1996), 19.

14. Mary Ann Glendon, *Rights Talk: The Impoverishment of Political Discourse* (New York: Free Press, 1991), 3.

15. See, e.g., Judith Shklar, *Legalism* (Cambridge: Harvard University Press, 1964), 1, describing American society as legalistic, and defining legalism as "the ethical attitude that holds moral conduct to be a matter of rule following, and moral relationships to consist of duties and rights determined by rules." But note that reverence for the great symbols of the law in this country has never been much cluttered by knowledge of their content. See Michael Kammen, *A Machine That Would Go of Itself: The Constitution in American Culture* (New York: Alfred A. Knopf, 1986).

16. Robert Bellah et al., *Habits of the Heart: Individualism and Commitment in American Life* (Berkeley: University of California Press, 2008); E. J. Dionne, *Our Divided Political Heart* (New York: Bloomsbury USA, 2012).

17. George W. Bush, First Inaugural Address, January 20, 2001, available online at Gerhard Peters and John T. Woolley, The American Presidency Project, http://www.presidency.ucsb.edu/ws/?pid=25853.

18. Bellah and his collaborators distinguish between civic republicanism and biblical religion as a source of this communitarian sentiment, but acknowledge their overlap; *Habits of the Heart*, 20–31.

19. Hillary Rodham Clinton, *It Takes a Village: And Other Lessons Children Teach Us* (New York: Simon and Schuster, 1996). Note that acknowledging the tradition of civic virtue in American life does not make it necessary for us to choose sides, or even wade into the dense academic underbrush of the debate over the relative importance of liberalism and republicanism in American thought. See Daniel T. Rodgers, "Republicanism: The Career of a Concept," *Journal of American History* 79, no. 1 (1992), 11–38. Pushing back against treatments like Louis Hartz, *The Liberal Tradition in America* (1955; New York: Harcourt Brace, 1991), historians began to point out the importance of republican ideas in early American history, which stressed the value of local, participatory democracy by a small, more or less homogenous community of civic-minded citizens who placed the welfare of the group over the success of the individual. There is no question that republicanism has played an important and too often neglected role in American thought. More than that, however, is a matter of dispute, as scholars disagree about the relative weight and enduring importance of the liberal and republican traditions. The debate seems to have died down of late as scholars have come to accept the wisdom of the historian Lance Banning's observation that intramural squabbles like these matter a great deal more to academics than to the people whose thought we purport to parse. Lance Banning, "Jeffersonian Ideology Revisited: Liberal and Classical Ideas in the New American Republic," *William and Mary Quarterly* 43, no. 1 (1986), 3–19. It requires no great stretch to suppose that a person can concern herself with both the rights of the individual and the welfare of the community without feeling a need either to weigh one value against the other or to choose whether her thought processes are predominantly liberal or republican.

20. Barack Obama, Remarks by the President in State of the Union Address, January 24, 2012, http://www.whitehouse.gov/the-press-office/2012/01/24/remarks-president-state-union-address.

21. Barack Obama, Commencement Address at Miami Dade College in Miami, Florida, April

29, 2011, available online at Peters and Woolley, American Presidency Project, http://www
.presidency.ucsb.edu/ws/?pid=90313.

22. McClosky and Zaller, *American Ethos*, 18.

23. Daniel Boorstin, *The Genius of American Politics* (Chicago: University of Chicago Press,
1958), 8–10. Boorstin believed this sense of "givenness" made Americans especially disin-
clined to political theory; ibid. Hartz made a similar point, in his typically more opaque
style, when he wrote, "It is only when you take your ethics for granted that all problems
emerge as problems of technique"; Hartz, *Liberal Tradition*, 10.

24. J. Hector St. John de Crèvecœur, *Letters from an American Farmer and Sketches of Eighteenth-
Century America* (New York: Penguin Classics, 1981), letter 3.

25. Ralph Waldo Emerson, *Fortune of the Republic* (Boston: Houghton, Osgood, 1879), 40.

26. Alan Wolfe, *One Nation After All: What Middle-Class Americans Really Think About God,
Country, Family, Racism, Welfare, Immigration, Homosexuality, Work, the Right, the Left, and
Each Other* (New York: Viking, 1998), 145–146.

27. William H. McNeill, *Mythistory and Other Essays* (Chicago: University of Chicago Press,
1986).

28. I use "myth" in the same way as Rogers Smith: "A civic myth is used to explain why persons
form a people, usually indicating how a political community originated, who is eligible for
membership, who is not and why, and what the community's values and aims are. . . . I
admittedly wish to highlight the unpalatable fact that stories buttressing civic loyalties virtually always contain elements that are not literally true. But these definitions also suggest,
correctly, that factual elements may well be present in myth, and especially that they may
contain accounts of the meaning of their social and natural worlds that people rightly find
convincing." Rogers M. Smith, *Civic Ideals: Conflicting Visions of Citizenship in U.S. History*
(New Haven: Yale University Press, 1997), 33.

29. Celeste Michelle-Condit and John Louis Lucaites, *Crafting Equality: America's Anglo-African
Word* (Chicago: University of Chicago Press, 1993), xvii.

30. See Daniel T. Rodgers, *Contested Truths: Keywords in American Politics Since Independence*
(New York: Basic, 1987).

31. Eric Foner, "The Meaning of Freedom in the Age of Emancipation," *Journal of American
History* 81, no. 2 (1994): 435–460, 437, quoting Ian C. Fletcher, "Rethinking the History of
Working People: Class, Gender, and Identities in an Age of Industry and Empire," *Radical
History Review* 56 (1993), 85. See also Robert Wuthnow, *The Restructuring of American Religion:
Society and Faith Since World War II* (Princeton: Princeton University Press, 1988), 277–282.

32. Michael Kammen, *Spheres of Liberty: Changing Perceptions of Liberty in American Culture*
(University of Wisconsin Press, 1986), 8.

33. *National Mut. Ins. Co. v. Tidewater Transfer Co., Inc.*, 337 U.S. 582 (1949) at 646 (Frankfurter,
J., dissenting).

34. See, e.g., McClosky and Zaller, *American Ethos*.

35. See, e.g., Huntington, *Who Are We?* For a discussion of both traditions, see Wuthnow, *Restructuring of American Religion*. For a critique of Huntington's view of Puritan history, see
David Little, "Calvinism and American National Identity," in *John Calvin's American Legacy*,
ed. Thomas J. Davis (Oxford: Oxford University Press 2010), 43–64.

36. Probably the most prominent in this camp is Hartz, *Liberal Tradition*. Hartz's work has been
criticized for its failure to discuss America's religious tradition. See, e.g., Richard J. Ellis,
"The Liberal Tradition in an Age of Conservative Power and Partisan Polarization," in *The
American Liberal Tradition Reconsidered: The Contested Legacy of Louis Hartz*, ed. Mark Hulliung (Lawrence: University of Kansas Press, 2010), 215–222.

37. *Elk Grove Unified School District v. Newdow*, 542 U.S. 1 (2004).

38. For an extended history of the pledge, see Jeffrey Owen Jones and Peter Mayer, *The Pledge: A History of the Pledge of Allegiance* (New York: Thomas Dunne, 2010); see also Daniel K. Williams, *God's Own Party: The Making of the Christian Right* (Oxford: Oxford University Press, 2010), 26–27.

39. *Newdow*, 542 U.S. at 17–18 (noncustodial father lacks standing to assert daughter's objection to pledge).

40. For a particularly thoughtful discussion of this problem from a conservative communitarian perspective, see Mary Ann Glendon, *Rights Talk: The Impoverishment of Political Discourse* (New York: Free Press, 1991).

41. Dionne, *Our Divided Political Heart.*

42. When radical abolitionists condemned slavery for its obvious tension with the egalitarian principle that "all men are created equal," defenders of the Peculiar Institution answered that Negros are not men, at least not as the Founders contemplated. As important, they stressed that slavery created in the freeman both a love of liberty and a passion for equality. In that way, slavery did not *threaten* timeless American values, it *protected* them, and an attack on slavery was an attack on America. For instance, the Alabama Fire Eater William Yancey wove these two strands of thought into a single speech for a Boston audience. "Your fathers and my fathers," Yancey said, "built this government on two ideas: the first is that the white race is the citizen, and the master race, and the white man is the equal of every other white man. The second idea is that the Negro is the inferior race." To the same effect, a writer in the staid *Southern Literary Messenger* undertook a detailed analysis of slavery throughout history. Ancient and medieval slavery, he said, when whites were enslaved to other whites, was an abomination because "races richly endowed by nature, and designed for high and lofty purposes, were kept from rising to their natural level." Not surprisingly, therefore, white slavery had disappeared before "the progress of truth, justice, and Christianity." Slavery of African-Americans, by contrast, had persisted precisely because it was fully compatible with the growth of liberty and equality in modern democracies. For the first quotation, see George M. Frederickson, *The Black Image in the White Mind: The Debate on Afro-American Character and Destiny, 1817–1914* (1971; Middletown, CT: Wesleyan University Press, 1987), 61, quoting a speech of Yancey's in Boston, October 12, 1860, and reprinted in the *Liberator,* October 26, 1860; the second quotation appears in Frederickson, *Black Image*, 62.

Under the attack that slavery was contrary to the liberal ideal of equality, equality in the slaveholding South (at least among white men) became a particularly cherished ideal and was vigorously thought to have taken root in the South more firmly and with greater success than in the abolitionist North. Speaking of the whites who occupied the lowest classes, one observer wrote, "It matters not that he is no slaveholder; he is not of the inferior race; he is a freeborn citizen. . . . The poorest meets the richest as an equal; sits at the table with him; salutes him as a neighbor; meets him at a public assembly, and stands on the same social platform." A republic based on slavery, wrote another, "elevates the character not only of the master, the actual owner of slaves, but of all who wear the colour of freeman." It was the South, therefore, that was the true champion of American ideals—a banner proudly upheld not in spite of slavery, but because of it, for slavery alone assured "the preservation of our Republic, in all its purity." Frederickson, *Black Image*, 62; Robert E. Bonner, *Mastering America: Southern Slaveholders and the Crisis of American Nationhood* (Cambridge: Cambridge University Press, 2009), 88.

In 1861, on the eve of war, Alexander H. Stephens, the newly elected vice president of the Confederate States of America, gave his famous "Cornerstone" speech in Charleston, South Carolina, in which this view achieved its fullest expression. "Many governments have been founded on the principles of subordination and serfdom of certain classes of the same race;

such were, and are, in violation of the laws of nature. Our system commits no such violation of nature's laws. With us, all the white race, however high or low, rich or poor, are equal in the eyes of the law. Not so with the Negro. Subordination is his place. He, by nature, . . . is fitted for that condition which he occupies in our system." The cornerstone of the new Confederate government, Stephens declared, rested "on the great truth that the Negro is not equal to the white man, that slavery—subordination to the superior race—is his natural or normal condition." In this view, slavery was not only compatible with American values but essential to its preservation. "Break down slavery," said Virginia Governor Harry Wise, "and you would with the same blow destroy the great democratic principle of equality among men." Quoted in Frederickson, *Black Image*, 63–64. Other writers similarly stressed the relationship between American republicanism and slavery. "The destruction of African slavery," said South Carolina Congressman Lawrence Keitt, "would be the destruction of republicanism"; Bonner, *Mastering America*, 107, quoting Keitt in *Southern Quarterly Review* 5 (1852), 538.

43. See, e.g., Smith, *Civic Ideals*, 518: "in modern cultures, myth-makers often have a degree of critical distance from their materials, so that they have greater awareness of their own constructive role. I therefore think that my emphasis on elite construction of myths for political purposes is appropriate, though I acknowledge that leaders often believe strongly in the moral truth of the civic myths they deploy" (internal quotations omitted).

44. For a wonderful account of the Constitution as a symbol, much revered but little understood, see Kammen, *A Machine That Would Go of Itself.*

45. On this score, it is certainly noteworthy that socialists in this country generally considered it necessary to defend their ideas in the language of the American Creed. See Merle Curti, *The Roots of American Loyalty* (New York: Columbia University Press, 1946), 210–211: "In contrast to this very small but highly vocal minority of the extreme left, most of the advocates of specific radical programs for the solution of economic ailments identified their creed with the traditionally American conception of loyalty to a land that provides everyone with fair opportunities to win the good life."

46. Ann Swidler, "Culture in Action: Symbols and Strategies," *American Sociological Review* 51, no. 2. (1986), 273–286.

47. In his lectures on the nature of history, the British historian E. H. Carr came up with a particularly apt metaphor to capture this idea. "The moral precepts we apply in history or in everyday life are like cheques in a bank; they have a printed and a written part. The printed part consists of abstract words like liberty and equality, justice and democracy. These are essential categories. But the cheque is valueless until we fill in the other part, which states how much liberty we propose to allocate to whom, whom we recognize as our equals, and up to what amount. . . . The conceptions are abstract and universal. But the content put into them has varied throughout history, from time to time and place to place; any practical issue of their application can be understood only in historical terms"; E. H. Carr, *What Is History?* (1961; Middlesex: Penguin, 1988), 82.

48. Alexis de Tocqueville, *Democracy in America*, vol. 2 (1840; New York: Vintage, 1945), 74.

49. Calvin Coolidge, "Education: The Cornerstone of Self-Government," Address to the Convention of the National Education Association, July 4, 1924, available online in Peters and Woolley, American Presidency Project, http://www.presidency.ucsb.edu/ws/?pid=24188.

50. William J. Clinton, Inaugural Address, January 20, 1993, ibid., http://www.presidency.ucsb .edu/ws/?pid=46366.

51. Hartz, *Liberal Tradition*, 145–150.

52. Ibid.

53. William J. Clinton, Inaugural Address, January 20, 1997, available online at Peters and

Woolley, American Presidency Project, http://www.presidency.ucsb.edu/ws/index.php?pid=54183#axzz1tvFQVW9p.

54. Remarks by the President at 2002 Graduation Exercise of the United States Military Academy, *Public Papers*, June 4, 2002, 1174. The president repeated these essential themes, often in nearly identical language, throughout his administration. On his last Fourth of July weekend in office, for instance, he told a national radio audience that "there is no American race, just an American creed. In the United States, we believe in the rights and dignity of every person. We believe in equal justice, limited government, and the rule of law. And we believe in personal responsibility and tolerance towards others. This creed of freedom and equality has lifted the lives of millions of Americans, whether citizens by birth or citizens by choice"; George W. Bush, The President's Radio Address, July 5, 2008, available online at Peters and Woolley, American Presidency Project, http://www.presidency.ucsb.edu/ws/?pid=77638.

55. Clinton, Inaugural Address, January 20, 1997.

56. John F. Kennedy, Inaugural Address, January 20, 1961, available online at Peters and Woolley, American Presidency Project, http://www.presidency.ucsb.edu/ws/?pid=8032.

57. Richard Nixon, Inaugural Address, January 20, 1969, ibid., http://www.presidency.ucsb.edu/ws/?pid=1941.

58. Bush, First Inaugural Address.

59. Boorstin, *Genius of American Politics*, 38, describing the "tendency to make the 'is' the guide to the 'ought.'"

60. E. H. Carr captured this well, though the occasion for his insight was a lecture to a British audience: "Every group has its own values, which are rooted in history. Every group protects itself against the intrusion of alien and inconvenient values, which it brands by opprobrious epithets as bourgeois or capitalist, or undemocratic and totalitarian, or, more crudely still, as un-English and un-American"; Carr, *What Is History?* 84.

61. Huntington, *American Politics*, 85–166. As Huntington put it, "In creedal passion periods, more people become intensely involved, committed to the realization of ideals, more agitated, more participant"; ibid., 108.

62. Ashley Parker, "Romney's Heated Exchange with a Veteran," *New York Times*, December 12, 2011.

63. McClosky and Zaller note that debates over the growth of the welfare state produced similar cleavages. American thought divided between the republican commitment to all members of a community and the liberal resistance to state-run assistance programs; McClosky and Zaller, *American Ethos*.

64. *Regents of the University of California v. Bakke*, 438 U.S. 265 (1978), 407.

65. See, e.g., Murray Edelman, *The Symbolic Uses of Politics* (Urbana: University of Illinois Press, 1964), 5–6: "For most men most of the time, politics is a series of pictures in the mind, placed there by television news, newspapers, magazines, and discussions. . . . It is central to its potency as a symbol that it is remote, set apart, omnipresent as the ultimate threat or means of succor, yet not susceptible to effective influence through any act we as individuals can perform." I do not mean to suggest that this idea originated with Edelman, though his use of it was pathbreaking. The notion can be traced at least to 1922, when Walter Lippmann wrote *Public Opinion* (1922; New York: Free Press, 1997).

66. This "top-down" approach to the formation of public opinion has to be qualified in one important respect. When personal experience allows people to assess the impact of a policy for themselves—when the issue is not remote, in other words—they are much less likely to accept uncritically the views of elites, who may be seen as out of touch with the reality on the ground. For example, recent scholarship about the course of desegregation in Atlanta during the civil rights era shows that working-class whites, whose neighborhoods were

typically the first to be desegregated and who therefore had firsthand experience with the process, often diverged in their views from the more moderate messages coming from business and political elites, who tended to live in distant, affluent parts of the city that were not at risk of desegregation. See Kevin M. Kruse, *White Flight: Atlanta and the Making of Modern Conservatism* (Princeton: Princeton University Press, 2005). As a general matter, however, the circumstances that have shaped the course of American thought since 9/11 are not of this sort. For instance, very few people have personal experience with interrogation techniques of any sort, and therefore cannot judge for themselves whether more aggressive methods are needed in a post-9/11 environment. Similarly, a substantial majority of Americans say they have "very little knowledge" or "none at all" about Islam. Notably, those who reported they do not know a Muslim were twice as likely to express "a great deal of prejudice" against them. See "Religious Perceptions in America, with an In-Depth Analysis of U.S. Attitudes Towards Muslims and Islam," Gallup, http://www.muslimwest facts.com/mwf/125315/Religious-Perceptions-America.aspx. In this environment, people are particularly apt to be influenced by elites who are presumed to know what the rest of us do not.

67. Dan M. Kahan and Donald Braman, "Cultural Cognition and Public Policy," *Yale Law and Policy Review* 24 (2006), 149.

68. Robert Spencer, *The Complete Infidel's Guide to the Koran* (Washington, DC: Regnery, 2009), 17.

69. Elise Foley, "Joe Walsh: Democrats Want Hispanics, African Americans 'Dependent on Government,'" *Huffington Post*, May 30, 2012, http://www.huffingtonpost.com/2012/05/30/joe-walsh-hispanics-african-americans_n_1557480.html; Elise Foley, "Joe Walsh: Jesse Jackson Trying to 'Keep African Americans Down on Some Plantation,'" *Huffington Post*, June 1, 2012, http://www.huffingtonpost.com/2012/06/01/joe-walsh-jesse-jackson-african-americans_n_1563099.html. A video of a representative portion of the town hall meeting is available at http://www.youtube.com/watch?v=K3iTbf9q6-s.

70. See Foley, "Walsh: Democrats Want Hispanics, African Americans 'Dependent'"; Foley, "Walsh: Jackson Trying to 'Keep African Americans Down on Some Plantation.'"

71. Robert Wuthnow, *America and the Challenges of Religious Diversity* (Princeton: Princeton University Press, 2005), 81, 316.

72. This was also the example Edelman used; Edelman, *Symbolic Uses*, 173–176.

73. John W. Dower, *War Without Mercy: Race and Power in the Pacific War* (New York: Pantheon, 1986), 302.

74. U.S. Senate, Committee on Armed Services and Committee on Foreign Relations, 82d Cong., 1 (1951), 312–313 (Hearings to Conduct an Inquiry into the Military Situation in the Far East and the Facts Surrounding the Relief of General of the Army Douglas MacArthur from His Assignments in that Area).

75. Dower, *War Without Mercy*, 309. Another example of this phenomenon was the rapid re-imagining of the Germans at the end of World War I. See Gary Gerstle, "The Immigrant as Threat to American Security: A Historical Perspective," in *The Maze of Fear: Security and Migration after 9/11*, ed. John Tirman (New York: New Press, 2004), 96–97.

76. Stuart Banner, *The Death Penalty: An American History* (Cambridge: Harvard University Press, 2003), 240–241.

77. Ibid., 244–246.

78. Ibid., 240–244.

79. Ibid., 267–268.

80. Ibid., 268.

81. Ibid., 268–269.

Chapter 3: The Dark Side of the Creed

1. For an extended discussion of this controversy, see the essays in Edward T. Linenthal and Tom Engelhardt, eds., *History Wars: The Enola Gay and Other Battles for the American Past* (New York: Henry Holt, 1996).

2. Today, the expression "a more perfect Union" is nearly as much of a cliché as "We the People." It therefore bears recalling that both are from the Preamble to the Constitution: "We the People of the United States, in Order to form a more perfect Union, establish Justice, insure domestic Tranquility, provide for the common defence, promote the general Welfare, and secure the Blessings of Liberty to ourselves and our Posterity, do ordain and establish this Constitution for the United States of America."

3. Lynne V. Cheney, *Telling the Truth: A Report on the State of the Humanities in Higher Education* (Washington, DC: National Endowment for the Humanities, 1992). For an account of some of the controversy surrounding this report, see Margaret MacMillan, *The Uses and Abuses of History* (London: Profile, 2009), 118–119.

4. Cheney, *Telling the Truth*, 44.

5. Dan Carter, *The Politics of Rage: George Wallace, the Origins of the New Conservatism, and the Transformation of American Politics* (New York: Simon and Schuster, 1995), 123.

6. Taylor Branch, *Parting the Waters: America in the King Years, 1954–63* (New York: Simon and Schuster, 1988), 906–909.

7. For accounts of Dr. King's "appropriation" by the political and cultural mainstream, see Denise M. Botsdorff and Stephen R. Goldzwig, "History, Collective Memory, and the Appropriation of Martin Luther King, Jr.: Reagan's Rhetorical Legacy," *Presidential Studies Quarterly* 35 (2005), 661; Francesca Polletta, "Legacies and Liabilities of Insurgent Past: Remembering Martin Luther King, Jr., on the House and Senate Floor," *Social Sciences History* 22 (1998), 479.

8. Roy Basler, ed., *The Collected Works of Abraham Lincoln*, vol. 2 (New Brunswick, NJ: Rutgers University Press, 1953), 406.

9. A number of scholars have recently made this point. See, e.g., Matthew D. Lassiter, *The Silent Majority: Suburban Politics in the Sunbelt South* (Princeton: Princeton University Press, 2006); Kevin M. Kruse, *White Flight: Atlanta and the Making of Modern Conservatism* (Princeton: Princeton University Press, 2005); George Lewis, *The White South and the Red Menace: Segregationists, Anticommunists, and Massive Resistance, 1945–1965* (Gainesville: University Press of Florida, 2004).

10. Hodding Carter, Jr., *Atlanta Journal*, September 3, 1948, quoted in Lillian E. Smith, *Killers of the Dream* (New York: W. W. Norton, 1961), 79. To put this in perspective, the South in the nineteenth century is often viewed as the very picture of a monolithic society, at least after the rise of northern abolitionism in the 1830s. Yet a leading scholar of southern dissent in the nineteenth century points out that there was substantially more dissent from the racial orthodoxy in the nineteenth-century South than there was in the first fifty years of the twentieth. Carl Degler, *The Other South: Southern Dissenters in the Nineteenth Century* (Gainesville: University Press of Florida, 2000), 371.

11. Paul M. Gaston, *The New South Creed: A Study in Southern Mythmaking* (New York: Alfred A. Knopf, 1970), 122–123.

12. U.S. Constitution Amendment XV.

13. Gaston, *New South Creed*, 131.

14. Ibid., 132.

15. Ibid., 135.

16. U.S. Constitution Amendment XIV.

17. The literature on nineteenth-century racist thought is voluminous. One of the best single-volume treatments is Thomas F. Gossett, *Race: The History of an Idea in America* (Dallas: Southern Methodist University Press, 1963); see also, e.g., Gaston, *New South Creed*, 125.

18. Quoted in Gaston, *New South Creed*, 137.

19. Ibid., 139.

20. Ibid., 140.

21. *Plessy v. Ferguson*, 163 U.S. 537 (1896).

22. Daniel Boorstin, *The Genius of American Politics* (Chicago: University of Chicago Press, 1958), 38.

23. See I. A. Newby, *Jim Crow's Defense: Anti-Negro Thought in America, 1900–1930* (Baton Rouge: Louisiana State University Press, 1965).

24. 106-a Cong. Rec. 4843 (1960) (statement of Sen. Long).

25. C. Vann Woodward, *Origins of the New South* (1951; Baton Rouge: Louisiana State University Press, 1971), 335–337. For a discussion of the early history of the poll tax, see Frank B. Williams, Jr., "The Poll Tax as a Suffrage Requirement in the South, 1870–1901," *Journal of Southern History* 18, no. 4 (1952), 469.

26. William M. Brewer, "The Poll Tax and the Poll Taxers," *Journal of Negro History* 42 (1944), 260, 264–265.

27. For an excellent account of the legislative debate over repeal of the poll tax, see Keith Finley, *Delaying the Dream: Southern Senators and the Fight Against Civil Rights, 1938–1965* (Baton Rouge: Louisiana State University Press, 2008), 56–104.

28. 90 Cong. Rec. 4172–4173 (May 10, 1944) (statement of Sen. McCarran).

29. Ibid. It is important to bear in mind that the partisan divisions we now take for granted were entirely different in the 1940s and 1950s. Senator McCarran, for instance, though a Democrat, was among the most conservative members of the Senate and is much better remembered today for his rabid anticommunism and enthusiasm for strict immigration quotas than for his support for civil rights. In the classic language of the American Creed, McCarran once decried the risk of uncontrolled immigration: "I believe that this nation is the last hope of Western civilization and if this oasis of the world shall be overrun, perverted, contaminated or destroyed, then the last flickering light of humanity will be extinguished. I take no issue with those who would praise the contributions which have been made to our society by people of many races, of varied creeds and colors. America is indeed a joining together of many streams which go to form a mighty river which we call the American way. However, we have in the United States today hard-core, indigestible blocs which have not become integrated into the American way of life, but which, on the contrary are its deadly enemies. Today, as never before, untold millions are storming our gates for admission and those gates are cracking under the strain. . . . I do not intend to become prophetic, but if the enemies of this legislation succeed in riddling it to pieces, or in amending it beyond recognition, they will have contributed more to promote this nation's downfall than any other group since we achieved our independence as a nation"; 83rd Cong. Rec. 1518 (March 2, 1953) (statement of Sen. McCarran).

30. 90 Cong. Rec. 4258 (May 10, 1944); see also ibid., 4260 (statements of Sen. Mead).

31. Ibid., 4260.

32. Ibid.

33. 90 Cong. Rec. 3763 (1944) (statement of Rep. Marcantonio).

34. 90 Cong. Rec. 4247 (May 10, 1944) (statement of Sen. George).

35. Ibid.

36. Ibid., 4255.

37. Ibid., 4173 (May 9, 1944) (statement of Sen. Connally).

38. Ibid., 4173–4174.

39. See, for instance, the extended remarks of Senator Bailey (D-NC). By the poll tax, "it is said to a man, 'If you do not pay your poll tax, you should not vote. If you are not willing to make any contribution for the schools and the police and the fire-protection systems and the prevention of the spread of disease—if you are unwilling to pay anything—why should anyone be greatly concerned as to whether you vote or do not vote?'" 90 Cong. Rec. 4246 (May 10, 1944) (statement of Sen. Bailey).

40. 90 Cong. Rec. 3763 (April 27, 1944) (statement of Rep. Sumners). The argument "that good citizenship required that electors also be taxpayers" has a long history and appears in the post-Reconstruction constitutional conventions at which the poll tax became law. Williams, "The Poll Tax as a Suffrage Requirement," 496. Williams correctly maintains that advocates of this philosophy "appear to have been fewer by the turn of the century"(496), but as the legislative arguments in 1944 make clear, they were by no means gone.

41. 90 Cong. Rec. 4176 (May 9, 1944) (statement of Sen. Connally).

42. Ibid., 4186.

43. Ibid.

44. Ibid., 4176 (statement of Sen. Russell). Or as Senator Walter George put it, "our Nation is divided into States not only for the purpose of local self-government, but also for the purposes of diluting the strength of the central government, preventing the spread of its power, and protecting the people against it"; ibid., 4247. In language that every modern student of campaign finance reform would immediately recognize, George cautioned that "in a country of this kind, a representative democracy, or a republic, there are temptations. There are temptations to cater to groups like those which are bringing pressure in connection with the pending proposed legislation, and to cater to demands such as those which have been made by labor organizations. Men can rise to power by way of catering. However, those who yield to such temptations should remember that in doing so they lay their self-respect upon the altar of their ambitions, and with their self-respect they surrender their country"; ibid., 4255.

45. It is worth pointing out that many members of the Southern Caucus were personally opposed to the poll tax, supported its repeal, and came from states that had already repealed it. Nearly to a man, however, the caucus insisted that this was a matter that could not be legislated by the federal government and must be left to the states. See "Poll Tax on Way Out, Russell Declares," *Atlanta Constitution*, November 20, 1942. As Keith Finley relates, their position on the poll tax stemmed from a fear of the camel's nose poking into the segregationist tent; Finley, *Delaying the Dream*, 62–63.

46. Bills were introduced in both the House and Senate. The text of each proposal is reproduced at Hearings to Prevent Discrimination in Employment, 78th Congress, Committee on Labor, June 1, 1944, 1–15.

47. Ibid., 1.

48. Ibid., 14 (statement of Rep. Scanlon).

49. Ibid.

50. Ibid., 16–17.

51. Report on H.R. 2232, The Fair Employment Practice Act, by the Committee on Labor, February 20, 1945, 1.

52. Hearings before the House Committee on Rules on H.R. 2232, 79th Congress First Session, March 8, April 19, 20, 25, 26, 1945, 7 (remarks of Rep. Norton).

53. Hearings to Prevent Discrimination in Employment, 78th Congress, Committee on Labor, June 1, 1944, 17 (remarks of Rep. Scanlon).

54. Report on H.R. 2232, The Fair Employment Practice Act, by the Committee on Labor, February 20, 1945, 1. The fear that political reform was really meant to impose "social equality"

was a bugbear that had haunted the South since Reconstruction. Degler, *Other South*, 242–249; Gaston, *New South Creed*, 140–141.

55. Report on H.R. 2232, The Fair Employment Practice Act, by the Committee on Labor, February 20, 1945, 9 (minority view of Rep. Fisher).

56. Hearings before the House Committee on Rules on H.R. 2232, 79th Congress First Session, March 8, April 19, 20, 25, 26, 1945, 58 (remarks of Rep. Rivers).

57. Ibid., 57.

58. See, e.g., Richard Epstein, *Forbidden Grounds: The Case Against Employment Discrimination Laws* (Cambridge: Harvard University Press, 1995).

59. Hearings before the House Committee on Rules on H.R. 2232, 79th Congress First Session, March 8, April 19, 20, 25, 26, 1945, 27 (remarks of Rep. Colmer).

60. Ibid. (remarks of Rep. Norton).

61. Ibid., 27–28.

62. Report on H.R. 2232, The Fair Employment Practice Act, by the Committee on Labor, February 20, 1945, 9 (minority view of Rep. Fisher).

63. For a discussion of the debate over *Brown*'s contested legacy, see Michael J. Klarman, *From Jim Crow to Civil Rights: The Supreme Court and the Struggle for Racial Equality* (New York: Oxford University Press, 2004), chapter 7; Tony Badger, "Brown and Backlash," in *Massive Resistance: Southern Opposition to the Second Reconstruction*, ed. Clive Webb (New York: Oxford University Press, 2005), 39–55.

64. Quoted in Lewis, *The White South and the Red Menace*, 73.

65. See the Mike Wallace Interview with James Eastland (July 28, 1957), available at http://www.hrc.utexas.edu/multimedia/video/2008/wallace/eastland_james_t.html.

66. Ibid.

67. 100-a Cong. 2d Sess., 6750 (1954).

68. 106-a Cong. Rec. 4854 (1960).

69. Ibid.

70. See *Congressional Record*, 84th Congress Second Session, vol. 102, part 4 (March 12, 1956) (Washington, DC: Government Printing Office, 1956), 4459–4460.

71. Ibid., 4459.

72. Ibid.

73. Ibid.

74. Ibid., 4460.

75. Ibid. For an interesting discussion of the southern elected officials who refused to sign the manifesto, and the desperate attempts by some liberals in the South to convince the drafters to tone down the manifesto's language, see Tony Badger, "Southerners Who Refused to Sign the Southern Manifesto," *Historical Journal* 42 (1999), 517.

76. Laura J. Scalia, "Who Deserves Political Influence? How Liberal Ideals Helped Justify Mid Nineteenth-Century Exclusionary Policies," *American Journal of Political Science* 42 (1998), 349, 375–376.

77. Robert C. Lieberman, "Ideas, Institutions, and Political Order: Explaining Political Change," *American Political Science Review* 96 (2002), 697, 702.

78. This relationship between stable values and constructed meaning also sheds light on another contentious issue in American thought: the persistence and occasional virulence of the so-called "culture wars." Compare James Davison Hunter, *Culture Wars: The Struggle to Define America* (New York: Basic, 1991) with Morris P. Fiorina et al., *Culture War? The Myth of a Polarized America* (White Plains, NY: Pearson Longman, 2007). There is no denying the intense partisan polarization between opposing political elites (and their most engaged supporters). See, e.g., Richard J. Ellis, "The Liberal Tradition in an Age of Conservative Power

and Partisan Polarization," in *The American Liberal Tradition Reconsidered: The Contested Legacy of Louis Hartz*, ed. Mark Hulliung (Lawrence: University of Kansas Press, 2010), 215–222. The rhetorical bombasts lobbed by these groups hardly seem to reflect the language of shared values. But in fact, as Samuel Huntington and Seymour Martin Lipset both explain, it is precisely because the values are shared that the rhetoric is heated. Samuel Huntington, *American Politics: The Promise of Disharmony* (New York: Simon and Schuster, 1981), 110–111; Seymour Martin Lipset, *American Exceptionalism: A Double-Edged Sword* (New York: W. W. Norton, 1996), 290. The rhetoric employed by these camps is simply evidence of the battle taking place in the public square to control the meaning given to these values, a meaning which will eventually be understood and used by the politically engaged and apathetic alike.

Chapter 4: Race and Religion in National Identity

1. International Mail Call, *Newsweek*, December 3, 2001.
2. Richard Herrnstein and Charles Murray, *The Bell Curve: Intelligence and Class Structure in American Life* (New York: Free Press, 1994); Jason DeParle, "Daring Research or 'Social Science Pornography'?: Charles Murray," *New York Times Magazine*, October 9, 1994. For a critique of some of the sources relied on in *The Bell Curve*, see Charles Lane, "The Tainted Sources of *The Bell Curve*," *New York Review of Books*, December 1, 1994.
3. Herrnstein and Murray, *Bell Curve*, 91.
4. For a collection of some of the hundreds of reviews, see Steven Fraser, ed., *The Bell Curve Wars: Race, Intelligence, and the Future of America* (New York: Basic, 1995); Russell Jacoby and Naomi Glauberman, eds., *The Bell Curve Debate: History, Documents, Opinions* (New York: New York Times Books, 1995); Howard L. Kaye, "Reviewing the Reviewers: The Bell Curve," *American Sociologist* 27 (1996), 79–86.
5. "The Bell Curve Rings the Cash Register," *Journal of Blacks in Higher Education* 20, no. 7 (Spring 1995), 10, citing "The Red and the Black: Tallying the Books '94," *Publishers Weekly* special supplement, March 20, 1995.
6. DeParle, "Daring Research."
7. Nicholas Lemann, *The Promised Land: The Great Black Migration and How It Changed America* (New York: Alfred A. Knopf, 1991), 6; Lawrence Bobo, James R. Kluegel, and Ryan A. Smith, "*Laissez-Faire* Racism: The Crystallization of a Kinder, Gentler, Antiblack Ideology," in *Racial Attitudes in the 1990s: Continuity and Change*, ed. Steven A. Tuch and Jack K. Martin (Santa Barbara, CA: Praeger, 1997), 33.
8. Bobo, Kluegel, and Smith, "*Laissez-Faire* Racism," 23–38; Doug McAdam, *Political Process and the Development of Black Insurgency, 1930–1970* (Chicago: University of Chicago Press, 1982).
9. Dorothy Roberts, *Fatal Invention: How Science, Politics, and Big Business Re-create Race in the 21st Century* (New York: New Press, 2011); Thomas F. Gossett, *Race: The History of an Idea in America* (Dallas: Southern Methodist University Press, 1963), chapters 16 and 17.
10. See, e.g., Mary L. Dudziak, *Cold War Civil Rights: Race and the Image of American Democracy* (Princeton: Princeton University Press, 2000), chapter 3; Azza S. Layton, *International Politics and Civil Rights Policies in the United States, 1941–1960* (New York: Cambridge University Press, 2000); Michael J. Klarman, *From Jim Crow to Civil Rights: The Supreme Court and the Struggle for Racial Equality* (New York: Oxford University Press, 2004), 182–186.
11. McAdam, *Political Process*, chapter 3; Thomas R. Rochon, *Culture Moves: Ideas, Activism, and Changing Values* (Princeton: Princeton University Press, 1998).
12. George W. Bush, Remarks at the Opening of the *Brown v. Board of Education* National His-

toric Site in Topeka, Kansas, May 17, 2004, available online at Gerhard Peters and John T. Woolley, The American Presidency Project. http://www.presidency.ucsb.edu/ws/?pid=63432.

13. Ibid.

14. Bobo, Kluegel, and Smith, "*Laissez-Faire* Racism," 29.

15. Howard Schuman, Charlotte Steeh, Lawrence Bobo, and Maria Krysan, *Racial Attitudes in America: Trends and Interpretation* (Cambridge: Harvard University Press, 1997), 104. Except where otherwise noted, the statistics in this note are from chapter 3 of *Racial Attitudes*, which contains an extended discussion of the trends. The reader should also consult the 2011 supplement, which provides the most current data. Fifty-five percent of white Americans surveyed in 1944 said that "white people should have the first chance at any job." By 1963 the number had fallen to 15 percent. By 1972 only 3 percent of Americans were of this view, a number so close to zero that pollsters thereafter dropped the question. Change came somewhat more slowly as the focus shifted from ending preferences that *favored* whites to ending those that *disfavored* blacks. Still, the change is now an accomplished fact. In 1942 nearly seven in ten white Americans favored segregated schools. In 1956, two years after the practice was struck down by the Supreme Court in *Brown*, the number had fallen to half, the great majority of whom were confined to the South. By 1970 only a quarter held this view. By 1982 the number had fallen to one in ten, and by 1995 to one in twenty-five. Fifty-five percent of white Americans in 1942 favored segregated transportation. Two decades later, nearly eight in ten opposed it, and by 1970 nearly nine in ten were against it, at which point pollsters dropped the question. In 1963, six in ten white Americans agreed that whites "had a right to keep blacks out of their neighborhood." By 1972 the number had fallen to four in ten. By 1996 only 13 percent believed whites had such a right, and 65 percent disagreed strongly. Even opposition to miscegenation—the great bugbear of segregationists—has fallen significantly. In 1958 only one in twenty-five white Americans approved of intermarriage between whites and blacks. Two decades later, one in three approved. It was not until 1991 that white America split evenly on this question, but by 1997, two in three approved, and by 2004, three in four. And by the twenty-first century, nearly 90 percent of white Americans opposed laws that would ban mixed marriages.

16. Paul M. Sniderman and Thomas Piazza, *The Scar of Race* (Cambridge: Harvard University Press, 1993), 40.

17. Schuman et al., *Racial Attitudes*, 106.

18. Ibid.

19. Bobo, Kluegel, and Smith, "*Laissez-Faire* Racism," 18.

20. Roberts, *Fatal Invention*, 81–82 and generally chapters 4–6.

21. Jennifer Hochschild, *Facing Up to the American Dream: Race, Class, and the Soul of the Nation* (Princeton: Princeton University Press, 1995), 62–63; Donald R. Kinder and Lynn M. Sanders, *Divided by Color: Racial Politics and Democratic Ideals* (Chicago: University of Chicago Press, 1996), 107; Bobo, Kluegel, and Smith, "*Laissez-Faire* Racism," 20, 38–41.

22. Lyndon B. Johnson, Commencement Address at Howard University: "To Fulfill These Rights," June 4, 1965, available online at Peters and Woolley, American Presidency Project, http://www.presidency.ucsb.edu/ws/?pid=27021.

23. Ibid. President Johnson's speech at Howard has been the inspiration for a great deal of excellent scholarship. The title for Nancy MacLean's 2006 book *Freedom Is Not Enough: The Opening of the American Workplace* (New York: Russell Sage Foundation; Cambridge: Harvard University Press, 2006), comes from a line in Johnson's speech: "But freedom is not enough. You do not wipe away the scars of centuries by saying: Now you are free to go where you want, and do as you desire, and choose the leaders you please." Ira Katznelson uses the speech as the opening scene of his book, *When Affirmative Action Was White* (New York: W. W. Norton, 2005).

24. Mark Baldassare, *Trouble in Paradise: The Suburban Transformation in America* (New York: Columbia University Press, 1986), chapter 1.
25. See, e.g., Matthew D. Lassiter, *The Silent Majority: Suburban Politics in the Sunbelt South* (Princeton: Princeton University Press, 2006), 218, 225–226, 289; Kevin M. Kruse, *White Flight: Atlanta and the Making of Modern Conservatism* (Princeton: Princeton University Press, 2005), chapter 9; Lisa McGirr, *Suburban Warriors: The Origins of the New American Right* (Princeton: Princeton University Press, 2001).
26. See, e.g., Nathan Glazer, *Affirmative Discrimination: Ethnic Inequality and Public Policy* (New York: Basic, 1975), chapter 5.
27. The history of modern conservatism has been exhaustively studied. See, e.g., George Nash, *The Conservative Intellectual Movement in America Since 1945* (Wilmington, DE: Intercollegiate Studies Institute, 2006); George Nash, *Reappraising the Right: The Past and Future of American Conservatism* (Wilmington, DE: Intercollegiate Studies Institute, 2009); Kim Phillips-Fein, *Invisible Hands: The Making of the Conservative Movement from the New Deal to Reagan* (New York: W. W. Norton, 2009); Joseph Lowndes, *From the New Deal to the New Right: Race and the Southern Origins of Modern Conservatism* (New Haven: Yale University Press, 2008); William C. Berman, *America's Right Turn from Nixon to Clinton* (Baltimore: Johns Hopkins University Press, 1998); Mary C. Brenna, *Turning Right in the Sixties: The Conservative Capture of the GOP* (Chapel Hill: University of North Carolina Press, 1995); John Ehrman, *The Eighties: America in the Age of Reagan* (New Haven: Yale University Press, 2005); Glenn Feldman, ed., *Painting Dixie Red: When, Where, Why, and How the South Became Republican* (Gainesville: University Press of Florida, 2011).
28. Carol A. Horton, *Race and the Making of American Liberalism* (New York: Oxford University Press, 2005), 201; see also MacLean, *Freedom Is Not Enough,* chapter 7; Glazer, *Affirmative Discrimination.*
29. Glazer, *Affirmative Discrimination,* 220.
30. Ibid., 220–221.
31. Ibid.
32. MacLean, *Freedom Is Not Enough;* Horton, *Race and the Making of American Liberalism.*
33. Ronald Reagan, Address Before a Joint Session of the Alabama State Legislature in Montgomery, March 15, 1982, available online at Peters and Woolley, American Presidency Project, http://www.presidency.ucsb.edu/ws/?pid=42269. The turn of phrase "tears of sorrow, tears of salvation" was a play on remarks Reagan had made six months earlier to Israeli Prime Minister Menachem Begin: "Well, with the help of God and us working together, perhaps one day for all the people in the Middle East, there will be no more tears of grief, only tears of salvation"; Ronald Reagan, Remarks at the Welcoming Ceremony for Prime Minister Menahem Begin of Israel, September 9, 1981, ibid., http://www.presidency.ucsb.edu/ws/?pid=44219.
34. Ronald Reagan, Remarks at the Tuskegee University Commencement Ceremony in Alabama, May 10, 1987, ibid., http://www.presidency.ucsb.edu/ws/?pid=34256.
35. Ronald Reagan, The President's News Conference, February 11, 1986, ibid., http://www.presidency.ucsb.edu/ws/?pid=36870. For an extended look at Reagan's use of Martin Luther King as part of his effort to roll back the civil rights achievements of the 1960s, see Denise M. Bostdorff and Steven R. Goldzwig, "History, Collective Memory, and the Appropriation of Martin Luther King, Jr.: Reagan's Rhetorical Legacy," *Presidential Studies Quarterly* 35, no. 4 (2005).
36. Bobo, Kluegel, and Smith, "*Laissez-Faire* Racism."
37. James J. Kilpatrick, *The Southern Case for School Segregation* (New York: Crowell-Collier, 1962), 26.

38. Quoted in MacLean, *Freedom Is Not Enough*, 236.

39. Ronald Reagan, Message to the Congress of Racial Equality on the Observance of Martin Luther King, Jr. Day, January 16, 1986, available online at Peters and Woolley, American Presidency Project, http://www.presidency.ucsb.edu/ws/?pid=37235.

40. Ibid.

41. Ronald Reagan, Radio Address to the Nation on Civil Rights, June 15, 1985, ibid., http://www.presidency.ucsb.edu/ws/?pid=38782.

42. Ibid.

43. See, e.g., Sniderman and Piazza, *Scar of Race* (61 percent of white Americans agree "blacks on welfare could get a job if they really tried," 43 percent agree that "if blacks would only try harder, they would be just as well off as whites," 42 percent believe "black neighborhoods tend to be run down because blacks simply don't take care of their property," and 22 percent agree that "blacks are more violent than whites"); Kinder and Sanders, *Divided by Color*, 107 (61 percent agree that "most blacks who receive money from welfare programs could get along without it if they tried").

44. Kinder and Sanders, *Divided by Color*, 107.

45. Ibid., 106–114.

46. A prominent variant of the individualist argument places the blame for persistent racial disparities on black "culture," which is said to discourage the ethic of personal sacrifice and hard work supposedly prized by the rest of society. High levels of crime, drug use, unemployment, and illegitimate births simply reflect the dominant preferences of black culture. But this variant, like the emphasis on pure individualism, accepts and depends on group stereotypes and a blameless state, insisting that overrepresentation by some groups in certain activity reveals something fundamental about the group rather than anything nefarious about the state. See, e.g., Dinesh D'Souza, *The End of Racism: Principles for a Multiracial Society* (New York: Free Press, 1996), chapter 12. For a vigorous response to these arguments, see Michael K. Brown et al., *White-Washing Race: The Myth of a Color-Blind Society* (Berkeley: University of California Press, 2005).

47. See, e.g., Gordon W. Allport, *The Nature of Prejudice* (1954; New York: Perseus Books, 1979), 9: "A certain man happened to know three Englishmen personally and proceeded to declare that the whole English race had the common attributes that he observed in these three. There is a natural basis for this tendency. Life is so short, and the demands upon us for practical adjustments so great, that we cannot let our ignorance detain us in our daily transactions. We have to decide whether objects are good or bad by classes. We cannot weigh each object in the world by itself. Rough and ready rubrics, however coarse, have to suffice."

48. Sniderman and Piazza, *Scar of Race*, 37: "the person who believes that most Jews engage in shady practices and that Jews are indifferent to the well-being of those who are not Jewish tends also to believe that most blacks have a chip on their shoulder and take advantage of welfare."

49. See Gallup, Inc., *Religious Perceptions in America: With an In-depth Analysis of U.S. Attitudes Toward Muslims and Islam* (2009), 12: "The variable most strongly linked to self-reported prejudice toward Muslims is self-reported prejudice toward Jews. Respondents who say they feel 'a great deal' of prejudice . . . toward Jews are about 32 times as likely to report feeling 'a great deal' of prejudice toward Muslims." See also Karen Stenner, *The Authoritarian Dynamic* (New York: Cambridge University Press, 2005), chapter 9 ("intolerance of racial diversity, political dissent, and moral deviance are all primarily driven by authoritarianism, fueled by the impulse to enhance unity and conformity, and manifested under conditions of normative threat, that is, conditions that threaten oneness and sameness" [269]); Donald R. Kinder and Cindy D. Kam, *Us Against Them: Ethnocentric Foundations of American Opinion*

(Chicago: University of Chicago Press, 2009), chapters 1 and 4; Marc J. Hetherington and Jonathan D. Weiler, *Authoritarianism and Polarization in American Politics* (New York: Cambridge University Press, 2009), chapters 4 and 5; Jennifer L. Merolla and Elizabeth J. Zechmeister, *Democracy at Risk: How Terrorist Threats Affect the Public* (Chicago: University of Chicago Press, 2009).

50. Robert D. Putnam and David E. Campbell, *American Grace: How Religion Divides and Unites Us* (New York: Simon and Schuster, 2010), 7–10.

51. Ibid., 112.

52. Will Herberg, *Protestant, Catholic, Jew: An Essay in American Religious Sociology* (1955; Chicago: University of Chicago Press, 1983), 74.

53. Ibid., 78.

54. Ibid., 75.

55. Ibid., 257–258.

56. Ibid., chapter 3; the quotation is on 28.

57. Ibid., 36–37. For a discussion of Herberg's contemporaries and successors who shared the view of both the "triple melting pot" and the barriers that separated one pot from another, see Robert Wuthnow, *The Restructuring of American Religion Since World War II* (Princeton: Princeton University Press, 1988), 71–80.

58. Putnam and Campbell, *American Grace*, 373–375.

59. Ibid., 375.

60. Ibid., chapter 3.

61. Ibid., 137; Wuthnow, *Restructuring of American Religion*, 89.

62. Putnam and Campbell, *American Grace*, 160.

63. Robert Wuthnow, *America and the Challenges of Religious Diversity* (Princeton: Princeton University Press, 2005), 259–285.

64. Alan Wolfe, *The Transformation of American Religion: How We Actually Live Our Faith* (Chicago: University of Chicago Press, 2003), 262.

65. See, e.g., Diana L. Eck, *A New Religious America: How a "Christian Country" Has Become the World's Most Religiously Diverse Nation* (New York: HarperOne, 2001), 6–7; 29–30; Wuthnow, *America and the Challenges of Religious Diversity*, 37–74.

66. Putnam and Campbell, *American Grace*, 3–4, 16–17, 121–127.

67. Ibid., 16–17; 121–127.

68. Ibid., 122–123; 564–566.

69. Ibid., 150–153; 505–508.

70. Stephen Prothero, Introduction, *A Nation of Religions: The Politics of Pluralism in Multi-Religious America*, ed. Stephen Prothero (Chapel Hill: University of North Carolina Press, 2006), 8.

71. James Davison Hunter and David Franz, "Religious Pluralism and Civil Society," in Prothero, *Nation of Religions*, 256–273.

72. Pew Forum on Religion, February 2002, retrieved July 1, 2012 from iPoll Databank, Roper Center for Public Opinion Research, University of Connecticut, http://www.ropercenter .uconn.edu/data_access/ipoll/ipoll.html.

73. Wuthnow, *America and the Challenges of Religious Diversity*, 159–187.

74. Ibid., 191–197.

75. Ibid., 170–172, 200.

76. Ibid., 200, 210.

77. The political scientists Clyde Wilcox and Carin Larson define "Christian Right" as "a social movement that attempts to mobilize evangelical Protestants and other orthodox Christians into conservative political action." Clyde Wilcox and Carin Larson, *Onward Christian Sol-*

diers? The Religious Right in American Politics (Boulder, CO: Westview, 2006), 6. Because the movement also includes a small number of conservative Jews, I prefer the broader term "Religious Right," but otherwise mean the same thing.

78. Stenner, *Authoritarian Dynamic*, 277; emphasis in original.

79. Sniderman and Piazza, *The Scar of Race*, 53.

80. Stenner, *Authoritarian Dynamic*, 81; emphasis in original. Other scholars have pointed to ethnocentrism rather than authoritarianism as the key to understanding American opinion regarding certain social policies, including the war on terror. See Kinder and Kam, *Us Against Them*. But Kinder and Kam understand ethnocentrism as "prejudice, broadly conceived," meaning favoritism toward in-groups and hostility toward out-groups; ibid., 11, 52–55, 85. Stenner, meanwhile, describes authoritarianism as a psychological predisposition that "inclines one toward attitudes and behavior variously concerned with structuring society and social interactions in ways that enhance sameness and minimize diversity of people, beliefs, and behaviors"; *Authoritarian Dynamic*, 16. When the threat to "sameness" is the constructed barbarian at the gate, it would seem that ethnocentrism and authoritarianism converge. Kinder and Kam, *Us Against Them*, 87–88; but see ibid., 88–89, insisting that ethnocentrism is a superior predictor to authoritarianism of attitudes about the war on terror.

81. See, e.g., Daniel Williams, *God's Own Party: The Making of the Christian Right* (Oxford: Oxford University Press, 2010).

82. John C. Green, "What Happened to the Values Voter? Believers and the 2008 Election," *First Things*, March 2009, 45; Esther Kaplan, *With God on Their Side: George Bush and the Christian Right* (New York: New Press, 2005), 3.

83. Phil Hirschkorn and Jennifer De Pinto, "White Evangelicals Are Half of GOP Primary Voters," *CBS News*, March 15, 2012, available at http://www.cbsnews.com/8301-503544_162 -57398385-503544/white-evangelicals-are-half-of-gop-primary-voters/.

84. Quoted in Kaplan, *With God on Their Side*, 75.

85. Bill Moyers, "9/11 and God's Sport," *Crosscurrents*, Winter 2006, 442–454.

86. Ibid., 450, 453.

87. Hetherington and Weiler, *Authoritarianism and Polarization*, 158.

88. Thomas E. Mann and Norman J. Ornstein, "Let's Just Say It: The Republicans Are the Problem," *Washington Post*, April 27, 2012.

89. Ibid.

90. "Former Republican Senator Criticises Party," *Financial Times*, September 1, 2011, video available at http://video.ft.com/v/1138459180001/Former-Republican-senator-criticises-party.

91. Josh Rogin, "Hagel: Reagan Wouldn't Identify with Today's GOP," *Cable*, May 11, 2012.

92. Mike Lofgren, "Goodbye to All That: Reflections of a GOP Operative Who Left the Cult," Truthout.org, September 3, 2011, available at http://truth-out.org/index.php?option=com_ k2&view=item&id=3079:goodbye-to-all-that-reflections-of-a-gop-operative-who-left-the -cult.

93. Ibid.

94. Ibid.

95. Ashley Southall, "Republicans Apologetic After Raising Issue of Obama's Birthplace," *New York Times*, May 24, 2012; Richard A. Oppel, Jr., "After Pressing Attacks on Obama, Romney Surrogate Later Apologizes," *New York Times*, July 17, 2012.

Chapter 5. The Punitive Turn

I am indebted to my colleague, the historian Michael Sherry, for the turn of phrase that I have used for the chapter title. See Michael Sherry, "Dead or Alive: American Vengeance Goes

Global," *Review of International Studies* 31 (2005), 245, 258; Michael Sherry, *Go Directly to Jail: The Punitive Turn in American Life* (forthcoming).

1. See, e.g., Jonathan Simon, *Governing Through Crime: How the War on Crime Transformed American Democracy and Created a Culture of Fear* (New York: Oxford University Press, 2007); David Garland, *The Culture of Control: Crime and Social Order in Contemporary Society* (Chicago: University of Chicago Press, 2002); Bruce Western, *Punishment and Inequality in America* (New York: Russell Sage Foundation, 2006); Katherine Beckett and Steve Herbert, *Banished: The New Social Control in Urban America* (New York: Oxford University Press, 2010); Anne-Marie Cusac, *Cruel and Unusual: The Culture of Punishment in America* (New Haven: Yale University Press, 2009).

2. Stanley Cohen, *Visions of Social Control: Crime, Punishment, and Classification* (Cambridge: Polity, 1985).

3. Ronald Bayer, "Crime, Punishment, and the Decline of Liberal Optimism," *Crime and Delinquency* 27 (1981), 169–190, 172. This was believed true even for African-American crime in the era of Jim Crow. See, e.g., Brenda Z. Seligman, "Race and Crime," *Man* 45 (1945), 44 ("The high criminality of the Negro has been examined sociologically, and American criminologists are practically unanimous in considering the solution to be in differences of education and economic and social status. The Negro criminal is the victim of a vicious circle of social, biological, and economic causes. He adjusts better qua criminality in the southern states than the northern, where the proportion of crime is highest in the overcrowded slums of the great cities"); Mary Huff Diggs, "Some Problems and Needs of Negro Children as Revealed by Comparative Delinquency and Crime Statistics," *Journal of Negro Education* 19 (1950), 290 ("a community has just as much juvenile misconduct as it deserves [and] an absence of such problems means an adequately financed and directed network of social agencies and facilities for all children within a community").

4. Juvenile crime was thought particularly susceptible to environmental explanations. "The cause of the current acts of juvenile delinquency," a *Nation* editorialist wrote in 1950, "is not mysterious. . . . They are painfully poor and since they in turn find it increasingly difficult to get part time jobs they swarm about the city streets with nothing to do, frustrated in all their desires"; Bayer, "Crime, Punishment," 174, quoting Carey McWilliams, "Nervous Los Angeles," *Nation*, June 10, 1950, 570.

5. Lyndon B. Johnson, Remarks on the City Hall Steps, Dayton, Ohio, October 16, 1964, available online at Gerhard Peters and John T. Woolley, The American Presidency Project, http://www.presidency.ucsb.edu/ws/?pid=26621.

6. Bayer, "Crime, Punishment," 171, quoting "Crime Waves and Scapegoats," *Commonweal*, August 9, 1946, 396.

7. *Report of the National Advisory Commission on Civil Disorders* (Washington, DC: Government Printing Office, 1968), 1.

8. Ibid.

9. Quoted in Kim Phillips-Fein, *Invisible Hands: The Businessmen's Crusade Against the New Deal* (New York: W. W. Norton, 2010), 68.

10. Quoted in Katherine Beckett, *Making Crime Pay* (New York: Oxford University Press, 1997), 35.

11. Ibid., 37.

12. Republican Party Platform of 1968, available online at Peters and Woolley, American Presidency Project, http://www.presidency.ucsb.edu/ws/index.php?pid=25841#ixzz1QOXYSgjy.

13. "Nation: Lurching Off to a Shaky Start," *Time*, September 20, 1968, http://www.time.com/time/magazine/article/0,9171,838728,00.html.

14. Ibid.

15. Quoted in Beckett, *Making Crime Pay*, 34.

16. Democratic Party Platform of 1964, available online at Peters and Woolley, American Presidency Project, http://www.presidency.ucsb.edu/ws/index.php?pid=29603#axzz1QOWXMdxn.

17. Ibid.

18. Democratic Party Platform of 1968, ibid., http://www.presidency.ucsb.edu/ws/index.php?pid=29604.

19. Ibid.

20. Ibid.

21. Ibid.

22. "Nation: Lurching Off to a Shaky Start"; Beckett, *Making Crime Pay*, 38.

23. Beckett, *Making Crime Pay*, 38.

24. Quoted ibid., 48.

25. Quoted ibid.

26. Quoted ibid., 49.

27. Quoted ibid., 47.

28. Quoted ibid.

29. Democratic Party Platform of 1988, available online at Peters and Woolley, American Presidency Project, http://www.presidency.ucsb.edu/ws/index.php?pid=29609.

30. Republican Party Platform of 1988, ibid., http://www.presidency.ucsb.edu/ws/index.php?pid=25846.

31. See Marshall Frady, "Death in Arkansas," *New Yorker*, February 22, 1993, 132.

32. Craig Wolff, "Youths Rape and Beat Central Park Jogger," *New York Times*, April 21, 1989. See also Chris Smith, "Central Park Revisited," *New York*, http://nymag.com/nymetro/news/crimelaw/features/n_7836/; Tracy Connor, "48 Hours: Twisting Trail to Teens' Confessions," *New York Daily News*, October 20, 2002; Maureen Callahan and Brad Hamilton, "The Return of the Central Park 5," *New York Post*, March 27, 2011.

33. *New York Daily News*, April 21, 1989. Image available at http://www.nydailynewspix.com/sales/searchResults.php?searchAction=advSearch&searchDisplay=A&searchAction=advSearch&numFields=1&searchVal=&location_0=Category_ms&value_0=COV&type_0=all&bool_0=AND&start=315619200&end=631238400.

34. Quoted in Lynnell Hancock, "The Press and the Central Park Jogger," http://www.4efren.com/resources/The+Press+and+the+Central+Park+Jogger.pdf.

35. Quoted ibid.

36. Michael Stone, "What Really Happened in Central Park: The Night of the Jogger and the Crisis of New York," *New York*, August 14, 1989.

37. Ibid.

38. Smith, "Central Park Revisited."

39. Julia Dahl, "We Were the Wolf Pack: How New York City Tabloid Media Misjudged the Central Park Jogger Case," Poynter.org, June 16, 2011, http://www.poynter.org/latest-news/top-stories/135971/we-were-the-wolf-pack-how-new-york-city-tabloid-media-mangled-the-central-park-jogger-case/.

40. "The Law and the Street Gang Menace," *Chicago Tribune*, October 1, 1993.

41. Joe Domanick, "Prisoners of Panic," *Los Angeles Times*, January 6, 2008.

42. J. Q. Wilson, "Crime," in *Crime and Public Policy*, ed. J. Q. Wilson and J. Petersilia (San Francisco: Institute of Contemporary Studies, 1995), 492.

43. John J. DiIulio, Jr., "The Coming of the Super-Predator," *Weekly Standard*, November 27, 1995.

44. Ibid.

45. Ibid.

46. Ibid.

47. Ibid.
48. William Bennett, John J. DiIulio, Jr., and John P. Walters, *Body Count: Moral Poverty . . . and How to Win America's War Against Poverty and Drugs* (New York: Simon and Schuster, 1996).
49. Ibid., 27.
50. DiIulio, "Coming of the Super-Predator."
51. Ibid.
52. Ibid.
53. Suzanne Fields, "The Super-Predator," *Washington Times*, October 17, 1996. See also, e.g., Sharon Mack, "The Age of the Super Predator: Mainers Say Soaring Juvenile Crime Portends Need for System Overhaul," *Bangor Daily News* (Maine), April 24, 1996 ("The Super Predator, Portland Police Chief Mike Chitwood explains, is a male, 14 to 17 years old, with no remorse and no fear. He is young and heartless and has no sense of the future"); Warren Richey, "Teen Crime Trend Puts Them Behind Adult Bars," *Christian Science Monitor*, June 2, 1997 ("America is being threatened by a growing cadre of cold-blooded teens called 'superpredators'").
54. "The Psychological Side of Lawlessness and the Central Role of Incarceration," *Tampa Tribune*, August 5, 1997.
55. Gene Koprowski, "The Rise of the Teen 'Super-Predator,'" *Washington Times*, October 23, 1996.
56. Richard Zogling, "Now for the Bad News: A Teenage Timebomb," *Time*, January 15, 1996, 52.
57. Ted Gest and Victoria Pope, "Crime Time Bomb: Rising Juvenile Crime, and Predictions That It Is Going to Get Worse, Are Prodding Cities, States, and Congress to Seek a Balance Between Tougher Laws and Preventive Measures," *U.S. News and World Report*, March 17, 1996.
58. Cited in Steve Macek, *Urban Nightmares: The Media, the Right, and the Moral Panic Over the City* (Minneapolis: University of Minnesota Press, 2006), 109.
59. Alas, it is ever thus, as the sociologist Edward Shils observed during the McCarthy era: "In the United States the rule of law is deeply rooted in the interests of institutions and in a powerful tradition. Alongside of it, however, runs a current of thought and sentiment, a disposition towards ideological enthusiasm and political passions, which proclaim great crises and announce their disbelief in the capacities of ordinary institutions and their leaders to resolve them"; *The Torment of Secrecy* (New York: New Press, 1956), 161.
60. The three preceding quotations are taken from David S. Tanenhaus and Steven A. Drizin, "Owing to the Extreme Youth of the Accused: The Changing Legal Response to Juvenile Homicide," *Journal of Criminal Law and Criminology* 92 (2001–2002), 641, 641. Of course, the halcyon days of spitballs and outhouses never existed. A close study of the juvenile code in Chicago, for instance, shows that it was written with an eye to all manner of juvenile delinquent, and that early-twentieth-century legislators were no more indifferent to the risk of violent juvenile crime than we are today; ibid., 648–649.
61. Ibid., 642.
62. Ibid., 643.
63. Ibid.; see also Amnesty International, "Betraying the Young: Children in the U.S. Justice System," November 1998, http://www.amnesty.org/en/library/info/AMR51/060/1998.
64. *Morning Edition*, National Public Radio broadcast, June 25, 1996.
65. Charles Puzzanchera, "Juvenile Arrests: 2008," U.S. Department of Justice, Office of Justice Programs, Office of Juvenile Justice and Delinquency Prevention, December 2009, http://www.ncjrs.gov/pdffiles1/ojjdp/228479.pdf. There were, of course, variations within offense categories, and rates for robbery showed a significant increase. "The number of ju-

venile arrests in 2008 for forcible rape was less than in any year since at least 1980, and the number of juvenile aggravated assault arrests in 2008 was less than in any year since 1988. In contrast, after also falling to a relatively low level in 2004, juvenile arrests for murder increased each year from 2005 to 2007, then declined 5% in 2008. However, juvenile arrests for robbery increased more than 46% since 2004"; ibid., 4. Still, overall arrest rates for juveniles have fallen significantly, and with the exception of robbery, from 1999 to 2008 rates for juveniles fell even more than the rates for adults in every category of violent or serious offense; ibid. For discussions and debunking of the superpredator myth, see, e.g., Franklin Zimring, *American Youth Violence* (Oxford: Oxford University Press, 1998), chapter 1; Franklin Zimring, "The Youth Violence Epidemic: Myth or Reality," *Wake Forest Law Review* 33 (1998), 727; Mark Soler et al., "Juvenile Justice: Lessons for a New Era," *Georgia Journal on Poverty Law and Policy* 16 (2009), 487; Lara Bazelon, "Exploding the Superpredator Myth: Why Infancy Is the Preadolescent's Best Defense in Juvenile Court," *New York University Law Review* 75, no. 159 (2000), 159.

66. "Youth Violence: A Report of the Surgeon General," U.S. Department of Health and Human Services, January 2001, http://www.ncbi.nlm.nih.gov/books/NBK44294/.

67. Ibid., 5. The authors said the rise in juvenile violence "resulted primarily from a relatively sudden change in the social environment—the introduction of guns into violent exchanges among youths. The violence epidemic was, in essence, the result of a change in the presence and type of weapon used, which increased the lethality of violent incidents"; ibid., 49.

68. Elizabeth Becker, "As Ex-Theorist on Young 'Superpredators,' Bush Aide Has Regrets," *New York Times*, February 9, 2001.

69. Ibid.

70. John J. DiIulio, Jr., "Jail Alone Won't Stop Juvenile Super-Predators," *Wall Street Journal*, June 11, 1997.

71. Becker, "Ex-Theorist." And in the case that played such an outsized role in creating the national image of the juvenile superpredator, it was not God but DNA that brought the case back to prominence. DNA evidence eventually exonerated the five boys who had been convicted in the attack of the Central Park jogger. A young man named Matias Reyes, himself only seventeen, had committed the assault. Five months after this attack, he was arrested for the attempted rape of one woman and the rape and murder of another. The boys, like so many other juveniles, had confessed falsely after hours of coercive interrogations. Smith, "Central Park Revisited"; Callahan and Hamilton, "Return of the Central Park Five."

72. Though he wrote about the new penology in the context of racial profiling, I believe William Rose meant the same thing when he referred to "a new way of talking about danger." See William Rose, "Crimes of Color: Risk, Profiling, and the Contemporary Racialization of Social Control," *International Journal of Politics, Culture and Sociology* 16, no. 2 (2002), 179, 185.

73. Andrew Vachss, "Sex Predators Can't Be Saved," *New York Times*, January 5, 1993; see also John Douard, "Sex Offender as Scapegoat: The Monstrous Other Within," *New York Law School Law Review* 53 (2008–2009), 31.

74. Vachss, "Sex Predators Can't Be Saved"; see also Andrew Vachss, "How to Handle Sexual Predators," *World and I*, August 1993: "There is an old saying about monsters that we ought to heed: You don't know where they're going, but you can always tell where they've been. Once an offender has shown us he has clearly embarked on the predator's bloody road, it is our responsibility to make that road a dead end."

75. Consider, for instance, the remarks of Congressman McCollum in support of the Sexual Offender Tracking and Identification Act of 1996: "It is well recognized that sexual predators are remarkably clever and persistently transient. The offenders are not confined within state lines, and neither should our efforts to keep track of them"; McCollum, Sexual Of-

fender Tracking and Identification Act of 1996, Cong. Rec. H11132, quoted in Mona Lynch, "Pedophiles and Cyber-Predators as Contaminating Forces: The Language of Disgust, Pollution, and Boundary Invasions in Federal Debates on Sex-Offender Legislation," *Law and Social Inquiry* 27 (2002), 529, 545.

76. See, e.g., Andrew Vachss, "If We Really Want to Keep Our Children Safe . . .," *Parade*, May 2, 1999: "Predatory pedophiles are experts at camouflage. Virtually all of their approaches to children are made under a benign guise—offering 'friendship' or 'understanding.' For every child molester who leaps out of a van wearing a ski mask to grab a victim, there are thousands whose weapons are deception and guile."

77. See, e.g., Philip Jenkins, *Moral Panic: Changing Concepts of the Child Molester in Modern America* (New Haven: Yale University Press, 1998), 189–214.

78. Lynch, "Pedophiles and Cyber-Predators," 553, quoting Biden, Sexual Offender Tracking and Identification Act of 1996, Cong. Rec. 142: S3423.

79. These provisions survived due process challenges in *Kansas v. Hendricks*, 521 U.S. 346 (1997) and *Kansas v. Crane*, 534 U. S. 407 (2002). In *United States v. Comstock*, 130 S. Ct. 1949, 1957 (2010), the Court held that Congress had authority under the Necessary and Proper Clause to enact a federal version of this statute.

80. See Charles Patrick Ewing, *Justice Perverted: Sex Offense Law, Psychology, and Public Policy* (New York: Oxford University Press, 2011), xvi–vii. Ewing relies on the 2004 National Crime Victimization Survey, compiled by the Department of Justice, which found that approximately a quarter of rapes and sexual assaults against adult women were committed by strangers. For children, Ewing points out that "strangers were the perpetrators in only 3.0 percent of the cases involving girls 0 to 5 years old, 4.8 percent of those involving girls 6 to 11, 10 percent of those involving girls 12 to 17, 3.5 percent of those involving boys 0 to 5, 4.6 percent of those involving boys 6 to 11, and 7.6 percent of those involving boys 12 to 17"; ibid., xvii.

81. Ibid., 33–35; see also Bureau of Justice Statistics, U.S. Department of Justice, "Recidivism of Sex Offenders Released from Prison in 1994," November 2003, 2 (finding that approximately 43 percent of sex offenders and 68 percent of non–sex offenders were rearrested for any type of crime within three years of release).

82. Ewing, *Justice Perverted*, 35–36; see also Frederick E. Vars, "Rethinking the Indefinite Detention of Sex Offenders," *Connecticut Law Review* 44 (2011), 161.

83. For an account of the life cycle of the dangerous sex offender in the public imagination, see Jenkins, *Moral Panic*.

84. See generally Ulrich Beck, "The Terrorist Threat: World Risk Society Revisited," *Theory, Culture, and Society* 19, no. 4 (2002), 39 ("The hidden central issue in world risk society is *how to feign control over the uncontrollable*"), emphasis in original; Ulrich Beck, *Risk Society: Towards a New Modernity* (London: Sage, 1992); Jonathan Simon, "Sanctioning Government: Explaining America's Severity Revolution," *University of Miami Law Review* 56 (2001), 217, 238 ("The federal government and at least some states, including highly visible ones like Florida, Texas, and California, have begun to make rituals of reassurance a primary government activity").

85. See "Correctional Populations in the United States, 2009," *Bureau of Justice Statistics*, December 2010, appendix, table 1, http://bjs.ojp.usdoj.gov/content/pub/pdf/cpus09.pdf. With respect to the total prison population, there is at least some reason to hope. The total number of people incarcerated in 2009 fell by approximately forty-eight thousand, which was the first annual decline since the Bureau of Justice Statistics began reporting the data in 1980; ibid., table 1. The incarceration *rate* has declined steadily since the early 1980s; ibid. Joseph Kennedy used this same rhetorical device more than ten years ago, pointing

out that "we have more people under criminal justice supervision than we have living in Indiana, Washington, Missouri, Tennessee, Wisconsin, Maryland, or any one of thirty other states and that we currently have enough jail and prison capacity to incarcerate every woman, man, and child in Manhattan with room to spare." See Joseph E. Kennedy, "Monstrous Offenders and the Search for Solidarity Through Modern Punishment," *Hastings Law Journal* 51 (2000), 829, 832. Since then, the numbers have grown considerably.

86. "World Prison Population List," *King's College London, International Centre for Prison Studies* 8 (2009), http://www.prisonstudies.org/images/downloads/wppl-8th_41.pdf. Though the United States clearly has the highest incarceration *rate* in the world, the total number of prisoners in China may be modestly higher than in the United States, depending on the number of people held by the Chinese government in "administrative detention"; ibid. For the statistics on the growth in the number of prisons, see Sarah Lawrence and Jeremy Travis, "The New Landscape of Imprisonment: Mapping America's Prison Expansion," *Urban Institute* (2004), 8.

87. Ashley Nellis, "Throwing Away the Key: The Expansion of Life Without Parole Sentences in the United States," *Federal Sentencing Reporter* 23, no. 1 (2010), 27.

88. "Correctional Populations, 2009," table 1.

89. Western, *Punishment and Inequality in America*, 3, 16.

90. See Leena Kurki and Norval Morris, "The Purposes, Practices, and Problems of Supermax Prisons," *Crime and Justice* 28 (2001), 385.

91. Daniel P. Mears, "A Critical Look at Supermax Prisons," *Corrections Compendium* 30 (2005), 6–7. Counting the number of prisoners in supermax is often complicated by a lack of consensus on what constitutes a supermax facility. In Mears's research, 95 percent of supermax wardens agreed on the following definition: "A supermax is defined as a stand-alone unit or part of another facility and is designated for violent or disruptive inmates. It typically involves up to 23-hour per day, single-cell confinement for an indefinite period of time. Inmates in supermax housing have minimal contact with staff and other inmates"; ibid., 49.

92. Lance Tapley, "Supermax Torture in America," *Boston Review*, November–December 2010.

93. For a discussion of the minor variations in conditions at supermax prisons, see Kurki and Morris, "Purposes, Practices," 394–410; see also, e.g., *Madrid v. Gomez*, 889 F. Supp. 1146 (N.D. Cal. 1995) (conditions at Pelican Bay, in California); *Ruiz v. Johnson*, 37 F. Supp. 2d 855 (S.D. Tex. 1999) (supermax in Texas); "Cold Storage: Super-Maximum Security Confinement in Indiana," *Human Rights Watch*, 1997; "Red Onion State Prison: Super-Maximum Security Confinement in Virginia," *Human Rights Watch*, 1999.

94. Kurki and Morris, "Purposes, Practices," 407.

95. See, e.g., Laura LaFay, "7 New Prisons Will Handle Growing Inmate Count," *Virginian-Pilot*, August 23, 1997 ("Red Onion, which will house 1,267 prisoners and employ about 400 people, has been designed for what Corrections Director Ron Angelone likes to call 'the worst of the worst.' 'These are hardcore, violent, predatory individuals who are a risk to other individuals and to staff,' he said"); Cathy Frye, "'Super Max' to House 'Worst of Worst,'" *Arkansas Democrat Gazette*, December 17, 1999; Karen Grigsby Bates, "A Cell in Super Max Prison," *National Public Radio*, May 4, 2006 (federal supermax at Florence "is designed to isolate what's often described as the worst of the worst of the prison population").

96. Kurki and Morris, "Purposes, Practices," 395.

97. Ibid., 395–396.

98. Ibid., 395.

99. See, e.g., Interim Report of the Special Rapporteur of the Human Rights Council on Torture and Other Cruel, Inhuman or Degrading Treatment or Punishment, United Nations Gen-

eral Assembly, Sixty Sixth Session, August 5, 2011; Stuart Grassian, "Psychiatric Effects of Solitary Confinement," *Journal of Law and Policy* 22 (2006), 325, 333–338.

100. See, e.g., Marc Mauer, "Mass Imprisonment and the Disappearing Voters," in *Invisible Punishment: The Collateral Consequences of Mass Imprisonment,* ed. Marc Mauer and Meda Chesney-Lind (New York: New Press, 2002), 50–51 ("Forty-eight states and the District of Columbia do not permit prison inmates to vote; thirty-two states disenfranchise felons on parole; and twenty-eight disenfranchise felons on probation. In addition, in thirteen states a felony conviction can result in disenfranchisement, generally for life, even after an offender has completed his or her sentence"); "Federal Statutes Imposing Collateral Consequences Upon Conviction," U.S. Department of Justice, Office of the Pardon Attorney, http://www.justice.gov/pardon/collateral_consequences.pdf, 1 [hereinafter OPA Federal Summary] ("The great majority of states impose some type of restriction on the ability of convicted felons to vote").

101. Christopher Uggen, Jeff Manza, and Melissa Thompson, "Citizenship, Democracy, and the Civic Reintegration of Criminal Offenders," *Annals of the American Academy of Political and Social Science* 605 (2006), 281, 297 (forty-seven states restrict an individual's right to serve on a jury after a felony conviction); OPA Federal Summary, 2–3 (conviction in federal or state court of any crime punishable by more than one year disqualifies a person from serving on a jury).

102. Jeremy Travis, "Invisible Punishment: An Instrument of Social Exclusion," in Mauer and Chesney-Lind, *Invisible Punishment,* 15, 24 ("The Public Housing Assessment System, established by the federal government, creates financial incentives for public housing agencies to adopt strict admission and eviction standards to screen out individuals who engage in criminal behavior"); OPA Federal Summary, 4 (federal courts "may impose certain occupational restrictions as a condition of probation or supervised release").

103. For residence restriction of sex offenders, see "No Easy Answers: Sex Offender Laws in the US," *Human Rights Watch,* 2007: "At least 20 states have enacted laws that prohibit certain sex offenders from living within a specified distance of schools, daycare centers, parks, and other places where children congregate. . . . In addition, hundreds of municipalities (in states with and without residency restriction statutes) have also passed similar ordinances." For restrictions on the right to move freely within a community, but not targeted at sex offenders alone, see Beckett and Herbert, *Banished.* For related restrictions on the right to travel, see Travis, "Invisible Punishment," 24: "In 1992, Congress passed a law requiring states to revoke or suspend the drivers' licenses of people convicted of drug felonies, or suffer the loss of 10 percent of the state's federal highway funds."

104. Travis, "Invisible Punishment," 24: after welfare reform law was enacted in 1996, the federal government required states to "permanently bar individuals with drug-related felony convictions from receiving federally funded public assistance and food stamps during their lifetime." Drug offenders may also be denied federal retirement benefits, Social Security, disability, and benefits for military service. Additionally, people convicted of drug-related and fraud-related felonies are permanently excluded from any federal health care program and some state health care programs; see OPA Federal Summary, 8–9.

105. Nora V. Demleitner, "Preventing Internal Exile: The Need for Restrictions on Collateral Sentencing Consequences," *Stanford Law and Policy Review* 11 (1999), 153, 158; Travis, "Invisible Punishment," 24 ("The Higher Education Act of 1998 suspends the eligibility for a student loan or other assistance for someone convicted of a drug-related offense").

106. Felons are barred from a number of different professions, including most commonly employment that requires contact with children, health service positions, and security ser-

vices. In some states, however, this prohibition has been extended to positions like acupuncturist and cosmetologist; Manza, Uggen, and Thompson, "Civic Reintegration," 298.

107. See, e.g., ibid., 296 ("Former felons must fulfill the *duties* of citizenship, but their conviction status effectively denies their *rights* to participate in social life"); Travis, "Invisible Punishment," 19 ("These punishments have become instruments of 'social exclusion'; they create a permanent diminution in social status of convicted offenders, a distancing between 'us' and 'them'").

108. Dan Kahan, "What Do Alternative Sanctions Mean?" *University of Chicago Law Review* 63 (1996), 591, 632–633 (internal citations omitted). Professor Kahan believes that shaming penalties represent a "feasible alternative to imprisonment for many offenses"; ibid., 594. For a contrary view, see James Q. Whitman, "What Is Wrong with Inflicting Shame Sanctions," *Yale Law Journal* 107 (1998), 1055. Professor Whitman properly focuses on the harm of shaming penalties *to society* rather than to the offender: "The most compelling arguments against such humiliation sanctions do not, in fact, involve the way we deal with the *offender* at all. . . . In the last analysis, we should think of shame sanctions as wrong because they involve a species of lynch justice, and a peculiarly disturbing species of lynch justice at that—a species of official lynch justice. The chief evil in public humiliation sanctions is that they involve an ugly, and politically dangerous, complicity between the state and the crowd. . . . They represent an unacceptable style of governance through their play on public psychology"; ibid., 1059.

109. Kahan, "Alternative Sanctions," 633–634.

110. Ibid.

111. Though I have stressed the role of state and federal legislatures and executives in this process, it is important to understand that the judiciary has also joined in the punitive turn. See Joseph Margulies, "Deviance, Risk, and Law: Reflections on the Demand for Preventive Detention," *Journal of Criminal Law and Criminology* 101, no. 3 (2011), 729–780.

112. See, e.g., Mark Warr, "Public Opinion on Crime and Punishment," *Public Opinion Quarterly* 59, no. 2 (1995), 296–310, 300.

113. See Task Force on Federalization of Criminal Law, "The Federalization of Criminal Law," *American Bar Association*, 1998; John S. Baker, "Measuring the Explosive Growth of Federal Criminal Legislation," *Federalist Society for Law and Public Policy*, 2004; John S. Baker, "Revisiting the Explosive Growth of Federal Crimes," Heritage Foundation Legal Memorandum, June 16, 2008. The ABA Task Force notes that 40 percent of the federal crimes were enacted since 1970. I arrive at the figure in the text by factoring in the growth since 1998, which included an increase of more than 10 percent in the period 2000–2008 alone.

114. See "Table of OJP Awards by State and Solicitation as of September 30, 2011," Office of Justice Programs, http://www.ojp.usdoj.gov/pfig?OCOM_STATE_SOL_TITLE&P_FISCAL_YEAR=2011; "Table of OJP Awards by State and Solicitation as of September 30, 2010," Office of Justice Programs, http://www.ojp.usdoj.gov/pfig?OCOM_STATE_SOL_TITLE&P_FISCAL_YEAR=2010.

115. Eric Pianin, "Senate Ties Crackdown on Drunk Drivers to State Highway Aid," *Washington Post*, March 5, 1998; *South Dakota v. Dole*, 483 U.S. 283 (1987).

116. The Drug-Free Workplace Act of 1988, Pub. L. No. 100-690, §§5151–5160, 102 Stat., 4304–4308 (1988).

117. Brian Z. Tamanaha, *On the Rule of Law: History, Politics, Theory* (New York: Cambridge University Press, 2004), 7–10.

118. Harry S. Truman, Address at the Laying of the Cornerstone of the New U.S. Courts Building for the District of Columbia, June 27, 1950, available online at Peters and Woolley, American Presidency Project, http://www.presidency.ucsb.edu/ws/?pid=13539#axzz1xafg1yjk.

President Eisenhower had much the same vision, as he revealed in a 1958 speech to mark the first Law Day: "Americans live, every day of our lives, under a rule of law. Freedom under law is like the air we breathe. People take it for granted and are unaware of it—until they are deprived of it. What does the rule of law mean to us in everyday life? Let me quote the eloquent words of Burke: 'The poorest man may, in his cottage, bid defiance to all the forces of the Crown. It may be frail; its roof may shake; the wind may blow through it; the storms may enter; the rain may enter—but the King of England cannot enter; all his forces dare not cross the threshold of that ruined tenement!'"; Dwight D. Eisenhower, Statement by the President on the Observance of Law Day, April 30, 1958, ibid., http://www.presidency .ucsb.edu/ws/?pid=11366. We recognize Eisenhower's sentiment even as we forgive his mistake—it was not Edmund Burke he was quoting but William Pitt, who also reminded us, "Where law ends, tyranny begins."

119. Lyndon B. Johnson, Statement by the President Following the Signing of Law Enforcement Assistance Bills, September 22, 1965, ibid., http://www.presidency.ucsb.edu/ws/index .php?pid=27270#axzz1uCdjAWjk.

120. Ibid, emphasis added.

121. Ibid.

122. Ronald Reagan, Remarks on Signing Executive Order 12360, Establishing the President's Task Force on Victims of Crime, April 23, 1982, ibid., http://www.presidency.ucsb.edu/ ws/?pid=42437.

123. Ronald Reagan, Remarks at the Annual Meeting of the American Bar Association in Atlanta, Georgia, August 1, 1983, ibid., http://www.presidency.ucsb.edu/ws/?pid=41664.

124. Ronald Reagan, Remarks at the Annual Conference of the National Sheriff's Association in Hartford, Connecticut, June 20, 1984, ibid., http://www.presidency.ucsb.edu/ws/?pid= 40074.

125. George H. W. Bush, Remarks at the Attorney General's Crime Summit, March 5, 1991, http://bushlibrary.tamu.edu/research/public_papers.php?id=2764&year=1991&month=all.

126. George H. W. Bush, Remarks on Police Brutality and an Exchange with Reporters, March 21, 1991, http://bushlibrary.tamu.edu/research/public_papers.php?id=2813&year=1991& month=all.

127. George H.W. Bush, Radio Address to the Nation on the Administration's Domestic Agenda, June 22, 1991, http://bushlibrary.tamu.edu/research/public_papers.php?id=3124&year= 1991&month=all.

128. Bill Clinton, Remarks Announcing the Anticrime Initiative and an Exchange with Reporters, August 11, 1993, available online at Peters and Woolley, American Presidency Project, http://www.presidency.ucsb.edu/ws/index.php?pid=46979.

129. Indeed, at a more general level, the punitive response is not confined to criminology. Daniel Rodgers has recently shown how the steps leading up to the Welfare Reform Act of 1996 followed much the same pattern: the demonization of the poor, who were exclusively to blame for their poverty, and who must be punished by removing the incentives in welfare which encourage them to remain impoverished. See Daniel Rodgers, *Age of Fracture* (Cambridge: Belknap Press of Harvard University Press, 2011), 201–209.

Chapter 6. "A Fight for Our Principles"

1. This literature is voluminous. For discussions of the language of the post-9/11 era, see Richard Jackson, *Writing the War on Terrorism: Language, Politics, and Counter-Terrorism* (Manchester: Manchester University Press, 2005); Stuart Croft, *Culture, Crisis, and America's War on Terror* (Cambridge: Cambridge University Press, 2004); Jeff Lewis, *Language*

Wars: The Role of Media and Culture in Global Terror and Political Violence (New York: Pluto, 2005); Brigitte L. Nacos, Yaeli Bloch-Elkon, and Robert Y. Shapiro, *Selling Fear: Counterterrorism, the Media, and Public Opinion* (Chicago: University of Chicago Press, 2009); Pippa Norris, Montague Kern, and Marion Just, eds., *Framing Terrorism: The News Media, the Government and the Public* (New York: Routledge, 2003); Jeff Birkenstein, Anna Froula, and Karen Randell, eds., *Reframing 9/11: Film, Popular Culture, and the "War on Terror"* (New York: Continuum, 2010); Anthony DiMaggio, *When Media Goes to War: Hegemonic Discourse, Public Opinion, and the Limits of Dissent* (New York: Monthly Review Press, 2009).

2. Joseph Margulies, "The Myth of Wartime," review of *Wartime: An Idea, Its History, Its Consequences* by Mary L. Dudziak, H-Net Reviews, April 2012, https://www.h-net.org/reviews/showpdf.php?id=35306. The best articulation of the myth of deviation and redemption is probably Geoffrey Stone, *In Perilous Times: Free Speech in Wartime from the Sedition Act of 1798 to the War on Terrorism* (New York: W. W. Norton, 2004); see also William H. Rehnquist, *All the Laws but One: Civil Liberties in Wartime* (New York: Alfred A. Knopf, 1998); Mark Tushnet, "Defending Korematsu? Reflections on Civil Liberties in Wartime," *Wisconsin Law Review* 273 (2003), 304; Bruce Ackerman, "The Emergency Constitution," *Yale Law Journal* 113 (2004), 1029. Candor compels the acknowledgment that I too initially saw things this way; see Joseph Margulies, *Guantánamo and the Abuse of Presidential Power* (New York: Simon and Schuster, 2006), 149–150. For a more extended critique of this view, see Joseph Margulies and Hope Metcalf, "Terrorizing Academia," *Journal of Legal Education* 60 (2011), 433.

3. CBS News/New York Times Poll, September 2001, retrieved July 6, 2012, from the iPoll Databank, Roper Center for Public Opinion Research, University of Connecticut, http://www.ropercenter.uconn.edu/data_access/ipoll/ipoll.html. The researcher who wants to examine the arc of public opinion since September 11 is immediately confronted by a bewildering collection of polls. In addition to consulting the individual polling organizations, I have found two databases to be particularly useful. The first is the iPoll databank, cited above, compiled by Roper Center for Public Opinion Research, which allows the user to search thousands of polls by scores of companies, filtered by keyword and date. The second is the Association of Religion Data Archives, available at http://www.thearda.com/Archive/browse.asp, which allows researchers to search polling data specific to religion and religiosity in the United States. In addition to these two, the American Enterprise Institute has created a fairly comprehensive collection of post-9/11 polls associated with the war on terror. The most recent update is current through August 2011; see "Attitudes Towards the War on Terror and the War in Afghanistan: A Ten-Year Review," American Enterprise Institute, August 2011, available at http://www.aei.org/files/2011/08/25/Attitudes-Towards-the-War-on-Terror-and-the-War-in-Afghanistan-August-2011.pdf. Citations to this document in the text are in the form "AEI Polling, [page]." The AEI collection, however, shows only the "top-line" numbers and does not include more detailed data broken down by other factors, such as demographics or party affiliation, which are generally available in the iPoll and ARDA databanks. In addition, the AEI researchers made the decision to exclude some polls, apparently because of their obvious bias. Because even biased polling can reveal something important, these are often worth consulting, if only to show how some pollsters were trying to influence the debate by manipulating public opinion to create the false appearance of consensus for one position or another.

4. Quoted in Nacos, Bloch-Elkon, and Shapiro, *Selling Fear*, 4.

5. Jackson, *Writing the War on Terrorism*, 38.

6. George W. Bush, Remarks Following a Meeting with the National Security Team, September 12, 2001, available online at Gerhard Peters and John T. Woolley, The American Presidency Project, http://www.presidency.ucsb.edu/ws/?pid=58058.

7. George W. Bush, Remarks in a Telephone Conversation with New York City Mayor Rudolph W. Giuliani and New York Governor George E. Pataki and an Exchange with Reporters, September 13, 2001, ibid., http://www.presidency.ucsb.edu/ws/?pid=58062.

8. George W. Bush, Remarks at the National Day of Prayer and Remembrance Service, September 14, 2001, ibid., http://www.presidency.ucsb.edu/ws/?pid=63645.

9. George W. Bush, Remarks in a Meeting with the National Security Team and an Exchange with Reporters at Camp David, Maryland, September 15, 2001, ibid., http://www.presidency.ucsb.edu/ws/?pid=63199.

10. Quoted in Nacos, Bloch-Elkon, and Shapiro, *Selling Fear*, 3.

11. Ibid., 2–3.

12. Margulies, "Myth of Wartime."

13. Bush, Remarks Following a Meeting with the National Security Team. The President repeated this language November 10 in an address to the U.N. General Assembly: "We know that evil is real, but good will prevail against it." George W. Bush, Remarks to the United Nations General Assembly in New York City, November 10, 2001, available online at Peters and Woolley, American Presidency Project, http://www.presidency.ucsb.edu/ws/?pid=58802.

14. George W. Bush, Address to the Nation from Atlanta on Homeland Security, November 8, 2001, ibid., http://www.presidency.ucsb.edu/ws/?pid=62836.

15. John Diamond and Bob Kemper, "Bush Lining Up Allies for Retaliation," *Chicago Tribune*, September 13, 2001.

16. Quoted in Jackson, *Writing the War on Terrorism*, 48.

17. Robin Wright, "Bush Prepares to Hit Back," *Pittsburgh Post-Gazette*, September 13, 2001.

18. Robert J. Caldwell, "America's Call to Arms," *San Diego Union-Tribune*, September 16, 2001.

19. For a fascinating discussion of American expectations associated with "wartime," and the difficulties occasioned by the use of that term when "wartime" is all the time, see Mary L. Dudziak, *Wartime: An Idea, Its History, Its Consequences* (New York: Oxford University Press, 2012).

20. Muneer Ahmed, "A Rage Shared by Law: Post-September 11 Racial Violence as Crimes of Passion," *California Law Review* 92 (2004), 1261, 1265–1266.

21. Ernst-Ulrich Franzen, "The Enemy Is Terrorism," *Milwaukee Journal Sentinel*, September 17, 2001.

22. Judy Mann, "Our Vengeance Must Be Patient, Wise," *Washington Post*, September 14, 2001.

23. "Bigotry Is Beneath Us," *Denver Post*, September 18, 2001.

24. Jacquielynn Floyd, "Our Fury: Handle with Care," *Dallas Morning News*, September 13, 2001.

25. "Angry Backlash Makes Difficult Situation Worse," *San Antonio Express-News*, September 14, 2001.

26. Herbert G. Klein, "New Threats and New Challenges," *San Diego Union-Tribune*, September 12, 2001.

27. Zev Chafets, "Arab Americans Have to Choose," *New York Daily News*, September 16, 2001.

28. Sam McManis, "American Muslims Fear Retribution," *San Francisco Chronicle*, September 13, 2001.

29. "Bigotry Is Beneath Us."

30. "Angry Backlash."

31. Mann, "Our Vengeance."

32. Floyd, "Our Fury."

33. Mann, "Our Vengeance."

34. Floyd, "Our Fury."

35. Michael Novak, "President of All the People," in *Who Belongs in America: Presidents, Rheto-*

ric, and Immigration, ed. Vanessa B. Beasley (College Station: Texas A&M University Press, 2006), 19–20.

36. On the surpassing importance of presidential rhetoric in shaping national identity, see, e.g., Vanessa B. Beasley, *You, the People: American National Identity in Presidential Rhetoric* (College Station: Texas A&M University Press, 2004); Beasley, *Who Belongs in America;* Denise M. Bostdorff, *The Presidency and the Rhetoric of Foreign Crisis* (Columbia: University of South Carolina Press, 1994).

37. George W. Bush, Address to the Nation on the Terrorist Attacks, September 11, 2001, available online at Peters and Woolley, American Presidency Project, http://www.presidency .ucsb.edu/ws/?pid=58057; George W. Bush, Address Before a Joint Session of the Congress on the United States Response to the Terrorist Attacks of September 11, September 20, 2001, ibid., http://www.presidency.ucsb.edu/ws/?pid=64731; George W. Bush, Remarks to the United States Attorneys Conference, November 29, 2001, ibid., http://www.presidency .ucsb.edu/ws/?pid=73556.

38. Bush, Remarks in a Telephone Conversation.

39. George W. Bush, Remarks at the Islamic Center of Washington, September 17, 2001, available online at Peters and Woolley, American Presidency Project, http://www.presidency .ucsb.edu/ws/?pid=63740.

40. Bush, Address Before a Joint Session of the Congress on the United States Response to the Terrorist Attacks of September 11.

41. George W. Bush, Remarks on the Celebration of Eid al-Fitr and an Exchange with Reporters, December 17, 2001, available online at Peters and Woolley, American Presidency Project, http://www.presidency.ucsb.edu/ws/?pid=73485.

42. Ibid.

43. H. Con. Res. 227, 147 Cong. Rec. H5691–5698 (daily ed., September 14, 2001), and Cong. Rec. S9859 (daily ed., September 26, 2001), available at http://www.gpo.gov/fdsys/pkg/ BILLS-107hconres227enr/pdf/BILLS-107hconres227enr.pdf.

44. Ibid.

45. Ibid.

46. Ibid.

47. Cong. Rec. S9859 (daily ed., September 26, 2001), available at http://www.gpo.gov/fdsys/ pkg/BILLS-107hconres227enr/pdf/BILLS-107hconres227enr.pdf.

48. Statement of Rep. Martin Frost (D-TX), quoted in "Standing by the President," *Dallas Morning News,* September 22, 2001.

49. Quoted in "Bigotry Is Beneath Us." Cheney went on to say, "We have many Arab-Americans who are first-class citizens," which not only damns with faint praise but repeats a common mistake, that all Arabs are Muslim.

50. Brigitte L. Nacos and Oscar Torres-Reyna, "Framing Muslim-Americans Before and After 9/11," in Norris, Kern, and Just, *Framing Terrorism,* 147.

51. Ibid.

52. Ibid.

53. Ibid.

54. Ibid.

55. George W. Bush, Remarks to the UNITY: Journalists of Color Convention and a Question-and-Answer Session, August 6, 2004, available online at Peters and Woolley, American Presidency Project, http://www.presidency.ucsb.edu/ws/?pid=63453.

56. Ibid.

57. Susan Sontag, Talk of the Town, *New Yorker,* September 24, 2001.

58. Ibid.

59. Raymond J. Haberski, Jr., "Susan Sontag and the 9/11 Haze," U.S. Intellectual History: The Blog of the Society for U.S. Intellectual History, September 7, 2011, http://us-intellectual-history.blogspot.com/2011/09/susan-sontag-and-911-haze.html.

60. Jonathan Alter, "Blame America at Your Peril," *Newsweek*, October 14, 2001.

61. Alexander Cockburn, "And Now for a Note of Good Cheer," *Nation*, October 15, 2001.

62. Michael Massing, "Press Watch," *Nation*, November 5, 2001.

63. Gallup/CNN/USA Today Poll, November 2001, retrieved June 21, 2012, from iPoll Databank.

64. IPSOS-Reid Poll, October 2001, retrieved June 24, 2012, ibid. IPSOS-Reid also asked whether American media was "only giving one side of the issues and not really reporting the Muslim side." While four in ten couldn't say one way or another, nearly a quarter of the respondents completely agreed, and just over a third completely disagreed. At the very least, these results suggest some skepticism about undifferentiated claims of American benevolence; ibid.

65. See, e.g., Ramesh Ponnuru, "The Uses of War," *National Review Online*, September 14, 2001, available online: http://old.nationalreview.com/ponnuru/ponnuru091401.shtml.

66. Deborah Schildkraut, "The More Things Change . . . American Identity and Mass and Elite Responses to 9/11," *Political Psychology* 23, no. 3 (2002), 511, 525–526.

67. Ibid.

68. Table 1, Hate Crime Statistics, 2001, Federal Bureau of Investigation, 2002, available at http://www.fbi.gov/about-us/cjis/ucr/hate-crime/2001.

69. Stanley Cohen, "A Study in Nativism: The American Red Scare of 1919–20," *Political Science Quarterly* 79 (1964), 52, 52.

70. Diana L. Eck, *A New Religious America: How a "Christian Country" Has Become the World's Most Religiously Diverse Nation* (New York: HarperOne, 2001), 8.

71. Table 1, Hate Crime Statistics, 2001.

72. The entire set of FBI Hate Crime Statistics through 2010, the last year for which data are available as of this writing, can be found at http://www.fbi.gov/about-us/cjis/ucr/ucr#cius_hatecrime.

73. For one of the few articles that gives credit where credit is due, see Samuel G. Freedman, "Six Days After 9/11, Another Anniversary Worth Honoring," *New York Times*, September 17, 2012. My thanks to Scott Hibbard for bringing this to my attention.

74. See Submission to United States Commission on Civil Rights, Testimony of Dr. James J. Zogby, October 12, 2001, 4–5, available at http://aai.3cdn.net/4a210464aeb6bbc959_y6m6bxt2w.pdf.

75. Bush, Address Before a Joint Session of the Congress on the United States Response to the Terrorist Attacks of September 11.

Chapter 7. "We Need to Bring the News to People"

1. "Spirit of America: Words of Wisdom. The Leaders," *Newsweek*, September 27, 2001.

2. Ted Szulc, "Journey of Faith," *National Geographic*, December 1, 2001.

3. Anna Quindlen, "A Quilt of a Country," *Newsweek*, September 27, 2001. Terkel was in turn quoting Leonel Castillo, the former director of the Immigration and Naturalization Service.

4. Ibid.

5. Quoted in Diana L. Eck, *A New Religious America: How a "Christian Country" Has Become the World's Most Religiously Diverse Nation* (New York: HarperOne, 2001), xvii.

6. Kenneth L. Woodward, "A Peaceful Faith, a Fanatic Few," *Newsweek*, September 24, 2001. The reference in the text refers to a photo accompanying this article.

7. Laurie Goodstein, "Stereotyping Rankles Silent, Secular Majority of American Muslims," *New York Times*, December 23, 2001.

8. Ibid.

9. Ibid.

10. Robert Worth, "For Arab-Americans, a Time of Disquiet," *New York Times*, September 30, 2001.

11. Only a few questions have been asked throughout the post-9/11 period without changes in the wording. ABC and CBS have both asked whether respondents have a favorable or unfavorable view of Islam. Pew has asked whether "the terrorist attacks . . . are the start of a major conflict between the people of America and Europe versus the people of Islam, or is it only a conflict with a small, radical group?" Respondents fairly consistently attribute the attack to a small, radical group. And CBS has asked this question: "How likely do you think it is now that Arab Americans, Muslims and immigrants from the Middle East will be singled out unfairly by people in this country—very likely, somewhat likely, not too likely or not at all likely?" The results consistently show that the great majority of Americans think some members of these groups will be singled out unfairly. See, e.g., CBS News/New York Times Poll, September 2001, retrieved June 22, 2012, from iPoll Databank, Roper Center for Public Opinion Research, University of Connecticut, http://www.ropercenter.uconn.edu/data_access/ipoll/ipoll.html. In September 2001, 87 percent said that unfair treatment was likely or somewhat likely, but this wording does not differentiate among Arab Americans, Muslims, and "immigrants from the Middle East." When the question is confined to Muslims, the results have been very different. In 2007 *Newsweek* asked whether Muslims were "unfairly singled out for scrutiny by law enforcement." More than half of the respondents (and more than two-thirds of the Republicans) said they were not; Princeton Survey Research Associates International/Newsweek Poll, July 2007, retrieved June 22, 2012, ibid. That question has not been repeated.

12. Los Angeles Times Poll, February 1993, retrieved June 15, 2012, ibid.

13. Ibid.

14. American Attitudes Toward Islam, March 1993, retrieved June 15, 2012, ibid.

15. Barna Research Group Poll, July 1995, retrieved June 15, 2012, ibid.

16. Taking America's Pulse II Survey, January 2000, retrieved June 16, 2012, ibid.; For Goodness Sake Survey, November 2000, retrieved June 16, 2012, ibid.

17. ABC News Poll, October 2001, retrieved June 15, 2012, ibid. Asked by *Newsweek*, "Thinking of the terrorists who attacked the United States (World Trade Center and the Pentagon) last month (September 11, 2001), do you think their views are close to the mainstream teachings of Islam, or do you think they're part of a radical fringe?" 87 percent of respondents attributed the attacks to a radical fringe, only 7 percent to mainstream Muslims; 5 percent had no opinion. Asked, "From what you know about Islam and its religious teachings, do you think the suicide bombings and other violence by some followers of Islam . . . represent a perversion of Islam by extremists or reflect an important part of Islam's teachings?" 70 percent said the attacks represent a perversion of Islam by extremists, 18 percent said they reflected an important part of Islam's teachings, and 12 percent said they didn't know. The question was asked three times (twice in December and once in January 2002), each time getting comparable results; Princeton Survey Research Associates/Newsweek Poll, December 2001, retrieved June 15, 2012, ibid.

18. In the three times the question was asked, Republican support for the proposition that the attacks were "a perversion of Islam" was 73 percent, 74 percent, and 71 percent. Democrats and independents supported the proposition in similar numbers (72 percent, 72 percent and 68 percent for Democrats and 68 percent, 70 percent, and 75 percent for independents).

19. The breakdown by political affiliation of people who attributed the attacks to the "radical fringe" was Democrat 86 percent, Republican 89 percent, independent 88 percent. The breakdown by ideology was conservative 88 percent, moderate 87 percent. There were not enough self-reported liberals to report results in that category. ABC News Poll, October 2001, retrieved June 15, 2012 from iPoll Databank.

20. Pew Research Center for the People and the Press and the Council on Foreign Relations, "America's Place in the World," October 15–21, 2001, http://www.people-press.org/files/legacy-questionnaires/141.pdf. Asked in a Civil Liberties survey, "Do you think the terrorist attacks (on the World Trade Center and the Pentagon, September 11, 2001) are the start of a major conflict between the people of America and Europe versus the people of Islam, or is it only a conflict with a small, radical group?" 63 percent of respondents said that it was a conflict with a radical group, 28 percent expected a major conflict, and 9 percent said they didn't know or refused to answer. Asked, "How do you think most Muslim Americans feel about the terrorists' acts? Do you think they are more sympathetic to the terrorists' acts than other Americans, or about the same as other Americans on this?" 81 percent said that Muslim-Americans felt about the same as other Americans, 12 percent said Muslims were more sympathetic to the terrorists' acts, and 7 percent said they didn't know; Civil Liberties Survey, October 2001, retrieved June 15, 2012, from iPoll Databank.

21. ABC News Poll, October 2001, retrieved July 11, 2012, ibid.

22. Ibid.

23. ABC News/Washington Post Poll, August 2010, retrieved July 12, 2012, ibid. CBS News has asked a similar question over the post-9/11 period ("What is your impression of the religion called Islam? As of today, is it very favorable, somewhat favorable, somewhat unfavorable, very unfavorable, or haven't you heard enough about that to say?"), and has obtained comparable results. The percentage of self-identified Republicans who have a favorable view of Islam has fallen by more than 50 percent (from 31 percent in February 2002 to 14 percent in November 2011). Among Democrats, the percentage has climbed modestly, and among independents it has fallen modestly. The results are available on the Roper Center Public Opinion Archives by searching the database for polls regarding Islam conducted by CBS News between 2001 and 2012. The November 2011 results in the Roper database do not break down the results by party identification. Those results may be found at "CBS News Polls, 11/11/11," CBS News, available at http://www.cbsnews.com/8301-250_162-57323535/cbs-news-polls-11-11-11/?tag=contentMain;contentBody.

24. "American Views on Arab and Muslim Americans," Arab American Institute, September 2010, available at http://www.aaiusa.org/page/-/Images/Polls/AAIPoll%20Report-Sept2010.pdf.

25. Ibid.

26. Ibid.

27. A November 2001 poll taken by the Pew Research Center for People and the Press, for instance, found that roughly six in ten Americans did not know anyone who is Muslim. Pew Research Center for People and the Press, November 2001, retrieved June 24, 2012, from iPoll Databank. The results did not much differ when broken down by party membership. A follow-up by the same organization in 2010 produced similar results; Pew Research Center for People and the Press, August 2010, retrieved June 24, 2012, ibid. It should be noted that some polls show a higher degree of familiarity. An ABC News poll in 2010, for example, found that roughly 50 percent of Americans know someone who is Muslim. ABC News/Washington Post Poll, August 2010, retrieved June 24, 2012, ibid. For the "close friend" data, see CBS News/New York Times Poll, September 2010, retrieved June 25, 2012, ibid.

28. Pew Religion and Public Life Survey, 2007, available at http://www.thearda.com/Archive/Files/Analysis/RELPUB07/RELPUB07_Var89_1.asp.

29. See, e.g., Esther Kaplan, *With God on Their Side: George W. Bush and the Christian Right* (New York: New Press, 2005), 72.

30. See, generally, Thomas S. Kidd, *American Christians and Islam: Evangelical Culture and Muslims from the Colonial Period to the Age of Terrorism* (Princeton: Princeton University Press, 2009), chapter 8.

31. These comments, and many others in the same spirit, are collected ibid., 147–164.

32. See Robert Wuthnow, *America and the Challenges of Religious Diversity* (Princeton: Princeton University Press, 2005), chapters 6 and 7.

33. American Enterprise Institute for Public Policy Research, Address by Newt Gingrich, "America at Risk: Camus, National Security, and Afghanistan," July 29, 2010, available at http://www.aei.org/files/2010/07/29/Address%20by%20Newt%20Gingrich07292010.pdf.

34. E.g., Norman L. Geisler and Abdul Saleeb, *Answering Islam* (Grand Rapids, MI: Baker, 2002), 84.

35. Ergun Caner and Emir Caner, *Unveiling Islam* (2002; Grand Rapids, MI: Kregel, 2009), 48.

36. Robert Spencer, *The Truth About Muhammad: Founder of the World's Most Intolerant Religion* (Washington, DC: Regnery, 2006), 10–11.

37. Geisler and Saleeb, *Answering Islam*, 319; Caner and Caner, *Unveiling Islam*, 51: "Jesus did not command the murderous crusaders. Muslim apologists do not present a powerful argument for Muhammad's worthiness when they equate his penchant for bloodshed to the Christian armies, who disobeyed Scripture."

38. Richard Cimino, "'No God in Common': American Evangelical Discourse After 9/11," *Review of Religious Research* 47, no. 2 (2005), 162–174.

39. Ibid., 166, 168.

40. Caner and Caner, *Unveiling Islam*, 77, 184.

41. Ibid., 184.

42. Geisler and Saleeb, *Answering Islam*, 328–329.

43. Caner and Caner, *Unveiling Islam*, 11.

44. Whittaker Chambers, *Witness* (Washington, DC: Regnery Gateway, 1952).

45. See, e.g., Ellen Schrecker, *Many Are the Crimes: McCarthyism in America* (Boston: Little, Brown, 1998), 74–75, 132–133.

46. Ray Allen Billington, *The Protestant Crusade, 1800–1860: A Study of the Origins of American Nativism* (Chicago: Quadrangle Paperback, 1964), 71–108.

47. Caner and Caner, *Unveiling Islam*, 63; emphasis in original.

48. Robert Spencer, *The Complete Infidel's Guide to Islam (and the Crusades)* (Washington, DC: Regnery, 2005), 114, quoting Muhammed Ibn Ismaiel Al-Bukhari, *Sahi al-Bukhari: The Translation of the Meanings*, trans. Muhammad M. Khan (Riyadh: Darussalam, 1997), vol. 1, book 2, no. 25.

49. Geisler and Saleeb, *Answering Islam*, 7.

50. Robert P. Jones, Daniel Cox, William Galston, and E. J. Dionne, "What It Means to Be an American: Attitudes in an Increasingly Diverse America Ten Years After 9/11," Public Religion Research Institute and Brookings Institution, September 2011, available at http://publicreligion.org/site/wp-content/uploads/2011/09/PRRI-Brookings-What-it-Means-to-be -American-Report.pdf.

51. Daniel Pipes, "How Dare You Defame Islam?" *Commentary*, November 1999, 41. Pipes is one of the most prominent voices in the secular conservative camp, a position explained in part by the fact that many of his arguments predate September 11.

52. Bassam Tibi, *Islam and Islamism* (New Haven: Yale University Press, 2012), 6.

53. Pipes, "How Dare You Defame Islam?"

54. Gingrich, "America at Risk."

55. Tibi, *Islam and Islamism*, 106.
56. Daniel Pipes, "The Danger Within: Militant Islam in America," *Commentary*, November 2001, 19.
57. Ibid.
58. Steven Emerson, *American Jihad: The Terrorists Living Among Us* (New York: Free Press, 2002), 159–160. The statistic traces its origin to remarks made by a Muslim cleric in 1999 at a State Department forum; ibid. The cleric, Muhammad Hisham Kabbani, later expanded on his views in an interview with the *Middle East Quarterly*. See "Muhammad Hisham Kabbani: 'The Muslim Experience in America is Unprecedented,'" *Middle East Quarterly* 7, no. 2 (2000), 61.
59. Emerson, *American Jihad*, 203–204.
60. Ibid., 203–240. The attack on CAIR is especially widespread in conservative circles. An editor at *Commentary*, for instance, described CAIR as "a group that has defended Islamic terrorism and attempted to silence those who expose it"; Naomi Schaefer, "Vishnu in Pittsburgh," *Commentary*, September 2001, 73, review of Eck, *New Religious America*.
61. See, e.g., Jones et al., "What It Means," 26.
62. Kidd, *American Christians*, 8.
63. Billington, *Protestant Crusade*, quoting *The Wide-Awake Gift: A Know-Nothing Token for 1855* (New York: Derby, 1955), 69–70.
64. Ibid., quoting Samuel F. B. Morse, *Imminent Dangers to the Free Institutions of the United States Through Foreign Immigration* (New York: E. B. Clayton, 1835), 9–17.
65. Ibid., 429, 435.
66. Paul Blanshard, *American Freedom and Catholic Power* (1949; Beacon, 1958), 1.
67. Paul Blanshard, *Communism, Democracy, and Catholic Power* (Beacon, 1951), 4–5.
68. Mark Massa, "Catholic-Protestant Tensions in Post-War America: Paul Blanshard, John Courtney Murray, and the 'Religious Imagination,'" *Harvard Theological Review* 95, no. 3 (2002), 319–339; John T. McGreevy, *Catholicism and American Freedom* (New York: W. W. Norton, 2003), 166–167.

Chapter 8. "A War for the Survival of America"

1. Barack Obama, Remarks in Cairo, June 4, 2009, available online at Gerhard Peters and John T. Woolley, The American Presidency Project, http://www.presidency.ucsb.edu/ws/?pid=86221.
2. For an account of the controversy surrounding the Cordoba House and the role of the anti-Islamic narrative in generating opposition to it, see Deepa Kumar, *Islamophobia and the Politics of Empire* (Chicago: Haymarket, 2012), 165–169.
3. Quoted ibid., 167. The speaker was Mark Williams, who was eventually expelled from the national Tea Party Federation for a mock letter to Abraham Lincoln that read in part: "We Coloreds have taken a vote and decided that we don't cotton to that whole emancipation thing. Freedom means having to work for real, think for ourselves, and take consequences along with the rewards. That is just far too much to ask of us Colored People and we demand that it stop!" A spokesperson for the federation called the letter "clearly offensive." Williams's remarks about Islam, by contrast, did not prompt such denunciations by the right; Helen Kennedy, "Tea Party Express Leader Mark Williams Kicked Out over 'Colored People' Letter," *New York Daily News*, July 18, 2010.
4. Jay Nordlinger, "The Terrible Truth," *National Review*, September 19, 2001.
5. Wajahat Ali, Eli Clifton, Matthew Duss, Lee Fang, Scott Keyes, and Faiz Shakir, "Fear, Inc.: The Roots of the Islamophobia Network in America," Center for American Progress, Au-

gust 2011, available at http://www.americanprogress.org/wp-content/uploads/issues/2011/ 08/pdf/islamophobia.pdf; see also Kumar, *Islamophobia*, 169–192. Though Kumar praises the authors of "Fear, Inc." for the thoroughness of their report, she criticizes them for failing to recognize the extent to which the anti-Islamic narrative is part of and dependent on main-stream American discourse; Kumar, *Islamophobia*, 176. In that regard, I do not share her view.

6. Ali et al., "Fear, Inc."

7. See Act! For America, www.actforamerica.org.

8. For a critique of this literature, see Justin Vaisse, "Eurabian Follies: The Shoddy and Just Plain Wrong Genre That Refuses to Die," *Foreign Policy*, January–February 2010.

9. Melanie Phillips, "Look Here," *National Review Online*, September 11, 2008, available online at http://www.nationalreview.com/articles/225613/look-here/melanie-phillips?pg=1.

10. Ibid.

11. Daniel Johnson, "Terror and Denial," *Commentary*, July–August 2006, reviewing Melanie Phillips, *Londonistan: How Britain Is Creating a Terror State Within* (New York: Encounter, 2006).

12. George Weigel, "Europe's Two Culture Wars," *Commentary*, May 2006.

13. Ibid.

14. U.S. Department of State, Passport Statistics, available at http://travel.state.gov/passport/ ppi/stats/stats_890.html.

15. Debbie Schlussel, "Donald Trump, Dhimmi: Miss Hezbollah Rima Fakih Wins Miss USA; Rigged for Muslima? Miss Oklahoma's Arizona Immigration Answer," May 16, 2010, avail-able at http://www.debbieschlussel.com/22000/donald-trump-dhimmi-miss-hezbollah-wins -miss-usa-was-contest-rigged-for-muslima-hezbollah-supporter-miss-oklahomas-great -arizona-immigration-answer/.

16. Bill O'Reilly, "Talking Points Memo and Top Story," Fox News, September 9, 2010.

17. Alex Alexiev, "Jihad, Inc.—Domestic Terrorism Is Not the End of the Islamists' American Project," *National Review*, December 7, 2009.

18. Ibid.

19. Ibid.

20. Ibid.

21. Ibid.

22. Ibid.

23. *Glenn Beck Show*, Fox News, April 14, 2011.

24. Robert Spencer, *Stealth Jihad: How Radical Islam Is Subverting America Without Guns or Bombs* (Washington, DC: Regnery, 2008), 13.

25. Mark Steyn, *America Alone* (Washington, DC: Regnery, 2006).

26. Ibid.

27. The proposal provided that Oklahoma judges, "when exercising their judicial authority, shall uphold and adhere to the law as provided in the United States Constitution, the Okla-homa Constitution, the United States Code, federal regulations promulgated pursuant thereto, established common law, the Oklahoma Statutes and rules promulgated pursuant thereto, and if necessary the law of another state of the United States provided the law of the other state does not include Sharia Law, in making judicial decisions. The courts shall not look to the legal precepts of other nations or cultures. Specifically, the courts shall not con-sider international law or Sharia Law. The provisions of this subsection shall apply to all cases before the respective courts including, but not limited to, cases of first impression"; Enrolled House Joint Resolution No. 1056, 52nd Oklahoma Legislature, 2d Sess., May 2010.

28. James C. McKinley, Jr., "Judge Blocks Oklahoma's Ban on Using Shariah Law in Court," *New York Times*, November 29, 2010.

29. "Taking Issue with Selective Friendliness," *Journal Record* (Oklahoma City), September 22, 2010.

30. "Judge Blocks Oklahoma's Ban."

31. *Awad v. Ziriax et al.*, 754 F. Supp. 2d 1298 (W. D. OK. 2010).

32. House Resolution No. 1055, Introduced by Rep. Reynolds, 53rd Oklahoma Legislature, 1st Sess., January 2011 (calling for Congress to impeach Judge Miles-LaGrange); *Awad v. Ziriax*, 670 F. 3d 1111 (10th Cir. 2012).

33. M. Scott Carter, "Oklahoma House Passes Bill Restricting Foreign Laws," *Journal Record* (Oklahoma City), March 21, 2011.

34. "A Matter of Law," *Journal Record* (Oklahoma City), December 1, 2010; "Judge Blocks Oklahoma's Ban."

35. The most assiduous chronicler of this legislation has been Bill Raftery, who maintains a blog for Gavel to Gavel, which tracks state legislation of relevance to the courts. See www .gaveltogavel.us.

36. 2012 Washington State Republican Party Platform, June 2, 2012, available at http://clallam republicans.org/wp-content/uploads/2012/05/2012_wsrp_platform.pdf.

37. Republican Party of Minnesota—2012 Standing Platform, available at http://www.mngop .com/pdfs/platform.pdf.

38. American Enterprise Institute for Public Policy Research, Address by Newt Gingrich, "America at Risk: Camus, National Security, and Afghanistan," July 29, 2010, available at http:// www.aei.org/files/2010/07/29/Address%20by%20Newt%20Gingrich07292010.pdf.

39. "The Marriage Vow: A Declaration of Dependence on Marriage and Family," Family Leader, available at http://www.washingtonpost.com/wp-srv/hp/ssi/wpc/nation/MARRIAGE-VOW .pdf; Sandhya Somashekhar, "Bachmann Signs Socially Conservative Pledge on Homosexuality, Marriage," *Washington Post*, July 8, 2011.

40. Scott Keyes, "Herman Cain Tells ThinkProgress 'I Will Not' Appoint a Muslim in My Administration," ThinkProgress, March 26, 2011, available at http://thinkprogress.org/ politics/2011/03/26/153625/herman-cain-muslims/.

41. *Awad*, 754 F. Supp. 2d at 1301.

42. Robert Spencer, "The Necessity of Anti-Sharia Laws," *American Thinker*, March 13, 2012.

43. Ibid.

44. The comments accompany Spencer's article and are available at http://www.american thinker.com/2012/03/the_necessity_of_anti-sharia_laws_comments.html#disqus_thread.

45. There have been many questions about the Arab Spring, for instance, or the Arab-Israeli conflict, but questions that probe hostility to Arabs in the United States have practically disappeared. There are occasional exceptions, however. In 2006, *Time* asked whether people favored requiring Arab-Americans to carry identification cards issued by the federal government. Respondents were split: 47 percent said yes, 50 percent said no. Unlike when the question is about Muslims, the results *did not* skew along partisan lines. Time/SRBI Poll, August 2006, retrieved June 25, 2012, from iPoll Databank, Roper Center for Public Opinion Research, University of Connecticut, http://www.ropercenter.uconn.edu/data_access/ ipoll/ipoll.html.

46. Michael Shear, "Race and Religion Rear Their Heads," *New York Times*, May 18, 2012.

47. Robert Wuthnow, *America and the Challenges of Religious Diversity* (Princeton: Princeton University Press, 2005), 57; "Mapping the Global Muslim Population: A Report on the Size and Distribution of the World's Muslim Population," Pew Forum on Religion and Public Life, October 7, 2009, available at http://www.pewforum.org/Mapping-the-Global-Muslim -Population.aspx.

48. Transcript of CNN National Security Debate, November 22, 2011, available at http://archives .cnn.com/TRANSCRIPTS/1111/22/se.06.html.

49. See, e.g., Aliyah Shahid, "Rick Santorum Gives Green Light to Racial Profiling of Muslims," *New York Daily News*, November 23, 2011.

50. Sam Harris, "In Defense of Profiling," April 28, 2012, available at http://www.samharris .org/blog/item/in-defense-of-profiling.

51. See Project Reason, http://www.project-reason.org/about/.

52. ABC News Poll, October 2001, retrieved October 4, 2012, from iPoll Databank. Consistent with other polling done immediately after September 11, it bears noting that the results of this poll did not diverge by ideology or political party. Republicans and conservatives were no more likely to favor giving the police this power than were Democrats or independents; ibid.

53. "Abusive and Invasive Searches," available at http://www.akdart.com/airline3.html.

54. Ibid.

55. Robert P. Jones and Daniel Cox, "Old Alignments, Emerging Fault Lines: Religion in the 2010 Election and Beyond," Public Religion Research Institute, November 2010, available at http://publicreligion.org/site/wp-content/uploads/2011/06/2010-Post-election-American -Values-Survey-Report.pdf.

56. Ibid.

57. Ibid. The Public Religion Research Institute repeated this question in a smaller tracking survey in February 2012. Unfortunately, however, the institute released only the topline data and did not break down the results by political party. Still, the percentage of people who believed that American Muslims wanted to establish shari'a in the United States had declined significantly. See "Religion and Politics Tracking Survey," Public Religion Research Institute, February 2012, available at http://publicreligion.org/site/wp-content/uploads/ 2012/02/January-Follow-up-Topline.pdf.

58. Baylor University, Baylor Religion Survey (Waco, TX: Baylor Institute for Studies of Religion, 2005), available at http://www.thearda.com/Archive/Files/Descriptions/BRS2005.asp.

59. Robert P. Jones, Daniel Cox, William Galston, and E. J. Dionne, "What It Means to Be an American: Attitudes in an Increasingly Diverse America Ten Years After 9/11," Public Religion Research Institute and Brookings Institution, September 2011, available at http:// publicreligion.org/site/wp-content/uploads/2011/09/PRRI-Brookings-What-it-Means-to-be -American-Report.pdf.

60. Ibid.

61. Early in the post-9/11 period, for instance, ABC News asked whether Islam was a violent religion. Most people said no, and, consistent with other polls at the time, the partisan differences were modest. In 2003, however, ABC changed the wording to ask whether "mainstream Islam" was violent. The problem with this language, of course, is that it directs respondents to accept the differentiation between an Islam that is inside and outside the "mainstream," then asks only about the former. The results, therefore, cannot fairly be compared with questions that do not make this distinction.

62. CBS News/New York Times Poll, May 2011, retrieved July 20, 2012, from iPoll Databank; 60 Minutes/Vanity Fair Poll, April 2011, retrieved ibid.

63. Jones et al., "What It Means."

64. Spencer, *Stealth Jihad*, 7.

65. Ibid., 6.

66. Eric Bolling, "Imam to Make Case for Ground Zero Mosque," Fox News, December 28, 2010.

67. Ali, et al., "Fear, Inc."

68. Ibid.

69. The letters are available on Congresswoman Bachmann's website. See http://bachmann .house.gov/news/documentsingle.aspx?DocumentID=303218.

70. Frank Gaffney, "The Muslim Brotherhood in America: A Course in Ten Parts," Center for Public Security, available at http://muslimbrotherhoodinamerica.com/.

71. Ibid.

72. Statement by Senator John McCain on the Matter of Recent Attacks Made on Huma Abedin, July 18, 2012, available at http://www.mccain.senate.gov/public/index.cfm?FuseAction =PressOffice.PressReleases&ContentRecord_id=9acf4627-0fad-89d1-d5d3-dda642179bca.

73. Ibid.

74. Ibid.

75. Ibid.

76. Ed Rollins, "Bachmann's Former Campaign Chief—Shame on You, Michele," Fox News, July 16, 2012, available at http://www.foxnews.com/opinion/2012/07/18/bachmann-former -campaign-chief-shame-on-michele/.

77. Stephanie Condon, "Bachmann Under Fire from More Republicans," CBS News, July 19, 2012, available at http://www.cbsnews.com/8301-503544_162-57475759-503544/bachmann -under-fire-from-more-republicans/.

78. "The American Divide: How We View Arabs and Muslims," Arab American Institute, August 23, 2012, available at http://www.aaiusa.org/reports/the-american-divide-how-we-view -arabs-and-muslims.

79. "For Second Straight Year, PBS Most Trusted Name in News," *Public Policy Polling,* January 17, 2012.

Chapter 9. "Think the Unthinkable"

1. Quoted in Brigitte L. Nacos, Yaeli Bloch-Elkon, and Robert Y. Shapiro, *Selling Fear: Counterterrorism, the Media, and Public Opinion* (Chicago: University of Chicago Press, 2009), 5.

2. Dan Balz, "Bush Confronts a Nightmare Scenario," *Washington Post,* September 12, 2001.

3. David Rieff, "Fear and Fragility Sound a Wake-Up Call," *Los Angeles Times,* September 12, 2001.

4. Walter J. Boyne, "Why? We're Slack," *Newsday,* September 12, 2001.

5. Carla Marinucci, "President's Defining Moment," *San Francisco Chronicle,* September 14, 2001.

6. *Meet the Press with Tim Russert,* NBC television broadcast September 16, 2001.

7. Todd Purdum, "After the Attacks: The Strategy; Leaders Face Challenges Far Different From Those of Last Conflict," *New York Times,* September 15, 2001, http://www.nytimes.com/ 2001/09/15/us/after-attacks-strategy-leaders-face-challenges-far-different-those-last-conflict .html?pagewanted=all.

8. Philip Gailey, "We Must Trust Our Leaders to Make Wise Choices," *St. Petersburg Times,* September 16, 2001 ("shadowy and elusive enemy"); Ann Scott Tyson, "US Calculates a War with Little Room for Error," *Christian Science Monitor,* September 18, 2001 (war on terror "will be a long, open-ended campaign against an elusive enemy capable of continually reinventing itself"; "'People talk blithely about invading or sending in ground troops,' says Anthony Cordesman, a former defense official now at CSIS. 'A ground invasion of Afghanistan makes no sense whatsoever. You'd be invading a country to try to chase down someone who can run and hide almost everywhere'"); Diane Carmen, "Hart: 'Hope Is Best Weapon,'" *Denver Post* ("the enemy is elusive. It's turning up in Hamburg, Amsterdam, Delray Beach and Jersey City. Its soldiers represent not a country, but an ideology").

9. Debra Pickett, "Who Are Our Allies Now?" *Chicago Sun-Times,* September 16, 2001.

10. Tom Mashberg, "Attack on America; Experts: It May Be Hard to Link bin Laden," *Boston Herald,* September 13, 2001: "blending in locally, earning money at simple jobs and all the while planning this major action on their own."

11. William J. Broad and Melody Petersen, "A Nation Challenged: The Biological Threat," *New York Times*, September 23, 2001, http://www.nytimes.com/2001/09/23/us/nation-challenged-biological-threat-nation-s-civil-defense-could-prove-be.html?pagewanted=all.

12. Michael D. Lemonick, "Bioterrorism: The Next Threat?" *Time*, September 24, 2001, http://www.time.com/time/nation/article/0,8599,176066,00.html; Jim Rutenberg, "A Nation Challenged: The Media; Talk of Chemical War Grows Louder on TV," *New York Times*, September 27, 2001. CIA Director George Tenet had warned Congress in 2000 that a number of groups were seeking "germ, chemical, radiological, or nuclear arms," and that operatives of Osama bin Laden trained to conduct attacks with toxic chemicals or biological toxins. But in 2000, warnings like this attracted little attention.

13. Don Melvin and Deborah Scroggins, "A Patron for Radical Groups," *Atlanta Journal-Constitution*, September 13, 2001. The Chechen–bin Laden story apparently originated with a 1999 article in the Arabic newsmagazine *Al-Watan*. It continues to circulate. See Youssef Bodansky, *Chechen Jihad: Al Qaeda's Training Ground and the Next Wave of Terror* (New York: Harper, 2007).

14. Rutenberg, "A Nation Challenged."

15. Ibid.

16. Ibid.

17. See, e.g., Eleanor Clift, "Capitol Letter: Duck and Cover," *Newsweek*, November 15, 2001.

18. Melody Petersen and Robert Pear, "A Nation Challenged: Cipro; Anthrax Fears Send Demand for a Drug Far Beyond Output," *New York Times*, October 16, 2001, http://www.nytimes.com/2001/10/16/business/a-nation-challenged-cipro-anthrax-fears-send-demand-for-a-drug-far-beyond-output.html?pagewanted=all.

19. "*48 Hours*: Bioterror Fear on Rise," CBS News, http://www.cbsnews.com/2100-18559_162-313592.html.

20. In response to a request under the Freedom of Information Act, the Department of Justice released an exhaustive summary of the anthrax attacks and subsequent investigation. See United States Department of Justice, Amerithrax Investigative Summary, available at http://www.justice.gov/amerithrax/docs/amx-investigative-summary.pdf. The report confirms that investigators "vigorously pursued the possibility that the letters were the result of a state-sponsored attack, and specifically focused on those governments known to have, or have had, an offensive biological weapons program. Task force investigators also exhaustively explored the possibility that al Qaeda or another international terrorist organization may have been responsible for the 2001 attacks, conducting witness interviews and evidence collection efforts on six continents with its liaison partners overseas. While it is undoubtedly true that al Qaeda was seeking to establish an offensive bioweapons program in 2001 (see *The 9/11 Commission Report: Final Report of the National Commission on Terrorist Attacks upon the United States*, chapter 5.1, p. 151), task force agents were unable to find any link between al Qaeda and the letter attacks in the United States, or even that, at the time of the attacks, any al Qaeda operatives had access to the type and quality of anthrax pathogen used in the 2001 attacks"; ibid., 16.

21. David Johnston and Philip Shenon, "A Nation Challenged: The Investigation; Agency Offers No Information About Threats," *New York Times*, October 12, 2001.

22. "Gephardt Thinks Anthrax, Terror Attack Linked," CNN, October 23, 2001, http://articles.cnn.com/2001-10-23/health/anthrax.gephardt_1_gephardt-anthrax-cases-central-mail-facility?_s=PM:HEALTH.

23. Julian E. Zelizer, *Arsenal of Democracy: The Politics of National Security from World War Two to the War on Terrorism* (New York: Basic, 2010), 445.

24. Kevin Cullen, "Fighting Terror: The Investigation; Indictment Expected in Hijackings; Suspect Is Called Would-Be Pilot; Anthrax Tie Seen to Conspiracy," *Boston Globe* November 7, 2001.

25. Kenan Malik, "Don't Panic," *New Statesman*, October 8, 2001, http://www.kenanmalik.com /essays/bioterrorism_print.html.

26. Sharon Begley, "Unmasking Bioterror," *Newsweek*, October 8, 2001.

27. Ibid.

28. Fred Guterl, "The Nagging Fear of Nukes," *Newsweek*, October 8, 2001. After the bioterror scare had faded, *Newsweek* used similar language to describe the risk of "a serious cyber-attack by Islamic militants." Quoting an unnamed "intelligence source," the magazine said, "It's not a question of if. It's a question of when"; Mark Hosenball, "Islamic Cyberterror," *Newsweek*, May 20, 2002.

29. "Old Scourges and New," *Economist*, October 6, 2001.

30. Transcript of Press Conference by President Bush, October 11, 2001, http://archives.cnn .com/2001/US/10/11/gen.bush.transcript/.

31. Leonie Huddy et al., "Threat, Anxiety, and Support of Antiterrorism Policies," *American Journal of Political Science* 49, no. 3 (2005), 593–608. Other polls showed similar results. Four polls taken by CBS News/New York Times from September 20 to December 10, 2001, for instance, showed that anywhere from 76 to 88 percent of respondents in a national survey believed a terror attack in the next few months was either very or somewhat likely. Available at http://documents.nytimes.com/new-york-times-cbs-news-poll#document/p25 (question 87).

32. Jay Winik, "Security Comes Before Liberty," *Wall Street Journal*, October 24, 2001.

33. Ibid.

34. Ibid.

35. Bob Drogin and Gregg Miller, "Spy Agencies Facing Questions of Tactics," *Los Angeles Times*, October 28, 2001.

36. Ibid.

37. Ibid.

38. Walter Pincus, "Silence of 4 Terror Probe Suspects Poses Dilemma," *Washington Post*, October 21, 2001. Shah was misidentified in the *Post* article as Ayub Ali Khan.

39. Ibid.

40. Ibid.

41. "This and Far More," *Omaha World Herald*, October 29, 2001.

42. "Interview with Eric Haney," *Fox News Edge*, Fox News, October 22, 2001.

43. "Interview with Larry Johnson," *Fox News Edge*, Fox News, October 26, 2001.

44. "Interview with Eric Haney," *The O'Reilly Factor*, Fox News, November 5, 2001.

45. Ibid.

46. "Anti-Terrorism Bill/Gallup-CNN-USA Today Poll on 'Torture,'" *Talk of the Nation*, National Public Radio, October 30, 2001.

47. Ibid.

48. Ibid.

49. Ibid.

50. Clarence Page, "Confess . . . or Else," *Chicago Tribune*, October 31, 2001.

51. Ibid.

52. Rekha Bashu, "Don't Let Terrorists Rob Us of Our Basic Rights," *Orlando Sun-Sentinel*, October 25, 2001.

53. "Tortured Logic," *Houston Chronicle*, October 27, 2001.

54. Tony Batt, "Delegation Opposed to Torture Tactics," *Las Vegas Review Journal*, October 26, 2001.

55. Ibid.

56. Both letters appeared in the *Washington Post*, October 23, 2001. The first was written by

John Hannon of Hyattsville, Maryland, the second by Josh Hilgart of Washington. On the use of letters to the editor as a gauge of public thought, see Andrew J. Perrin, "National Threat and Political Culture: Authoritarianism, Antiauthoritarianism, and the September 11 Attacks," *Political Psychology* 26, no. 2 (2005), 167.

57. "Target Terrorism: Forcing Suspects to Talk," *Crossfire*, CNN, October 25, 2001, http://transcripts.cnn.com/TRANSCRIPTS/0110/25/cf.00.html.

58. Jonathan Alter, "Time to Think About Torture," *Newsweek*, November 4, 2001; the ellipsis is Alter's.

59. Ibid.; emphasis Alter's.

60. Ibid.

61. Alexander Cockburn, "The Wide World of Torture," *Nation*, November 9, 2001; Alisa Solomon, "The Case Against Torture," *Village Voice*, December 4, 2001.

62. *The McLaughlin Group*, November 13, 2001.

63. Jim Rutenberg, "Torture Seeps into Discussion by News Media," *New York Times*, November 5, 2001. Alter would later insist he had been misunderstood, and that he was "against court-sanctioned, physical torture," and in favor of "court-sanctioned sodium pentothal"; ibid. This, however, does not explain his apparent support for transferring presumptively innocent defendants to third countries for torture.

64. *Nightline*, October 11, 2001.

65. Ibid.

66. Ibid.

67. Alan M. Dershowitz, "Is There a Torturous Road to Justice?" *Los Angeles Times*, November 8, 2011.

68. Ibid.

69. Tina Hesman, "U.S. Now Might Have to Consider What Once Was Unthinkable, Dershowitz Says," *St. Louis Post-Dispatch*, November 4, 2001.

70. Scott Martelle, "The Truth About Truth Serum," *Los Angeles Times*, November 5, 2001.

71. David Kohn, "Legal Torture?" *60 Minutes*, CBS News, http://www.cbsnews.com/2100-18560_162-324751.html; Alan Dershowitz, "Want to Torture? Get a Warrant," *San Francisco Chronicle*, January 22, 2002.

72. Suzy Hansen, "Why Terrorism Works," *Salon*, September 12, 2002.

73. *Newark Star-Ledger*, November 11, 2001; *Hamilton Spectator*, January 23, 2002.

74. Alan M. Dershowitz, *Why Terrorism Works: Understanding the Threat, Responding to the Challenge* (New Haven: Yale University Press, 2002), 13.

75. Ibid., 24–25; emphasis Dershowitz's.

76. Ibid., 182.

77. Dershowitz described his proposal in much these terms: "If the reason you permit nonlethal torture is based on the ticking bomb case, why not limit it exclusively to that compelling but rare situation? Moreover, if you believe that nonlethal torture is justifiable in the ticking bomb case, why not require advance juridical approval—a 'torture warrant'? That was the origin of a controversial proposal that has received much attention, largely critical, from the media. Its goal was and remains to reduce the use of torture to the smallest amount and degree possible, while creating public accountability for its rare use. I saw it not as a compromise with civil liberties but rather as an effort to maximize civil liberties in the face of a realistic likelihood that torture would, in fact, take place below the radar screen of accountability"; ibid., 141.

78. In fact, many opponents of lynching made a similar argument. They recognized its inevitability, despite its savagery, particularly in cross-racial crimes. To limit the practice, they advocated more widespread use of capital punishment. In that way, legal lynching became the

analogue to the torture warrant. See Amy Louise Wood, *Lynching and Spectacle: Witnessing Racial Violence in America: 1890–1940* (Chapel Hill: University of North Carolina Press, 2010), 26–27, 50–52.

79. Jed Babbin, "The Silence of the Lambs: Torture Is Not Appropriate Treatment for Terrorists," *Washington Times*, March 21, 2002.

80. Ibid.

81. See, e.g., Alan Dershowitz, "Torture, Accountability, and Name-Calling, Part II," *Huffington Post*, November 19, 2007, http://www.huffingtonpost.com/alan-dershowitz/torture-account ability-an_1_b_73405.html.

82. Hansen, "Why Terrorism Works."

83. William F. Buckley, Jr., "Tortured Thought," *National Review*, January 29, 2002; see also Steve Chapman, "No Tortured Dilemma," *Washington Times*, November 5, 2001; Philip B. Heymann, "Torture Should Not Be Authorized," *Boston Globe*, February 16, 2002; Richard A. Posner, "The Best Offense," *New Republic*, September 2, 2002. Dershowitz always acknowledged the force of this critique. He responded to it on a number of occasions. See, e.g., Alan Dershowitz, "Yes, It Should Be 'On the Books,'" *Boston Globe*, February 16, 2002; Dershowitz, *Why Terrorism Works*, 151–163. For a particularly thoughtful discussion of Dershowitz's proposal, without the histrionics, see John T. Parry, "Torture Warrants and the Rule of Law," *Albany Law Review* 71, no. 3 (2008), 885. Parry's article was part of a symposium dedicated to Dershowitz's scholarship. In the same volume, Dershowitz expands on his defense of the torture warrant. See Alan Dershowitz, "Visibility, Accountability, and Discourse as Essential to Democracy: The Underlying Theme of Alan Dershowitz's Writing and Teaching," *Albany Law Review* 71, no. 3 (2008), 731, 750–757. Parry also collects most of the legal scholarship generated by the proposal.

84. George W. Bush, The President's News Conference, October 11, 2001, available online at Gerhard Peters and John T. Woolley, The American Presidency Project, http://www .presidency.ucsb.edu/ws/?pid=73426.

85. Brooks Egerton, "Even Here, Afghan Widow Can't Forget Horrors," *Dallas Morning News*, October 13, 2001; Dareen Barbee, "After Horrors and Death, Afghan Refugee Says She Feels Safe at Last," *Fort Worth Star-Telegram*, October 20, 2001. A week later, the *Dallas Morning News* followed Ms. Ghafoori as she traveled to a school in Duncanville, Texas, near Dallas, to speak with a group of third-graders; Brooks Egerton, "Afghan Widow Gives Youngsters a Firsthand History Lesson: 'I'm So Grateful I'm Here,' She Tells Duncanville Students," *Dallas Morning News*, October 26, 2001: "'Since I've come to this country, I've seen nothing but kindness,' said the Afghan widow, who escaped her homeland's madness last year and reached North Texas a few weeks ago. 'I'm so grateful I'm here.'"

86. Egerton, "Afghan Widow Gives Youngsters a Firsthand History Lesson."

87. Ibid.

88. Niraj Warikoo, "America Responds: Anthrax Refugees Haunted by Old, New Fears," *Detroit Free Press*, October 16, 2001.

89. Ibid.

90. Max Singer, "Better Than Retaliation," *National Review*, September 18, 2001.

91. Ibid.

92. "War on Terror: The Hunt for the Killers," Fox News, October 15, 2001. Mugniyah was killed in February 2008. Some sources attribute the killing to Israel; others to an internal faction within Hezbollah. See "Hezbollah's Most Wanted Commander Killed in Syria Bomb," Reuters, February 13, 2008, http://www.reuters.com/article/newsOne/idUSL1350754620080213.

93. Alexandra Marks, "The Beginnings of Justice Against Al Qaeda," *Christian Science Monitor*, October 18, 2001.

94. Ibid.

95. Roy Gutman, "Training in Terror," *Newsweek*, October 26, 2001, http://www.msnbc.msn .com/id/3067505/t/training-terror/#.T8000sWRZI0.

96. For some of the many other stories in this vein, see, e.g., Margery Eagen, "War on Terrorism; Afghan Atrocities Coming into Focus," *Boston Herald*, September 23, 2001; Robert Salladay, "New Kind of Enemy, New Kind of Response; Civilization Confronts Warriors Who Have No Limits," *San Francisco Chronicle*, September 30, 2001. Other commentary took a slightly different tack, demonizing the Taliban but warning against violent reprisals that would only add to the misery in Afghanistan. See, e.g., Jan Jarboe Russell, "Like Us, Afghan People Victims," *San Antonio Express-News*, September 20, 2001; Anne Brodsky, "Victims of Taliban Violence, Threats, Terror," *Cleveland Plain Dealer*, September 26, 2001; Belquis Ahmadi, "Wounds of September 11, 2001, Will Not Be Healed Through More Attacks," *Ascribe Newswire*, September 25, 2001. There is nothing uniquely American about this process. See, e.g., Christina Lamb, "War on Terror: Police Butchers: Taliban's Torturer," *Mirror* [England], October 1, 2001; Frank O'Donnell, "Afghan Escapee Tells of Life as a Torturer," *Scotsman*, October 1, 2001; Ian Traynor, "The Terrorism Crisis: Inside Afghanistan: Afghan Chaos Explodes Across Region: First Reports Emerge of Systematic Torture That Is Forcing Afghans to Flee," *Guardian*, September 30, 2001; Cole Moreton, "America at War: Afghans in Britain—'We Came Because You are Civilised,'" [London] *Independent*, September 23, 2001; Laura Bracken, "Afghan People Are Victims, Too," *Toronto Star*, September 21, 2001; Margaret Wente, "The Taliban's Forgotten War on Women," *Globe and Mail* [Canada], September 20, 2001.

97. Gallup/CNN/USA Today Poll, October 2001, retrieved July 4, 2012, from iPoll Databank, Roper Center for Public Opinion Research, University of Connecticut, http://www.roper center.uconn.edu/data_access/ipoll/ipoll.html. People who identified themselves as Republicans were more likely than independents or Democrats to support torture, but even Republican support for torture did not exceed 50 percent; ibid.

98. See, e.g., *Talk of the Nation*, National Public Radio, October 30, 2001.

99. See, e.g., John Zaller, *The Nature and Origins of Mass Opinion* (New York: Cambridge University Press, 1992).

100. TIPP/Investor's Business Daily/Christian Science Monitor Poll, November 2001, retrieved July 4, 2012, from iPoll Databank. Gallup repeated its poll in January and November 2005, during a substantially different threat environment. Here, even with the same wording as in 2001, the percentage of people who supported torture fell to 39 percent and 38 percent, respectively. For a summary of the polling data on torture from October 2001 through the beginning of 2009, including the wording used, see Paul Gronke and Darius Rejali, "U.S. Public Opinion on Torture, 2001–2009," *Journal of Political Science and Politics* 43 (2010), 437–444.

101. Fox News/Opinion Dynamics Poll, March 2002, retrieved July 4, 2012, from iPoll Databank.

102. Unfortunately, partisan divisions at the popular level on this issue are difficult to assess during the first months after September 11. Of the polls taken in 2001 and 2002, only the Gallup poll in October 2001 broke down the results by party identification.

103. James R. Petersen, "Thinking About Torture: Is It Time to Get Out the Rubber Hoses?" *Playboy*, March 2002. For some of the commentary during this period, see "Torture? Using Torture as a Means to Get Terrorists and Other Criminals to Talk," *60 Minutes*, January 20, 2002; Alisa Solomon, "The Case Against Torture," *Village Voice*, December 4, 2002; John Riley, "The War on Terror; Probe Stymied by Silence; Weighing How to Get Suspects to Cooperate," *Newsday*, November 4, 2001; Rowland Nethaway, "Torturing Terrorists for Info

Should Not be a Question of 'If' but 'How,'" Cox News Service, January 23, 2002; John Parry and Walsh White, "Should We Torture Terrorists?" *Pittsburgh Post-Gazette*, November 18, 2001; Mark Sauer, "Agonizing over Torture," Copley News Service, December 10, 2001; Tom Farmer, "Debate Arises over Torture," *Boston Herald*, January 22, 2002; Darius Rejali, "Tortured Truth," *Miami Herald*, February 10, 2002. The *Washington Post* followed up its own column with an editorial from Douglas Johnson, the executive director for the Center for Victims of Torture. Contrasting "us" with "them," Johnson noted that torture was "highly effective for gaining confessions from innocent people." Rather than "doing the hard work of investigation, police in countries permitting torture rely on confessions for the sake of efficiency. It becomes less important to actually solve a crime and do justice than to create a statistic of effectiveness"; Douglas Johnson, "Torture Isn't the Way to Make Them Talk," *Washington Post*, October 30, 2001.

104. *Today*, NBC News Transcripts, January 29, 2002; Murphy quoted in Jim Rutenberg, "Torture Seeps."

Chapter 10. "Can You Think of Anything More Un-American?"

1. Two polls in 2003 asked about torture, with revealing results. In September, ABC News asked whether respondents supported the federal government sending prisoners to third countries to be tortured for information. By roughly a three-to-one ratio, people were opposed to the idea, results that did not vary either by party membership or by political ideology. Indeed, conservatives were even more opposed to the idea than liberals or moderates. ABC News Poll, September 2003, retrieved July 4, 2012, from iPoll Databank, Roper Center for Public Opinion Research, University of Connecticut, http://www.ropercenter.uconn .edu/data_access/ipoll/ipoll.html. In March, Fox News asked, "If there were a possibility that a member of your own family could be saved, then would you favor or oppose allowing the government to use physical torture to obtain information from terrorist prisoners?" Even when framed this way, fewer than one in four supported torture, and six in ten were opposed. Fox News/Opinion Dynamics Poll, March 2003, retrieved July 4, 2012, ibid. In the same poll, Fox also asked whether the federal government should be allowed to use "any means necessary" to protect the country from terrorist attacks, including torture. Respondents were evenly split, with 44 percent in favor, 42 percent opposed, and 9 percent unsure; ibid.

2. For *Entertainment Weekly*, see http://www.ew.com/ew/gallery/0,,20268279,00.html#2060 0339.

3. See, e.g., Dennis Broe, "Fox and Its Friends: Global Commodification and the New Cold War," *Cinema Journal* 43 (2004), 97; Steven Keslowitz, "*The Simpsons, 24*, and the Law: How Homer Simpson and Jack Bauer Influence Congressional Lawmaking and Judicial Reasoning," *Cardozo Law Review* 29 (2008), 2787.

4. "'24' and America's Image in Fighting Terrorism: Fact, Fiction, or Does it Matter?" Heritage Foundation, June 23, 2006, http://www.heritage.org/events/2006/06/24-and -americas-image-in-fighting-terrorism-fact-fiction-or-does-it-matter.

5. "From 2002 through 2005, the Parents Television Council counted 624 torture scenes in prime time, a six-fold increase. UCLA's Television Violence Monitoring Project reports 'torture on TV shows is significantly higher than it was five years ago and the characters who torture have changed. It used to be that only villains on television tortured. Today, "good guy" and heroic American characters torture—and this torture is depicted as necessary, effective and even patriotic'"; Maura Moynihan, "Torture Chic: Why Is the Media Glorifying Inhumane, Sadistic Behavior?" Alternet, February 3, 2009, http://www.alternet.org/media/124739.

6. Human Rights First et al., "By the Numbers: Findings of the Detainee Abuse and Account-ability Project," April 2006, http://www.chrgj.org/docs/By_The_Numbers.pdf.

7. See, e.g., "US Detainee Death Toll 'Hits 108,'" BBC News, March 16, 2005, available at http://news.bbc.co.uk/2/hi/americas/4355779.stm.

8. Douglas Jehl, "Army Details Scale of Abuse in Afghan Jail," *New York Times*, March 12, 2005.

9. Ibid.

10. Ibid.

11. Tim Golden, "In U.S. Report, Brutal Details of 2 Afghan Inmates' Deaths," *New York Times*, May 20, 2005.

12. Limbaugh's comments are widely available and quoted at length in Dick Meyer, "Rush: MPs Just 'Blowing Off Steam,'" CBS News, December 5, 2007, http://www.cbsnews.com/2100-500159_162-616021.html.

13. George W. Bush, Statement on United Nations International Day in Support of Victims of Torture, June 26, 2004, available online at Gerhard Peters and John T. Woolley, The Ameri-can Presidency Project, http://www.presidency.ucsb.edu/ws/?pid=72674.

14. See, e.g., Inquiry into the Treatment of Detainees in U.S. Custody, Report of the Committee on Armed Services, United States Senate, 110th Cong., 2nd Sess. (November 20, 2008), 16–38; David Cole, *The Torture Memos: Rationalizing the Unthinkable* (London: Oneworld, 2009), 1–40; "Declassified Narrative Describing the Department of Justice Office of Legal Counsel's Opinions on the CIA's Detention and Interrogation Program," April 22, 2009, ibid., 275–291. What promises to be the definitive account of the CIA program is not avail-able as of this writing. For several years, the Senate Select Committee on Intelligence has been reviewing the program. Staff members have reviewed more than six million pages of records. The committee's final report is expected to be more than five thousand pages and "will provide a detailed, factual description of how interrogation techniques were used, the conditions under which detainees were held, and the intelligence that was—or wasn't—gained from the program." See "Joint Statement from: Senator Dianne Feinstein (D-Calif.), Chairman, Senate Intelligence Committee; Senator Carl Levin (D-Mich.), Chairman, Senate Armed Services Committee, April 27, 2012," Dianne Feinstein: United States Senator for California, April 27, 2012, http://www.feinstein.senate.gov/public/index.cfm/files/serve?File_id=026a329b-d4c0-4ab3-9f7e-fad5671917cc.

15. Cole, *Torture Memos*, 15.

16. ICRC Report on the Treatment of Fourteen "High Value Detainees" in CIA Custody, Febru-ary 2007, http://assets.nybooks.com/media/doc/2010/04/22/icrc-report.pdf.

17. Ibid.

18. Cole, *Torture Memos*, 5.

19. Ibid.

20. Memorandum for Alberto R. Gonzales, Counsel to the President, Re: Standards of Conduct for Interrogation under 18 U.S.C. 2340–2340A, United States Department of Justice, Au-gust 1, 2002, reprinted in Cole, *Torture Memos*, 41–93.

21. Harold Hongju Koh, "Friedmann Award Essay: A World Without Torture," *Columbia Journal of Transnational Law* 43 (2005) 641, 647.

22. Cole, *Torture Memos*, 17–18.

23. 151 Cong. Rec. S8836–8895, National Defense Authorization Act for Fiscal Year 2006 (daily ed., July 25, 2005).

24. 151 Cong. Rec. S8790.

25. Josh White and R. Jeffrey Smith, "White House Aims to Block Legislation on Detainees," *Washington Post*, July 23, 2005; Eric Schmitt, "Cheney Working to Block Legislation on De-tainees," *New York Times*, July 24, 2005.

26. White and Smith, "White House Aims"; Sheryl Gay Stolberg, "As August Recess Looms, Congress Finds High Gear," *New York Times,* July 27, 2005.

27. Reuters, "Bush Threatens Defense Bill Veto, Warning on Prisoners," *Washington Post,* September 30, 2005 (renewed threat of veto by White House); Liz Sidoti, "Senate to Engage in Debate over Detainees," Associated Press, October 5, 2005 (McCain vows to press forward). More than fifty editorials supporting Senator McCain's proposed amendments are available at http://www.humanrightsfirst.org/wp-content/uploads/pdf/edit-mccain-amend-081805 .pdf, including editorials from the *Washington Post, Miami Herald, New York Times, Newsday, Seattle Times, St. Louis Post-Dispatch, Minneapolis Star-Tribune, Salt Lake City Tribune,* and *Houston Chronicle.*

28. "Preventing Prisoner Abuse: The Answer Is Easy—or Is It?" *Philadelphia Inquirer,* October 12, 2005.

29. "Torture Is Un-American and Just Doesn't Work," *Modesto Bee* (California), October 26, 2005.

30. "No Exemptions on Torture: Cheney Shouldn't Try to Shield CIA from Ban," *Dallas Morning News,* October 27, 2005.

31. "This Should Be Simple: U.S. Doesn't OK Torture," *Des Moines Register,* October 11, 2005.

32. 151 Cong. Rec. S11114, October 5, 2005, http://frwebgate.access.gpo.gov/cgi-bin/getpage.cgi ?dbname=2005_record&page=S11114&position=all.

33. "Binding the Hands of Torturers," *New York Times,* October 8, 2005; Charles Babbington, Shailagh Murray, "Senate Supports Interrogation Limits; 90–9 Vote on the Treatment of Detainees Is a Bipartisan Rebuff of the White House," *Washington Post,* October 6, 2005; see also Eric Schmitt, "Senate Moves to Protect Military Prisoners Despite Veto Threat," *New York Times,* October 6, 2005.

34. George W. Bush, "President's Statement on Signing of H.R. 2863, the 'Department of Defense, Emergency Supplemental Appropriations to Address Hurricanes in the Gulf of Mexico, and Pandemic Influenza Act, 2006,'" December 30, 2005, http://georgewbush-white house.archives.gov/news/releases/2005/12/20051230-8.html.

35. Charlie Savage, "Bush Could Bypass New Torture Ban; Waiver Right Is Reserved," *Boston Globe,* January 4, 2006.

36. These memos did not become public until they were released by the Obama administration in April 2009; Cole, *Torture Memos,* 10. An extended discussion of the political machinations surrounding the McCain amendments appears in Joseph Margulies, *Guantánamo and the Abuse of Presidential Power* (New York: Simon and Schuster, 2006), from which this more abbreviated discussion is adapted.

37. AEI Polling, 54–57, 136–137.

38. George W. Bush, Remarks on the War on Terror, September 6, 2006, available online at Peters and Woolley, American Presidency Project, http://www.presidency.ucsb.edu/ws/ ?pid=779.

39. Ibid.

40. Ibid.

41. Ibid.

42. Office of the Director of National Intelligence, Summary of the High Value Terrorist Detainee Program, http://s3.amazonaws.com/propublica/assets/detention/dni_highvalue detainee_program_060906.pdf.

43. Ibid.

44. AEI Polling, 137–138.

45. Remarks by Richard B. Cheney, American Enterprise Institute, May 21, 2009, http://www .aei.org/article/foreign-and-defense-policy/regional/india-pakistan-afghanistan/remarks-by -richard-b-cheney/.

46. Marc Thiessen, *Courting Disaster: How the CIA Kept America Safe and How Barack Obama Is Inviting the Next Attack* (New York: Free Press, 2010).

47. Ibid., 12.

48. This explains why, as noted earlier, even American socialists tried to present their arguments in creedal terms. Merle Curti, *The Roots of Loyalty* (New York: Columbia University Press, 1946), 210–211. Anything that cannot be articulated in these terms is literally inconceivable for most Americans.

49. See, e.g., Charles Krauthammer, "The Truth About Torture: It's Time to Be Honest About Doing Terrible Things," *Weekly Standard*, December 5, 2005. Professor Dershowitz's proposal also falls in this category.

50. Thomas Sowell, "Tortured Reasoning," *Human Events*, November 22, 2005.

51. "Topics and Guests for Tuesday, Oct. 15," *The Big Story with John Gibson*, Fox News, October 15, 2002.

52. "Interview with Wayne Simmons," *The Big Story with John Gibson*, Fox News, January 6, 2005.

53. Ibid.

54. Ibid.

55. Ibid.

56. Sean Hannity and Alan Colmes, "Guests Debate Legality of Gitmo Interrogation Practices," Fox News, December 1, 2004.

57. "Interview with Wayne Simmons."

58. Sean Hannity and Alan Colmes, "Does CIA Go Too Far Questioning al Qaeda Members?" Fox News, May 13, 2004.

59. Charles Krauthammer, "Truth About Torture."

60. Joseph Farah, "Waterboarding Is Not Torture," *Human Events*, January 9, 2008.

61. "Hard Measures: Ex-CIA Head Defends Post-9/11 Tactics," *60 Minutes*, CBS News, April 29, 2012, transcript available at http://www.cbsnews.com/8301-18560_162-57423533/hard -measures-ex-cia-head-defends-post-9-11-tactics/.

62. 155 Cong. Rec. S 1617, 1640 (February 5, 2009).

63. "Talking Points Memo and Top Story," *The O'Reilly Factor*, Fox News, September 8, 2006.

64. Sowell, "Tortured Reasoning."

65. "Hard Measures."

66. "President Obama Addresses the Nation on Secret Trip to Afghanistan," *Hannity Show*, Fox News, May 1, 2012.

67. See Mission Statement, National Religious Campaign Against Torture, http://www.nrcat .org/index.php?option=com_content&task=view&id=443&Itemid=319.

68. A euphemism like this is an example of what the sociologists Stanley Cohen and Lisa Hajjar call "interpretive denial." Stanley Cohen, *States of Denial: Knowing About Atrocities and Suffering* (Cambridge: Polity, 2001), 103; Lisa Hajjar, "Torture and the Future," *Middle East Report*, May 2004 ("'Interpretative denial' is when a state refutes allegations by saying that what happened is not torture but 'something else'—like 'moderate physical pressure' or 'stress and duress'").

69. Neal Desai et al., "Torture at Times: Waterboarding in the Media," Joan Shorenstein Center on the Press, Politics and Public Policy, April 2010, 8–10, http://dash.harvard.edu/ bitstream/handle/1/4420886/torture_at_times_hks_students.pdf?sequence=1.

70. Ibid., 11. The *New York Times* did so almost 85 percent of the time (28 of 33), the *Los Angeles Times* more than 90 percent (21 of 23), and the *Wall Street Journal* 75 percent (3 of 4).

71. Mark Bowden, "The Dark Art of Interrogation," *Atlantic*, October 2003, 58.

72. For some of the accounts of the connection between the enhanced techniques and the *Kubark Manual*, see, e.g., Mark Danner, "US Torture: Voices from the Black Sites," *New York*

Review of Books, April 9, 2009; Margulies, *Guantánamo and the Abuse of Presidential Power;* Mark Danner, "The Logic of Torture," *New York Review of Books,* June 24, 2004; Jane Mayer, *The Dark Side: The Inside Story of How the War on Terror Turned into a War on American Ideals* (New York: Doubleday, 2008); Alfred W. McCoy, *A Question of Torture: CIA Interrogation from the Cold War to the War on Terror* (New York: Metropolitan, 2006). For an extended discussion of the *Kubark Manual,* see Steven M. Kleinman, "KUBARK Counterintelligence Interrogation Review: Observations of an Interrogator, Lessons Learned, and Avenues for Further Research," in Educing Information: Interrogation: Science and Art: Foundations for the Future, February 2006, http://www.fas.org/irp/dni/educing.pdf.

73. See, e.g., Gary Cohn and Ginger Thompson, "When a Wave of Torture and Murder Staggered a Small U.S. Ally, Truth Was a Casualty," *Baltimore Sun,* June 11, 1995; Ginger Thompson and Gary Cohn, "A Carefully Crafted Deception," *Baltimore Sun,* June 18, 1995; Ginger Thompson and Gary Cohn, "Honduras Charges Soldiers," *Baltimore Sun,* July 26, 1995; Gary Cohn, Ginger Thompson, and Mark Matthews, "CIA Training Manual Shows Tortures Used in Central America," *Baltimore Sun,* January 28, 1997.

74. "Torture, CIA Style; Intelligence Agency Once Taught Psychological Torture," *Houston Chronicle,* February 2, 1997.

75. "Torture, CIA-Style: Notorious Manual Offered Tips on 'Coercive' Interrogation," *Pittsburgh Post-Gazette,* January 29, 1997.

76. "The CIA's Textbook on Torture," *St. Louis Post-Dispatch,* February 7, 1997.

77. Quoted in Cohn and Thompson, "When a Wave of Torture and Murder Staggered a Small U.S. Ally."

78. Mark Matthews, "Probe Demanded into Use of CIA Torture Manuals; Latin American Official Calls for Independent Probe," *Baltimore Sun,* January 29, 1997; see also Cohn, Thompson, and Matthews, "CIA Training Manual Shows Tortures"; Walter Pincus, "CIA Manual Discussed 'Coercive' Interrogation; Latin Countries Used 1983 Training Book," *Washington Post,* January 28, 1997; Mark Matthews, "U.S. Manuals Taught Murder, Kennedy Says; Allies Trained in Use of Torture in 1980s," *Baltimore Sun,* March 7, 1997.

79. John Monahan, "Brown Defends Waterboarding; Coakley Slams JFK Ads," *Worcester Telegram Gazette,* January 5, 2010, http://www.telegram.com/article/20100105/NEWS/100109910/1116#.

80. The candidates' views on this matter have been collected and appear at procon.org, which describes itself as "an independent, nonpartisan" public charity, and are available at http://2012election.procon.org/view.answers.election.php?questionID=1717#mitt-romney.

81. All polling results are available on iPoll Databank. The detailed results for July 2004 poll are at Pew Research Center for the People, July 2004, retrieved July 5, 2012, ibid., while the results for the August 2011 poll are at Pew Research Center for the People, August 2011, retrieved July 5, 2012, ibid.

82. Other polls show the same trend, though the wording demands that we approach the results with caution. In May 2004 (just after the initial disclosures from the Abu Ghraib prison), nearly six in ten Republicans told ABC News that torture was "never acceptable." By June 2009 nearly seven in ten Republicans took the opposite view. In the latter poll, however, ABC prefaced the question by pointing to President Obama's insistence that his administration would never use torture. Republican responses may therefore have been animated in part by animosity toward President Obama rather than by enthusiasm for torture. Compare ABC News/Washington Post Poll, May 2004, retrieved July 5, 2012, ibid., with ABC News/Washington Post Poll, June 2009, retrieved July 5, 2012, ibid. The polling by Pew, however, does not suffer this limitation.

83. Most often, this debate focuses on the information that led to the raid on bin Laden in 2011

and the interrogation of Abu Zubaydah in 2002. On the former, Leon Panetta, then the director of the CIA and later the secretary of defense, told NBC News that it was impossible to know whether lawful, noncoercive methods could have secured the same information. See Transcript of Brian Williams' Interview with CIA Director Leon Panetta, available at http://www.nbcuniversal.presscentre.com/content/detail.aspx?ReleaseID=4722; see also Marian Wang and Braden Goyette, "Bin Laden Reading Guide: How to Cut Through the Coverage," Pro Publica, May 3, 2011, available at http://www.propublica.org/blog/item/bin-laden-reading-guide-how-to-cut-through-the-coverage. As for the latter, Ali Soufan, the former FBI agent who participated in Zubaydah's interrogation, has consistently said that the actionable intelligence from Zubaydah was secured through noncoercive rather than enhanced interrogations. See, e.g., Testimony of Ali Soufan before the Subcommittee on Administration Oversight and the Courts, Senate Judiciary Committee (May 13, 2009), available at http://www.judiciary.senate.gov/hearings/testimony.cfm?id=e655f9e2809e547 6862f735da14945e6&wit_id=e655f9e2809e5476862f735da14945e6-1-2.

Chapter 11. "Must We Sell Our Birthright?"

1. See, e.g., Harumi Befu, "Demonizing the 'Other,'" in *Demonizing the Other: Anti-Semitism, Racism, and Xenophobia,* ed. Robert S. Wistrich (New York: Routledge, 2003), 17–30; Henri Zukier, "The Transformation of Hatred: Anti-Semitism as a Struggle for Group Identity," ibid., 118–130.

2. E.g., George W. Bush, Remarks in a Meeting with the National Security Team and an Exchange with Reporters at Camp David, Maryland, September 15, 2001, available online at Gerhard Peters and John T. Woolley, The American Presidency Project, http://www.presidency.ucsb.edu/ws/?pid=63199 ("a group of barbarians have declared war on the American people"); Ruben Navarrette, "Can We Be as Tough as We Are Compassionate?" *Dallas Morning News,* October 12, 2001 ("Retired Gen. Barry McCaffrey was right when . . . he detailed the sort of covert military exercises that one can, and must, employ to exterminate these vermin"); Steve Chapman, "A War That We Can't Avoid—and a War That We Can," *Chicago Tribune,* October 11, 2001 (bin Laden's "network has to be eradicated"); Letters to the Editor, *St. Louis Post-Dispatch,* September 17, 2001 ("Terrorism is a cancer. You do not negotiate with cancer. You do not seek to reason with cancer. You do not pacify cancer. You do not expect cancer to honor the Geneva Conventions. You surgically remove a cancer where possible or you irradiate or you chemically poison it. Your sole objective is to kill it. You never win, but you hope for remission and remain ever-vigilant").

3. George W. Bush, Remarks at the Chief Executive Officers Summit in Shanghai, October 20, 2001, available online at Peters and Woolley, American Presidency Project, http://www.presidency.ucsb.edu/ws/index.php?pid=63185&st=&st1=.

4. Evan Thomas, "The Day That Changed America," *Newsweek,* December 31, 2001.

5. Evan Thomas, "How He'll Haunt Us," *Newsweek,* December 31, 2001.

6. One of the most thoughtful discussions of the subhuman/superhuman terrorist appears in Richard Jackson, *Writing the War on Terrorism: Language, Politics, and Counter-Terrorism* (Manchester: Manchester University Press, 2005), especially chapter 4. As Jackson observes (108–109): "In a series of constructions which sit uneasily with their simultaneous depiction as cowards, crazed fanatics, evildoers and faceless villains, the terrorists are made out to be formidable and frightening foes. . . . There would be no advantage for officials to admit that terrorists are normally rather incompetent and no match for the resources, training and expertise of counter-terrorist units, particularly those of the world's most powerful states; or that they were rather ordinary people just like everyone else. Instead, the authori-

ties make terrorists out to be incredibly sophisticated and fearsome agents—super-terrorists, as it were." For an attempt to debunk the myth of the superhuman terrorist, see John Mueller, "Is There Still a Terrorist Threat? The Myth of the Omnipresent Enemy," *Foreign Affairs* 85, no. 5 (2006), 2–8.

7. John W. Dower, *War Without Mercy: Race and Power in the Pacific* (New York: Pantheon, 1986), especially chapter 5, "Lesser Men and Supermen"; see also, e.g., Nathaniel Pfeffer, "Japanese Superman? That, Too, Is a Fallacy," *New York Times Magazine*, March 22, 1942.

8. Ellen Schrecker, *Many Are the Crimes: McCarthyism in America* (Boston: Little, Brown, 1998), 135.

9. Ibid. 198.

10. Jackson, *Writing the War on Terrorism*, 111.

11. Tom W. Smith, Kenneth A. Rasinski, and Marianna Toce, "America Rebounds: A National Study of Public Response to the September 11th Terrorist Attacks," National Opinion Research Center, Preliminary Findings, October 25, 2001, http://www.unc.edu/courses/2008 spring/poli/472h/001/Course%20documents/RESOURCES/Misc/National%20Tragedy %20Study.pdf. The NORC did a follow-up study in 2002, in which the earlier results regarding support for democracy were revised upward slightly. See Kenneth A. Rasinski, Jennifer Berktold, Tom W. Smith, and Bethany L. Albertson, "America Recovers: A Follow-Up to a National Study of Public Response to the September 11th Terrorist Attacks," National Opinion Research Center, August 7, 2002, http://www3.norc.org/NR/rdonlyres/E80028D8 -96BB-47EF-90A3-B69D253D8652/0/pubresp2.pdf.

12. See Chapter 6.

13. "National Security Strategy of the United States of America," September 2002, 30, http:// www.state.gov/documents/organization/63562.pdf.

14. *Youngstown Sheet & Tube Co. v. Sawyer,* 343 U.S. 579 (1952) (Jackson, J., concurring).

15. The entire set of amicus briefs, including the five filed in support of the United States, is available at http://www.hamdanvrumsfeld.com/briefs.

16. See Priscilla Ray, "Report of the Council on Ethical and Judicial Affairs: Physician Participation in Interrogation," American Medical Association, 2006, http://www.ama-assn.org/ resources/doc/ethics/ceja_10a06.pdf; "Leave No Marks: Enhanced Interrogation Techniques and the Risk of Criminality," Physicians for Human Rights and Human Rights First, August 2007, https://s3.amazonaws.com/PHR_Reports/leave-no-marks.pdf; "Report of the American Bar Association on Signing Statements," American Bar Association, August 7–8, 2006, http://www.americanbar.org/content/dam/aba/migrated/leadership/2006/annual/daily journal/20060823144113.authcheckdam.pdf.

17. George W. Bush, Address to a Joint Session of Congress and the American People, September 20, 2011, http://georgewbush-whitehouse.archives.gov/news/releases/2001/09/2001 0920-8.html.

18. The list of organizations, law professors, and computer scientists who joined the coalition, as well as its statement, is available at www.indefenseoffreedom.org.

19. Ibid.

20. Ibid.

21. See John Ashcroft and Joseph Mueller, Press Briefing, FBI Headquarters, September 28, 2001, available at http://www.justice.gov/archive/ag/speeches/2001/agcrisisremarks9_28 .htm; John Ashcroft, Prepared Remarks for the US Mayors Conference, Washington, DC, October 25, 2001, http://www.justice.gov/archive/ag/speeches/2001/agcrisisremarks10_25.htm. see also Supplemental Declaration of James S. Reynolds, ¶2, *Center for National Security Studies v. Department of Justice*, No. 01-2500; Statement of Kate Martin, Director, Center for National Security Studies, Before the Judiciary Committee of the United States Senate, on

DOJ Oversight: Preserving Our Freedoms While Defending Against Terrorism, November 28, 2001, available at www.cnss.org.

22. See "The September 11 Detainees: A Review of the Treatment of Aliens Held on Immigration Charges in Connection with the Investigation of the September 11 Attacks," Department of Justice, Office of the Inspector General, http://www.justice.gov/oig/special/0306/full.pdf.

23. Jodi Wilgoren, "A Nation Challenged: The Interviews; Prosecutors Begin Effort to Interview 5,000, but Basic Questions Remain," *New York Times*, November 15, 2001; Memorandum from Kenneth L. Wainstein, Director, Executive Office for U.S. Attorneys, U.S. Department of Justice, to the Attorney General and Deputy Attorney General re: *Final Report on Interview Project*, February 15, 2002, http://www.scribd.com/doc/17819468/T5-B61-VIP-Fdr-21502-Wainstein-Memo-Re-Final-Report-on-Interview-Project-225, 6. In March, Ashcroft announced plans to interview another three thousand people, but it appears that the Department of Justice never released the results of this follow-up program. John Ashcroft, "Eastern District of Virginia/Interview Project Results Announcement," Richmond, VA, March 20, 2002, http://www.justice.gov/archive/ag/speeches/2002/032002agnewsconferenceedva interviewprojectresultsannouncement.htm.

24. "Washington Post-ABC News Poll: America at War," *Washington Post*, November 28, 2001, http://www.washingtonpost.com/wp-srv/politics/polls/vault/stories/data112801.htm.

25. "Constitutional Challenges," *Milwaukee Journal Sentinel*, November 16, 2001.

26. "Secret Detentions Needlessly Undercut Public Justice," *USA Today*, November 2, 2001.

27. "An Un-American Secrecy," *Los Angeles Times*, November 17, 2001.

28. "Unseemly Secrecy," *St. Petersburg Times*, October 6, 2001.

29. Ashcroft, Prepared Remarks for the US Mayors Conference.

30. Quoted in Julian E. Zelizer, *Arsenal of Democracy: The Politics of National Security from World War Two to the War on Terrorism* (New York: Basic, 2010), 446.

31. Electronic copies of the requests and responses, along with other related information, can be found at http://www.cnss.org/arrests.htm.

32. Letter to Attorney General John Ashcroft from Senators Russell Feingold, Patrick Leahy, and Edward Kennedy and Representatives Jerrold Nadler, Robert Scott, and John Conyers, October 31, 2001. A copy of the letter appears on the website of the Center for National Security Studies and is on file with the author.

33. Letter to Attorney General John Ashcroft from Senator Patrick Leahy, Chairman, Senate Judiciary Committee, November 7, 2001; emphasis Leahy's. A copy of the letter, with the senator's handwritten comments, appears on the website of the Center for National Security Studies and is on file with the author.

34. Neil A. Lewis and Christopher Marquis, "A Nation Challenged: Immigration; Longer Visa Waits for Arabs; Stir over U.S. Eavesdropping," *New York Times*, November 10, 2001.

35. Editorial, "Must We Sell Our Birthright for Security?" *Chicago Tribune*, November 15, 2001.

36. Beryl Howell, "Seven Weeks: The Making of the USA Patriot Act," *George Washington Law Review* 72 (2004), 1145, 1179.

37. Ibid., 1169 fn. 155, quoting 147 Cong. Rec. S10,686 (daily ed. October 15, 2001) (statement of Sen. Biden).

38. Ibid., 1154.

39. Ibid., 1154–1158.

40. Quoted ibid., 1159.

41. Quoted ibid., 1161.

42. Quoted ibid., 1166.

43. Ibid., 1178.

44. USA Patriot Act of 2001, H.R. 3162 (2001).

45. Zelizer, *Arsenal of Democracy*, 445–446.

46. Nancy Talanian and Kit Gage, Foreword to David Cole and James X. Dempsey, *Terrorism and the Constitution: Sacrificing Civil Liberties in the Name of National Security*, 3rd ed. (New York: New Press, 2006), xv.

47. Resolution No. 13, Series of 2002, "Expressing the Commitment of the City and County of Denver to Civil Rights and Liberties," March 18, 2002, http://www.bordc.org/detail.php ?id=166.

48. Ibid.

49. The Bill of Rights Defense Committee maintains a list of all resolutions passed, as well as their text. They may be examined at http://www.bordc.org/list.php?sortChrono=1.

50. *Hamdan v. Rumsfeld*, 548 U.S. 557 (2006).

51. Military Order, Detention, Treatment, and Trial of Certain Non-Citizens in the War Against Terrorism, November 13, 2001, 66 Fed. Reg. 57833 (November 16, 2001); William Safire, "Kangaroo Courts," *New York Times*, November 26, 2001.

52. Testimony of Attorney General John Ashcroft, Senate Committee on the Judiciary, December 6, 2001, http://www.justice.gov/archive/ag/testimony/2001/1206transcriptsenatejudiciary committee.htm.

53. Ibid.

54. "Ashcroft's Zeal Rules Out Honest Debate," *Newsday*, December 8, 2001.

55. *Detroit Free Press v. Ashcroft*, 303 F. 3d 681 (6th Cir. 2002) (secret hearings unconstitutional); *North Jersey Media Group v. Ashcroft*, 308 F. 3d 198 (3rd Cir. 2002) (secret hearings not unconstitutional), *cert. denied*, 123 S. Ct. 2215 (2003); *Center for National Security Studies v. Department of Justice*, 215 F. Supp. 2d 94 (D.D.C. 2002), *rev'd by Center for National Security Studies v. Department of Justice*, 331 F. 3d 918 (D.C. Cir. 2003).

56. For an extended discussion of the use of judicial decisions as rhetorical resources in the construction of narratives about national identity, see Joseph Margulies and Hope Metcalf, "Terrorizing Academia," *Journal of Legal Education* 60 (2011), 433.

57. "A Win for Open Trials," *New York Times*, August 28, 2002; see also Danny Hakim, "A Nation Challenged: The Detainees; Transcripts Offer First Look at Secret Federal Hearings," *New York Times*, April 22, 2002.

58. See, e.g., Joseph Margulies, *Guantánamo and the Abuse of Presidential Power* (New York: Simon and Schuster, 2006).

59. "Editorial: A Nation of Laws," *Buffalo News*, July 1, 2004.

60. "Curbing Government," *Milwaukee Journal Sentinel*, June 29, 2004.

61. "Editorial: Justice Delivered," *Pittsburgh Post-Gazette*, July 2, 2004.

62. "Editorial: The Rights of Detainees," *Boston Globe*, June 29, 2004.

63. "Editorial: Administration's Rogue Lawlessness Checked," *Ft. Lauderdale Sun-Sentinel*, July 2, 2004.

64. "It's Called Democracy," *Los Angeles Times*, June 29, 2004.

65. Cf. "Our Turn: High Court Upholds Basic U.S. Principles," *San Antonio Express-News*, July 3, 2004 ("Not only was the U.S. Supreme Court right to reject President Bush's policy of holding 'enemy combatants' in prison indefinitely without trial or access to lawyers, a majority of the court also was refreshingly decisive on the issue"); "Editorial: No Blank Check," *St. Louis Post-Dispatch*, June 29, 2004 ("The U.S. Supreme Court soundly rejected on Monday President George W. Bush's extraordinary claim that he could classify people as enemy combatants and order them held indefinitely without access to a lawyer or a day in court"); "Our Opinions: Justices Duly Uphold Due Process," *Atlanta Journal-Constitution*, June 29, 2004 ("This is a major victory for those who believe the U.S. Constitution guarantee of due

process applies all the time, during war and peace"); "Editorial: Return to Balance," *Baltimore Sun,* June 29, 2004 ("The Supreme Court's decision provides much-needed reassurance—both at home and abroad"); "Editorial: War No Excuse to Deny Suspects Their Due," *Chicago Sun-Times,* June 30, 2004 ("We believe, like the high court, that a state of war should never give a president a 'blank check'"); "Editorial: Due Process in a Time of Crisis," *Denver Post,* June 30, 2004 ("Acting in Americans' best interests, the U.S. Supreme Court on Monday ruled that enemy combatants in U.S. custody have legal rights"); "Opinion: The Right Decisions on Prisoners," *Rocky Mountain News,* June 29, 2004 ("The two decisions leave much for the lower courts to sort out, but the high court made a welcome statement that the U.S. Constitution can't be waived"); "Detainees," *Minneapolis Star-Tribune,* June 30, 2004 ("The decision is a triumph for a bedrock principle of American democracy—one that President Bush and his Administration should never have violated"); "Due Process Applies to All," *Newsday* (New York), June 29, 2004 ("Yesterday's historic Supreme Court decisions guaranteeing enemy combatants in United States custody their day in court are an important triumph for the rule of law"); "Reaffirming the Rule of Law," *New York Times,* June 29, 2004 ("Fortunately, this court appears to be mindful of the mistakes of the past"); "Editorial: Court Says No, No, and No," *Oregonian,* June 29, 2004 ("The justices had to push back and insist on the rule of law—even when lawless enemies keep national security at risk"); "Opinion: Rule of Law II," *San Diego Union-Tribune,* June 29, 2004 ("In their rulings, the justices reaffirmed the most basic rights of Americans"); see also Margulies, *Guantánamo,* 103–155.

66. "ABC News/Washington Post Monthly Poll," June 2004, http://www.icpsr.umich.edu/icpsrweb/ICPSR/studies/04112/version/1; "The New York Times/CBS News Poll," July 11–15, 2004, http://www.nytimes.com/packages/html/politics/20040717_poll/20040717_poll_results.pdf.

67. Ian McAllister, "A War Too Far? Bush, Iraq, and the 2004 Presidential Election," *Presidential Studies Quarterly* 36, no. 2 (2006): 260–280, 266.

68. Paul R. Abramson et al., "Fear in the Voting Booth: The 2004 Presidential Election," *Political Behavior* 29, no. 2 (2007): 197–220, 202–203.

69. James Risen and Eric Lichtblau, "Bush Lets U.S. Spy on Callers Without Courts," *New York Times,* December 16, 2005; Eric Lichtblau and James Risen, "Top Aide Defends Domestic Spying," *New York Times,* February 7, 2006. The administration had considered but rejected a proposal that would have allowed the NSA to listen in on purely domestic conversations, opting instead for a requirement that at least one participant in the conversation be overseas. When the NSA program was first revealed, the *Times* indicated it was initially authorized in 2002. But in February 2006, then–Attorney General Gonzales testified in Congress that it began only a few weeks after September 11, much earlier than originally thought. It was retroactively authorized in October 2001, when Bush signed the secret order. For a useful and accessible summary of the controversy, see "The NSA Wiretapping Program," *For the Record: A Publication of the Center for Law and Security at the NYU School of Law* 1 (2007), http://www.lawandsecurity.org/Portals/0/Documents/NSA_jan_07.pdf.

70. David Ignatius, "Revolt of the Professionals," *Washington Post,* December 21, 2005.

71. Hope Yen, "Probe Sought on NSA Surveillance," *Washington Post,* December 19, 2005; Dan Eggen and Charles Lane, "On Hill, Anger and Calls for Hearings Greet News of Stateside Surveillance," *Washington Post,* December 19, 2005; James Gordon Meek, "W Spy Uproar Heats Up. Two GOP Senators Join Growing Chorus of Dems Seeking Probe," *New York Daily News,* December 21, 2005.

72. Geoffrey R. Stone, "So Much for Protecting the Constitution," *Chicago Tribune,* December 21, 2005.

73. "Big Brother Bush: Has This Administration Gone Too Far?" *Philadelphia Daily News*, December 19, 2005.

74. "Want to Snoop in America? Get a Court Order," *USA Today*, December 19, 2005.

75. "Warrantless Surveillance," *St. Petersburg Times*, December 18, 2005.

76. David G. Savage, "Words, Deeds on Spying Differed," *Los Angeles Times*, January 26, 2006.

77. See Foreign Intelligence Surveillance Act of 1978 Amendments Act of 2008, P.L. 110–261 (July 10, 2008).

78. "Transcript: Former Vice President Gore's Speech on Constitutional Issues," *Washington Post*, January 16, 2006, http://www.washingtonpost.com/wp-dyn/content/article/2006/01/16/AR2006011600779.html.

79. Ibid.

80. Charlie Savage, "Bush Challenges Hundreds of Laws," *Boston Globe*, April 30, 2006.

81. Ibid.

82. Ibid.

83. "President Bush: Making Congress a Lapdog," *Milwaukee Journal Sentinel*, May 4, 2006.

84. Tom Henderson, "King George Picks and Chooses the Laws He'll Obey," *Lewiston Morning Tribune*, May 15, 2006.

85. "The Fall of the House of Bush," *Philadelphia Daily News*, May 22, 2006.

86. Cox News Service, "Election's Underlying Issue: Price of Unchecked Power," *Waco Tribune*, May 18, 2006.

87. Ibid.

88. Quoted in Henderson, "King George."

89. "Hold Bush Accountable," *Roanoke Times*, May 12, 2006.

90. "Presidential Power: Veto, Schmeto," *Seattle Post-Intelligencer*, May 8, 2006.

91. "Shield Reporters from Bush-Think; Administration Acts Like First Amendment Doesn't Apply to It," *Buffalo News*, May 24, 2006.

92. Ibid.

93. "Hold Bush Accountable."

94. Arthur M. Schlesinger, Jr., *The Imperial Presidency* (New York: Houghton Mifflin, 1973).

95. Arthur M. Schlesinger, Jr., "So Much for the Imperial Presidency," *New York Times*, August 3, 1998.

96. Andrew Rudalevige, "George W. Bush and the Imperial Presidency," in *Testing the Limits: George W. Bush and the Imperial Presidency*, ed. Mark Rozell and Gleaves Whitney (New York: Rowman and Littlefield, 2009), 243.

97. Darrell West, "Bush Taps America's New Fear," *Chicago Tribune*, March 18, 2003.

98. Peter Irons, *War Powers: How the Imperial Presidency Hijacked the Constitution* (New York: Metropolitan, 2005).

99. Charlie Savage, *Takeover: The Return of the Imperial Presidency and the Subversion of American Democracy* (New York: Back Bay, 2007).

100. *The Imperial Presidency and the Consequences of 9/11: Lawyers React to the Global War on Terrorism* (Westport, CT: Praeger Security International, 2007).

101. Gene Healy, "The Imperial Presidency and the War on Terror," Cato Institute, April 1, 2006, http://www.cato.org/research/articles/cpr28n2-1-060401.html; Gene Healy, "Learning to Love the Imperial Presidency: How Conservatives Made Peace with Executive Power," *Reason*, October 2007, http://www.cato.org/publications/commentary/learning-love-imperial-presidency.

102. House Committee on the Judiciary Majority Staff Report to Chairman John C. Conyers, Jr., *Reining in the Imperial Presidency: Lessons and Recommendations Relating to the Presidency of George W. Bush* (2009), 25.

103. Ibid., 26.

104. Quoted in Zelizer, *Arsenal of Democracy*, 494.

105. On that score, it is certainly true that many major media outlets were initially quite defer-
ential. On September 17, 2001, for instance, CBS anchorman Dan Rather appeared as a
guest on the *Late Show with David Letterman* and broke into tears as he discussed the attacks. "George Bush is the president," Rather said. "He makes the decisions, and, you know,
just as one American, he wants me to line up, just tell me where"; quoted in Brigitte L.
Nacos, Yaeli Bloch-Elkon, and Robert Y. Shapiro, *Selling Fear: Counterterrorism, the Media,
and Public Opinion* (Chicago: University of Chicago Press, 2009), 6. And the abject failure
by the media to hold the president's feet to the fire during the run-up to the invasion of Iraq
was the Fourth Estate's darkest hour of the post-9/11 period. For the mea culpa by the *New
York Times*, see Editors, "The Times and Iraq," *New York Times*, May 26, 2004.

    The media continue to be excoriated for these lapses. One author denounced the main-
stream press as simply a mouthpiece for official propaganda, claiming that editors and
journalists in the United States willingly narrowed public debate after September 11 "to the
spectrum of agreement and disagreement expressed by America's bipartisan political
elite"; Anthony DiMaggio, *When Media Goes to War: Hegemonic Discourse, Public Opinion,
and the Limits of Dissent* (New York: Monthly Review Press, 2009), 13. Another team of
prominent scholars has pronounced a similar judgment, insisting "the media reported
and amplified whatever messages the administration put out, and ignored topics and problems that the administration did not want to discuss. Overall, the press failed at its long-
standing 'watchdog' function"; Nacos, Bloch-Elkon, and Shapiro *Selling Fear*, xii.

    Notwithstanding the respect I have for these authors, I view things somewhat differ-
ently. On the one hand, scores of journalists and editors refused to become silent partners
in the war on terror. Some of the most important excesses of the Bush administration came
to light only because the mainstream press uncovered and relentlessly publicized topics
"that the administration did not want to discuss," including most prominently the CIA
black sites, the Abu Ghraib torture scandal, the warrantless wiretap program, and the ex-
cessive use of signing statements. In very large part, the master narrative owes its success
to the willingness of the press to perform its "watchdog" function. On the other hand, with
the notable exception of Dana Priest at the *Washington Post*, much of the mainstream press
continues to ignore many other aspects of the post-9/11 transformation.

106. See, e.g., Andrew C. McCarthy, "Lawfare Strikes Again," *National Review Online*, June
12, 2007, http://www.nationalreview.com/articles/221258/lawfare-strikes-again/andrew-c
-mccarthy. The term still gets frequent play at the *Review*. See, e.g., David French, "The Gaza
Flotilla and Lawfare," *National Review Online*, June 29, 2011, http://www.nationalreview
.com/corner/270805/gaza-flotilla-and-lawfare-david-french.

107. Pauline Jelinek, "Defense Official Resigns Over Remarks," *Washington Post*, February 2,
2007. The official, Cully Stimson, later joined the staff of the Heritage Foundation, a conservative think tank.

108. Stephen J. Whitfield, *The Culture of the Cold War* (Baltimore: Johns Hopkins University
Press, 1996), 59.

Chapter 12. The Paradox of the Obama Era

1. Quoted in Julian E. Zelizer, *Arsenal of Democracy: The Politics of National Security from World
War Two to the War on Terrorism* (New York: Basic, 2010), 490. On the role of Hurricane
Katrina in the anti-Bush narrative, see Brigitte L. Nacos, Yaeli Bloch-Elkon, and Robert Y.
Shapiro, *Selling Fear: Counterterrorism, the Media, and Public Opinion* (Chicago: University
of Chicago Press, 2009), 166–169.

2. For an account of the U.S. attorney scandal and its fallout, see Memorandum from Representative John Conyers, Jr., to the Members of the House Judiciary Committee regarding the attempts by the committee to secure information from executive branch officials relevant to the scandal. The memo is available at http://media.washingtonpost.com/wp-srv/politics/documents/contempt_memo_072407.pdf. In addition, a collection of coverage by the *Washington Post* on the scandal is available at http://www.washingtonpost.com/wp-dyn/content/linkset/2007/03/05/LI2007030500666.html.

3. CBS News, "Bush's Final Approval Rating: 22 Percent," February 9, 2009, available at http://www.cbsnews.com/2100-500160_162-4728399.html.

4. "Bush the Arrogant: President Bush's Latest Permutation of Crisis Management Is the Last Straw. But Who Best to Roll Back the Excesses?" *Los Angeles Times*, September 28, 2008.

5. Ibid.

6. Bob Lewis, "Obama First Democrat to Take Virginia in 44 Years," Associated Press, November 4, 2008; Franco Ordonez, "Is Obama Running Scared in North Carolina?" McClatchy Newspapers, March 6, 2012.

7. The results are available at a number of websites, including one maintained by the *New York Times* at http://elections.nytimes.com/2008/results/president/votes.html.

8. Michael Grunwald, "One Year Ago: The Republicans in Distress," *Time*, May 9, 2009; Joe Rothstein, "Can the Republican Party Survive the 2008 Elections?" *U.S. Politics Today*, October 8, 2008, available at http://uspolitics.einnews.com/article/557738-can-the-republican-party-survive-the-2008-elections; David Brooks, "Darkness at Dusk," *New York Times*, November 20, 2008.

9. See, e.g., "Barack Obama: The War We Need to Win," available at http://obama.3cdn.net/417b7e6036dd852384_luzxmvlo9.pdf ("Guantanamo has become a recruiting tool for our enemies. The legal framework behind Guantanamo has failed completely, resulting in only one conviction. President Bush's own Secretary of Defense, Robert Gates, wants to close it. Former Secretary of State Colin Powell wants to close it. The first step to reclaiming America's standing in the world has to be closing this facility. As president, Barack Obama will close the detention facility at Guantanamo. He will reject the Military Commissions Act, which allowed the U.S. to circumvent Geneva Conventions in the handling of detainees. He will develop a fair and thorough process based on the Uniform Code of Military Justice to distinguish between those prisoners who should be prosecuted for their crimes, those who can't be prosecuted but who can be held in a manner consistent with the laws of war, and those who should be released or transferred to their home countries"); CBS News, January 11, 2009 ("But I don't want to be ambiguous about this. We are going to close Guantanamo and we are going to make sure that the procedures we set up are ones that abide by our Constitution"), available at http://www.cbsnews.com/stories/2009/01/11/national/main4713038.shtml.

10. See e.g., Matthew Ivey, "A Framework for Closing Guantánamo Bay," *Boston College International and Comparative Law Review* 32 (2009), 353, 354–355 (collecting references to calls for the prison to be closed).

11. Aaron Gould Sheinin, "Former Secretaries of State: Close Guantánamo," *Atlanta Journal-Constitution*, March 27, 2008.

12. Renee Schoof, "Congress Letter to Bush: Close Guantanamo," McClatchy Newspapers, June 29, 2007, available at http://mcclatchydc.com/100/story/17486.html. The article also includes the text of the letter. See also, e.g., 152 Cong. Rec. S6047 (daily ed. June 19, 2006) (statement of Sen. Bingaman); 152 Cong. Rec. S7290-04 (daily ed. July 11, 2006) (statement of Sen. Durbin); 153 Cong. Rec. E979-05 (daily ed. May 8, 2007) (speech of Rep. Harman); 153 Cong. Rec. H7080-05 (daily ed. June 26, 2007) (statement of Rep. Moran); 155 Cong. Rec. S779 (daily ed. January 22, 2009) (statement of Sen. Dodd); posting of Sen. Dianne

Feinstein to The Hill, June 28, 2007, http://thehill.com/opinion/letters/6777-setting
-acceptable-conditions-for-military-detentions-trials.

13. National Defense Authorization Act for Fiscal Year 2008, Sec. 1066 (3) & (4), Sense of Congress Regarding Detainees at Naval Station, Guantanamo Bay, Cuba. In July 2007 the Senate voted 94–3 in support of a nonbinding "Sense of the Senate" resolution, offered by Senator Mitch McConnell (R-KY) and introduced during discussion of the College Cost Reduction Act, to the effect that prisoners at Guantánamo "should not be released into American society, nor should they be transferred stateside into facilities in American communities and neighborhoods"; 153 Cong. Rec. S. 9661, 9668 (July 20, 2007). Though conservatives would point to this vote during the Obama administration as evidence of public sentiment, it must be read in light of the subsequent vote of both chambers in December 2007 which called for an end to indefinite detentions at Guantánamo and for prompt repatriation of those prisoners designated for release or transfer. It is nonetheless true that support for closing the base was substantially greater than for moving the prisoners to the United States.

14. Exec. Order No. 13,492, 74 C.F.R. 4897 (January 22, 2009); Exec. Order No. 13,491, 74 C.F.R. 4893 (January 22, 2009). For a list of the generals in attendance, see Background: President Obama signs Executive Orders on Detention and Interrogation Policy, January 22, 2009, available at http://www.whitehouse.gov/the-press-office/background-president-obama-signs
-executive-orders-detention-and-interrogation-polic.

15. On support for trials in the civilian system, see, e.g., Jon Cohen and Jennifer Agiesta, "Public Supports Closing Guantanamo; In Poll, Most Agree with President's Plan to Shutter the Facility within a Year," *Washington Post*, January 22, 2009, available at http://www.washingtonpost.com/wp-dyn/content/article/2009/01/21/AR2009012103652.html; Jon Cohen, "WaPo-ABC Poll on Gitmo," *Washington Post*, January 21, 2009, available at http://www.washingtonpost.com/wp-srv/politics/documents/postpoll011709.html.

16. AEI Polling, 152–155. Some polls were certainly less supportive of the move, particularly if the questions were specifically worded to direct respondents to perceived problems with the president's proposal. Fox News, for instance, often asked whether it was a "good idea" or a "bad idea" for the president to have ordered the base closed "before there is a plan on where the prisoners will be located." When the question was framed that way, 63 percent of respondents thought it was a bad idea. When the questions were framed in a more neutral way, however, virtually every poll in January 2009 showed that support for closing the base approached or exceeded 50 percent; ibid.

17. Ibid., 152–158.

18. In a poll conducted a little more than a year after Obama took office, for instance, respondents preferred trial by military commission 55 percent to 39 percent; ABC News/Washington Post Poll, February 2010, retrieved July 10, 2012, from iPoll Databank, Roper Center for Public Opinion Research, University of Connecticut, http://www.ropercenter.uconn.edu/data_access/ipoll/ipoll.html.

19. Teresa Watanabe and Paloma Esquivel, "Muslims Say FBI Spying Is Causing Anxiety; Use of an Informant in Orange County Leads Some to Shun Mosques," *Los Angeles Times*, March 1, 2009; Matt Apuzzo and Adam Goldman, "With CIA Help, NYPD Moves Covertly in Muslim Areas," Associated Press, August 24, 2011; Matt Apuzzo and Adam Goldman, "Inside the Spy Unit That NYPD Says Doesn't Exist," Associated Press, August 31, 2011 ("New York Police Department officials and a veteran CIA officer built an intelligence-gathering program . . . to map the region's ethnic communities and dispatch teams of undercover officers to keep tabs on where Muslims shopped, ate, and prayed").

20. Michael Powell, "In Police Training, a Dark Film on U.S. Muslims," *New York Times*, January 24, 2012.

21. These provisions are contained in the controversial National Defense Authorization Act of 2012. The core of the controversy is whether the law permits the military detention of American citizens seized in the United States. Unlike for foreign nationals, it is clear the bill does not *require* military detention of citizens. It is less clear, however, whether such detention is authorized. The bill itself is deliberately vague, saying only that it does not purport to expand existing authority. The Supreme Court, however, has never ruled explicitly on whether military detention of a citizen is authorized in a post-9/11 setting when the civilian courts are open and functioning. National Defense Authorization Act for Fiscal Year 2012, Sec. 1021–1029, H.R. 1540, 112th Cong., 1st Sess. (2011), available at http://www.gpo.gov/fdsys/pkg/BILLS-112hr1540enr/pdf/BILLS-112hr1540enr.pdf.

    The provisions that limit transfers from Guantánamo are also included in the 2012 NDAA. They were first passed in 2010 as part of the National Defense Authorization Act of 2011. Congress prohibited the use of Defense Department funds to bring a prisoner at Guantánamo to the United States for any reason, including prosecution. Congress also barred the use of funds to modify any mainland site for Guantánamo prisoners, which nixed the Obama administration's plan to reconfigure the unused prison at Thomson, Illinois. Congress also insisted that no Department of Defense funds be used to transfer any prisoner to another country unless the receiving state agreed to unprecedented intrusions on its sovereignty. See National Defense Authorization Act for Fiscal Year 2011, Sec. 1032–1034, H.R. 6523, 111th Cong. (2010), available at http://www.gpo.gov/fdsys/pkg/BILLS-111hr6523eh/pdf/BILLS-111hr6523eh.pdf.

22. Fawaz A. Gerges, *The Rise and Fall of Al Qaeda* (New York: Oxford University Press, 2011).

23. "Bin Laden Files Show Qaeda Leader's Waning Sway," CBS News, March 21, 2012, available at http://www.cbsnews.com/8301-505263_162-57401421/bin-laden-files-show-qaeda-leaders-waning-sway/?tag=strip. The most complete cache of material taken from the bin Laden raid and available as of this writing has been assembled by the Combatting Terrorism Center at West Point. See "Letters from Abbottabad: Bin Laden Sidelined?" Combatting Terrorism Center at West Point, May 3, 2012, available at http://www.ctc.usma.edu/wp-content/uploads/2012/05/CTC_LtrsFromAbottabad_WEB_v2.pdf.

24. In the 2009 National Threat Assessment, Blair described the global economic freefall as the greatest threat to national security and said that "because of the pressure we and our allies have put on al-Qa'ida's core leadership in Pakistan and the continued decline of al-Qa'ida's most prominent regional affiliate in Iraq, al-Qa'ida today is less capable and effective than it was a year ago." See Intelligence Community Annual Threat Assessment, Given to the Senate Select Committee on Intelligence, February 12, 2009, available at http://www.dni.gov/files/documents/Newsroom/testimonies/20090212_testimony.pdf. The assessment in 2010, given shortly after the failed Christmas attack, was considerably less sanguine. Still, Blair ranked cyberattacks as the number one threat to national security, followed by continued instability in the global economy, and did not retreat from his 2009 position that the United States was "turning a corner on violent extremism." See Intelligence Community Annual Threat Assessment, given to the Senate Select Committee on Intelligence, February 2, 2010, available at http://www.dni.gov/ files/documents/Newsroom/testimonies/20100202_testimony.pdf.

25. Statement for the Record on the Worldwide Threat Assessment of the U.S. Intelligence Community for the House Permanent Select Committee on Intelligence, February 3, 2011, available at http://www.dni.gov/testimonies/20110210_testimony_clapper.pdf.

26. Unclassified Statement for the Record on the Worldwide Threat Assessment of the US Intelligence Community for the Senate Select Committee on Intelligence, January 31, 2012, available at http://www.dni.gov/files/documents/Newsroom/testimonies/20120131_testimony_ata.pdf.

27. John O. Brennan, "The Efficacy and Ethics of U.S. Counterterrorism Strategy," Speech at the Woodrow Wilson International Center for Scholars, April 30, 2012, available at http://www.wilsoncenter.org/event/the-efficacy-and-ethics-us-counterterrorism-strategy.

28. See "Letters from Abbottobad," 2–3, 9–13. "Far from being in control of the operational side of regional jihadi groups, the tone in several letters authored by Bin Ladin makes it clear that he was struggling to exercise even a minimal influence over them. It is further evident that although he did not consider publicly dissociating (*tabarru' min*) himself and al-Qa'ida from the actions of regional groups, . . . Bin Ladin largely disapproved of their conduct"; ibid., 13.

29. Jonathan Masters, "Al Qaeda in Iraq," Council on Foreign Relations, March 14, 2012, available at http://www.cfr.org/iraq/al-qaeda-iraq/p14811#p5; Gerges, *Rise and Fall*, 107–112.

30. See 2009 and 2012 Threat Assessments.

31. "A False Foundation? AQAP, Tribes and Ungoverned Spaces in Yemen," Combatting Terrorism Center at West Point, September 2011, 152–153, available at http://www.ctc.usma.edu/wp-content/uploads/2011/10/CTC_False_Foundation2.pdf; see also Jonathan Masters, "Al-Qaeda in the Arabian Peninsula (AQAP)," Council on Foreign Relations, December 7, 2011, available at http://www.cfr.org/yemen/al-qaeda-arabian-peninsula-aqap/p9369#p5.

32. Adla Massoud, "Interview with Richard Barrett," Al Jazeera, January 21, 2010, available at http://www.aljazeera.com/focus/2010/01/20101177513563176.html.

33. "A False Foundation?" 153.

34. "Homegrown Terror on the Rise in 2009," Fox News, December 17, 2009, available at http://www.foxnews.com/story/0,2933,580173,00.html.

35. Erick Stakelbeck, "2009: The Year of Homegrown Jihad," Christian Broadcasting Network, January 28, 2010, available at http://www.cbn.com/cbnnews/us/2010/January/Homegrown-Terror-A-Bigger-Problem-than-We-May-Know/.

36. Charles Kurzman, "Muslim-American Terrorism in the Decade Since 9/11," Triangle Center on Terrorism and Homeland Security, February 8, 2012, available at http://tcths.sanford.duke.edu/ documents/Kurzman_Muslim-American_Terrorism_in_the_Decade_Since_9_11.pdf. This is the third of three reports published to date in this series. Predecessors, published in 2010 and 2011, are available at http://kurzman.unc.edu/muslim-american-terrorism. For an extended discussion of the relative absence of Muslim violence in the post-9/11 era, see Charles Kurzman, *The Missing Martyrs: Why There Are So Few Muslim Terrorists* (New York: Oxford University Press, 2011).

37. Federal Bureau of Investigation, Uniform Crime Report, *Crime in the United States, 2010*, Expanded Homicide Data, available at http://www.fbi.gov/about-us/cjis/ucr/crime-in-the-u.s/2010/crime-in-the-u.s.-2010/offenses-known-to-law-enforcement/expanded/expand homicidemain.pdf.

38. Kurzman, "Muslim-American Terrorism."

39. Gerges, *Rise and Fall*, 159–165.

40. Kurzman, "Muslim-American Terrorism."

41. Jonathan Masters, "Militant Extremists in the United States," Council on Foreign Relations, February 7, 2011, available at http://www.cfr.org/terrorist-organizations/militant-extremists-united-states/p9236.

42. "The Second Wave: Return of the Militias," Southern Poverty Law Center, August 2009, 13, available at http://www.splcenter.org/sites/default/files/downloads/The_Second_Wave.pdf; "Terror from the Right," Southern Poverty Law Center, November 2011, available at http://www.splcenter.org/get-informed/publications/terror-from-the-right.

43. Rich Lowry, "The Abdulmutallab Travesty," *National Review Online*, January 26, 2010, available at http://www.nationalreview.com/articles/229023/abdulmutallab-travesty/rich-lowry.

44. *The Sean Hannity Show*, Fox News, January 4, 2010.

45. Marc Thiessen, "New Poll: 58 Percent Say Waterboard Abdulmutallab, 71 Percent Say Hand Him to the Military," *National Review Online,* January 1, 2010, available at http://www .nationalreview.com/corner/192138/new-poll-58-percent-say-waterboard-abdulmutallab -71-percent-say-hand-him-military/marc. It should be noted that this particular poll was conducted by Rasmussen Reports, which, even more than Fox News, conducts its polling in a way to maximize the appearance of conservative viewpoints. The firm has been attacked for its inaccuracy and bias. See, e.g., Nate Silver, "Rasmussen Polls Were Biased and Inaccurate; Quinnipiac, SurveyUSA Performed Strongly," *New York Times,* November 4, 2010. Still, other polls taken at approximately the same time showed substantial support for waterboarding and military tribunals, though not at the level found by Rasmussen. See, e.g., "Waterboarding Terror Suspects Unacceptable to Half of Americans," Angus Reid Public Opinion, February 24, 2010, available at http://www.visioncritical.com/wp-content/uploads /2010/02/2010.02.24_Waterboard.pdf: 39 percent of Americans, and 58 percent of Republicans, support water-boarding; 57 percent of Americans, and 77 percent of Republicans, support "enhanced interrogation techniques." On military commissions, see, e.g., Economist /YouGov Poll, March 13–16, 2010, available at http://media.economist.com/images/pdf/ Toplines20100318.pdf: 58 percent of Americans favor military commissions.

46. Stephen Schwartz, "Recruiters for Jihad; Meet the Tablighi Jamaat—Right Here in the U.S.A.," *Weekly Standard,* January 28, 2002. Other articles presented no inkling that Reid was anything other than a criminal who should be prosecuted to the full extent of the law. See, e.g., Deroy Murdock, "Right Country, Wrong Camp," *National Review Online,* January 25, 2002, http://www.nationalreview.com/articles/205127/right-country-wrong-camp/deroy -murdock; Robert A. Levy, "Not on Our Soil," *National Review,* January 25, 2002 ("Plain and simple, military tribunals have no business on U.S. soil. So far, President Bush seems to agree. He should say so, unequivocally and soon"); Theodore Dalrymple, "Just Your Average Shoe-Bomber: 'Not a Bad Lad,' and How Not to Be Had," *National Review,* January 28, 2002.

47. See President Barack Obama, Remarks on National Security at the National Archives, May 21, 2009, transcript available at http://www.whitehouse.gov/the_press_office/Remarks-by -the-President-On-National-Security-5-21-09/.

48. Ibid.

49. Ibid.

50. Joshua Green, "Strict Obstructionist," *Atlantic,* January–February 2011.

51. "Ingraham Angle," *The O'Reilly Factor,* Fox News, January 22, 2009.

52. *Sean Hannity Show,* Fox News, January 23, 2009.

53. *Sean Hannity Show,* Fox News, January 26, 2009.

54. The transcripts can be retrieved via a lexisnexis search of Fox News in the News and Business Database.

55. By my count, Fox News attacked the president's decision about Guantánamo on 73 of 120 days in the four months between February 1 and May 31, 2009, and never went an entire week without bringing it up. On most of those days, it was discussed during several programs.

56. John Yoo, "Obama Made a Rash Decision on Gitmo," *Wall Street Journal,* January 29, 2009.

57. *Hannity's America,* Fox News, February 1, 2009.

58. Pew Research Center for the People and the Press, September 2008, retrieved July 8, 2012, from iPoll Databank; Pew Research Center for the People and the Press, March 2009, retrieved ibid.; Pew Research Center for the People and the Press, July 2010, retrieved ibid.

59. "Very Close Race in Both Alabama and Mississippi," *Public Policy Polling,* March 12, 2012.

60. Stephanie Condon, "Poll: One in Four Americans Think Obama Was Not Born in U.S.," CBS News, April 21, 2011; "Poll Shows 3 percent Now Think Obama Born Abroad," CNN, May 5, 2011.

61. David Cole, "Obama and Terror: The Hovering Questions," *New York Review of Books,* July 12, 2012, reviewing Daniel Klaidman, *Kill or Capture: The War on Terror and the Soul of the Obama Presidency* (New York: Houghton Mifflin Harcourt, 2012), and Jack Goldsmith, *Power and Constraint: The Accountable Presidency After 9/11* (New York: W. W. Norton, 2012).

62. The letter was introduced into the Congressional Record by Sen. Dianne Feinstein (D-CA). See Congressional Record: February 3, 2011 (Senate), S549–S551; the letter is also widely available online, e.g., at http://www.fas.org/irp/congress/2011_cr/s289.html.

63. Jim Abrams, "Patriot Act Extension Signed by Obama," Associated Press, May 27, 2011.

64. Ibid.

65. Dana Priest and William M. Arkin, *Top Secret America: The Rise of the New American Security State* (New York: Little, Brown, 2011).

66. James Bamford, "The NSA Is Building the Country's Biggest Spy Center (Watch What You Say)," *Wired,* March 15, 2012.

67. See, e.g., Clara Gutteridge, *East Africa's War on Terror* (London: Hurst, forthcoming 2013); Alex Perry, "Countering al-Shabab: How the War on Terrorism Is Being Fought in East Africa," *Time,* July 3, 2012; Jeremy Schahill, "The CIA's Secret Sites in Somalia," *Nation,* August 1–8, 2011.

68. See, e.g., Lisa Hajjar, "Anatomy of the US Targeted Killing Policy," *Middle East Report* 42, no. 264 (2012); Jo Becker and Scott Shane, "Secret 'Kill List' Proves a Test of Obama's Principles and Will," *New York Times,* May 29, 2012.

69. Gerges, *Rise and Fall,* 6.

70. Quoted ibid., 6–7.

71. On the rise and role of presidential rhetoric, see Jeffrey K. Tulis, *The Rhetorical Presidency* (Princeton: Princeton University Press, 1987).

72. Editorial, "KSM Hits Manhattan—Again," *Wall Street Journal,* November 14, 2009.

73. Charles Krauthammer, "New York Travesty," *Chicago Tribune,* November 23, 2009.

74. "GOP Blasts Terrorism Trial Decision," United Press International, November 13, 2009, http://www.upi.com/Top_News/US/2009/11/13/GOP-blasts-terrorism-trial-decision/UPI-93971258171262/.

75. Ibid.

76. Gordon Cucullu, "Terrorists on Trial in NYC Is an Unacceptable Risk," *Human Events Online,* November 15, 2009, http://www.humanevents.com/article.php?id=34439.

77. Charlie Savage, "In a Reversal, Military Trials for 9/11 Cases," *New York Times,* April 4, 2011. There is some indication that Holder understood the need to mount a vigorous media campaign in defense of the decision to try the 9/11 conspirators in federal court, but that he was overruled by Obama's former Chief of Staff Rahm Emanuel. See Cole, "Hovering Questions."

78. *United States v. bin Laden et al.,* S(9) 98 Cr. 1023 (LBS) (S.D.N.Y. 1998), available at http://news.findlaw.com/hdocs/docs/binladen/usbinladen1.pdf.

79. Benjamin Weiser, "Detainee Acquitted on Most Counts in '98 Bombings," *New York Times,* November 17, 2010.

80. *In re* Terrorist Bombings of U.S. Embassies in East Africa, 552 F.3d 93, 101–102 (2d Cir. 2008) (affirming the life sentences imposed upon three of the four defendants and noting that the fourth withdrew his appeal before it reached the Second Circuit).

81. *United States v. Ghailani,* 686 F. Supp. 2d 279, 284 (S.D.N.Y. 2009).

82. Ibid.

83. Warren Richey, "Ghailani Verdict Could Signal an End to Civilian Terror Trials," *Christian Science Monitor,* November 17, 2010, http://www.csmonitor.com/USA/Justice/2010/1117/Ghailani-verdict-could-signal-an-end-to-civilian-terror-trials.

84. *United States v. Ghailani,* 2010 WL 4006381, at *1 and note (October 6, 2010). As Judge

Kaplan's order notes, the government asked that the court "assume for purposes of deciding the motion that everything Ghailani said from the minute he arrive[d] in CIA custody till the minute he [got] to Guantanamo at least is coerced"; see also Daphne Eviatar, *Liz Cheney & Co. Have Little Faith in U.S. Law,* Huffington Post, October 8, 2010, http://www.huffington post.com/daphne-eviatar/critics-of-ghailani-rulin_b_755611.html.

85. Richey, "Ghailani Verdict."

86. Senator Mitch McConnell, Statement before the U.S. Senate, November 18, 2010, transcript available at http://mcconnell.senate.gov/public/index.cfm?p=PressReleases&ContentRecord _id=dodda13f-9e94-485e-8c3d-78c213bbfb8d.

87. Liz Cheney, "Statement on Ghailani Verdict," Keep American Safe, http://www.keepamerica safe.com/?page_id=6398.

88. Jennifer Rubin, "The Ghailani Debacle," *Commentary,* November 17, 2010, http://www .commentarymagazine.com/blogs/index.php/rubin/381533.

89. John McCormack, "Peter King Rips Obama on Ghailani Verdict," *Weekly Standard,* November 17, 2010, http://www.weeklystandard.com/blogs/peter-king-rips-obama-ghailani-verdict _518137.html.

90. David Cole, "A Fair Trial, Without Torture's Taint," *New York Times,* November 19, 2010, http://www.nytimes.com/roomfordebate/2010/11/18/prosecuting-terrorists-in-federal-court/ a-fair-trial-without-tortures-taint.

91. Amy Davidson, "The Ghailani Verdict," *New Yorker,* November 17, 2010, http://www.new yorker.com/online/blogs/closeread/2010/11/the-ghailani-verdict.html.

92. Center for Constitutional Rights, "Center for Constitutional Rights Responds to Ghailani Verdict," November 17, 2010, http://ccrjustice.org/newsroom/press-releases/center-consti tutional-rights-responds-ghailani-verdict.

93. Scott Horton, "The Verdict on Ghailani," *Harper's,* November 18, 2010, http://www.harpers .org/archive/2010/11/hbc-90007816. Horton also pointed out that Ghailani may not have been subject to trial by military commission, since the government's allegations related to a 1998 bombing and predated the U.S. entry into the war; ibid.

94. Cheney, "Statement on the Ghailani Verdict."

95. Campbell Craig and Fredrik Logevall, *America's Cold War: The Politics of Insecurity* (Cambridge: Harvard University Press, 2009).

96. David Halberstam, *The Best and the Brightest,* 20th anniversary ed. (New York: Random House, 1992), 108–109, quoted in Craig and Logevall, *America's Cold War,* 82.

97. "Fox News Poll: Voters Approve President's Decision to Resume Gitmo Tribunals," Fox News, March 14–16, 2011, available at http://www.foxnews.com/politics/2011/03/24/fox-news-poll -voters-approve-presidents-decision-resume-gitmo-tribunals/.

98. See, e.g., Adam J. Berinsky, *In Time of War: Understanding American Public Opinion from World War II to Iraq* (Chicago: University of Chicago Press, 2009); William Howell and Douglas Kriner, "Political Elites and Public Support for War" (unpublished manuscript, 2007, on file with author), http://www.ipr.northwestern.edu/publications/papers/cab/Howell Kriner07.pdf: "Whereas most citizens have immediate experiences on which to draw when formulating their domestic policy preferences, on questions of foreign policy these citizens lack direct experience or knowledge; and consequently, . . . citizens rely on elites both to acquire and process information about foreign affairs." For a discussion of survey data demonstrating voter ignorance about foreign affairs over many decades, see, e.g., Herbert H. Hyman and Paul B. Sheatsley, "Some Reasons Why Information Campaigns Fail," *Public Opinion Quarterly* 11 (1947), 412–423; Stephen E. Bennett, "'Know-Nothings' Revisited: The Meaning of Political Ignorance Today," *Social Science Quarterly* 69 (1988), 476–492; Stephen E. Bennett, "'Know-Nothings' Revisited Again," *Political Behavior* 18 (1996), 219–231.

99. A variant of this experiment became part of the 2010 midterm elections. In New Jersey, Jon Runyan, the Republican challenger to incumbent Democrat John Adler, vowed that he would vote to repeal the Obama health care law even though he hadn't read it. See "John versus Jon: Adler and Runyan Debate," *South Jersey*, October 27, 2010, available at http://www.southjersey.com/articles/?articleID=23276. Runyan won.

100. ABC News/Washington Post Poll, November 2001, retrieved July 9, 2012, from iPoll Databank.

101. CBS News/New York Times Poll, December 2001, retrieved July 9, 2012, ibid.

Chapter 13. All Will Be as It Ought to Be

1. See E. H. Carr, *What Is History?* (1961; Middlesex: Penguin, 1988).

2. Charlie Savage, "Election to Decide Future Interrogation Methods in Terrorism Cases," *New York Times*, September 27, 2012. The internal campaign memo is available at http://www.documentcloud.org/documents/441318-romney-campaign-interrogation-policy.html.

3. Savage, "Election to Decide Future Interrogation Methods."

4. Facts About the Death Penalty, Death Penalty Information Center, January 27, 2012, http://www.deathpenaltyinfo.org/documents/FactSheet.pdf; Year End Report, Death Penalty Information Center, December 2011, http://www.deathpenaltyinfo.org/documents/2011__Year__End.pdf.

5. U.S. Department of Justice, Office of Justice Programs, Bureau of Justice Statistics: Total Corrections Population, December 2011, available at http://bjs.ojp.usdoj.gov/content/pub/pdf/p10.pdf; Nicole Porter, "The State of Sentencing 2011: Developments in Policy and Practice," The Sentencing Project, February 2012, http://sentencingproject.org/doc/publications/publications/sen_State_of_Sentencing_2011.pdf.

6. U.S. Census Bureau, Age and Sex Composition, May 2011, http://www.census.gov/prod/cen2010/briefs/c2010br-03.pdf.

7. Porter, "State of Sentencing 2011," 1–4.

8. The debate is at Cong. Rec. 111th Congress, S11148, S11155-S11169, S11170-S11171 (November 5, 2009).

PERMISSIONS

INDEX